RETHINKING SEXUAL HARASSMENT

Rethinking
Sexual Harassment

Edited by

Clare Brant and Yun Lee Too

Pluto Press

LONDON • BOULDER, COLORADO

First published 1994 by Pluto Press
345 Archway Road, London N6 5AA
and 5500 Central Avenue, Boulder, Colorado 80301, USA

94 95 96 97 5 4 3 2 1

British Library Cataloguing in Publication Data
A catalogue record for this book is available from the British Library

Library of Congress Cataloging in Publication Data
Rethinking sexual harassment / edited by Clare Brant and Yun Lee Too.
  293 p. 22 cm.
  Includes bibliographical references and index.
  ISBN 0-7453-0837-6
  1. Sexual harassment. 2. Sexual harassment of women. 3. Feminist
theory. I. Brant, Clare, 1960– . II. Too, Yun Lee.
HD606.3.R47 1994
331.4'133—dc20   94–25614
                                                                 CIP

ISBN 0 7453 0837 6 Hardback
ISBN 0 7453 0838 4 Paperback

Designed and produced for Pluto Press by
Chase Production Services, Chipping Norton, OX7 5QR
Typeset from authors' disk by Stanford DTP Services, Milton Keynes
Printed in the EC by TJ Press, Padstow

Contents

Illustrations

The authors and publisher acknowledge with thanks the permission to reproduce illustrations granted by artists and other agencies. Every effort has been made to contact copyright holders, but we apologise if by any chance a request has not been received.

For any kind of lasting illumination the focus must be on the history routinely ignored or played down or unknown. For the kind of insight that invites reflection, language must be critiqued.

Toni Morrison, *Race-ing Justice, En-gendering Power*

Acknowledgements

This book is the result of many discussions and exchanges going back a number of years for both editors. We have people to thank in several countries, both jointly and separately, including members of the Women Tutors' Group in Oxford from its inception in 1985, especially Niki Lacey, and its subgroup on sexual harassment, especially Liz Frazer, and all those who contributed to the Sexual Harassment Working Party in Cambridge, 1989–91, especially Leela MadhavaRau and Kathryn Packer. We also acknowledge the valuable work of Women Against Sexual Harassment (WASH); the Prevention of Professional Abuse Network (POPAN); the Sexual Harassment/Assault Advising, Resources, and Education Program (SHARE) at Princeton University, especially Myra Hindus and Siobhan Gibbons; the Canadian Association Against Sexual Harassment in Higher Education (CAASHE), especially Nancy Adamson and Paddy Stamp; and Women in Medicine, especially Dr Susan Bewley and Dr Helen Salisbury.

For helpful ideas at an early stage of the book, we thank Jeff Hearn and Elizabeth Stanko; for material support and advice of various kinds, we are grateful to Duncan Campbell, David Cooper, Simon Evans, Loraine Gelsthorpe, Mary Jacobus, Leo Sharpston, Tony Smith, the tutorial staff of Gonville and Caius College, Cambridge, and Rhona Watson and Roland Thomas of the Marshall Economics Library, Cambridge.

We would both like to express our gratitude to Sara Dunn for her encouragement and to our editor at Pluto Press, Anne Beech, for her faith in our project.

Yun Lee would like to thank personally Helen Elsom and Hilary Mackie for being there.

Clare would like to thank Sarah Spiller, Vicki Bertram, Jo Collinge and Zoë Penn for all the pleasures of friendship and for all the inspiration of their feminisms. Mimi and Cadbury contributed inimitable sagacity, companionship and comic relief. Most of all, heartfelt gratitude to Ewen Green for all his support, practical suggestions, forbearance and humour.

Notes on Contributors

Padma Anagol-McGinn is lecturer in history at Bath College of Higher Education. She has research interests in gender history and South Asian history.

Jane Beckett is lecturer in the history of art and cultural studies in the School of World Art Studies and Museology, University of East Anglia.

Gargi Bhattacharyya is lecturer in Cultural Studies at Birmingham University.

Clare Brant is a lecturer in English at King's College, London. She has edited with Diane Purkiss *Women, Texts and Histories 1575–1760* (London: Routledge, 1992). She has also published articles on eighteenth-century literature and women's writing, and on twentieth-century culture and gender.

Suzanne Gibson is lecturer in law and fellow of New College, Oxford. She is currently writing a play about an eighteenth-century woman called Mary Tofts, who claimed she gave birth to rabbits.

Ros Hunt is a priest in the Church of England and works with survivors of sexual abuse.

Ruth Jamieson is a doctoral student in the Faculty of Social and Political Sciences, University of Cambridge. From 1984 to 1989 she worked for the Department of Justice in Canada doing evaluation research on legal aid, the organisation of legal services and sexual assault legislation. Her research interests include social regulation, and the relationship between gender, law and the state.

Celia Kitzinger is director of women's studies in the Department of Social Sciences at Loughborough University (UK), author of *The Social*

Construction of Lesbianism (London: Sage, 1987), co-author (with Rachel Perkins) of *Changing Our Minds: Lesbian Feminism & Psychology* (London: Onlywomen and New York: New York University Press, 1993) and co-editor (with Sue Wilkinson) of *Heterosexuality: A Feminism & Psychology Reader* (London: Sage, 1993).

Diane Purkiss is lecturer in English at the University of Reading. She has co-edited *Women, Texts and Histories 1575–1760* (London: Routledge, 1992) and has also edited the works of Elizabeth Cary and Aemilia Lanyer. She has published articles on early modern and modern women's writing, and is working on a book on women and cinema with Clare Brant.

Suzanne Raitt is lecturer in English at Queen Mary and Westfield College, University of London. Most recently she is the author of *Vita and Virginia: The Work and Friendship of V. Sackville-West and Virginia Woolf* (Oxford: Oxford University Press, 1993).

Yun Lee Too is lecturer in classics and ancient history at the University of Liverpool. She has recently completed a book, *The Rhetoric of Identity in Isocrates: Text, Power, Pedagogy* (Cambridge University Press, forthcoming). Her research interests are literary and cultural history and politics in antiquity; she is writing a book on the idea of ancient literary criticism.

Helen Watson is an anthropologist who has worked on women and Islam, migration and urban poverty, and sectarianism and nationalism in Ireland. She is a fellow of St John's College and lecturer in the Department of Social Anthropology, University of Cambridge.

1

Introduction

Clare Brant and Yun Lee Too

For just over 20 years, the term 'sexual harassment' has been in use as a way of addressing and naming a serious issue. The law, the media, institutions, employers and individuals recognise the term and use it to describe unwanted sexual attention. Sexual harassment has been taken up in anti-discrimination laws and made a focus for workplace codes and a key issue in contemporary debates about gender relations. Sexual harassment has been in many ways a success story for late twentieth-century feminism: since its arrival on the agenda, it has attracted attention and support and effected considerable political and social changes. The success of sexual harassment both as a term in itself and as an indicator of larger feminist concerns is evident from how it has catalysed responsiveness to other categories of harassment, such as those concerning race, sexual orientation and disability.

But has the language of sexual harassment gone as far as it can or in the direction that it should? The apparent success of this language has made it harder to question. The term has moved into a variety of contexts – for instance, from trade unions to churches or the armed forces – guaranteeing its currency but, in the process of doing so and perhaps in order to be able to do so, it has kept a relatively invariable meaning. Indeed, the workplace origin of the discourse, for example, is still so influential that it is difficult to apply sexual harassment to situations which involve working at home or just being at home. Unease about this rigidity has emerged from several different quarters. Originally, action on sexual harassment was thought to be a matter of implementing legislation or codes, but increasing complexity shows that such measures do not provide an infallible solution. So universities, for instance, which were among the first institutions to be persuaded to have sexual harassment policies, have in many cases had to redraft them to accommodate other harassment categories, such as race, sexual orientation and disability, and to acknowledge that they cannot act in isolation from legal authorities.[1]

There is also unease about the term, not as to whether it is too fixed but as to whether it is clear enough. For all that it has become familiar

1

in everyday language, widely recognised and institutionalised in policy and in law, it remains embroiled in controversy. Confusion about what we mean by sexual harassment comes from those sympathetic to the issue as well as those hostile to it. Charges of exaggeration, oversimplification, inadequacy or inflexibility can be made by feminists who find the available discourse not always helpful in describing experiences of sexual harassment. Most recently, debates concerning 'date rape' have raised questions parallel to those around sexual harassment – for example, anxieties about consent and proof. These debates have done little to contribute to the understanding of sexual harassment, and indeed in some ways they have made it harder to address the uses and complications of the language of sexual harassment. This makes it all the more important to review sexual harassment, and to do so in full awareness of how it has become entangled with other contentious issues.

Rethinking Sexual Harassment offers an opportunity to reflect upon how we think about, speak about and deal with a pressing issue. It does so from within feminism and in a way which contributes constructively to potential practice. This book does not question the experience of unwanted sexual attention, nor does it suggest that we abandon the term sexual harassment – that would be to risk having to reinvent the wheel. Rather, it aims to raise consciousness about the discourse of sexual harassment and the adequacy of practice based on this language. It examines how generalising elements in accounts of sexual harassment have been of benefit in drawing attention to widespread experiences, but are now also a hindrance, as they turn common ground into fixed ideological terrain. The chapters analyse patterns in accounts of harassment to illuminate the causes of sexual harassment, and the cultural structures which affect our perceptions of it. But this is not to suggest that experience of harassment is uniform. The contributors to *Rethinking Sexual Harassment* also consider what is specific to harassment in different contexts, whether institutional, geographical or historical. They show how simplified narratives and explanations of harassment disguise complexity for particular social reasons.

FEMINISM AND SEXUAL HARASSMENT

Feminism continues to be the political scenario where the term sexual harassment is asserted, negotiated and fought over. Some imaginative effort has been made to find it a context in the discourse of citizenship and ethics,[2] though, as Catharine MacKinnon has observed about refusals to recognise rape as a war crime, human rights which predominantly affect women are too likely to stay obstinately gendered as women's issues.[3] So sexual harassment has been particularly associated with women's access to employment, and with feminist incentives to improve conditions and mobility for women in employment.[4] In the twentieth century, the world of work is widely recognised as a sphere of movement – literally, economically and socially. One explanation of the origins of sexual harassment describes it as a consequence of women's entry into this most visible form of the public sphere.[5] In leaving behind the protection as well as the restriction of the family, the principal scene of the private sphere, women then have to invoke the state, or its instrument, the law, as a defence.[6] This explanation, however, has some shortcomings. Besides overlooking the issue of domestic violence in the home, it tends to fuse the history of women's work with the history of the post-industrial workplace. If sexual harassment was aimed at women to deter them from working, one would expect to see more of it during industrialisation's expansion of workforces or, earlier, among working-class women. That more research is still needed here is shown by Lin Farley, who first gave sexual harassment a genealogy back to the nineteenth century. But the examples she gave concern men who ruin women's employment chances by accusing the *women* of sexual impropriety.[7] Farley's history offered an understanding of harassment which reverses twentieth-century understandings that it is women who blow the whistle on *men's* sexual impropriety, though of course the earlier instances can be read as men disguising their behaviour by preemptive accusations. Nineteenth-century sources also provide evidence of unwanted sexual attention on the street, which, although historically specific, has reinforced associations between sexual harassment and the public sphere both then and now.

Farley's work is extremely important because her consciousness-raising study conducted with working women in upstate New York first put the term sexual harassment on an established footing. The participants in the study found that they were all subject to unpleasant and uninvited behaviours, and agreed that 'The male behaviour eventually required a name, and *sexual harassment* seemed to come about as close to symbolising the problem as language would permit.'[8] The connection between sexual harassment and work was cemented by Catharine MacKinnon's pathbreaking book, *Sexual Harassment of Working Women*, published in 1979.[9] Although its immediate concern was with sex discrimination law, this book gained classic status not least because it brought together legal specialists and a wider audience. Subsequent political developments in America and, a little differently, in Britain during the 1980s made it difficult for feminists to locate harassment in spheres other than work, though they could and did ensure that the idea of sexual harassment was addressed across a wide field of employment areas. With recession and conservative social and economic policies making women additionally vulnerable at work, sexual harassment was an important way of drawing attention to power imbalances between the sexes.

Another strand of feminism, often running concurrently with that outlined above, has interpreted sexual harassment in the light of a radical feminist agenda. This strand links sexual harassment to rape as an invasion of women's bodies and space, and as a type of sexual encounter in which the oppressor's object is not the procuring of sex but the expression of power. Sexual harassment is seen as patriarchy's everyday way of intimidating women; either, as we have seen, in order to keep them out of the workplace altogether (particularly in historically male-dominated areas of employment), or to keep them in lowly and low-paid positions. The significance of sexual harassment then becomes not so much its effect on women's work as its public challenge to women's claims to rights over their own bodies. Like rape, sexual harassment could also be used to target and punish women troublesome to men. Radical feminism historically employed and still employs a totalising rhetoric as a polemical strategy in the face of a disbelieving or hostile patriarchal establishment. While the issue of harassment has no exact equivalent to the strategically provoking slogan used to raise consciousness about rape, 'All men are rapists', radical feminists have done much to expose the widespread sexism of male attitudes to women, and to implicate that general sexism as a cause of harassment both in and beyond the workplace. They emphasise that not only is the working world dominated by men, but that the whole world is dominated by men. Harassment by women, besides being statistically negligible, could never have the same cultural weight, because society would never support harassing women as it does harassing men.

This line of thought has connected workplace harassment to the wider world in some helpful ways. In stressing continuities, however, it discards differences to the point of making cultural context oddly invisible again. By effacing distinctions between public and private spheres, and by dismissing national, institutional and local factors which contribute to experiences of harassment and, importantly, shape people's perceptions of harassment, it has led feminists such as Sue Wise and Liz Stanley to the dramatic – and despairing – conclusion that, for women, all life is sexual harassment.[10] Similarly global was Carrie Herbert's suggestion that sexual harassment was analogous to foot-binding in China or female circumcision in Africa.[11] These parallels may encourage community between women, but they also lead people who are hostile to feminism, or to this kind of feminism in particular, to respond with charges of exaggeration and fear-mongering, and hence to doubt whether sexual harassment actually exists.

The attention drawn to sexual harassment by different kinds of feminists has made it a barometer of social attitudes towards women. Like rape and abortion, it provides a touchstone against which social attitudes can be tested, and changes measured, whether those changes involve progress or resistance. But it has also taken on a topical aspect as a zeitgeist issue. So Susan Faludi draws on government statistics and contradictory official pronouncements to argue that 'annual charges of sexual harassment nearly doubled between 1981 and 1989'.[12] Activism in peace movements during the 1980s offered feminists a way to critique male aggression as a historical but also an urgent problem; likewise, sexual harassment, though it seems a modern phenomenon, points to how old obstacles to equality could be given a contemporary guise.

This strange and potentially contradictory mixture of the long-standing and topical, the individual and social, makes sexual harassment a difficult issue for feminism and explains its propensity for making visible divisions among feminists. Recent attacks from positions professedly within feminism claim that belief in sexual harassment – as a material aspect of life for women, and as a concept – is damaging.[13] Such feminists see it as a shibboleth among younger women deluded by 'victim feminism', and view commitment to its eradication as a sign of joyless, sexless self-oppression. What starts as a valuable concern about orthodoxy and conformity in feminist discourse turns into either a dismissal of the subject or a redefinition of its terms. For Camille Paglia, though the issue of sexual harassment is 'one of the solid innovations of contemporary feminism', undue attention to it increases the risk that 'women are being returned to their old status of delicate flowers who must be protected from assault by male lechers'.[14] For Katie Roiphe, feminist emphasis on sexual harassment and date rape encourages women to play weak too readily.[15] These writers see women who make unnecessary complaints of sexual harassment (as they define 'unnecessary'), 'complainants' in the legal sense, as 'complainers' in the literary sense, voluble malcontents in a poor cause. More qualified criticism argues that a focus on sexual harassment can seem to portray women consistently as victims. Without denouncing feminists as self-oppressed, Naomi Wolf implies that a focus on sexual harassment represents women as lacking in sexual initiative, roused only in response to predators. She cautions, 'We must be wary of new definitions of sexual harassment that leave no mental space to imagine girls and women as sexual explorers and renegades.'[16] Wolf advises women to oppose feminist prophets of doom so long as their alleged fixation on harassment and date rape distracts women from other issues.

The feminist backlash denounces 'victim feminism' for infantilising women, making them feel helpless by focusing on their vulnerability to rape, date rape and sexual harassment, and by underplaying the capacity of women to achieve position and authority. The opponents of 'victim feminism' claim for themselves the original feminist programme of empowering women in a world which structurally and systematically disadvantages them. They attribute to 'victim feminists' anxieties which, with horrible irony, mirror patriarchal concerns for women's purity and chastity. They see the cause of feminism endangered by women 'crying wolf' about rape and harassment, and demanding protection rather than taking action themselves. While other feminists might agree that a culture of dependency should be avoided, this line of argument oversimplifies: it tends to assume, for instance, or to assume that feminists against harassment assume, that the right to say 'no' to undesired sexual initiatives means an unwillingness to say 'yes' to desired sexual activity. It may well be that American feminists' pre-occupation with women's refusals – 'No means No' – has led them to neglect to ask whether women's positive invitations are also misheard. But this is not the only important issue missed by opponents of victim feminism. In certain contexts (large organisations or universities, for instance), it may be both physically possible and institutionally desirable to provide some protection against sexual violence – especially when these authorities may be legally liable for negligence if they do not do so.[17] Those who criticise such measures as overprotective overlook, firstly, whether they are effective and, secondly, whether they aggravate inequalities: women who do not live on campuses or work in the mini-states of institutions do not have the luxury of despising protection. Such critics make pampered students synecdochal of all women.[18]

The opponents of 'victim feminism' attack what they perceive to be flaws in the ways in which we currently talk about harassment and rape. In doing so, they propose to reform the discourse by getting rid of it. But they fail to recognise how those involved in harassment and rape-campaigning support and celebrate strength. Taking action on rape and sexual harassment has not always been seen as a sign of weakness: it takes courage to say that you have been raped or harassed when the odds are stacked against you in law courts and society at large. If the odds have improved a fraction, this is thanks to feminism. Acknowledging the possibility of sexual harm acknowledges the reality of sexual harm. More alarmist aspects may be educational or preventative, comparable to road safety campaigns which play on the shock value of 'worst case' images and narratives in the hope of reducing danger and encouraging responsible behaviour. Furthermore, the image of the powerless, complaining woman that critics of 'victim feminism' present us with is not one which originates in feminism. The weak, feckless victim is an image of misogynist myth. It is all too often what the law requires women to be if they are to be credible when they make a charge of rape or harassment. Feminism rejects this stereotype of women, despite the fact that the law tends to treat women who are seen to be in any way assertive or sexually active – the very women Paglia and Roiphe regard themselves as inventing – as responsible for harm done to them. Yet again, with media encouragement, feminism is found guilty of the very stereotypes it opposes.

Critics of 'victim feminism' paint with the same broad brush as their opponents. They ironically reinstate the absolutism they oppose, by reducing all feminist language to one supposed orthodoxy. *Rethinking Sexual Harassment* questions absolutist aspects of the language of sexual harassment for quite a different reason: to draw attention to differences within the experience we have monolithically termed 'sexual harassment' for convenience. Standard definitions of the term do acknowledge difference; most assert that it covers a range of behaviours, from verbal abuse to sexual assault. But besides the variety of these behaviours, the contexts in which they take place and the structural facts which affect their origins and developments also introduce further differences. Sexual harassment needs a common language, but it must be responsive to such differences.

DISCOURSE

Raising consciousness through symbolic action is harder to do for sexual harassment than it is for other forms of sexual violence such as rape or assault, although universities in the United States often employ drama and play-acting to orient their students in delicate issues of sexual politics. Where 'Take back the Night' marches reclaim dark streets and no-go neighbourhoods, there is no equivalent protest activity and show of solidarity against sexual harassment. It is hard to organise a shoulder-to-shoulder march through an office. But it is a tenet of feminist theory that naming behaviours is empowering because language can make forms of oppression visible; this is particularly so in the case of sexual harassment because the phenomenon may itself be verbal. Appropriate discourse helps to inform people about the nature of sexual harassment; it also offers those who have been harassed a therapeutic recognition of their pain. The optimistic believe it contributes to a climate in which harassers will be deterred or encouraged to stop by recognising the trauma they inflict.

Fixing names on problems like sexual harassment can make analysis more rigid. It can also lead to cliché which puts imaginative limits on understanding. Even expressions which wear well can settle into unthinking familiarity – for instance, the terms 'victims' and 'survivors' portray people who have been harassed (or raped or abused) as having been overwhelmed or transformed utterly. Conventional wisdom is that such experiences are shattering to a sense of self, but it is hard to agree or disagree when such a limited vocabulary is available. To continue to recognise and question the limits and meanings of the terms we use for harassment, rape and abuse prevents analytical rigidity. It sets the scene for the production of a more sensitive and responsive language.

There are several conventional ways of communicating the experience of sexual harassment. One of these is the survey, favoured by all parts of the media.[19] Surveys have authority because they are perceived as offering objective evidence about which groups are being harassed – 'hard' facts for the phallically minded. Clinical data do affirm the occurrence and frequency of harassment. But surveys cannot simultaneously speak to the ways in which individuals are harassed, nor can they disclose anything about resistance to harassment. Surveys dealing in numbers, percentages and monosyllabic responses can only articulate in limited ways factors that may make a difference to the ways in which people experience harassment – gender, race, sexuality, class, age, religion. Since surveys require 'experts' to decode and interpret them, discursive control is further removed from those who have been harassed.

Another genre in harassment discourse is the personal narrative, which seems to offer an alternative to the abbreviated language of surveys. This is the story told to friends, to counsellors, to therapists, and sometimes also to oneself. Feminism has frequently agreed with psychoanalysis that talking helps one to feel better: by responding with belief, an audience makes the story therapeutic for the narrator, who may also find community through hearing similar stories from others. The personal narrative is also a story that may be published for public consumption.[20] Or it may be more private. Harassment advisers often encourage those who come to them to write 'letters' to their harassers, telling the latter how they perceive their actions and are hurt by them, and asking them to stop.[21] These letters are not usually meant to be sent, but they allow the person who is being harassed to recognise what is happening to her, to believe in her own perceptions and experiences, and to articulate her feelings in a situation where communication has broken down. Though therapeutic models of story-telling have been helpful to feminism, the father-figures of psychoanalysis and religion have also been ready with paternalist and misogynist responses to accounts of harassment. All personal narratives risk being seen as motivated by the desire to seek approval from an audience. This can cast doubt on the speaker's integrity, and implicitly establishes the audience, rather than the speaker herself, as the authority for the story. The importance of the audience as interpreter was evident in the United States Senate confirmation hearings of November 1991 involving Anita Hill and Clarence Thomas, where what officially mattered was not whether there had or had not been sexual harassment, but whether sexual harassment, if proven, made Clarence Thomas unfit to be a Supreme Court judge. With this end in mind, the uses to which truth would be put affected people's sense of what was plausible. Competing stories disrupted a notion of absolute truth, obliging audiences to assess relative credibility – a relativity made even more contentious in the Hill–Thomas case by deep cultural prejudices about race, class and gender.[22] Stories of harassment are always potentially inflammatory, given the difficulty of proving allegations and the symbolic use to which they are put.

LIMITATIONS OF DISCOURSE

The media play an important role in creating and reinforcing the discourse of sexual harassment. Many people learn about sexual harassment from the media, and many have their perceptions of harassment shaped by or in response to media representations. Newspaper and television stories in particular tend to concern themselves with sensational aspects of cases – for instance, spectacular settlements or damages awards, or details likely to strike the public as bizarre, perverse, repulsive, transgressive or in some way illustrative of the intrusion of forbidden sex into everyday life. Thus the alleged pubic hair on a Coke can in the Hill–Thomas case became a point of media obsession.[23] The guilt or innocence of the accused then seems to turn literally on a hair's breadth evidence; in turn, feminist insistence on the reality of sexual harassment is seen to rest on minute and fragile proofs. Media interest in minutiae can be helpful, in so far as it recognises the significance of detail, but it can create an atmosphere in which the striking detail rather than grinding mundanity is what makes harassment believable. Details, moreover, often relate to intimate matters, and their publication can be humiliating. Scrutiny of the lives, habits and past sexual histories of the parties involved leads to invasion of privacy in sexual harassment actions as it does in rape trials. Besides, the sensationalism and selectivity that often enter into media reporting of sexual harassment cases are self-interested, necessary ingredients of newsworthy stories.

Newspapers repeatedly headline stories of workplace harassment with the phrase 'sex pest' to describe alleged harassers.[24] Less of a mouthful than 'sexual harasser', the words are usefully graphic. But the shift from 'sexual' to 'sex' introduces a simpler reading: the stress on sex excludes possibilities of seeing harassment as anything more than the overflow of instinctive urges. 'Pest' points to a group of creatures who behave systematically, but who are simultaneously a local and limited irritant. Metaphors of insects and beasts disconnect such descriptions from human responsibility and agency, except in so far as they figure masculine sexuality as naturally, and hence properly, predatory.[25] On the one hand, this language requires women to brush off such behaviours as merely irritating. 'Sex pest' turns sexual harassment into a caricature quest for sex; it diminishes sexual harassment to a mite-size problem. On the other hand, it places women as passive recipients of animal passions to which they are 'naturally' subject. There are important arguments as to whether it is helpful to place sexual harassment on a continuum of sexual violence and, if so, where to place it, but these metaphors efface all those questions in favour of no argument at all, leading to the representation of harassment as something trivial.

Besides media highlighting, there are other ways too in which discourse about sexual harassment has become limited. Institutions have provided images which have been influential in shaping stereotypes. Aggregations of the discourse around individuals in contexts such as the academy, the church and the workplace suggests that these figures have almost themselves become institutions.[26] But the familiar images of lecherous professor, dirty boss and clerical abuser actually mask the institutions with which they are associated. Focus on these individuals tends to locate power in personalities rather than professions; it skims over how power accrues to them from their authority within their institution, and from the status of that institution in wider society. Understanding institutional power may lead to unfixing the stereotype of male-harasser and female harassed, as – to a degree – Michael Crichton does when he identifies corporate authority with a female harasser in his novel *Disclosure*. 'The advantage of a role-reversal story is that it may enable us to examine aspects concealed by traditional responses and conventional rhetoric', he asserts.[27] Though *Disclosure* reverses one role in terms of plot, it uncritically upholds a gamut of misogynist stereotypes about women. The explanation of sexual harassment in terms of an imbalance of power, such as Crichton uses, has a more general shortcoming too. It does not necessarily provide greater understanding of how women in authority may be empowered differently from men; it also fails to address how masculinity varies among empowered men.

The power model also ignores extensive evidence which suggests that harassment from peers or juniors can be more common than harassment by people in positions of authority. Power is not a pure or unmediated force but an amalgam of influences with material contexts. If 'peer harassment' has proved inexplicable, and hence all too often invisible, it is because 'equals' cannot be mapped onto a power game and because power models fail to explain how 'equals' may after all be advantaged by institutional factors. This also implicitly explains why things do not always get better when more women hold power in institutions. The stereotype of the lecherous doctor harassing nurses, an image which also overlooks other hospital workers such as ancillaries, support staff, technicians and administrators, simplifies the gendering of authority in medical culture. A survey of women doctors, for instance, showed that harassment came more from male patients than from those in charge.[28] Some stereotypes persist as shorthand for truths, but they also serve to mask equally real though more diffuse contributory factors. Institutional codes and laws address some of these factors in helping individuals who want redress against harassers. Such measures may begin to address the relative advantaging and disadvantaging of groups within an institution or culture. In this sense, doctors or patients who harass nurses will have their individual identities related to a group identity and the empowerment of that group. But disciplinary action has the effect of reindividualising: a harasser is punished as a singular instance, an exception, to those rules maintained for the benefit of all groups, however empowered.

There are a number of other problems with how individuals and institutions dominate the discourse of sexual harassment. Institutions impose static roles on people because these help to structure an institution.[29] But these may be at odds with how people prefer to see themselves, or may only apply to selective aspects of the working world or the working day. Management theory increasingly requires workers to make no distinction between a working identity and a leisure personality, in order that employees should bring to the service of employers those skills which they use creatively for themselves out of hours.[30] Executive culture, some professions and certain kinds of work also erase boundaries between social and business skills so that the issue of authority upon which power models of harassment depend is neither straightforwardly institutional nor clearly personal. An institution is also likely, sometimes for more benign purposes such as administrating equal opportunities policies, to locate its members within fixed categories of sex, race and ability. The process of calling stereotypes into question can depend on fixing these categories even as, ironically, they qualify others: so a *female* boss or a *black* priest or even a *short* policeman may challenge institutional stereotypes, but at the same time they can evoke negative assumptions about the competence and authority of women, black people and short people in general. Institutional categories have been a particular problem for women belonging to ethnic minorities, where they have been obliged to decide if they have been harassed on grounds of sex or race.

MEDIA

Workplace constraints on personal identities are now deeply entrenched. They are welcome in so far as they prevent action on sexual harassment from dissolving into chaotic individualism and, to the extent that they identify group interests, they may help many feminists' commitment to collectivity. But they also ultimately serve corporate goals and economic ideologies in which private profit comes before community gain. In so far as market forces can make use of sex in the workplace, there is an incentive to regulate it. Sexual harassment then becomes a waste of human resources (in the case of women workers, this is nearly always seen as a waste of her time rather than her harasser's). But policies can represent the end of institutional responsibilities rather than their start: as with law, once a policy is in place it becomes the responsibility of individuals to make use of it. The existence of legal and paralegal redress does not mean individuals are able to use it, but it becomes their failure, rather than an institution's, if they do not. By such means, action on sexual harassment reaches an impasse or fizzles out. To show people as more than sexual beings, or to decommodify sexuality, would be an alternative way to defuse the implications of sexuality in the workplace. It could be argued that the more aspects of themselves which people can keep, the less they are trapped into ambiguously sexualised identities as workers – although this would mean being aware of how non-working aspects of identity involve sexuality. From this perspective, better childcare and initiatives to acknowledge men's familial relationships are as relevant as more refined policies in reducing sexual harassment in the workplace.[31]

The importance of the law with reference to harassment will be discussed more fully later, but it is relevant here to note that the law also works to shape and limit discourse. In particular, the laws of libel prevent certain stories from being told, at least as their tellers would prefer. The combination of media and legal discourses in trial reporting, and their cultural influence, mean that court cases are frequently presented as the only or the most important paradigm of sexual harassment. Hence feminists are often under pressure to respond to sexual harassment in this context as something topical and controversial, leaving little space for critiques of how legal requirements affect both plaintiff's and defendant's accounts.[32] Topicality is by its nature hard to sustain, and this leaves feminists continually trying to keep harassment from fading as an issue. Topicality also makes it hard to speak authoritatively on the subject without mastery of the latest cases. Legal and media paradigms thus become inescapable, regardless of other sources of knowledge feminists could draw on. Those concerned end up lurching from event to event; historical continuity gives way to a collection of discrete episodes. This also makes it harder to invoke certainties of interpretation, as every case can claim to be *sui generis*.

Uncertainties

Public uncertainty about definitions of sexual harassment, and the separation of harassment into different types, are perfectly illustrated in a curious board game called *Harassment*, released in 1992 to favourable reviews. This claims to be 'The game that lets you be the judge'. A series of cases describes actions, situations or verbal exchanges which may or may not be harassment. You win not by correctly stating whether or not a scenario is harassing, but by correctly predicting the majority opinion of your fellow players. The game presents definitions of harassment as unstable, relative and contestable. Points are given to reward good guesses rather than for identifying any truth. Arguments for and against a reading of harassment are spelled out in differently coloured booklets, and the outcome is voted on using differently coloured cards. The 'yes' booklet and cards, the ones claiming harassment has taken place, are a sensationalist and aggressive red; the 'no' booklet and cards are absolutist black: case closed. Throughout the case book, resemblance to real persons is disavowed; as the manufacturers say, it must be entirely coincidental that the first case involves a character called Anita complaining belatedly about the behaviour of another character called Clarence just as he is about to be appointed to high office. In the booklets which present the arguments (as opposed to the case book which presents the stories), there is a repeated printed message that 'The arguments presented in this game do not constitute legal opinions and are presented for entertainment only.' This reminds players that, for all the vitality of public debate, in the end ruling definitions come from the courts, not from ordinary people. Yet the courts need these people, as the pretend court of the game admits, in the form of an invitation to players from the manufacturers to send in experiences of harassment. The game addresses 'harassment' rather than 'sexual harassment', but this ostensibly wider remit does not clarify categories by extending them. On neutral bits of the game – the box cover, the playing board, the judge's booklet – background lettering lists sexual, age, religious, gender, racial and ethnic harassments as relevant categories. Black lettering printed on grey makes the metaphorical uncertainty of distinctions between different types of harassment literally a grey area.

Perhaps the most popular cliché in the discourse on sexual harassment is uncertainty, above all uncertainty about whether or not a particular person was harassed. The grey areas which certain celebrity male authors have favoured are ones which undermine sexual harassment as a plausible concept. Interpretative difficulties in David Mamet's play *Oleanna* and Michael Crichton's novel *Disclosure* are attributed to the unreliability of women, either because they are mentally unstable or because they have compromising sexual histories. In both cases, there are strong echoes of old misogynist stereotypes of mendacious or impure women. There seems little to choose between supposing this to be part of either a postmodern ironic consciousness or a backlash against feminism which need not bother with irony as a disguise for misogyny.[33] The commercial and to some extent critical success of these texts shows that controversial representations of sexual harassment all too often depend on exhausted clichés. The disconnection of media understanding of harassment makes it harder to spot clichés as such; still, even clichéd controversy sells copy.

The cliché of uncertainty also manifests itself in a question commonly asked by people possibly sympathetic to the concept of harassment but anxious lest it be applied unequally. This is uncertainty as to whether or not women also harass, and so whether sexual harassment is a legitimate feminist issue. The question 'What about women who harass men?' forms the plot of Crichton's *Disclosure*. The raising of this possibility might be defended as a liberal desire to be fair in acknowledging that individuals of either sex may harass – although Crichton's characterisation of the female boss as harasser reveals anxieties about 'women on top' which are hardly even-handed. But this liberal perspective is problematic. It conceals a fiction, namely that harassing effaces any social difference or structural inequality between men and women. It pretends that men and women operate on a terrain which is neutral rather than one contoured by inequalities.[34] It treats female and male harassers as equal in the narrow context of harassment, but does not engage with how women and men are not equal in the wider world. The second problem with the raising of this question is that, although it allows for complications in the basic scenario of sexual harassment, it restricts those complications to a simplistic reversal of gender roles. Replacing a predatory male by an aggressive female does nothing to illuminate how sex and power operate together in harassment, and does nothing to extend representations of harassment beyond the conventionally heterosexual. The implication is always, 'What about women who harass heterosexual men?' The question shuts down possibilities of harassment on grounds of other sexual orientations; nor does it make room for women's harassment of women and men's of men. It demands feminism should concede that female harassers may be as numerous as male harassers. But this numbers game is never equal: one woman harassing is as threatening as ten men. The supposed perversity of women who harass outweighs the frequency of men who harass. As long as the question 'What about women who harass?' assumes this agenda, it is difficult to explore how and why women may indeed harass.[35]

Liberal concerns are valuable in so far as they promote ideals of fair play and raise doubts, albeit limited ones, about stereotypes. But some liberal concerns are themselves less fair than others. In his highly publicised book *Illiberal Education: The Politics of Sex and Race on Campus*, Dinesh D'Souza cites what he takes to be institutional excesses committed on behalf of minorities. His examples purport to show how policies against racial and sexual harassment have curtailed opportunities for expression in universities and so have violated the fundamental right to freedom of expression.[36] By drawing attention to the exceptional instances where harassment policies have failed, at least according to his account, D'Souza redefines concern with harassment as a form of oppression by minority interests and their bleeding-heart supporters without recognising that harassment policies have in many instances succeeded, either in resolving specific cases or in creating better work, professional or study environments.

Attacks such as this imply that feminism is irredeemably partisan to women, and that 'liberalism' is more compatible with social justice than feminism is. They also express liberal ambiguity about the independent standing of academic institutions. In North America generally, and the United States in particular, the academy operates as a microcosm. It can appear to be a smaller version of the macrocosmic nation – for instance, when patterns in campus behaviour are taken as indicators of national tendencies. Hence the media interest in the fortunes of issues such as date rape and political correctness on campus, with both of which sexual harassment has been associated. But the academy also appears to be an enclosed world, the proverbial ivory tower, whose particular culture is not duplicated anywhere else: it may be geographically detached, in terms of a campus; or socially separate, in terms of class and economic privilege. Other ambiguities are also at work. On the one hand, teaching is an intellectual affair: it cultivates brains. On the other, being mostly young, single and sexually active, students are interested in their own and each others' bodies. And in so far as college sports offer a route to fame and fortune, the academy promotes the body. This might look like a split version of a supposedly antique ethos, *mens sana in corpore sano*. But, as British public schools exemplified during the nineteenth century, living as a brain in a body, or having to choose between living as a brain or as a body, is not the same as being a person: such dualism is hospitable to harassment as a way of coping with the gaps.[37] Life is also harder for women in a culture where it can be socially smart to be dumb, and where an athletic female body can be valorised through fewer and less prestigious sports than are available to her male peers.[38] These sorts of tensions, exacerbated by the licence given to fraternities and their culture in the United States and their equivalents elsewhere, are local factors which make harassment on campuses harder to eradicate.

The discomfort of American liberals at initiatives which promote group rather than individual rights stems from a view of education as enlightening for individuals, or as enabling for people in human rather than political ways. This plays down the fact that all forms of knowledge have values assigned to them – which liberals elsewhere do recognise in debates over the canon. Doubt about how the academy performs as a workplace gives it some licence not to follow procedures used elsewhere in the working world. What is the product of education? – learning? transferable skills? social skills? But if you can teach students a number of things, why not also teach them political correctness? Uncertainty about whether the miniature society of the academy mirrors or differs from the rest of the world has made it a prime site for arguments about sexual harassment. Those who believe in intervention as a way of improving social relations look to campus policies as an example, however imperfect, of progress. In contrast, those who privilege the resources of the individual see harassment policies as overly protectionist or directive. For feminism, the former belief points to material benefits in that institutions can be persuaded or pressured to commit resources such as sexual harassment officers, night-lighting and personal safety alarms: resources rarely available outside the academic community. The price paid is living by institutional rules which ultimately serve institutional interests, admit of little uncertainty, and allow little room for development or change.

COMPLICATIONS

Uncertainty can be controlled by clichés which overcompensate. But it is important to realise that a degree of uncertainty is built into standard definitions of sexual harassment. Sexual harassment is often described as 'unwanted attention', which may include words, looks or physical contact; it implies a lack of consensus and a lack of consent.

When sexual harassment is presented as a lack of consent, it would seem easy enough to identify: the harassed individual only has to say she or he did not want the attention. Yet consent is a contentious area, as campaigns against 'date rape' illustrate. These have focused on claims that men found it hard to tell 'yes' from 'no', or might reasonably take 'no' to be a coded form of 'yes', and have insisted on the obviousness of 'no' – 'No means No'. This shifts emphasis from the difficulty of knowing what went on between two protagonists, a common way of denying rape and sexual harassment, to the difficulty of interpreting something indisputably said.

That consent is by no means a simple matter to sort out is acknowledged by the inclusion of *quid pro quo* scenarios in definitions of sexual harassment in the United States. *Quid pro quo* suggests a situation where the harasser offers something in return for unwanted sex – the proposal of sex for promotion by a boss to a worker, the suggestion of a 'lay for an A' by a lecherous professor to his student, or alternatively a favour in return for a special consideration. It marks a situation in which the appearance of a bargain or contract might appear to call 'no', or unwillingness to participate, into question. It is a provision that suggests the need to reassert the 'unwanted' nature of the attention or proposal when 'no' appears to be compromised by the return that supposed agreement to sex or sexual attention will bring.

Consent can be understood to be the indicator of an individual's wants or desires. Lack of consent may, however, as the *quid pro quo* provision recognises, be related to impersonal factors. An inability to give consent on equal terms lies at the heart of the theory which regards sexual harassment as an issue of power. Power is the capacity to disregard or override consent. You cannot refuse the boss or the professor because they have hierarchical power over you; you cannot refuse your co-worker or acquaintance because they have the power to confuse and threaten you. Or you can refuse them loudly and clearly, but their power not to hear you can wipe out your power to speak.[39] Feminists have rightly insisted on the truth of these situations. It is worth considering further how we understand consent is not straightforward.

Consent can be interestingly complicated by environments. For instance, in medicine, when someone becomes a patient she gives implicit consent to medical treatment even if that involves discomfort, pain, touching of intimate body parts or invasive examination. It is generally assumed by doctor and patient that the patient will allow these things to happen because they are in her immediate or longterm interests. Nevertheless, she is being asked or expected to consent to activities which go against the grain of average experience; for instance, being undressed in the presence of a complete stranger or being intimately examined. One common way to reduce embarrassment is by detachedly seeing yourself as an object. But such objectivity qualifies consent, since consent presumes a whole person wholly willing to cooperate. (From the doctor's point of view the situation is also strange, although the rewards of a professional persona are compensation for not acting like an ordinary person.) Objectification is a form of damage limitation; it may be preemptive, or a reaction to shock – so rape victims often distance themselves, describing rape as something done to their bodies but not to themselves as persons. Objectification points to duress under which consent cannot be free. The stress of undergoing defamiliarising medical procedures, particularly if a patient is confused or weak or in pain, puts constraints on consent. Awareness of how vulnerability can make consent incomplete makes many doctors careful about ensuring that patients give a fuller and more informed consent than is registered by the simple signature usually required of them by law.

Medicine clearly demonstrates how notions of consent can be stretched. Patients agree to what they would not normally allow to happen, and though formal consent procedures appear to allow full subjectivity, the institutional context gives greater value to the doctor's specialised knowledge than to the patient's experience of her own body. The law recognises a need for safeguards in some circumstances; for example, where a person's voice is involuntarily silent, in an anaesthetised or unconscious body or, less clearly, where voices are likely to be socially devalued, as in the cases of people with learning difficulties or prisoners. But it disregards consent in other circumstances: people with religious views at odds with medical orthodoxy may have their lack of consent overturned. In this sense, the law controls definitions of 'unwanted attention' in medical contexts. One surprising and helpful point of comparison with sexual harassment shows how fine distinctions between wanted and unwanted attentions can be legally sustained by consent: where vaginal examinations are conducted for teaching purposes, rather than for diagnosis or treatment in the patient's interest, doctors now have to obtain explicit consent.[40] Whether beneficial to a wider community or not, the opportunity for medical students to get 'hands-on' experience has been deemed to be invasively unwanted attention. In fact, doctors who fail to obtain this explicit consent can be charged with battery in the UK, or with assault in the US.

Consent implies the possibility of reciprocity, of an offer and an agreement to an offer. As the example of medical culture shows, consent is not a simple or predictable concept. In English law, several other areas illustrate confusions in the legal uses of consent. You can consent to injure yourself, for instance through sado-masochistic practices or dangerous sports, but you can be charged with assault if injury results.[41] Consent as part of a two-way system of communication, rather than a one-way process of assent, is also complicated by technology. To what are you consenting if you answer a ringing phone or plug into an electronic network? The impersonality of the technology means there is no person present to say 'no' to. Harassing phone calls are frightening and intimidating because the recipient usually has no way of determining whether or not the phone call is an unwanted attention until she picks up the phone. Similarly with computer pornography: the screen viewer is unable to anticipate the pornographic image or comment, and therefore cannot choose not to receive it. Cyberporn, or pornography stored in space on networks, is a growing means of harassment in offices. Just as workers personalise office space with pot-plants or postcards, so computer users treat personal network space as 'home', where they can freely indulge in 'male only' pursuits. Again, it is impossible to refuse pornographic material spread around in this way because the computer user is in the situation of being 'tuned-in', of being receptive. Significantly, the existence of contractual agreements not to misuse technology points to recognition of its potential for abuse.[42]

LEGAL RECOURSES

One obvious response to sexual harassment is to seek redress through legal or paralegal resolution. Many of those who have tried this approach find it less than satisfactory: as with cases of rape, the ordeal in court or at a tribunal can be as traumatic as the original crime. But the law provides at least a limited means of redress against harassment; it also contributes key paradigms to discourse on harassment, and acts as a forum in which social attitudes to harassment can be tested and challenged. Since law is such a powerful force in determining how sexual harassment is recognised and upheld, it is helpful to bear in mind how the law varies from country to country, and from period to period. Since it is beyond the scope of this book to undertake a comprehensive survey, the following observations point only in general ways to how different kinds of law construct sexual harassment.

European Union law treats sexual harassment under a provision regarding the desirability of 'equal treatment of men and women'.[43] It defines such harassment as including behaviour which 'affects [a] person's access to vocational training, continued employment, promotion or salary', or which 'creates an intimidating, hostile or humiliating work environment for the recipient' of such behaviour. European Union law favours establishing general principles – in this instance, the right to a certain kind of working environment – to which specific cases can appeal. In Britain and the United States, sexual harassment can be treated as a form of sex discrimination.[44] Broadly speaking, the law offers two possibilities: either support in terms of general rights, as expressed in some part of a national or supranational constitution or equivalent, or support by case law, in which a case must match not a principle but a precedent in the form of judgements made in previous cases. In both approaches, the law treats sexual harassment not as a hermetic category but in relation to other discourses, either of equality of opportunity, especially in legislation relating sexual harassment to the workplace, or to entitlements or rights. Sexual harassment also has to fit into frameworks of legal thought which govern other offences against the person, such as rape. Moreover, constructions of sexual harassment have to be compatible with concepts of harm and responsibility, and with how these concepts treat gender.

A historical example shows how contemporary legal attitudes make assumptions about gender roles which are different from those of the past. Ancient Roman law made provision for injuries to the person. In *Justinian's Institutes*, a law code compiled under the Emperor Justinian in AD 533, we find prohibitions against following the *materfamilias* or matriarch of the family and adolescents of both sexes, and against threats to any citizen's modesty or *pudicitia*. The latter prohibition, *sive cuius pudicitia attemptata esse dicetur*, literally 'if anyone's modesty is said to have been threatened', has been rendered in one modern translation as 'sexual harassment'.[45] But this interpretation ignores several things. A careful consideration of the text reveals that the law was most immediately concerned with the protection of citizens other than the authoritative *paterfamilias*. The law was paternalistic in intent, designed to protect individuals who were potentially vulnerable because they were not adult male Romans. Roman law indicated that this harm affected both a woman or juvenile herself *and* also the patriarchal family and the society to which the individual belonged. The parallel for this injury in modern law is not sexual harassment, but the negative construction placed on it by people who object that feminist concern with harassment and rape turns women into victims who have to be protected. In contrast, contemporary legislation on sexual harassment recognises women as individuals with rights under the law, ostensibly protecting the right of working women to be able to work free from sexual harassment, although in practice these rights are bound up with often unreasonable expectations about available actions. But we might also ask whether the focus of modern legislation on sexual harassment as a violation of workplace rights is really a wider construction of women's social value. Where women were constructed by Roman law as signifiers of morality, under late twentieth-century capitalism women have rights in the public sphere when they are economically useful.

This is not in any way to underestimate the slog feminists have faced in getting employers to adopt equal opportunity policies. But the comparative lack of action on domestic violence, for example, does suggest that the progress of women in the public sphere, however frustratingly slow, has been greater than in the private sphere. To take one instance, legal responsiveness to sexual harassment has left a married, working woman better protected against her boss than against her husband. The success in gaining recognition for sexual harassment as an issue may even be unwittingly contributing to women's continuing disadvantage outside the world of work. Campaigns against sexual harassment have been seen as demeaning to women: 'protection' has been reviled as an agenda on the grounds that women are feisty enough to see off threats without help. In a very different context, 'protection' is now also a key euphemism in the capitalist marketing of products for menstruating women. Perhaps either of these developments is enough to discredit the term as used originally in feminism, as any effort made by women for women to overturn inequality, injustice or oppression. The problem with protection is that now it is coming to be read as a form of paternalism. The irony is excruciating: after decades of women struggling to think through their mothers, feminism still cannot be, however clumsily, maternalism. The location of sexual harassment away from the family intensifies the contradiction: neither the working women nor the college students who feature so prominently in the standard scenarios of sexual harassment can easily be discursively connected to a possible source of advice and support – their mothers, or a generation of older women, who have seen sexual harassment or its like before.

Feminism has, for obvious reasons, rarely received good press. This book's critique of the dominant discourse of sexual harassment, as used by feminists, non-feminists and anti-feminists, should not be mistaken as in any way sympathetic to the spurious concept of 'post-feminism'. Feminism can make a vital and creative difference to global problems. Some areas of environmentalism, for instance, are in danger of restating an uncritical gender politics by exalting a feminine Nature which needs to be protected against despoliation. With new technologies – biotechnologies, computing and electronic-imaging technologies, reproductive technologies – proliferating, concerns about how they are transforming the world, and how they are affecting women's lives for both better and worse, urgently need very public feminist input. The debate about sexual harassment in America, so crystallised and catalysed by the Clarence Thomas confirmation hearings in the Senate, involves national aspects of culture which do not all transplant well: so the litigiousness of American society shapes and constrains discourse and proceedings in a way unparalleled elsewhere.[46]

CONTENTS OF THE BOOK

Rethinking Sexual Harassment does not purport to offer a 'grand theory' of sexual harassment, nor an explanation of sexual harassment as a problem simply of 'sex' or 'power' or 'patriarchy'. Any such theory lends itself to polarised debates, to simplistic yes–no and is–isn't arguments, which risk reducing the issue to one of whether sexual harassment is *actually* a problem. Since the simple answer is not necessarily or always the best one, this book offers different ways to speak about and approach sexual harassment. It argues that things are more complicated than we might have liked to admit in the past in the hope that in future they will be less prone to oversimplification and stereotype. *Rethinking Sexual Harassment* takes an interdisciplinary and multidisciplinary approach. From this perspective, the different chapters assess and interrogate the effectiveness of current ways to deal with harassment, and suggest where, why and how they need to be rethought. Contributors from the fields of law, literary criticism, sociology, psychology, theology, anthropology, history, art and cultural studies bring insights from their particular disciplines to bear on the topic. In so doing they show how diversity, even debate, is productive for the language of harassment: it can produce more flexible thinking about sexual harassment through plural and mobile representations.

The book is divided into three parts. The first of these, 'Stories', focuses on what sense of rules, legal paradigms, group stories and personal identity shapes our recognition of harassment stories. This section's mix of analysis, data-based interpretation and personal writing shows how various methodologies, singly and in creative combination, can provide new understanding of sexual harassment. The second part, 'Categories', investigates typology, asking whether all women benefit equally from privileging 'sexual' as the prime term in harassment. It also compares representation of sexual harassment with other categories of sexual harm. Imaginative juxtapositions and dismantlings of the term sexual harassment show how its current applications could be changed. The third part, 'Contexts', explores and diversifies the study of sexual harassment historically, geographically and culturally; through lively and close readings of texts, a picture of sexual harassment emerges as a varied and complex phenomenon which deserves correspondingly detailed interpretation.

But the chapters have many other points of overlap and contact. Recognition of sexual harassment as a phenomenon is inescapably tied to how stories of sexual harassment are understood and accepted. Helen Watson reveals that in offering stories of why sexual harassment occurs, men and women provide gender-specific accounts. She interprets these competing explanations in terms of how they appeal to larger cultural narratives about interactions between men and women. Other contributors optimistically suggest how some of these oppressive discursive institutions might be transformed for the better. Suzanne Gibson examines the process by which legal discourse comes into being. She observes that, if legal and legalistic language is rule-like and apparently prescriptive, rule-like language can also be rewritten. Rules are shorthand for larger narratives of what an ideal situation is perceived to be; they require interpretation, which gives feminists an opportunity to challenge meanings. Ruth Jamieson gives us an example of how language can be transformed from within, using existing legal terms to spotlight the conceptual gaps and weaknesses in legal representations of women and sexual harm.

Several chapters explore how subjectivity affects perceptions and accounts of harassment, whether oral, verbal or visual. Gargi Bhattacharyya looks at how public and private meanings operate simultaneously through commodification and consumption. She demonstrates, moreover, how viewers can recover agency supposedly denied by harassing representations which treat women as sex objects. The 'sex gone wrong' explanation of sexual harassment favoured by Helen Watson's male respondents leaves 'wrongness' pitifully unglossed, as no more than an accident. Celia Kitzinger shows how being 'in the wrong' in terms of sexuality leads to the deliberate threat, and actuality, of being beaten up, while Ruth Jamieson argues that legal systems place women 'in the wrong' for supposedly failing to read risk adequately. The frequency with which men describe sexual harassment as 'harmless' or 'just a bit of fun' has added to the caricature of unamused feminists as humourless. All the contributors write conscious of, and sometimes consciously about, the many ironies they live by in simultaneously resisting and rethinking sexual harassment.

In an attempt to offer genuine alternatives to dominant American models, several chapters also reflect upon the contemporary discourse of sexual harassment by looking at other historical and cultural contexts. They illuminate current constructions of harassment by investigating their origins. Diane Purkiss draws on material from antiquity to show how the eroticisation of imparting knowledge fashions the figures of both teacher and student in contemporary education; while Padma Anagol-McGinn explores how sexual harassment under colonialism affects perceptions of race, class, gender and community on the part of both colonised and colonising peoples. Jane Beckett investigates how feminist images of sexual harassment employ tropes which can 'rewrite' scenarios of harassment in order to educate and inspire resistance. In the process, she shows how visual languages do not simply mirror written texts of sexual harassment.

The chapters also have in common explorations of differences and specificities beyond those of gender, particularly by reexamining how sexual harassment is currently related to sexual violence. The book as a whole does not suggest that the discourse of sexual harassment is infinitely extendable to other forms of harassment, such as those involving race or sexuality, or to other forms of sexual violence, such as rape or sexual abuse; although in various ways the contributors look at how factors like ethnicity, sexuality, age and religious belief coexist alongside gender and complicate it in the context of sexual harassment. Indeed, the book questions whether it is helpful that sexual harassment has become the dominant paradigm and other categories subsidiary. Rather than extending the categories of harassment unthinkingly, the contributors explore complications along their boundary lines. Celia Kitzinger calls for the creation of a category of 'lesbian harassment' to address this problem, arguing that general and institutional refusals to admit the harassment of lesbians as such and the sexual harassment of women often mask homophobic anxieties regarding lesbians. Suzanne Raitt shows that assumptions about age are intricately at work, and gendered, in commonly made distinctions between sexual harassment and sexual abuse. Sexual harassment characteristically belongs in the public sphere, so harm done to children, who have a limited place in the public sphere, uses terms other than sexual harassment to describe unwanted sexual attention. Ros Hunt also demonstrates how young people in particular who become vulnerable to unwanted sexual attention in a Christian context find themselves in a contradictory relation to the language of their faith. Gargi Bhattacharyya shows how racial harassment can involve stereotypes not only of racial identity but also of heterosexuality: harassing images project fantastical sexualities for black and Asian women as pornographic objects of desire. In contrast, Padma Anagol-McGinn's study of Eve-teasing in India makes clear that this form of unwanted sexual behaviour expresses anxiety about the Westernisation of women. National meanings are significant – a point underlined by the felicitous use of 'seku hara' as the Japanese vernacularisation of sexual harassment.

Contributors show that issues of power, consent and subjectivity are variable. Where feminism has long argued that sexual harassment is about power, namely male power directed against women, many of the chapters in *Rethinking Sexual Harassment* demonstrate that power is by no means abstract and uniform. They unpack 'power', showing that it is not an unassailable monolith but has variable and distinct attributes. These analyses show that sexual harassment is a product of local factors, and that recognition of this has benefits for all parties involved. By examining the problem of harassment across different categories and contexts, such as rape, abuse and racial harassment, the contributors to this work make clear that it is no longer possible to essentialise power as simply or uniformly a male characteristic. Moving away from the preoccupation with harassment as a workplace phenomenon by which harassment is usually understood to take place in offices or factories, they expose how impersonal structures are at work in situations of harassment, and how physical and institutional spaces form and assist scenarios of harassment. Ruth Jamieson examines how the issue of sexual harassment takes up the model of the 'reasonable man' from law, especially as regards rape; this, in conjunction with ideas about female behaviour which have little to do with reality, works to the serious disadvantage of women. In the academy, as Diane Purkiss argues, the professor's authority, a complex construction of gender, intellect and historical credential, places students at an institutional disadvantage; while Ros Hunt demonstrates how religious virtues of faith and forgiveness can be appropriated by those who deny the occurrence of sexual harassment and abuse in the church. We suggest that a similar awareness of local features might be applied to other social fields such as the police, armed forces, prisons, sports or medicine.

In expanding a classic workplace focus to encompass other spheres of harassment, the book engages with ideas of space and how they shape the experience of harassment. If workplace harassment has been explained as a response to women's emergence into a previously male environment, Celia Kitzinger examines lesbian harassment as a result of their visibility in public, while Padma Anagol-McGinn looks at how Eve-teasing overspills the neat boundaries of the workplace as a scene of harassment to include the process of travelling to work. Suzanne Gibson and Suzanne Raitt investigate how public, domestic and personal space have contested meanings, particularly gendered meanings, and rethink the manner in which these concepts of space structure our understanding of harassment. On the other hand, if these chapters reveal the liabilities of different spaces, Jane Beckett explores how representations of the street can provide women artists with ways of articulating and annulling threat.

Rethinking Sexual Harassment says that we need more than the summarising 'tag', the slogan and the fixed category to deal effectively with sexual harassment. But the book's space is finite, and it does not claim to treat sexual harassment comprehensively. The contributions show what more can be done with what we already have; they reveal how a wider framework of ideas and a deeper field of focus can stimulate fresh thinking and action on sexual harassment. By bringing together areas of thought and experience previously considered separately, we aim to enlarge the range of resources available to understand and oppose harassment, and not only in the forms discussed here. We dedicate this book to all those who share that project.

Notes and References

1. Some harassment policies, for example, include rape as the far end of the spectrum of unwanted sexual attention. This means possible clashes of responsibility with the police and judiciary over rape as a criminal matter which should not be left to civil institutions to sort out.
2. See Jeffrey Minson, *Questions of Conduct: Sexual Harassment, Citizenship, Government* (London: Macmillan, 1993).
3.
   Human rights principles are based on experience, but not that of women ... When things happen to women that also happen to men, like being beaten and disappeared and tortured to death, the fact that they happened to women is not counted in, or marked as, human suffering ... What happens to women is either too particular to be universal or too universal to be particular, meaning either too human to be female or too female to be human.

   Catharine A. MacKinnon, 'Crimes of War, Crimes of Peace',
   in Stephen Shute and Susan Hurley (eds),
   On Human Rights: The Oxford Amnesty Lectures 1993
   (New York: Basic Books, 1993), pp. 84–5.

4. Forms of unwanted sexual attention directed at women in the nineteenth century and earlier suggest that, from a historical perspective, the most consistent contributory factor may be mobility – principally economic, but also social and physical. In the early modern period, verbal sexual abuse between women was significant as a way of policing class and livelihood. On this immense topic, the editors have benefited from the insights of Anna Clark, Alison Gill, Laura Gowing and Judith Walkowitz, among other historians.
5. Jeff Hearn, for instance, points out how sexual harassment was recognised as a workplace issue in the period 1870–1920. See Hearn, *Men in the Public Eye: The Construction and Deconstruction of Public Men and Public Patriarchies* (London: Routledge, 1992), especially

pp. 174–80. Hearn gives instances of sexual harassment in different employments – mining, weaving, retailing – and how each produced different conditions for sexual harassment. But the generalising concept of 'the workplace' erases historically specific class and gender relations. More particularly, it masks the anachronism of 'sexual harassment' as a label for behaviours before the 1970s.

6. Elizabeth Fox-Genovese notes the appeal of this interpretation – and its inadequacy. See *Feminism without Illusions: A Critique of Individualism* (Chapel Hill, NC: University of North Carolina Press, 1991), p. 66.

7. Lin Farley, *Sexual Shakedown: The Sexual Harassment of Working Women on the Job* (New York: Warner, 1978), for example pp. 35–7.

8. Farley, *Sexual Shakedown*, p. xi. It would be interesting to know, particularly since Farley stresses the importance of origins (p. xiii), from where the women drew on the term. Might police harassment, a staple complaint in cop shows of the time, have been a source?

9. Catharine A. MacKinnon, *Sexual Harassment of Working Women: A Case of Sex Discrimination* (New Haven, Conn.: Yale University Press, 1979).

10. See for instance Sue Wise and Liz Stanley, *Georgie Porgie: Sexual Harassment in Everyday Life* (London: Pandora, 1987), pp. 116–20.

11. See Carrie Herbert, *Talking of Silence: The Sexual Harassment of Schoolgirls* (London: Falmer, 1989), pp. 132–45, especially p. 139.

12. Susan Faludi, *Backlash: The Undeclared War against Women* (London: Chatto and Windus, 1991), pp. 401–2.

13. Katie Roiphe, *The Morning after: Sex, Fear and Feminism* (London: Hamish Hamilton, 1994); see reviews by Ruth Picardi, 'Culture of Complaint', *New Statesman and Society* (January 1994), p. 37, and Katha Pollitt, 'Not Just Bad Sex', *New Yorker* (4 October 1993), pp. 220–4.

Those hostile to 'victim feminism' (such as Roiphe) and to 'puritan feminism' (such as Paglia) tend to treat sexual harassment and date rape together as symptomatic, and to address them in the context of concern about young women and/or campus culture. See Camille Paglia, 'The MIT Lecture: Crisis in the American Universities', in Paglia, *Sex, Art and American Culture: Essays* (Harmondsworth: Penguin, 1993), pp. 249–98.

14. Camille Paglia, 'The Strange Case of Clarence Thomas and Anita Hill', *Sex, Art and American Culture*, pp. 46–7.

15. Roiphe, *The Morning after*, especially 'Introduction'.

16. Naomi Wolf, *Fire with Fire: The New Female Power and How It Will Change the 21st Century* (London: Chatto and Windus, 1993) p. 205.

17. The first case involving sexual harassment in a university, *Alexander Yale* (459 F. Supp. 1 [D. Conn.] 1977), was brought against Yale University for lack of responsiveness to sexual harassment. The suit was unsuccessful, on the grounds that 'no plaintiff could represent a class of sexually harassed women students to whom the university had allegedly been unresponsive because each incident is 'necessarily personal and particularized'. See MacKinnon, *Sexual Harassment of Working Women*, p. 85. But the subsequent widespread adoption of sexual harassment policies did prevent this kind of legal action.

18. Or synecdochal of all women in one ethnic group: 'what's happening is that we have a white middle-class problem. I don't notice so many Hispanic women and African-American women going around and carrying on like this': Camille Paglia, 'The MIT Lecture', p. 260. Or from an article on *Schindler's List*:

> This cult of victimhood, which Spielberg can't escape from, is now a growing force in a particular American discourse, the cult of 'survival' and 'endurance'. The new Holocaust Museum in Washington can hardly contain its visiting crowds, and has plugged into a certain 'politically correct' idea of everyone as a survivor of some real or imagined trauma. Young women in college who have been harassed, even verbally, by male fellow students are classed as survivors.
>
> Simon Louvish, 'Witness', *Sight and Sound* 4 (3) (March 1994), p. 14.

This is also the case in Britain, where Oxbridge students are further figured as synecdochal of all students, despite many students being not at all well-heeled or pampered, but increasingly deep in debt.

19. For instance, for television, the 1993 MORI poll for the BBC. For newspapers and magazines, see for example Eleni Kyriacou, 'Hands Off', *New Woman* (October 1993), pp. 44–7; or the survey at La Sapienza University, Rome, reported in the *Times Higher Education Supplement* 114 (11 March 1994), p. 10.

20. See for instance A.C. Sumrall and D. Taylor, *Sexual Harassment: Women Speak Out* (Freedom, Calif.: Crossing Press, 1992); and L. Armstrong, *Kiss Daddy Goodnight: A Speak-out on Incest* (New York: Pocket Books, 1978). These titles evoke the 'speak-out', a ritualistic occasion where women are encouraged to share bad experiences with an audience.

21. See Bernice R. Sandler, 'Writing a Letter to the Sexual Harasser: Another Way of Dealing with the Problem', Project on the Status and Education of Women (Washington, DC: Association of American Colleges, 1983).

22. See Toni Morrison (ed.), *Race-ing Justice, En-gendering Power: Essays on Anita Hill, Clarence Thomas, and the Construction of Social Reality* (London: Chatto and Windus, 1993), passim.
23. See for instance Jane Mayer and Jill Abramson, 'The Surreal Anita Hill', *New Yorker* (24 May 1993), pp. 90–6, especially p. 93.
24. For recent relevant articles, the editors consulted CD 'Profiles', a compact disc database providing references to articles in major newspapers worldwide.
25. Paedophiles, rapists, murderers and serial killers are associated with monsters and beasts. The colloquial 'office wolf' is perhaps a halfway point; an article by Rebecca Walker on sexual harassment evokes this threatening predatory imagery with the title, 'The Art of the Beast', *Trouble and Strife* 23 (Spring 1993), pp. 33–7. This discourse, however, is not gender-exclusive: 'sharking' describes women looking for sex on an evening out.
26. See for example Billie Wright Dziech and Linda Weiner, *The Lecherous Professor: Sexual Harassment on Campus* (Boston, Mass.: Beacon, 1984).
27. Michael Crichton, *Disclosure* (London: Century, 1994), 'Afterword', no page number.
28. *New England Journal of Medicine* (23 December 1993); also 'Female MDs Harassed by Male Patients: Poll', *Toronto Star* (23 December 1993), front page headline.
29. 'Institutions create shadowed places in which nothing can be seen and no questions asked. They make other areas show finely discriminated detail, which is closely scrutinized and ordered.' Mary Douglas, *How Institutions Think* (London: Routledge, 1987), p. 69. Though it is sometimes convenient to treat individuals and institutions as opposites, as Mary Douglas argues, institutions are made up of individuals.
30. See J. Hearn, D. Sheppard, P. Tancred-Sheriff and G. Burrell (eds), *The Sexuality of Organisation* (London: Sage, 1989). Employees can also be prevented from personalising office space by open-plan design or so-called 'hot-desking', where business is transacted at any unoccupied desk.
31. Another instance of workplace needs shaping individual identities is the issue of recreation. Employers used to encourage workplace team sports; now health is narcissistically individualised in workplace gyms. Adrienne Rich suggested imaginative solutions to the conflict between institutional and community needs. Twenty years on, her social vision is still as remote as ever. See her 'Toward a Woman-Centered University', (1973–4); reprinted in Rich, *On Lies, Secrets and Silence: Selected Prose 1966–1978* (London: Virago, 1980 repr. 1986); see especially pp. 148–9.

32. See Morrison, *Race-ing Justice*, p. xi: 'For any kind of lasting illumination the focus must be on the history routinely ignored or
played down or unknown. For the kind of insight that invites
reflection, language must be critiqued.'

    In 'The Private Parts of Justice', Andrew Ross discusses the
complex effects of the apparent suspension of legal and media
'rules' in the Hill–Thomas hearings:

    > the prosaic shock-effect of Hill's plain-style description of everyday
    > sexist behaviour broke the viewer's first law of mainstream news reporting
    > – your own politics, if they return, always return to you in alienated form.
    > That was how it felt, at least until the spin people broke the trance at
    > the end of each session of the hearings. Without their contextualising,
    > the feel of the testimony announced that the rules were being challenged,
    > especially the separation between private and public that is as rigorously
    > observed in TV land as it is regulated in the law of the land.
    >
    > In Morrison (ed), *Race-ing Justice*, p. 47.

33. One men's magazine foregrounded pecuniary rather than literary
considerations, headlining an article on Crichton 'Cashing in on
Sexual Harassment'; see *Esquire*, February 1994.
34. In *Disclosure* Crichton uses an image of the symmetrical halves of
a Rorsach test ink blot to suggest that the parts he reverses are equal.
35. For instance, where many men use touch, women and some men
may be more likely to use the telephone as a means of harassing.
36. Dinesh D'Souza, *Illiberal Education: The Politics of Race and Sex on
Campus* (New York: Vintage, 1992), pp. 142–3.
37. Bullying and homoerotic attachments in the British school and
university world of 'hearties and aesthetes' could be seen as historical
forms of sexual harassment.
38. Though class, race and above all economic forces have a strong
influence in the world of male college sports.
39. Power relations may appear to be straightforwardly a question of
gender, or they may bring into force a number of factors of which
gender may be one. For instance, gender intersects with race,
religion, politics and class for Irish people stopped and questioned
by police officers at British airports. When police go through or read
aloud their personal documents, '[i]n any other setting this type
of behaviour – where men use their position of authority to
intimidate and humiliate women – would constitute sexual
harassment. But because it takes place within a police setting this
overt force of sexism goes uncensored.' See Paddy Hillyard, *Suspect
Community: People's Experience of the Prevention of Terrorism Acts in
Britain* (London: Pluto, 1993) p. 56. Here hierarchies between men

and women are mirrored in the empowerment of British over Irish and police over civilians.

40. See Susan Bewley, 'The Law, Medical Students, and Assault', *British Medical Journal* 304 (June 1992), pp. 1551–3.

41. Cf. Operation Spanner in Britain 1993, which resulted in the jailing of members of a group of homosexual sado-masochists for consensual acts of genital torture. Also see 'Consent and Offences against the Person', Law Commission consultation paper no. 134 (London: HMSO, 1994).

42. There are anomalies in this area: for example, in British law the fax is treated as a form of post, via which it is illegal to send obscene material.

43. See Commission of the European Communities, 'Commission Recommendation of 27 November 1991 on the Protection of the Dignity of Women and Men at Work', *Official Journal of the European Communities*, L49 (24 February 1992).

44. On Title VII of the Civil Rights Act 1964, see Farley, *Sexual Shakedown*, especially pp. 133–46, and MacKinnon, *Sexual Harassment of Working Women*, p. 6.

45. P. Birks and G. McLeod, *Justinian's Institutes* (Ithaca, NY: Cornell University Press, 1987). The original text reads:

> sive quis iniuria autem committitur ... sive quis matrem familias aut praetextum praetextamve adsectatus fuerit, sive cuius pudicitia attemptata esse dicetur ... [literally, 'if any injury is committed ... if anyone follows the *materfamilias* or an adolescent male or female, or if any person's modesty has been threatened ...']
>
> (Book 4.1)

46. In *Moviewatch*, broadcast on Channel 4 on 9 March 1994, Jeff Barman, an attorney who has defended several Hollywood studios in cases of sexual harassment, commented: 'average settlements are well into the six and sometimes seven figures'. An unnamed woman speaking on the same television programme observed that, regardless of personal gain, large awards in favour of women bringing actions could have deterrent effects:

> if these guys get hit in their pocketbooks, they might not have their consciousness raised but they won't do it any more, and that's the reason for all the sexual harassment law suits, which is the only way anyone is going to learn this lesson is to get hit financially [sic].

The litigiousness of Americans can seem like a mixed blessing to non-Americans. This broadcast item also raised the question of renaming behaviours: here the general term 'sexual harassment' replaces the more culturally specific 'casting couch'.

Part I

Stories

2

Loose Rules and Likely Stories

Suzanne Gibson

PROLOGUE

I do not want to write this chapter. A faint, indefinable, but undeniable taint of incompetence hangs over it.

I started writing; I stopped; I wrote another article in the meanwhile. I have tried to wriggle out of writing my piece, but the book's editors will not let me. Usually I enjoy writing. It brings me (does this sound pretentious?) closer to myself. And so. And so, yes, there lies the dilemma.

Like other women who are contributing to this book (like many of the women who write about the subject),[1] I have my own memories of harassment.

The details of the particular episode I have in mind do not matter very much. It was not dramatic; merely sleazy, in a routine, mediocre sort of way. And it did not cause me very deep distress at the time. But to sit here now and think about it is to be reminded awkwardly, uncomfortably, of a young woman who was somehow set upon by sexual acts (it did not feel like men, like whole real people, but their acts) which she felt unable to repel. She thought she was waylaid by these acts because she had been foolish (too trusting); inexperienced (too sheltered); flattered (too vain). Those sexual ambushes seemed somehow to be her responsibility. And their cause appeared to be her own incompetence. What had to be accomplished in the aftermath, therefore, was the learning of the lessons. Wise up. Grow up. Eat humble pie. I became a renaissance woman of sexual wrong.

What we put, sometimes, some of us, between ourselves and the engulfing world, is our sense of competence. It seemed to me then that my repertoire of competencies should come to include not-attracting-unwanted-sexual-attention. The fact that unwanted sexual acts were foisted on me made me feel at first incompetent, and later defiant, tried by life. But I never felt altogether powerless, because I thought, erroneously or otherwise, that it was in my power to learn to behave so that these things would not happen to me again.

Harassment is, one way or the other, always about power; and also about defiance. People other than myself have claimed and asserted their remnant sense of competency or power by challenging the person who is harassing them. Sometimes that is the only way that the harassment will ever stop. One of the resources people will try to use against a harasser with greater social or institutional status than their own, is rules. This chapter is a reflection upon what happens to power when we wield rules, or sets of rules, against it.

THE RULES OF HARASSMENT

The long shadow of the law[2] falls far beyond the courtroom. Publicly reported judgements[3] of harassment cases are a tiny and unrepresentative sample of harassment disputes. Reported cases are a reliable guide neither to the hidden routines of harassment nor to the organisational responses to it. It is the impact reported cases have upon the thinking of company and labour lawyers, and the advice these lawyers give in turn to the companies and employers who are their clients, which give reported cases their import. In the case of sexual or racial harassment in particular,[4] we will most often locate law's influence lying under institutional codes of behaviour, in workplace grievance procedures, in the rules and regulations of private organisations.

What interests me is not so much what happens in the very few cases of harassment which go for adjudication by courts or public tribunals, but rather what might happen when organisations (colleges, companies, public bodies) set up their own rule-based systems of private adjudication. The situations I have watched developing in my mind's eye as I have written this chapter are those where accounts of harassment encounter law-like disciplinary systems and the adjudicators who work within them.

These systems may be described as law-like for two reasons. Firstly, in the advanced industrial economies of the world, organisations appear to have embraced mechanisms of internal control and dispute resolution which bear many of the hallmarks of modern law.[5] How do these codes of behaviour, disciplinary rules and sundry regulations express affinity with the legal ideal? The codes are impersonal, in the sense that they are held to apply equally to all members of the organisation and are promulgated in the name not of sovereign individuals but of collective or corporate order. The rules are not arbitrary or capricious, but justified and reasonable, in accord with the purposes and objectives of the organisation. These regulatory codes are open in the sense that they are made known to members of the organisational community. And they are closed in the sense that new rules are not applied retrospectively. The rules bind decision-makers within the organisation. There are avenues of appeal.

Secondly, organisational codes have become increasingly law-like as (in Britain) the legislature has stipulated that some types of management action may be scrutinised by an industrial tribunal.[6] These tribunals have scrutinised management decisions in accordance with a specific legal framework, and according to legalistic ideals. Employee dismissals should not be, in legal terms, unfair. So that natural justice may be served, tribunals may insist that, just as the decision to dismiss must be a legally fair decision, so too must be the procedures which precede it. And, as an employee may claim that she is unfairly dismissed when she feels compelled to resign a job which has been made intolerable to her, there should exist workplace grievance procedures which are also fair.[7]

Of course, the prescriptive requirements that I have written of here (the stipulation that procedures should be fair) do not emerge as direct commands to corporate bodies. They emerge, rather, through rights given to individuals (to claim compensation for discrimination, for example) which create, in turn, what seem to be corresponding duties in the organisations against which claims may be made. But these 'duties' are more truly warnings to employers to protect themselves from the adverse consequences of claims made against them.[8] It is perfectly possible for an organisation to buy itself out of its 'duties' to its members should it decide that the adverse consequences are less burdensome than the efforts necessary to avoid them. In this respect, feminist action within the institution is one of the 'costs' which the unethical employer would have to bear.

We weave our lives through webs of rules. When we go to school, to college or to work for large organisations, we will be taken to have acceded to the regulations and codes of private government. In this first section of this chapter, I contemplate some of the implications of living by the rules. In the second section, I consider what happens when the way we tend to think and talk about our individual lives – that is, through stories – confronts the way we tend to seek to organise our communal life – that is, through rules.

Philosophers of law have spent at least the last quarter century or so arguing over the nature of rules and their role in legal reasoning.[9] Our concern here is not so much with legal reasoning (decisions made by judges in courts) as with legalistic reasoning (decisions made by laypeople in the shadow of the law), and this serendipitously sets to one side some of the more persistent problems pressing modern jurisprudence. I have chosen the legal philosopher Frederick Schauer as our guide to the world of rules, as he has recently published an excellent account of some of the ways in which rules work in life as well as law.[10] I shall use his discussion as the basis for my own, which adds our specific concern with harassment codes to his general account.

Philosophers commonly draw a distinction between descriptive rules ('As a rule, men can't keep their hands to themselves') and prescriptive rules ('No Eve-teasing').[11] Interestingly, a similar problem can generate a differently accentuated descriptive rule ('As a rule, women travellers are harassed by men, not by other women'), resulting in an elliptically expressed but nevertheless equally prescriptive rule ('Ladies' Compartment').[12]

Descriptive rules, as Schauer observes, are very recognisably generalisations. If we choose to say that, *as a rule*, 'Men can't keep their hands to themselves', we are also implicitly recognising that there are occasions when they do. If, *as a rule*, strange women are more trustworthy than strange men, then also, sometimes, a woman may pick my pocket and a man will render me some assistance. Moreover, expecting that the phrase 'men can't keep their hands to themselves' will make sense to anyone is to know that listeners will refer to their stocks of social knowledge and appreciate that for the purpose of this utterance 'men' probably means 'strange men', and 'can't keep their hands to themselves' means 'touch inappropriately intimate parts of the body'.

Feminism has of course a distinguished history of locating and objecting to the iniquities of descriptive generalisation, starting with the use of 'man' to mean 'all men and women of the world', which leads us to Schauer's next observation. This is that descriptive generalisations suppress differences, something that is exemplified with some immediacy in feminist irritation at men and women being lumped together in the *general* term 'man' or 'he', a term which also bears the *particular* meaning 'human of the male (and not female) sex'. To return to our 'Eve-teasing' example, any definition of the term 'men' would include both homosexual and heterosexual men. Any desire on either of their parts to 'keep their hands to themselves' or indeed do otherwise will be stimulated by quite different motives and quite different objects. Equally, the privileged seats in the Ladies' Compartment may be occupied by either honest or dishonest 'women', women with whom one either might or might not prefer to travel.

The two prescriptive rules are generalisations derived, as Schauer points out all prescriptive rules must be, from calculations of probability. 'Ladies' Compartment' (put directly, 'Men keep out') and 'No Eve-teasing' respond to the same descriptive generalisation, 'Men can't keep their hands to themselves'. But the 'Ladies' Compartment' rule is derived from calculating the probability 'A woman travelling without a male protector is at risk', where the 'No Eve-teasing' rule is derived from calculating the probability 'Men will molest women in public places'.

Examining the rule 'Ladies' Compartment' more closely, we see that it apprehends all kinds of threats from men to unprotected women travellers over and above sexual harassment; and it addresses itself to the problem of women who have no male protector as well as, simultaneously, to the behaviour of some members of the category 'men'. Women's need for protection is one of the assumptions upon which this rule is based, and the lack of a protector one of the causal calculations which produces it. Assuming that every woman requires a guardian, the rule provides a substitute for the protective male in the shape of the 'Ladies' Compartment'. At the same time, since we cannot know in advance which individuals out of all men will offer such provocation as justifies exclusion, the rule simply excludes every man.[13]

Where the 'Ladies' Compartment' makes women's general need for protection the object of the calculation, the 'No Eve-teasing' rule makes men's behaviour its object. 'No Eve-teasing' lacks the clear protective intent of the rule 'Ladies' Compartment', because it is predicated upon the assumption that women will and must make short journeys without male guardians. And while derived from a similar descriptive generalisation 'sexual harassment', it is more specific, lacking the broad apprehension of harm which generates the 'Ladies' Compartment' rule. While this results in a less crude rule, one which does not exclude all men, good and bad, from certain areas, it also results in a less effective preventive measure. The rule merely serves to remind 'Eve-teasers' that public authorities disapprove of their behaviour, and they may therefore incur a sanction when they indulge it.

What is especially interesting to a lawyer (and a legal philosopher like Schauer) is what happens when adjudicators are invited to apply prescriptive rules derived, on the back of calculations of probability, from descriptive generalisations. The adjudicator will often encounter two distinct, albeit related, difficulties. One: although the meaning of the generalisation is clear to her, she thinks this a poor rule because the category seems to include or exclude too much. Two: the meaning of the generalisation is not clear to her and she has difficulty deciding what is to be included or excluded.

Difficulty number one is related to the accuracy of the original generalisation. At one level, the 'Ladies' Compartment' solution is an 'overinclusive' prescriptive rule: in determining that 'all men' will 'keep out' of the Ladies' Compartment, many (wholly innocent, delightful and attractive travelling companions?) will be excluded. At the same time, however, the 'Ladies' Compartment' represents an 'underinclusive' prescriptive rule: it permits all women to enter the compartment, even women whose behaviour may be as bad as that of the men who have justifiably been barred. (Hard to imagine, I know.)

The problem of over- or underinclusiveness emerges out of the probabilistic, causal generalisation we have made. As even ostensibly civilised men are capable of behaving in most unpleasant ways, it follows that any man, indeed all men, are potentially problems to the lone woman traveller. The fact that the *nasty man* will be indistinguishable, before the event, from the *only potentially nasty* man nullifies, for protective purposes, any distinction between the category 'nasty man' and the category 'all men'.

Difficulty number two is that of interpretation.[14] Unperturbed by the prospect of excluding delightful men and prepared to undertake the risk of including bad women, we may nevertheless not be able to agree on what a 'man' is, when it matters. Where a categorical 'Ladies' Compartment' type of rule is applied, an adjudicator may have to decide whether or not a given object falls within the prohibited class: that is, whether the person attempting to enter the compartment is a man for the purpose of the rule. What about a 15-year-old boy, or a very sick old man travelling with his attractive young daughter? Although the result remains under- or overinclusiveness, these two persons present us with rather different sorts of problem.

The problem with the 15-year-old boy is that he may fall within the definition of 'man' as far as some of the women in the compartment are concerned, and that of 'boy' in the eyes of the others. When does a 'boy' become a 'man'? One way of finding an answer to the question of interpretation would be to poll the women in the Ladies' Compartment (without explaining why) and adopt the definition of 'man' prevalent in that community of meaning. We could also poll the train in general (without explaining why) and this time arrive at an answer which included a man's view on what made a boy a man. Might it be different?

Another way of finding an answer, one which this time acknowledges the reason for the rule, would be to ask the women concerned to make their own calculation of the risks involved. We should ask them to decide at what age adolescent boys become likely to engage in sexual harassment, and select that age as the moment at which we start treating them as men. If we were then to put the question to the whole train and not just the women using the compartment, we might again get a different answer. Some men, for the right motives we hope, might wish the women to continue to be protected; while other men, we fear, might wish to take advantage of a newly voted-in lack of protection.

When we set about defining objects against the background of their purposes, we produce a far more complex, and sometimes contradictory, definition than would result from the first, entirely abstract, exercise we tried. A boy old enough, perhaps, to be interested in the 'manly' activity of sexual harassment might be thought too young to be involved in the 'manly' activity of war. So the women in the carriage might agree, quite reasonably, to exclude the boy as a 'man' from the carriage, and at the same time protect him as a 'boy' from wartime conscription.

The problem of interpretation presented by the sick old man is not so much that of appreciating the meaning of the category as that of appreciating the reason for the rule. Although as a 'man' our invalid falls unquestionably within the scope of the exclusion, there might be good reason to subvert the rule and allow him to accompany his daughter into the Ladies' Compartment. Such a decision could be consistent with the underlying purpose of the rule. The daughter could require protection from unwanted attention (the old man is in no position to defend her honour himself), and besides, the other women in the carriage would not be harmed (he is too ill to molest anyone).[15] I have presented the sick old man as a problem of interpretation, because that is what lawyers tend to argue is the problem when they wish to be seen to be playing by the rules as well as producing the right outcomes. But when we reexamine him, the sick old man is as much an example of the first difficulty, the wrong things excluded or too many things included, when the rule is applied, as he is an example of the second difficulty, that of interpretation. If the adjudicator thinks that, on a strict interpretation, it is a poor rule which excludes the old invalid, she may be tempted to argue for a looser 'interpretation', one which includes him. The line between a creative interpretation and an illegitimate one can be exceedingly thin, which is of course why lawyers spend so much time arguing over it.

Were the adjudicator now to turn to the prohibition on 'Eve-teasing', she would find herself confronted at the outset by a question of interpretation. Although the immediate problem of a specific kind of offensive behaviour has been directly addressed by the prohibition, anyone accused will be able to exploit the ambiguities which such a description of human behaviour invokes. What touching, where on the body, constitutes Eve-teasing? What if the touch was accidental? What if one touches an 'innocent' area with ill intent and a concupiscent eye? What if the woman invited it? What if the man was mistaken about the woman inviting it? And so on ...

Schauer argues that if the adjudicator intends to act with integrity and bind herself to the rules, it is the problem of under- or overinclusiveness which makes rule-based decisions interesting. A man tries to enter the Ladies' Compartment brandishing a knife and threatening to 'cut up all bitch whores': here, there will be no difference between the adjudicator applying the rule itself ('All men stay out') and directly applying the justification for the rule ('Women require protection from some men'). Now imagine that the people seeking access to the Ladies' Compartment are the sick old man and his daughter, while the knifeman goes on stalking the corridor. Most people would, I think, find it easy to subvert the rule on this occasion and let them in, but if our adjudicator is really committed to the rules as the basis for her decision she faces a challenging dilemma.

To summarise then, we have seen that prescriptive rules are derived by making causal inferences following from descriptive generalisations. One problem associated with generalisation is that it tends to suppress differences within the categories which the process of abstraction creates. Partly in consequence of this, generalised rules are prone, if we attend to the underlying reason for the rule, either to exclude matters which should be included, or to include matters which should be excluded. When this happens, the adjudicator committed to the rules is faced with the choice of either adapting the rule or arriving at an invidious outcome.

We have not yet completed our analysis of rules, but this is a good point at which to pause and consider how rule-making affects the way we think about harassment. First of all, what differences come to be suppressed when we creatively generalise about harassment? Next, what causal inferences underlie prescriptive rule-making in the domain of harassment? And then, what problem-solving categories (with what interpretative difficulties) emerge?

What Differences Come to be Suppressed?

'Harassment' as an abstract category covers a very diverse range of performed behaviours. Most codes on harassment acknowledge this when they accompany the codified abstraction of disciplinary regulations with a more detailed narrative description of harassing behaviour.[16] But this narrative itself often includes descriptive generalisations, referring, for example, to harassment on the basis of 'sex' or 'race'. Both 'sex' and 'race' are, I think, generalisations which suppress radically different constructions and perspectives: those of 'me' or 'we' and that of 'the Other'. The concept of 'sexual' harassment or 'racial' harassment starts with particulars, with known instances, with individual understandings and feelings about what the event meant to (primarily) the victim. From these particulars emerge the abstract references to a general class of behaviours, distinct because they still bear the traces of their racial or sexual origins. But when we use these qualifying adjectives descriptive precision arrives at the same moment as descriptive elision. Is race the same thing to a racist and a person from a racial minority? Is sex the same thing to men and to women?

If we answer 'no' to those questions, as I think we must, we see that the categories of 'race' and 'sex' suppress differences between individual perceptions (perpetrator and victim, say) of the same event (a racial attack). Equally, they suppress differences between group perceptions (men and women, say) of the same domain of human action and behaviour (sex). Behind the processes of abstraction which provide us with categories, and behind our efforts to communicate meaningfully with each other by reference to such categories, lie dramatically different experiences. Schauer thinks that rule-based decision-making becomes interesting when an over- or underinclusive rule has to be applied to an awkward instance. Similarly, it may be said of generalisations (sex, race) in general that they become interesting when the different stories which underlie them, and enable us as individuals to understand them, erupt through their surface. What is especially interesting is that individuals understand generalisations by explicating them through individually meaningful stories, and yet these generalisations are still regarded as just that: *generalisations*.

We have noted that prescriptive rules are derived from descriptive rules. But it is as much the case that, as rules come to be applied, the procedure will operate in reverse. The interpretation of prescriptive rules may both warp and reinforce their descriptive element. Where an abstraction has been made, application of the rule on any future occasion will require fresh consideration of the meaning of the abstraction. (What does 'men' mean for the purpose of deciding this case?) The content and meaning of the abstraction, precisely because it is an imprecise, possibly over- or underinclusive, generalisation are therefore apt to shift. ('Sick old males' are not 'men' for the purposes of this rule.) The shifted meaning that the prescriptive rule acquires will then confront the original descriptive rule, and the battle over meaning is enjoined. (What do you mean, sick old men may use the women's lavatories?)

The battle over meaning breaks out almost instantaneously with sexual harassment in particular. The differing experiences of men and women, their divergent understandings and expressions of sexual claims, yield to the individual quite different meanings when he or she reflects upon the generalisation 'sexual' for the purposes of harassment. These meanings are, as in the nature of many sexual meanings, highly contested. Except in the expression of the rule, the difference in sexual perspectives on harassment is barely suppressed at all, and at the point of the rule's application the jagged consequences of the differing perspectives erupt through its silky surface. The process of enforcing a

prescriptive rule against sexual harassment is as likely to result in a new
descriptive rule 'Women can be oversensitive and mendacious' as it is
to endorse the original 'Some men exploit their power in the workplace
to extract sexual favours'. The battle over meaning becomes a matter
of maintaining the original prescriptive rule 'No sexual harassment' in
the face of attempts to shift it to 'No sexual violence,' or even to 'No
defamation of (male sexual) character'.

What Causal Inferences Underlie Prescriptive Rule-making in the Domain of Harassment?

'[P]rescriptive generalisation', writes Schauer, 'commonly starts with a
particular, takes it as an exemplar of some more general category, and
then searches for the property of the particular that is causally relevant
to the occurrence of the more general category, [that is], the evil sought
to be eradicated'. Schauer has in view here a model of rule-making in
which reason will generally result in the declaration of a prohibition backed
up (if the prohibition is to prove effective) by a threat to punish trans-
gressors; and by the provision of a remedy to a complainant. It is helpful
to look at English law as well, as it were, from the opposite end of the
telescope; that is, by starting with the remedies which have been provided
and working out from there what evils it has been sought to eradicate.
What we find is that legal rules in the domain of harassment rest upon
a foundation of fragmented and narrowly drawn causal inferences.

   In both the common law and in statute, it is protection from continuing
harassment by means of an injunction which has been the subject of
legal rule-making. In the common law, the problem for those seeking
protection through the 'inherent jurisdiction' of the courts is that a
request for an injunction is not regarded in law as a cause of action in
itself. It is, rather, a remedy provided by the court in order to protect
an established legal interest. The interests which the courts have been
prepared to protect in the past have been those relating to the physical
sanctity of the person, so that an injunction to prevent further violence
could be sought in an action for damages for assault; those relating to
the sanctity of legal proceedings, so that injunctions may be granted
to protect litigants from their adversaries; those relating to the sanctity
of legal marriage, so that the privileged legal and social status of marriage
remained secure; and those relating to the sanctity of private property,
so that an injunction may be granted to exclude a bothersome interloper.
Until very recently, unless the victim of harassment could claim that
a physical assault was imminent, or that there were related legal proceedings underway, or that there was a property right to protect, no
injunctive protection would be forthcoming.[17]

Looking to statute law, injunctive relief against harassment is available through the domestic violence legislation[18] where the harassment amounts to 'molestation' by a sexual partner. Protection is, however, only available to married couples, or couples currently cohabiting as man and wife. The rules encapsulated in the domestic violence legislation of the 1970s reflect the immediate concerns, and presumptions of causal relevance, of the campaigners who fought for it: that is, wife-beating and 'common-law-wife'-beating. For these campaigners the marital or quasi-marital nature of the relationship between the abuser and his abused was causal relevance incarnate. It was the sex-specific nature of the intimate relationship which stimulated the abuse; it was the private nature of family life which allowed the abuse to proceed unchecked; and it was women's economic dependency in connubial or quasi-connubial relationships which prevented them from leaving an abusive partner.

So what are the sources of the modern harassment code? We have already seen that there are two quite distinct points of origin: the motives of the institution which decides to promulgate a code, and the legislative initiatives which have persuaded it that it may be effective to do so. The proximate calculation (the one made by employers, for instance) is of the economic consequences of failure to protect employees: the cost of any claim made by an aggrieved party, the costs of impaired performance in the workplace, the costs of poor labour relations, for example. Behind such calculations lie more remote inferences: those which produced the employment protection, and sex and race discrimination, legislation.

I cannot embark here upon a detailed inquiry as to origins. We may, though, at least observe an interesting historical progression. The highly *specific, legal* remedies of the common law have given way to far more *general, bureaucratic* ones, a pattern consistent with legal-historical trends at large. The shift from legal to bureaucratic rule solutions may have something to do with a difference in the way we now tend to make causal inferences, and thence derive rules. Or it may have something to do with how we now want rules to work for us.[19] Either way, both specificity and generality in rules have their own advantages and disadvantages.

What Problem-solving Categories (with What Interpretative Difficulties) Emerge?

We saw that the generalisations 'sexual' and 'racial' carry the advantage of reflecting the relatively concrete descriptions from which they are derived; and at the same time carry the disadvantage that, as generalisations, they are unlikely to mean the same thing to differently situated social actors. We have also noted that making causal inferences from too narrowly circumscribed descriptive generalisations results in historical absurdity. Every rule, therefore, balances generality against specificity. It must be sufficiently general to address all instances of the evil its promulgators sought to eradicate, and at the same time sufficiently specific to identify the evil with some precision. The dilemma which confronts us is whether to define harassment as generally as possible, in which case we risk the differences we suppress at the prescriptive level erupting uncontrollably in specific adjudications; or whether to define harassment as concretely as possible, in which case we risk consigning it to the wastebin of irrelevance.

To illustrate the dilemma, then. *A broad rule*: 'Harassment consists of ... unwelcome sexual advances ... such as may reasonably be expected ... seriously to disrupt the work or substantially to reduce the quality of life of the complainant.' Dr Sleaze tells the disciplinary panel (Chairman: Prof. Willing Dupe) that the sexual advances he made to his graduate student were 'not unwelcome'. Anyway, he will add, even had he been mistaken and they had been unwelcome, they were so trivial that no reasonable woman would have allowed them to affect her work or diminish her quality of life.[20] Dupe thinks Sleaze is an attractive man (as far as he can tell) and he hears evidence that the graduate student has had several affairs, including one with a teaching member of the faculty.[21] Does the plaintiff win her case? She does not. *A narrow rule:* 'Sexual relationships between students and teaching members of the faculty are not permitted.' Dr Sleaze points out to Prof. Dupe that he is not a member of the faculty but a visiting lecturer. At the next faculty meeting Prof. Dupe proposes that the rule be changed to encompass all student–teacher relationships. Now Dr Sleaze starts harassing his secretary. So at the next faculty meeting Prof. Dupe proposes ... And so on, until we arrive at the broad rule.

Well then, if rules perform for us so obdurately, why bother with them?

Schauer proposes a number of reasons for playing by the rules, of which the four that follow are perhaps the most compelling: rules are a reliable way of making decisions; they are an efficient way of making decisions; they generate stability; they constrain the decision-maker.

Firstly: rules are reliable. They are reliable, Schauer argues, in the sense that:

decision-makers who follow rules even when other results appear preferable enable those affected to predict in advance what the decisions are likely to be. Consequently, those affected by the decisions of others can plan their activities more successfully under a regime of rules than under more particularistic decision-making.[22]

Since rules create general categories in advance of the need for any given decision, rule-based decision-making should be, in principle, both simpler and more predictable. The adjudicator is required to consider only the pertinent categories, and this limited scope should result in a reduced range of possible outcomes. Interestingly, Schauer suggests that if all parties are likely to come to the same decision in the given circumstances, there would be little to be gained from having a rule: rules 'have their greatest marginal advantage when addressees and enforcers have ... different outlooks on decisions while still sharing a common language'.[23]

We could put the marginal advantage conclusion another, rather more blunt way. Rules are a tool to manage entrenched conflict, a tool we use when we anticipate the expression of opposing views, such as ideas about sexual or racial prerogative. Rephrasing Schauer's proposition helps us to see that being able to rely upon a rule is really being able to rely upon social power being allocated in a certain way. Rules settle the outcome in advance, in accordance with the rule-maker's view of what should, in principle, be the proper outcome of such disputes. But if we seek to rely upon rules in this way, we should remember the adjudicator's dilemma as she watches the sick father and the knifeman pacing in the corridor outside the Ladies' Compartment. Will we be able to trust the decision-maker to apply the rules appropriately?

Our second reason for playing by the rules is: rules are efficient. It would surprise the author of *Bleak House*, inventor of the celebrated case of *Jarndyce* v. *Jarndyce*, to hear that rules are an efficient way of making decisions.[24] But the contortions of Chancery litigation which Dickens satirised are not, I think, the invariable concomitant of rule-based decision-making. I think we may accept that simple rules inflexibly applied enable us to make unreflecting and rapid decisions. The invention of rules such as those Schauer lists – 'grey flannel suits for business; gowns at high table; no white shoes before Memorial Day' – allow us to 'eliminate the calculations, the anguish, and the expenditures that would otherwise be necessary, thereby freeing time, money, and mental space for more worthwhile endeavors'.[25] In more formal contexts, decision-making is streamlined when adjudicators 'are channelled by relatively precise rules into deciding cases on the basis of a comparatively small number of easily identified factors ([e.g.] Was the defendant driving faster than 55 miles per hour?)'.[26] We are returned here, are we not, to a dilemma we confronted earlier? If we define harassment

broadly (abstractly), we must anticipate lengthy and subversive argu-
mentation whenever we try to apply the rule. If we define harassment
narrowly (concretely), we may anticipate ease of enforcement in
situations where the rule applies. We must also anticipate, though, many
circumstances in which we feel morally the rule ought to apply and yet
discover it does not.

Third reason: rules create stability. Schauer argues that since rule-based
decision-making narrows (as we have seen) the range of potential
decisions, it makes departure from the status quo more difficult. This
quality of rules provides the argument, for example, both for and
against a written constitution: those *for* think that we should enshrine
our basic political freedoms now, while the going is good; those *against*
think that in future the going is as likely to get better as it is to get worse.
Those who have fought for codes on harassment know well that what
they fought for was to secure the principle 'harassment is wrong' within
the status quo.

Finally: rules constrain the decision-maker. Those who have fought
for codes on harassment also well know that what they were fighting
for were ways to constrain the decision-makers asked to deal with cases
of harassment. The difficulties of interpretation we considered as we
travelled in the Ladies' Compartment may give us cause to question
whether the decision-maker is always quite as constrained as we might
wish. This concern is especially likely to arise if we cannot choose
(whole train or Ladies' Compartment only?) the decision-makers. But
as long as the decision-maker can be made to submit to them, rules, as
the barons of Magna Carta fame were aware, are more trustworthy
than sovereign caprice and less equivocal than the sovereign's discretion.
Moreover, in so far as we use codes of rules to ensure that decision-makers
confront those and only those issues which the architects of a code deem
relevant, then so too do we use codes to ensure that the issue is actually
confronted, that some decision is indeed made. The American jurist Karl
Llewellyn has described one of law's jobs as the job of 'arranging the
say'; that is, of arranging for things to be said which must be heard if
social consensus is to be maintained.[27] Law-like rules determine that
the harassment complaint will be heard,[28] and they bestow authority
upon some law-like person to hear it.

The architects of a code will stipulate that certain carefully defined
behaviours are wrong, will nominate an appropriate person to deal with
complaints and will require an adjudicator to deal with a complaint
according to the rules. If our hopeful reliance upon rules is to be
justified, they will thereby have engineered a range of just outcomes
from an always as yet unknown panoply of unjust behaviours.

So just how hopeful should we be?

THE STORIES OF HARASSMENT

[A] conversation in Anne Tyler's novel *The Accidental Tourist*. Macon and Muriel have been living together, but Macon is still legally married to someone else. Macon makes a casual remark about Alexander, Muriel's son:

'I don't think Alexander's getting a proper education,' he said to her one evening.

'Oh, he's okay.'

'I asked him to figure out what change they'd give back when we bought the milk today, and he didn't have the faintest idea. He didn't even know he'd have to subtract.'

'Well, he's only in second grade,' Muriel said.

'I think he ought to switch to a private school.'

'Private schools cost money.'

'So? I'll pay.'

She stopped flipping the bacon and looked over at him. 'What are you saying?', she said.

'Pardon?'

'What are you saying Macon? Are you saying you're committed?'

Muriel goes on to tell Macon that he must make up his mind whether he wants to divorce his wife and marry her: she can't put her son in a new school and then have to pull him out when and if Macon returns to his wife. The conversation ends with Macon saying, incredulously, 'But I just want him to learn to subtract!'[29]

Deborah Tannen uses that fictional conversation to show that sometimes, when men and women argue, each will express a core concern which differs according to their sex. Muriel listens to what Macon says in ways Tannen suggests are womanly, with a mind attuned to issues of intimacy, and she responds to the 'metamessage' she hears: what is Macon saying about their relationship? Macon, on the other hand, speaks like a man, with a mind attuned to blunt action, and he affects to be concerned only with the immediate 'message': what about Alexander's education?

Thirty-five years of puzzlement lead me to believe that Tannen is right, that men and women do converse, all the while in a common language, about uncommonly different things. But while I find her study intriguing, it is not essential to my purpose that we wholeheartedly endorse her conclusions. I want to use Muriel and Macon's argument to make a point related to, but different from, Tannen's.

'What are you saying?', asks Muriel. 'Are you saying you're committed?' 'Committed' is a generalisation, an abstraction, which for Muriel in this story may mean many things: a higher standard of living (she is a single parent when she meets Macon); security; a caring father for her son; an awkward relationship with Macon's much grander family. For Macon, 'committed' means finally quitting another relationship, one which created his son and was crushed by the child's death; it means taking on a stepson; it means being confronted by his own emotional ambivalence. As readers of the novel, guided by an author, we can see what generally so painfully eludes us: the different stories which lie under and then erupt through the generalisations of the common language.

'Let us speak of a proper education,' starts Macon, with an abstraction. It lacks colour; Muriel is unmoved. So Macon tells her (part of) the story which lies under it: Alexander cannot subtract change. (What part of this tale does Macon not narrate: That his own parents thought maths was important? That he was embarassed by Alexander's stupidity? That people might think ignorant Alexander was his own child?) On Alexander's behalf, refracting Macon's focus, Muriel adds a detail to Macon's story: Alexander is young, still in the second grade. Only after Macon authors the story further with a future action, 'I'll pay', does it become clear that the Alexander story, and more especially Macon's abstraction 'education', bears a different meaning for the two adults. 'What are you saying?', demands Muriel at the point at which Macon's concerns turn to a future finally made concrete, a future which will affect her. And now her own abstraction, commitment, surfaces. Had Muriel started this conversation; had she turned to Macon and said, 'Let us speak of commitment,' each might have shared the telling of a similar Alexander story but this time as a means of illustrating, understanding, Muriel's own abstracted concerns.

The narrative element in Muriel and Macon's exchange is what enables them to understand each other, and to reckon on each other's abstractions. In ordinary conversation this is what makes life interesting, if troublesome, at the times we fail to realise that we need to know more of the story if we are truly to understand the abstraction.

But what if the abstraction is in the form of a prescriptive rule with which parties must comply and which some person must understand and enforce? Schauer, we know, thinks that rules become interesting where they are under- or overinclusive. But if we have such difficulties with abstraction, Macon and Muriel's difficulties, how are we to know what is supposed to be included in the rule or excluded from it? One way, of course, is to tell stories. We illustrate the rule with the colour of words. The catch is that we will be trying to tell these rule-bounding tales at the very same time as we are trying to apply a bounded rule. The most compelling narratives will be told in the course of testifying to the rule's breach; perhaps as I am seeking to justify myself, or as I am twisting and turning the story away from some untoward conclusion, or as I am in the process of coming to a judgement. The boundaries of the rule are not known until we do these things, but the point of having the rule is to impose boundaries upon such things. If harassment is an abstraction which has different meanings to differently situated social actors, it will be on the occasions when we seek to enforce the rules against it that this will become clear. And what then if the judges, the victim, the perpetrator, would all tell a different tale to explain to us what harassment means?

Academic lawyers have recently turned to consider the role of narrative in legal decision-making in their efforts to identify what really happens when living actors engage with law. For some, finding the true reasons for the relative unpredictability of legal outcomes remains a jurisprudential holy grail, and accounts of narrative structure and function have provided interesting new impetus to this pursuit. Others have identified the lawyer's client's commitment to his or her own story as a compelling professional issue, not least because some clients would rather tell their story than win their case. Both groups of writers are concerned, as we must be, with what makes a story convincing: so convincing, in the first case, that a judge will find law to accommodate it; so convincing, in the second case, that a client will choose to tell it even if that puts her cause itself at risk.[30]

In legal and law-like decision-making, the story we are searching for is the one which is not just good but also true. Only when we think we can know what actually happened and what ought (not) to have happened can we lay a rule over the range of social outcomes and produce its consequences: compensation; punishment; reparation. If we are to understand what happens or guess what will happen in decisions on harassment, we need to know three things. Firstly, what will make a story believable? By 'believable', I mean that the adjudicator will conclude at the end of the process of scrutiny that the alleged wrong was actually done. Secondly, what makes a story persuasive? By 'persuasive', I mean that the adjudicator will conclude when she evaluates the story that what was done was wrong and should be righted in some way. And thirdly, what happens when persuasive, believable stories encounter rules?

To our first question, then. Legal and law-like decision-making generally relies upon accounts by others (witnesses, plaintiff, defendant) of what actually happened. Exploring the question of how jurors decide what is true in the course of a criminal trial, W. Lance Bennett and Martha Feldman have concluded that the likelihood of a story being believed is heavily dependent upon its structural coherence. In experimental situations, they found that there was no statistical association between the actual truth of a story being told and the extent to which it was perceived to be true by those who heard it. It seems that when we are asked to act as arbiters of the truth, what apparently concerns us most is the degree of structural ambiguity in a story: the more there is, the less true we judge the story to be.

The likely-to-be-true story will convince us in relation to a 'setting' (a place of work, for example), a 'concern' (a request for sexual favours in exchange for securing a promotion, maybe) and a 'resolution' (the employee is not promoted, perhaps). But evidence of what actually happened brought in relation to each of these elements individually will not, in itself, convince us: we require, too, that the elements cohere into a satisfying whole. In the legal or quasi-legal hearing each element in the narrative is liable to contestation. The winner of the contest for truth, according to Bennett and Feldman, will be whichever party manages best to organise the play of doubt and ambiguity among and between the various elements.[31]

To some extent Bennett and Feldman's answer seems merely to put us one step back; we have now to explain why some arrangements of doubt and ambiguity are more or less convincing than others.[32] The reasons which persuade us to ascribe a high degree of structural coherence to a given story, and therefore believe it, are complex and largely outside the scope of this chapter. But I think we should be concerned for the extent to which harassment narratives, in terms of the categories with which we conventionally organise our understanding of the world, are often inherently incoherent. Sexual harassment, for instance, is frequently harassment precisely because it is perceived to be an *abuse* of power and, whether naive or not, an *inversion* of expectation; the world turned upside down. Furthermore, at the core of any given harassment story is an event which may have been witnessed by no-one; the meaning, even were it to be observed, may be unclear to all but the perpetrator and the victim; the effect of a 'perpetrator's' acts upon the 'victim' may genuinely be misunderstood or unintended; a victim may not react in the correct way; and a victim may have conflicting and confused feelings about his or her own story. Almost everything about the harassment narrative requires the listener to abandon habitual assumptions of normality.

The (to be no further explained) requirement of internal coherence reemerges in relation to our second question: what makes a story persuasive? We are not so much concerned now with whether we believe the story we have been told. Rather, we are concerned with whether this story discloses a compelling reason to decide the case in favour of its author. Here, we are returned to the question of the impact that the actual events have upon an arbiter armed with rules. The events are of course rarely presented to the arbiter as events. They are presented as stories of events. It has been argued in the legal and philosophical literature that the persuasive story, like the believable story, is in some way a familiar story; one which fits snugly within a framework of crucial intuitions and preconceptions. What makes a rule intelligible, what pulls a rule in a new direction or keeps it anchored close to its origins, is it seems an especially compelling 'pre-text': what has been described as an 'entrenched generalisation',[33] an 'idealized cognitive model'[34] or a 'stock story',[35] for example.

Because he supplies us with an interesting legal example, I have chosen Bernard Jackson to illustrate this point. 'Decision-making in adjudication', Jackson writes, 'consists in comparing a narrative constructed from the facts of the case with the underlying narrative pattern either explicit in or underlying the conceptualised legal rule'.[36] In a suggestive discussion of law's 'tendency to lose touch with its underlying narrative models', Jackson illustrates his own argument with an example from English criminal law. He points out that the social narratives which lie deep below the legal doctrine he discusses are discrepant: there are two incompatible narratives stitched together in the same generalisation. The generalisation with which he is concerned is contained in the Criminal Attempts Act: '[a] person may be guilty of attempting to commit an offence ... even though the facts are such that the commission of the offence is impossible'.[37] In respect of this law, there is, writes Jackson:

> a sense of unease ... In doctrinal discussion, the following two cases are sometimes contrasted. Case A: a thief puts his hand into an empty pocket, intending to steal whatever he can find in it. Case B: a man stabs a corpse, thinking it to be alive. Ought these two cases to be treated alike? In the first, we do not hesitate to say that the unlucky pickpocket should be convicted of attempted theft. But we are far more apt to hesitate before concluding that Case B should result in a charge of attempted murder. Why this difference? If we apply the abstract, conceptual language of the 1981 Act, there is clearly no difference between the two situations ... [But] in fact, 'attempt' cannot be charged in the abstract ... ; the defendant must always be charged with attempted something. And the something ([a] completed crime) which is attempted itself falls within one or other of the [stock] patterns of criminality ... This, I think, explains our different feelings towards Case A and Case B. Case A is a case of attempted theft, and theft falls historically within the pattern of 'manifest criminality', based upon the collective image of acting like a thief, which is at root a narrative of invasion of territory. If, then, we compare the narrative of the unsuccessful pickpocket with the narrative model of acting like a thief, we see that there is a sufficient basis of similarity: the unsuccessful pickpocket has indeed invaded the territory of the victim. On the other hand, murder falls ... into [the stock] pattern of 'harmful consequences', and [in Case B] those harmful consequences have not been produced (since the victim was already dead). The narrative of the corpse-stabber is in this sense more remote from the paradigm narrative of murder

than is that of the unsuccessful pickpocket from the collective image of
acting like a thief.[38]

In this discussion, Jackson focuses upon the legalistic-cum-cultural
stock narrative pattern which underlies different crimes and the legal
doctrines associated with them. Eventually, he anticipates, the criminal
law on attempts will come under pressure of reform because the relevant
statutory provision does not cohere with the underlying narrative
which provides the rationale for punishing attempts. What is interesting about Jackson's conceptualisation of the stock narratives of criminal
law is that he regards the deep narratives as more enduring than the
superficial, fly-by-night statutory provisions. He anticipates that it will
be the statute (as interpreted in case law) which changes, as the unvarying
deep narratives are played out over the surface of the rules.

But is it in principle equally possible that the underlying narrative
will adjust itself to cohere with the statutory provision? I pose that
question by way of introducing comment upon the connection between
Jackson's prognosis for the law on attempts and our own concerns. What
is the prognosis for rules against harassment? In Jackson's view, I think,
we must address our attention to the deep narratives which underlie a
code on harassment. Are they conducive to the outcomes we seek, of
reduced harassment and appropriate recompense?

I can claim to have done no more than speculate upon what may be
the deep narratives which underlie harassment. From the victim's point
of view (whether harassment is racial, sexual, whatever) I think that the
issue is, fundamentally, one of social and personal *integrity*. It is not quite
a matter of invaded territory, because the 'territory' is often ill defined
beforehand and quite altered afterwards. It is not quite a matter of harmful
consequence either, because (although there are harmful consequences
in the criminal sense, in some cases) ultimately the consequences may
be less significant than the act. 'Integrity', in the sense in which I mean
it, is about being able to construct and sustain a sense of oneself as sound,
as whole; not a person rotting at the centre or fractured into objecti-
fied, usable body parts. I think that in many respects the 'deep narrative'
of feminism is about that sort of integrity. I also think, sadly, that the
world is not generally cognisant of it as a deep theme.

Where the legal and lay world may not be receptive to a narrative of
integrity it is, unfortunately, receptive to the masculine narrative of the
mendacious woman. This is the woman who lies to deceive both men
and male lawmakers. The allegedly false allegation of rape (or indeed
harassment) is nowadays the most commonly rehearsed version of this
narrative.[39] But an earlier generation of judges was much excited by a

different version of this male incubus: the profligate wife deceitfully and dishonestly pledging her husband's credit.[40]

My observations would imply that the narratives available to facilitate the operation of harassment codes are rather weak, where those which are liable to impede them are rather strong. But if that dark speculation were true, how then would we account for the legal progress harassment has made in the United States?[41] The short answer must be that feminists working in the interstices of legal doctrine have made progress by exploiting the narrative opportunities which are available (such as those that buttress key principles of the US constitution), or by using narrative against itself (in the same way that Mary Wollstonecraft used liberalism against conservative liberals).[42] We live in a complex of multiple, conflicting narratives where individual stories will sometimes get heard by the same means as rainwater currently seeps through my roof. It trickles through structural fissures. I suspect therefore that the likelihood of predicting the impact of supporting or impeding narratives in advance of the legal or social developments they affect is slight, quite simply because there are so many narratives that they defy our capacity to model their effects.

We should recall the motives which inspire organisations to introduce and apply codes on harassment: the possibility of expensive actions brought by aggrieved employees; the desire to manage the workplace so that the workforce is fully productive; even the desire to act ethically. Whatever the narrative hindrances to harassment rules functioning effectively, there are here stock narrative opportunities to be exploited.

Our third question concerned what happens to stories when they reconnoitre with a rule. We have already seen some of the things which may happen, but there is an important perspective we have yet to consider. I suggested above that one of the ambiguities from which harassment narratives may suffer is the ambivalence of the victim; and as the response of the victim returns us to the theme of the prologue it is an appropriate issue to consider in closing this chapter.

Some of the most compelling accounts of storytelling in a legal context have been furnished by clinical academic lawyers particularly attuned to their clients' needs in negotiating legal processes.[43] Time and again they write of recognising the urgency with which the client tells his or her story; of coming to understand the importance to the client of being properly heard by an adjudicator; of observing the critical negotiation of dignity in a dispute disruptive to the client's self-esteem; of participating in the contest between the client, her lawyer and the adjudicator to define what the dispute is really about.

Take the case of Mrs G, for instance.[44] Mrs G was awarded some small sum in compensation for a car accident, and she was advised by her welfare worker that she could keep it and spend it without losing welfare benefits. She bought sanitary towels and a few good meals and 'Sunday shoes' for her children. Then she was told that the welfare worker had made a mistake and that she would be required to repay 'overpaid' benefit money. Mrs G could not repay it. She was living on the poverty line already. So she would have to go and plead her case to a tribunal. Her lawyer thought that the best strategy was to justify the expenditure on the basis of 'need'. But when it came to the tribunal, this client did not want to rest her case on the indignity of need. After all the discussion with her lawyer, after all her anxiety about having to repay money she no longer had and could not get, she just came right out and said it. She had bought her daughters good 'Sunday shoes', she said. These were not new shoes because the old ones were worn out, not shoes they would have needed in the eyes of a welfare agency, but just good shoes, for Sunday.

Why was it so important to Mrs G to say what she wanted, so important that she could risk losing her case? Perhaps because that was the only way that her integrity could be sustained. For this African-American mother rearing her children on the minimal provision of welfare payments, to be compelled to plead abject need was too great an indignity. The interesting epilogue to this story is that the case against Mrs G was dropped after the hearing. Although the tribunal did not actually make a finding in her favour, the welfare department ceased proceedings against her. Perhaps they did this because they wanted to respond to her need for dignity? If this were the reason for dropping the case, it would appear that the only way in which both sides, Mrs G and the welfare agency, could approach a discourse of integrity was to step aside from the discursive constraints of legal rules which structured the tribunal proceedings.

Or again, take the case of Dujon Johnson. Here we see a different response to the constraining force of legal discourse, the anger at not being heard at all whatever one says.[45] A young (black) man is stopped in his car for no substantial reason; after a little legal brinksmanship and some adverse comment by an intolerant judge, his case is dismissed. The anger which inspires his lawyer to write about these proceedings is the anger which his client feels when it becomes clear that his story is not being heard by anyone. His story is not heard by the lawyer, who, thinking like a lawyer, has composed his own, legally structured story about the case and is preparing to press that version upon the court. The story is not heard by the judge, who judges him by his colour alone. It is not heard by the court, because legal procedures permit the case to be dispatched without a full hearing. If one of law's jobs is the job of 'arranging the say', of allowing things to be said which should be said, Dujon Johnson's anger is precisely because he never gets to say anything at the say.[46]

So what do we learn from these accounts? I think we must occasionally stop and reflect upon what 'justice' may mean in harassment cases. Lawyers, as Trollope has observed,[47] are paid not to consider the justice of a case but to win it. Such moral neutrality (some would say vacuity) may justifiably be practised only by those to whom the lifestory does not matter, but for whom the legal outcome is everything. Whatever the nature of the hearing, and whether or not they are represented by a lawyer, all my reading and experience suggest that women (and others) who have been harassed have a very urgent need to tell their story and know that it has been properly heard. This is why I defined the issue of harassment as 'integrity'. We rebuild our integrity by engaging again with a world which validates our feelings, our sense of ourselves. Whatever may be their advantages, codes, laws and other rule-based systems may be a far from ideal theatre for such lifemaking performances.

We seem to have no alternative but to use rules as a means to fetter the exercise of the harasser's power. But we must also recognise that rules are a clumsy binding, ill suited to the tasks of recreating the lacy web of self-worth, or delineating the contours of a new concept of integrity. What do we mostly seek when we seek justice after harassment?

Notes and References

1. See for instance the closing remarks in the preface to Catharine MacKinnon's *Sexual Harassment of Working Women: A Case of Sex Discrimination* (New Haven, Conn.: Yale University Press, 1979).
2. 'Bargaining in the Shadow of the Law' was the title chosen by Mnookin and Kornhauser for their seminal article on the ways in which legal professionals negotiate financial settlements between divorcing couples (R.H. Mnookin and L. Kornhauser, 'Bargaining in the Shadow of the Law: The Case of Divorce', *Yale Law Journal* 88 (1979), p. 950). Although couples reach their own settlements through a process of lawyer bargaining, agreements between couples reflect the status quo achieved in the courts in litigated settlements, because these are used as a reference point in negotiations. Reported cases are a guide to what is fair, what may be thought to be just, or to what may reasonably be expected. The shadow of the law may therefore be said to fall over all those decisions which are determined by our knowledge of our legal rights or liabilities.

3. That is, cases reported in the professional literature lawyers use. Very few of these gain a pay-off for the victim which is higher than expected; in which the corporation (army, police force, courts of law) is supposed to embody high standards of moral rectitude; in which the victim's story was unlikely to be, but was in the event, believed. On this last, see the second half of this chapter.

4. Because of the impact on employers of the Sex Discrimination Act 1975 and Race Relations Act 1976. While no-one would describe the anti-discrimination regimes inspired by such legislation as rigorous, they have made it possible to assert that harassment on grounds of sex or race are clearly 'discriminatory' in law and that employers may be held liable for harassment.

5. See for example R.M. Unger, *Law in Modern Society* (New York: Free Press, 1976); and, rather differently, Judith Shklar, *Legalism* (Cambridge, Mass.: Harvard University Press, 1964).

6. The Employment Protection (Consolidation) Act 1978. In the United States, sexual harassment has been treated as discrimination inconsistent with a woman's constitutional right to equality and the law has developed through individual women bringing claims against their harassers upon this basis. A good critical summary of the current state of play in the US may be found in Ann C. Juliano, 'Did She Ask for It? The "Unwelcome" Requirement in Sexual Harassment Cases', *Cornell Law Review* 77 (1992), p. 1558.

7. See for example *Bracebridge Engineering Ltd.* v. *Darby* [1990] IRLR 3. Mrs Darby complained to the firm's general manager after suffering sexual harassment from two supervisors. The general manager investigated the incident and, faced with a blank denial by the workers concerned, decided to do nothing. Mrs Darby felt compelled to resign her job, and brought a successful claim of constructive dismissal through an industrial tribunal. The Employment Appeal Tribunal, which considered the company's appeal against the decision, confirmed the industrial tribunal's judgement.

8. There is a catch here, though. The enlightened employer who encodes harassment or equal opportunities procedures may be able to take advantage of those *precisely as a defence against* an employee who has suffered harassment but feels her complaint has not been adequately addressed by management. In *Balgobin and Another* v. *London Borough of Tower Hamlets* [1987] IRLR 401, the fact that the Borough had a (probably somewhat token) equal opportunities policy and had investigated (inconclusively) the women's complaints enabled them to establish a defence under s. 41 (3) of the Sex Discrimination Act:

In proceedings brought under this Act against any person in respect of an act alleged to have been done by an employee of his it shall be a defence for that person to prove that he took such steps as were reasonably practicable to prevent the employee from doing that act, or from doing in the course of his employment acts of that description.

9. Professor Herbert Hart started it all in *The Concept of Law* (Oxford: Oxford University Press, 1961) and in an earlier article, 'Positivism and the Separation of Law and Morals', *Harvard Law Review* 71 (1958), pp. 593–629, to which Professor Lon Fuller replied in the same issue at pp. 630–72. More recently, Professor Ronald Dworkin has questioned Hart's presentation of law as rules in *Taking Rights Seriously* (London: Duckworth, 1977). But this massive debate has spawned hundreds of contributions, of which those cited are merely the best known.

10. Frederick Schauer, *Playing by the Rules: A Philosophical Examination of Rule-Based Decision-making in Law and in Life* (Oxford: Clarendon, 1991).

11. 'Eve-teasing' is the term used in Pakistan and India (and possibly other Asian countries) to describe sexual harassment of women by strangers in public places. Signs prohibiting the activity are seen on Pakistani buses, for example. See Chapter 10 below. Indian women are organising against street harassment. On street harassment generally, see Cynthia Grant Bowman, 'Street Harassment and the Informal Ghettoization of Women', *Harvard Law Review* 106 (1993), pp. 517–80.

12. When I was travelling in India about 15 years ago, it was common to designate formally the end compartment of a compartment-and-corridor railway carriage as the 'Ladies' Compartment'. Women who wished to do so could travel in the compartment (provided there was space, which in my experience often there was not) at the same fare as applied to that carriage in general. I do not know whether Indian Railways still operate the practice. I am told that British trains used to be the same, and that there were also (and as I have seen in some stations, still are), as in India, separate ladies' and gentlemen's waiting rooms.

13. Unfortunately for women, calculations which assume women's need for male protection are prone to lead to topsy-turvy outcomes. In other societies at other times, women could equally well be discouraged or even prohibited from travelling alone; from this we learn that it is not perhaps so much that women need protection, as that men need to protect their property in women. The sexual balance of power will determine whether women will be protected from men

when they seek to do what men do unmolested, or whether men will seek to prevent women from doing these things at all.

14. Much jurisprudential thought has been expended upon this point. See the references at note 9 above.

15. Lon Fuller argued that these two (to me) different questions are really the same, as it is impossible to agree on even the core meaning of a word without referring to the purposes for which the word is selected. What view you take upon this depends upon what linguistic theory you choose to adopt, a matter beyond the scope of this chapter! See Lon Fuller, 'Positivism and Fidelity to Law: A Reply to Professor Hart', *Harvard Law Review* 71 (1958), p. 630.

16. Two examples will suffice. The first is from the 'Oxford University Code on Harassment':

> [H]arassment may be broadly understood to consist of unwarranted behaviour towards another person, so as to disrupt the work or reduce the quality of life of that person, by such means as single or successive acts of bullying, verbally or physically abusing, or ill-treating him or her, or otherwise creating or maintaining a hostile or offensive studying, working, or social environment for him or her. Harassment relating to another's sex, sexual orientation, religion or race are among the forms of harassment covered by this code. Unacceptable forms of behaviour may include unwelcome sexual advances, unwelcome requests for sexual favours, offensive physical contact or verbal behaviour of a sexual nature ... The abuse of a position of authority ... is an aggravating feature of harassment.

The Second is the Harvard Graduate School of Education Policy Statement on Harassment (which accompanies their 'Procedures for Resolving Complaints on Harassment'):

> Certain physical acts are impermissible. When they are based on such characteristics as race, ethnic group, religious belief, sex, sexual orientation, disability status or age, they constitute impermissible harassment. These physical acts include, but are not limited to, rape, assault, unwelcome touching, physical intimidation, defacing or damaging property, and interfering with freedom of movement. The fact that physical harassment may be accompanied by verbal or symbolic expression does not make the physical harassment less punishable.
>
> Certain purely verbal or symbolic expression may also constitute harassment. For example, unwelcome comments or suggestions of a sexual nature constitute sexual harassment if, from the standpoint of the reasonable person, they are sufficiently severe or pervasive to affect adversely an individual's working or learning environment; determination of what is reasonable will be made in accordance with [other procedural definitions].

Epithets, threats of violence, and other offensive verbal or symbolic expression may also constitute impermissible harassment. Depending on the circumstances, purely verbal or symbolic expression may be punished where it:

A.   Is addressed directly to an individual or a small group of individuals;

B.   Insults, stigmatizes or intimidates the individual or individuals on the basis of such characteristics as race, ethnic group, religious belief, sex, sexual orientation, disability status, or age; and

C.   Would be interpreted by a reasonable person as evincing grave disrespect or an intent to demean on part of the speaker or speakers.

17. For discussion of the general provision of injunctive relief in the context of domestic violence, see for example S.M. Cretney and J.M. Masson, *Principles of Family Law,* 5th edition (London: Sweet and Maxwell, 1990). The recently decided case of *Khorasandjian* v. *Bush* [1993] 3 All E.R. 669 appears to have opened up new avenues of protection in the inherent jurisdiction. On this case see further Joanne Conaghan's case note: 'Harassment and the Law of Torts', *Feminist Legal Studies* 1 (2) (1993), pp. 189–97.

18. Domestic Violence and Matrimonial Proceedings Act 1976, s.1; Domestic Proceedings and Magistrates Courts Act 1978, ss.16–18; Matrimonial Homes Act 1983, s.1 (2).

19. See L. Friedman, 'On Legal Development', *Rutgers Law Review* 24 (1969), p. 11, where he argues that modern law is not more rational than law used to be, but that people expect it to be so. This expectation perhaps impacts upon the way in which we then set out to design rules.

20. Naomi Cahn 'The Reasonable Woman Standard', *Cornell Law Review* 77 (1992), p. 1398.

21. He would be acting perfectly properly in hearing evidence as to the character and sexual behaviour of the complainant: see *Snowball* v. *Gardner Merchant* [1987] IRLR 397, in which the complainant objected to such evidence being brought. The Employment Appeal Tribunal ruled that the evidence was admissible.

22. By 'particularistic decision-making' Schauer means, approximately, using rules as a loose general guide in order to arrive at what appears to be a good outcome in the particular instance. See Schauer, *Playing by the Rules*, p. 137.

23. Schauer, *Playing by the Rules*, p. 139.

24.

Jarndyce and Jarndyce drones on. This scarecrow of a suit has, in course of time, become so complicated that no man alive knows what it means. The parties to it understand it least; but it has been observed that no two Chancery lawyers can talk about it for five minutes without coming to a total disagreement as to all the premises. Innumerable children have been born into the cause; innumerable young people have married into it; innumerable old people have died out of it. Scores of persons have deliriously found themselves made parties in Jarndyce and Jarndyce, without knowing how or why; ... Jarndyce and Jarndyce has passed into a joke.

Charles Dickens, *Bleak House* (1853)
(Harmondsworth: Penguin, 1971) p. 52.

25. Schauer, *Playing by the Rules*, p. 147.
26. Schauer, *Playing by the Rules*, p. 147.
27. Karl Llewellyn, 'The Normative, the Legal, and the Law-Jobs: The Problem of Justice Method', *Yale Law Journal* 49 (1940), p. 1355.
28. See the *Bracebridge Engineering* case cited in note 7 above.
29. Deborah Tannen, *You Just Don't Understand: Women and Men in Conversation* (London: Virago, 1992), quoting from Anne Tyler, *The Accidental Tourist* (New York: Knopf, 1985). The reader may be concerned by my switch from academic argument to fiction as the device I use to explain the way in which, firstly, abstractions need stories in order to be understood; and then, how misleading abstractions may be seen to be. I have chosen to use a fictional conversation to make my point because, as a reader of the fiction, I felt that it resonated with my own understanding of the hazards of human communication. I am therefore treating it, as does Tannen, as a realistic imitation of real-life conversation.
30. The best known accounts of legal storytelling, though, and from which much other work is derived, are concerned with slightly different matters. See for example Bennett and Feldman's study of juries and their response to stories: W.L. Bennett and M. Feldman, *Reconstructing Reality in the Courtroom* (New Brunswick, NJ: Rutgers University Press, 1981). Probably as well known is Sarat and Felstiner's work on lawyer–client interaction in the context of divorce; for example, A. Sarat and W.L.F. Felstiner, 'Law and Social Relations: Vocabularies of Motive in Lawyer/Client Interaction', *Law and Society Review* 22 (1988), p. 737. On finding law to accommodate the good story, see Bernard Jackson, *Law, Fact, and Narrative Coherence* (Liverpool: Deborah Charles, 1988). On clients sticking to their stories at all costs, see C.D. Cunningham, 'The Lawyer as Translator, Representation as Text: Towards an Ethnography of Legal Discourse', *Cornell Law Review* 77 (1992), p. 1298 and 'A Tale of Two Clients', *Michigan Law Review* 87 (1989), p. 2459. On feminist use of storytelling, see Kathryn Abrams, 'Hearing the Call of Stories', *California Law Review* 79 (1991), p. 971.

31. A very simplified account of Bennett and Feldman's work has been presented here. For an interesting discussion and criticism of some of the weaknesses in their approach, see Bernard Jackson, *Law, Fact, and Narrative Coherence.*

32. Jackson, *Law, Fact, and Narrative Coherence.*uses Greimasian semiotics to explain our ascriptions of narrative coherence.

33. Schauer, *Playing by the Rules.*

34. Steven Winter, 'Transcendental Nonsense, Metaphoric Reasoning, and the Cognitive Stakes for Law', *University of Pennsylvania Law Review* 137 (1989), p. 1105.

35. Gerry López, 'Lay Lawyering', *UCLA Law Review* 32 (1984), p. 1.

36. Jackson, *Law, Fact, and Narrative Coherence*, p. 101.

37. Criminal Attempts Act 1981, s.1 (2).

38. Jackson, *Law, Fact, and Narrative Coherence*, pp. 108–9. He cites George Fletcher, *Rethinking Criminal Law* (Boston, Mass.: Little, Brown, 1978).

39. The reader may imagine my mingled delight and despair when, having just completed a revision of this chapter, I turned to the hundredth issue of the *Oxford Magazine*. (This organ is editorially independent of the University of Oxford, but is circulated periodically inside the *Oxford Gazette*, which publication is in effect the university newsletter.) Entitled 'Sexual Harassment', the article purports to be a first-person account by 'H. Harris' of the effects of a false allegation of sexual harassment made against a colleague. 'Harris' reminisces, in C.P. Snow-ish style, about his service as a 'University elder' in disciplinary proceedings sometime in the 1960s; and about his subsequent discovery that the accused man was homosexual (and therefore *must* have been innocent!) and the woman accuser was now a permanent resident of a psychiatric hospital. It is only upon reaching the end of this account that one learns that, '[a]part from the narrator … all the characters in this tale are fictional'. Although the first person of the tale is clearly male ('No man who has taught undergraduates for any length of time can have failed to come across the pretty girl who sits in the front row and makes eyes at you all the way through your lecture'), we cannot automatically assume that the real 'H. Harris' is a man too. (As this book goes to press, I discover H. Harris is indeed a real person.) I shall not, therefore, cite this story as evidence of the nightmare brought forth by the male mind, although it is typical of the genre. It is a striking exemplar, however, of one person's use of narrative to understand and interpret the abstractions of a harassment code. Its final paragraph reads:

> This morning, a revised version of the rules for dealing with sexual harassment reached my desk. The new rules are all-inclusive: they deal in one and the same breath with sexual harassment, harassment on grounds of religion or colour, harassment of one undergraduate by another. It seems to me that there are distinctions to be made. It's unlikely now that I shall be asked to serve on another judicial panel, but if I am and it's a case of sexual harassment, I don't think I could bring myself to do it.

If the piece truly represents the narrator's views, his unwillingness to serve can only be welcomed.

40. On the distrust of women victims, see Susan Estrich, *Real Rape* (Cambridge, Mass.: Harvard University Press, 1987). I have referred to the false rape allegation in 'The Structure of the Veil', *Modern Law Review* 52 (3) (1989), p. 420, and to the profligate wife in 'Bellum Pax Rursum', *Journal of Legal History* 12, (2) (1991), p. 148.

41. See Juliano, 'Did She Ask for It?'

42. M. Wollstonecraft, *A Vindication of the Rights of Woman* (1792).

43. 'Clinical' academic lawyers teach law students how to perform the nitty-gritty involved in actually taking on a case. While learning legal doctrines – rules – is an important part of legal education, the law student must also acquire such professional skills as client interviewing, negotiation, and the drafting of documents like wills. In US law schools such skills are taught as part of the degree course, and 'professional' issues have concomitantly received greater attention.

44. Lucie White, 'Subordination, Rhetorical Survival Skills and Sunday Shoes: Note on the Hearing of Mrs. G', *Buffalo Law Review* 38 (1990), p. 1.

45. Cunningham, 'The Lawyer as Translator'.

46. Llewellyn, 'The Normative, the Legal, and the Law-Jobs'.

47. See especially *The Warden* (1855), in which Sir Abraham Haphazard Q.C., Attorney-General, represents the Bishop of Barchester: 'the justice of the [beneficiaries'] claim or the justice of [the Warden's] defence had never presented themselves. A legal victory over an opposing party was the service for which Sir Abraham was ... to be paid' (London: Everyman, (1991), p. 79).

Handwritten margin notes: *mens + ♀ Perceptions differ (legitimation?)*

Red Herrings and Mystifications: Conflicting Perceptions of Sexual Harassment

Helen Watson

This chapter compares the explanations of people accused of harassment with those of people making accusations. In the course of research I interviewed 60 people with the aim of eliciting personal accounts of the experience of harassment. The method of research was typically anthropological. An initial use of loosely structured interviews was followed by participant observation in a variety of informal meetings with groups of informants. Personal accounts of harassment were presented orally and first-person narratives were constructed as a basis for collective discussion of common experience. I worked in terms of two basic analytical categories: people accused of harassment, a total of 30 men; and people who had made a formal accusation of harassment, 30 women.[1] I was interested in gaining a broad, ego-centred view of harassment from both groups by concentrating on three open-ended research questions. How do you define the type of behaviour experienced? How has the experience influenced your perception of harassment? What underpins the type of behaviour named as harassment? The representations of harassment which emerged involve a shift from the specific to the general; moreover, attempts to explain personal experience often depended on this generalising tendency.

In the course of research it became evident that there was a significant difference in the explanations of harassment being constructed. This concerned how explanations of harassment represented the role of sex. The difference in explanations stems from divergent perspectives, those of accused or accuser. The alternative theories can be condensed into two propositions which explain 'what harassment is about'.[2] Implicit in the alternative positions is a parallel tension between what

65

is offered as explanation and what is avoided. For those who had been accused of harassment, the experience could be explained in terms of an actual or potential sexual encounter, based on a straightforward natural case of sexual attraction which had gone wrong. For those who had made an accusation of harassment, the behaviour they had been subject to could not be explained in relation to any single causal factor; indeed, a particular emphasis was given to the view that harassment was not associated with sexual attraction, repulsion or conflict. The small number of female respondents who mentioned sex in their accounts (three out of 30) stressed that any element of sexual attraction which might have been present initially was irrelevant in the light of subsequent events which led to the accusation being made. In response to direct questions on this issue each woman argued that, although there was some link between harassment and sex at an abstract level, the behaviour they had experienced had 'nothing to do with sex *per se*'. One woman's words reflect the general position:

> You can only say it [harassment] was about sex or sexual relations if you mean that it was all tied up with the kind of power games which men play with women all the time. You can only understand sexual harassment if you take a hard look at gender roles and who controls who in the workplace.

It is my suggestion that the greater the emphasis on harassment as a consequence of sexual attraction gone wrong, the greater the dominant appeal of an explanatory model. However, a question about the appeal of one type of narrative over another implies the importance of language in structuring perceived reality in relation to a gendered discourse of dominance. It has been observed that both public and private narratives of harassment have been adversely affected by harassment's 'name-lessness'. In Spender's terms, 'objects and events remain but shadowy entities when they are not named'.[3]

It is useful to examine representations of harassment in relation to the pattern of language used and the style of explanation offered, particularly in relation to that realm of power defined as the capacity to set an agenda, to say and thereby to establish what is or isn't relevant. The capacity to set an agenda is a relatively invisible process. It involves the ability to influence how certain issues are presented and understood by others, and represents a critical dimension of material and other more visible aspects of power relations. Beyond this there are disturbing implications for the formulation, implementation and functioning of public policy on harassment. Being in a position to manage power by influencing how 'facts' are presented to and perceived by a wider audience is of immense significance in harassment cases. A typical harassment case involves rival accounts which consist of mutually incompatible explanations. In such a contested situation, the advantage of 'credibility' for the individuals concerned as well as a wider 'audience' may be gained by a narrative which explains behaviour in terms of familiar or dominant norms and values. As comparison of conflicting explanatory theories will show, there are significant advantages in the presentation of harassing behaviour as a sexually inspired error or simple misunderstanding. I will suggest that a party accused of harassment who explains behaviour in such terms has 'set the agenda' in his own interest by appealing to a dominant model of contemporary gender relations.

The greater power of the narrative of harassment as 'sex gone wrong' derives from its foundation on a conceptual red herring. The term derives from fox-hunting: a dried, smoked herring if drawn across the fox's trail has a potent effect on the hounds, which throws the chase into disarray. Conceptual red herrings are of analytical interest in relation to the tensions between what people say and what they don't, what they offer as explanations for certain actions or behaviour and what they avoid. The simplifying reductionist model of harassment as sex gone wrong involves a classic Conan Doyle red herring which has the power to divert attention from the main question. Sherlock Holmes had the perspicacity to see through red herrings and ask why the dogs didn't bark in the night, but many of us may not.

The pervasive appeal of a red herring theory lies in its power to render alternative explanations unconvincing at best, irrelevant at worst. Mernissi has described the power of the pervasive discourse as 'one loud bell ringing alone ... it rings so loudly and has such powerful means at its disposal that it renders alternatives inaudible'.[4] It is important to examine why red herrings have such a potent effect, and why people in general appear to be so fond of them. In this respect the red herring of sexual attraction has the advantage of linking the explanation of harassment to an unambiguous view of behaviour which is 'natural' and 'inevitable'. Questions of 'truthful accounting' or 'what actually happened' are ultimately subsumed and problematised by the simplifying elements of the explanation.

Formal attempts to define sexual harassment include as common elements unsolicited and non-reciprocal behaviour which involves coercion, feelings of embarrassment, powerlessness, mental or physical pain, and behaviours presented in the form of sexual initiative which are reinforced by status and power positions. An institutional trade union definition exemplifies a typical formulation:

> Sexual harassment is a form of victimisation, the imposition of unwelcome attention or action on one person often by a person in a superior position. It is frequently a display of power over the recipient and is designed to undermine, isolate and degrade that person.

There has been much debate about the implications of various forms of definition, reinforced by the knowledge that sexual harassment is an imprecise term. In numerous studies a key debate is over the meaning and degree of emphasis to be given to the 'sexual' element of the behaviour. As Wise and Stanley argue, 'the fundamental issue ... is whether we should understand sexual harassment as a power behaviour or as a sexual behaviour'.[5] The crude question at the core of the problem has four critical components. Is sex the goal of sexual harassment? Is power being used to gain sex? Is sexual harassment an end in itself? Is it another patriarchal play and display of power?

A passing mention of some definitional concerns merely illustrates the problems of separating or fusing notions of power and sex. There is immediate significance in Simmel's comment that 'man's position of power does not only assure his relative superiority ... but it assures that his standards become generalised as generically human standards'.[6] A telling feature of the red herring theories is how sexual harassment *per se* seems to 'disappear' as a critical factor for investigation. The red herring explanation provides a misleading account of behaviour, combining power and sex in a peculiar way. Harassment is not represented as a variant of other forms of exploitation and discrimination inextricably linked to sexism, racism and so on. Those accused of harassment explain their behaviour as the cumulative result of a series of unfortunate misunderstandings and human errors which stem from the innocent, 'natural' source of sexual attraction. Here it is the sexual minus the harassment. This in itself is an interesting variation on the familiar theme of harassment being a matter of interpretation, in that it defines harassment as a misnamed non-event from the imagination of the accuser. In my initial interviews with men accused of harassment, each described how the accusation was a part of their accuser's 'imagination', 'fantasy' or 'dream world.'

It is possible to distil women's perceptions of harassment as presented in their narratives into three sets of issues.[7] Firstly, there is a concern that they could have overreacted, given their experience of the situation as emotionally charged and confusing. They feel it is feasible that they might have misunderstood or mismanaged their relationship with the alleged harasser. In this respect they see themselves as being partly to blame for subsequent events. There is a high degree of anxiety about the role of unconscious, non-verbal signals in their encounters with the accused. (Had they appeared to be encouraging his interest? Had they failed to maintain a balance between being friendly and distant in a close working relationship which entailed time spent eating and travelling together?) There is a similar retrospective concern with dress and image. (Had they dressed provocatively or frivolously? Should they have adopted an anonymous, unfeminine or asexual style of dress? Had they failed to project a serious, professional image?) A minority remain convinced that they should have explicitly stated that they were not interested in a sexual relationship with the accused.

A second set of factors concern views on alternative ways of coping with harassment and the different choices made as an individual's awareness of harassment developed. All the women had adopted a pattern of coping with harassment by a variety of strategies before making a formal accusation. Initial reactions involved giving the accused the benefit of the doubt and concluding that his actions were ambiguous, probably innocent. Following the transition from this position of doubt (they were misreading the other party's intentions), to one of certainty (they knew this wasn't a joke; the behaviour was unmerited, clearly discriminatory and intolerable), each woman was able to describe an incident or moment of time which marked her recognition of the behaviour as harassment. What is described as 'the moment of realisation' is said to have been accompanied by a sense of shock and self-criticism for the previous period of naivety and the attempt to ascribe innocent motives to the harassment. At this stage, all the women were prompted to choose other courses of action. In order of use during the period of harassment, the typical pattern of responses to harassment involved: ignoring the behaviour, trying to joke about it, seeking support from friends and colleagues, threatening formal action, making an accusation within the public arena. The value or effectiveness of each course of action seems to have altered with hindsight. At the time of research each woman was convinced that she dealt with the situation in an inadequate and strategically inept way.[8]

A third area of agreement concerns explanations of the motives of the accused and the consequences of taking action against him. All the women describe their experience as a dilemma based on the paradoxical outcome of action. The decision to make a formal accusation and bring the matter into the public domain is seen as an act of desperation, the last option open in a situation perceived as threatening sanity, health and happiness. To make a formal accusation is to take on the establishment in ignorance of the consequences, the act of a weak individual against a stronger opposition which tends to cluster around the accused. The outcome is to be labelled a troublemaker, to risk hostility or isolation from colleagues, to force others to take sides and in general to make the situation worse. Some women mention the parallel situation faced by victims of rape under cross-examination in court, when a woman might 'come to wonder why she hadn't just tried to forget it'. Another woman added, 'Facing up to the crime and having to deal with it in public is probably worse than suffering in silence. I found it to be a lot worse than the harassment itself.' Even those women who had initiated a public case which resulted in the harasser being disciplined stress that they would not take the same course of action again in a similar situation. There is full agreement with the perception that making an accusation is worse than having to tolerate the harassment on both a personal and a professional level.[9]

Institutional attempts to resolve cases are believed to be wholly biased in favour of the accused. Women feel that formal hearings operate in terms of a basic principle that it is preferable not to convict an actual harasser than to risk convicting an innocent party. There is agreement that hearings can be undermined by assumptions which work in favour of the accused. One commonly held view among the women is that their accusations were treated as if false or rooted in 'ulterior motives'. Women describe how during their hearings questions on contested issues were dominated by consideration of their sexual behaviour and 'general personal and private conduct'. The women argue that tribunals are also interested in establishing the extent to which 'professional motives inspired the accusation of harassment'.[10] One woman gave the following description of the conclusion made at her tribunal: 'He [the accused] had overall responsibility for my work and my progress report. I was in for promotion but wouldn't get it, so I must have made this accusation in order to discredit him and protect my career.'

The women's narratives tend to avoid theorising about harassment as a general phenomenon. One exception observes that the harassment of women may be related to men's enjoyment of power games. The women's accounts of harassment concentrate on the actual or potential threat of violence, the intolerable psychological pain, and confusion over how to interpret the motives of the accused and make an effective response. Some women argue that harassment tends to transform pre-existing relationships of authority into manipulated displays of dominance and subservience. Others express the concern that they were provoked into making an accusation which the harasser knew would be discredited. This 'trickery' is described as part of the 'conspiracy among men' to 'protect each other'. The women describe this 'closing of ranks' as a 'general tendency' among male workmates, although all mention that 'there is an increasing number of men unwilling to take part in this kind of behaviour'.

The accounts of the alleged harassers display a similar degree of consensus. Firstly, there is an overriding emphasis on how and why the accusation of harassment was false.[11] The premise of all explanations is that there was a simple misunderstanding and breakdown of communication with the accuser concerning a potential or actual sexual relationship. Those accused of harassment are commonly convinced that their accusers had been attracted to them before the misunderstanding developed. There are three variations on this general theme:

1. The alleged harasser had misread or overestimated the meaning of apparent signs of sexual attraction in the behaviour of the woman concerned. He had been guilty of a natural, human error of judgement at best. At worst, vanity, insensitivity or self-preoccupation had compounded the mistaken reading of sexual interest into a friendly working relationship.
2. He had interpreted the signals of mutual sexual interest correctly, but miscalculated the timing of his attempt to develop a sexual element in the friendship. He should have waited another week or two; he had handled the preliminary sexual initiative in a clumsy manner; or he had been swept away by his passionate feelings without due consideration for the object of his affection and/or lust.
3. He had been too slow to respond to the other party's evident sexual interest and had failed to recognise its decline. He had been too busy to act on the assumed mutual feelings that were developing until it was too late; he had not realised that the woman had had a change of heart; or he had simply missed his chance.[12]

A second common feature of accounts of being accused of harassment is the tendency to express and explain personal experience in terms of a general hypothesis of heterosexual relationships. For example, the men locate their experience within a broad framework which argues that false accusations of sexual harassment occur because modern relationships between men and women are complicated. Harassers concede that sexual harassment does exist, but it is very rare. In most cases of alleged harassment, 'men are not really guilty as charged'. The problem arises because men are not sure 'what women want' from a relationship. Traditional marital, domestic and public roles have undergone rapid change which makes sexual misunderstandings more likely.

Alternative versions of such theories involve discussions of factors which could cause a woman to make a false accusation of harassment. An abbreviated list of such factors includes menstruation, sexual frustration, paranoia (personal or feminist-inspired), wounded vanity following a bad experience with another man, the perception of personal insult or rejection, an inability to cope with competition and rivalry, and feminine vindictiveness or the desire for revenge (either against a specific individual or against men in general via any convenient male).

All the accused men share the view that procedures which existed to resolve harassment cases were biased in favour of the accuser. However, this mirror-image of the opinion of the women centres not on the advantages of the system for the opposing party, but on the personal, social and occupational disadvantages of having to face an accusation. An edited extract from one of the arguments presented will illustrate this basic difference of perspective:

> Once you get accused of harassment and your name is mentioned, whatever the outcome of the hearing, there will always be a question mark against it. You get labelled the office playboy, the smooth operator and this causes all kinds of problems in your future dealings with women ... The case nearly ruined my chances of good relationships with other women. I always worry about girlfriends finding out ... If you've just met a woman and get on well with her you start to wonder if she knows about it. What usually happens is if women know they'll act as if they're a bit suspicious of me.

All the men describe legislation against harassment as unjust. Rules prohibiting harassing behaviour and procedures for resolving accusations are said to be fundamentally flawed. The general view is that sexual harassment is a feminist invention which has the deliberate or unintended consequence of proscribing the 'normal' (inevitably sexual) relationships that develop when men and women work together.[13]

Parallels are drawn with what is described as a fashionable obsession with 'politically correct' and 'ideologically sound' behaviour. Although no one was able to provide a definition of these concepts which met with common agreement, all expressed the view that these trends had developed as a result of feminism. There was unanimous agreement with the comment that one woman's harassment was another's compliment. This remark, made in passing in the course of a discussion about 'what feminism was for' and 'what women wanted', inspired further interest among the group of twelve men involved in the links between 'the problem of feminism/the modern woman' and their own experience of a 'false' or 'malicious' accusation of harassment. The conclusion reached is that, because of feminism, 'all women are trapped in a dilemma of their own invention'; as women they must like to flirt and be complimented, but their anti-harrassment rules forbid the practice and appreciation of such actions.

In all harassers' accounts, there is an explicit overarching theme that the accusation of harassment has been caused by a misunderstanding centred on sexual attraction. No reservations are expressed about constructing a general explanatory theory of harassment from experiential evidence, nor is there any sense of hesitation in explaining the heterogenity of the female psyche or discussing women as a monolithic category with a female researcher.

Comparison of the explanatory styles of the two perspectives on harassment I have described reveals some fundamental differences. Implicit in the alternative positions is a tension between what has been presented as explanatory evidence and what has been avoided. In contrast to the single-focused confidence of the male model of harassment, women's representations project a mutifaceted view of the issue. The women's narratives of harassment avoid generalised statements and precise definitions of harassment derived from experience. A woman tends to associate the behaviour of her harasser with a situation or working relationship which made him feel insecure or challenged. The resulting harassment is seen as part of a cultural propensity for men to resort to any tactic which bolsters their position if they feel it to be under threat from women. The view that harassment behaviour involves a complex mix of status, authority and gender conflicts is rarely stated explicitly. Women come closest to making a direct connection when describing the tactical use of sexual attraction by the accused as 'an excuse', 'smokescreen' or 'cover' for attempts to undermine a professional rival. Among the women, harassment is classified only in terms of 'what it is not' in so far as it is not perceived to be connected to a misunderstanding about a potential sexual relationship. The women tend to be self-reflexive and open to a critical reassessment of their own role and reaction in relation to the harassment. There is a frank admission of the complexity of motives and actions involved, and there is consensus that harassment may only be understood by investigation of the motives and actions of both parties. In this respect, particular emphasis is given to the need to revise institutional procedures for dealing with harassment. The women argue that it is important to consider the constraints which force women to withdraw allegations of harassment, and agree that existing legislation should be informed by research into unresolved and abandoned cases.[14]

In contrast with the women's views, the harassers' accounts exhibit some quite different general features.There is a defensive style of explanation which gives primary focus to 'what went wrong' and 'why the accusation was false'. The general perception is that because harassment is 'too complex and confusing' a type of behaviour it cannot be codified or regulated by institutional legislation. The men explain that the allegations of harassment they faced derived from the 'ambiguous nature' of male–female relationships. They represent harassment as an inescapable consequence of the sexual dimension present in all male–female relationships. Allegations of sexual harassment are perceived as the 'natural result of unsuccessful sexual relationships'. The men's 'explanations' present harassment as inextricably linked to a 'natural' propensity for male–female relations to imply sex in so far as there is always a potential or actual sexual dimension to all social encounters.[15]

I want to return to the demystifying aspects of the red herring theory of harassment. This will involve a close examination of the men's representations of harassment, which are built on a generalising view of the 'inevitability of heterosexual attraction'. Analysis of harassers' 'explanations' in terms of the red herring of sex reveal certain advantages implicit in a reductionist theory of harassment. The men's focus on sex excludes the possibility of other primary causal factors and provides an unambiguous account of their behaviour: 'the allegation of harassment followed a failed sexual relationship' because 'harassment is about simple sexual miscommunication'. The absence of ambiguity in this representation of harassment may have wider social consequences in relation to how conflicting and contested narratives of the same event are resolved in the public domain. The general 'style of explanation' fits a familiar stereotypical male image of social processes in the heterosexual world.[16] In the same way that a distinction between harassment as 'typical' or 'aberrant' behaviour is a critical factor in how it is perceived by the individual concerned and by society at large, the red herring theory's evocation of a 'taken for granted, natural' state of affairs places it within a dominant cultural mainstream. A pastiche of the men's written narratives of the experience of being named harassers will illustrate how the red herring relates to what can be considered to be a dominant heterosexual male discourse:

> We know that sexual attraction is a powerful thing, it can be messy and complicated. It's a fact of life that flirtations, courtship signals and initial moves in a relationship can be misunderstood. Modern relationships are complicated because men haven't learned how to deal with modern women ... Accusations of harassment have to be understood within this framework.

The appeal to what is represented as 'commonsense knowledge' assumes the mutual understanding of an external audience. The power of the red herring theory lies in how it diverts attention from aberrant behaviour by emphasising a typical aspect of projected 'social reality': human relationships are frequently subject to problems of communication. Harassers comprehend and explain their behaviour within a public gender ideology which assumes that differences between the sexes explain everything. Theoretically there is agreement among the men that harassment is 'unacceptable behaviour', but if the general situation is understood in sexual terms, and as a consequence of the natural status quo, their conclusion is that nothing can be done to eliminate the root cause. In this context, a harasser projects his experience of a false allegation as an example of the injustice of anti-harassment legislation. The men share the view that legislation is biased in women's favour.[17] In general, the men's explanations of harassment 'naturalise' their behaviour and reduce harassment to a 'matter of sex gone wrong'. In one man's terms:

It's pointless to have rules saying what harassment is and isn't since people know that 99.9 per cent of cases are just mistakes – the situation a man can fall into in relationships with women without realising ... When a charge is made against you there's the attitude that it's not enough to say, 'Sorry, you misunderstood my intentions,' because she is after your blood. Once the formal rules are brought into play by the women's lobby, the system has to be on her side because they all see you as the guilty party because you're a man.

The red herring theory also relegates the contested issues of any case to secondary concerns. The men's explanations of harassment present the view that both parties were subject to a system of mutual misunderstanding in which imperfect signals were imperfectly received. According to their theory, the accused cannot be blamed, except for being human. The consequence of this style of explanation is that a smokescreen is drawn across the categories of truth and lie, perpetrator and victim. By a logical progression, the category of victim collapses and the search for blame is rendered futile: it can be concluded that neither party is at fault.

The red herring theory derives its appeal from the focus on sex as a fundamental force in human affairs. Sex is represented as a potent driving force in human life, the 'high-octane fuel of society'. I suggest that simplifying or reductionist theories are increasingly attractive in contemporary Western society. The men's reductionist explanations of harassment provide evidence of the particular advantages of presenting a simplified account of a complex phenomenon. The general preference may be for an explanation of hitherto complex or random phenomena in terms of causal factors and central influences, however chaotic or complex the actual processes involved.[18] Sex is especially useful in this respect, since it reduces behaviour to a simple matter of 'natural influences'. For instance, 'harassment has an innocent genesis in nature because we are subject to some inescapable basic instincts to which no blame can be attached.'

If sex is evoked in this determinist explanatory manner, three general advantages follow from the ascribed nature-based source of behaviour. It cuts through the red tape of ethics, and issues of responsibility, choice and will. It eliminates the problem of the audience having to 'play god', making an infallible judgement on action and intention that would demand impossible omniscience. It obviates the need to consider the tangle of cultural influences on behaviour, those complicating ideological, material or psychological factors which would entail a relativistic perspective at best, and willingness to confront the possibility that 'all is not what it seems' at worst.

Alternatively, the theory can assume a misogynist angle which enforces gender stereotypes. The premise that harassment is about sex gone wrong establishes men as natural seekers of sex and women as the natural objects of their quest. The accused's explanatory models of harassment reflect a phallocentric fantasy where sex makes the world go round; every man is a predator, every encounter with a woman is a kind of safari. The images of women in the harassers' red herring theory are the stuff of an adolescent wet dream: each woman has her place on the continuum from harlot to harridan. In this formulation false allegations of harassment may be explained by reference to gender-role stereotypes, women who are prone to dysfunctional or confused role play: the unnatural career women who have developed rejectionist tendencies vis-à-vis male colleagues; the faint-hearted feminists who get cold feet about embarking on the relationship they initially desired. This view fits other deeply embedded cultural stereotypes of the irrepressible office joker, the breast-fondler, the audition-couch approach to promotion and the humourless asexual feminist. Media coverage of the Tyson and Kennedy–Smith rape trials in 1992 and 1992/3, respectively, evoked a host of such stereotypes, apparently reflecting greater public interest in the issue of sex games and seductions gone wrong than in legal questions of violence and assault.

The final analytical issue to be discussed is perhaps the most important one, the inherent 'weak spot' in the red herring theory. The men's narratives and explanatory models of harassment depend on the construction of an unambiguous enemy (men-haters and deniers of sexual 'nature'), since the world must be seen to consist of rival camps in a natural battle of the sexes. The basic point is that the explanation of harassment in sexual terms is the only one which can maintain the conceptual and practical dominance of its advocates. The alternative theory, that harassment has little to do with sex, represents a shift of emphasis which would undermine the position of the accused. In the alleged harassers' accounts, factors such as material advantage, wage differentials, discriminatory legislation and equal opportunities are considered irrelevant to the crucial sexual dimension of the problem. My argument is that if an alleged harasser was to abandon the red herring of sex as an explanation for behaviour, he would have to consider the relevance of power-sharing, male dominance and hegemonic control

mechanisms in the workplace. It would be necessary to face the implications of men's sustained command of the public arena on the one
hand, and of their management of dominant ideology on the other.
The men's explanations of harassment effectively 'naturalise' patriarchy
via the red herring of sex. The 'explanation' is presented as part of 'how
the world really is through men's eyes'. The red herring theory depends
on representing 'men' and 'male experience' as undifferentiated and
homogeneous. Their narratives of harassment admit no possible dissent
or diversity among men. Typical comments in discussions about men
who had 'sided with the woman' in harassment cases are: 'What kind
of man would do that!', and 'You wouldn't think a man would fall for
such an unlikely story.' In short, any explanatory model of harassment
without sex as its primary causal factor not only implies potential
admission of individual guilt, but entails a reappraisal of existing patriarchal power structures.

Despite the increased public profile of sexual harassment, discussion
of my research with academic colleagues outside feminist or specialist
circles raised a set of issues of some relevance here.[19] These reactions
ranged from one extreme position to the other. At one extreme, there
is the argument that sexual harassment doesn't really exist: it is a 'fashionable' term invented by the feminist employment lobby and/or a simple
misclassification of a complex kind of behaviour which takes place in
that no-man's-land between potential and real sexual encounters. At
the other extreme, there is the view that sexual harassment is a universal
fact of life, ubiquitous and inevitable as long as there are encounters
between the male and female of the species.[20] The common implication in both reactions is the impossibility of dealing with sexual
harassment on an intellectual or a practical, institutional level.
Interpreting the actual experiences of harassment which I was research-
ing against such a backdrop reinforced my interest in the apparent
omnipresence of a red herring tendency. If harassment could be both
too simple and too complex a phenomenon to merit investigation, did
that not suggest a desire either to bury one's head in the sand or to theorise
the subject out of existence? It is notable that some colleagues chose
to focus on minutiae of the problem in much the same way and, with
the same consequences as my male subjects, concentrated on the red
herring in their narratives of harassment.

In conclusion, I found the appeal and general dominance of the red
herring theory surprising. In many ways, the men's representations and
explanatory models of harassment provide a disturbing picture of contemporary perceptions of the pattern of heterosexual relations. The
general question seems to be how men and women are to form relationships when the pre-war, pre-feminist pattern of gender roles has been

broken. There is a sense of crisis in the face of irrevocable change; the *ancien régime* has been replaced by new rules, roles and responsibilities, although no one seems sure what they are. At an abstract level this may be part of the crisis of culture in the First World. Discussion of the late-twentieth-century break between 'the word and the world' and the loss of faith in metanarratives can throw some light on this problem. At a human, social level an obvious dilemma is that there are rarely unambiguous rules of behaviour: more often than not people juggle with a collection of fragmentary models of and for reality. Perhaps in this context it is not so surprising that the search for red herrings is so popular.

Notes and References

1. Research was carried out during 1991–3. Sixty cases of harassment were considered in detail, an equal number of 'accusers' and 'accused'. These were selected from a total of 272 responses to an advertisment placed in ten newspapers and journals. The newspapers included three national daily broadsheets, three local or regional weekly papers, two journals aimed at a professional/middle-class female readership, and two journals aimed at a professional, male readership. Each case had occurred in an institutional setting, whether a place of employment, or an educational or entertainment establishment (sports clubs and leisure centres) in the southeast of England. Despite the different environments, harassment had involved individuals who were in frequent contact with each other. In cases where harassment had not occurred at work, the individuals were in relationships similar to those of the workplace, requiring systematic cooperation and collaboration – people described their relationships with the 'other party' as 'just like he'd been a colleague'. A wide range of cases of harassment were described, from ones alleging rape to others which centred on persistent verbal insults. All cases had been discussed within a formal institutional framework for resolving harassment, but more than half had remained unresolved (the allegation being withdrawn). The timescales in the cases ranged from four months to three years. All alleged harassers were male, aged from 15 to 49, and all the objects of harassment were female, aged 25–47. The average age at the time of harassment was 36 for males, 27 for females. I would like to thank each person involved for their frank cooperation in this research, and I respect their desire for anonymity.
2. Where I paraphrase informants' statements I have tried to use their words and remain faithful to the style in which they were expressed.

3. D. Spender, *Man Made Language* (London: Routledge and Kegan Paul, 1980), p. 172. Also see S. Ardener (ed.), *Perceiving Women* (London: Dent, 1975); D. Cameron, *Feminism and Linguistic Theory* (London: Macmillan, 1985); C. Herbert, *Talking of Silence: The Sexual Harassment of Schoolgirls* (London: Falmer, 1989).

4. F. Mernissi, *Doing Daily Battle* (London: Zed, 1984) p. 4.

5. S. Wise and L. Stanley, *Georgie Porgie: Sexual Harassment in Everyday Life* (London: Pandora, 1987) p. 53. Also see C. MacKinnon, *Sexual Harassment of Working Women: A Case of Sex Discrimination* (New Haven, Conn.: Yale University Press, 1979); L. Farley, *Sexual Shakedown: The Sexual Harassment of Women on the Job* (New York: Warner, 1978); S. Read, *Sexual Harassment at Work* (Feltham: Hamlyn, 1982); A. Sedley and M. Benn, *Sexual Harassment at Work* (London: National Council of Civil Liberties, 1982); N. Hadjifotiou, *Women and Harassment at Work* (London: Pluto, 1983); Herbert, *Talking of Silence*.

6. Cited by V. Hey, *Patriarchy and Pub Culture* (London: Tavistock, 1986), p. 6. See L. Kelly, 'The Continuum of Sexual Violence' in J. Hanmer and M. Maynard (eds), *Women, Violence and Social Control* (London: Macmillan, 1987).

7. It is important to state that I am discussing a Western industrial setting. I am not convinced that the remarks made here can be applied to other cultural contexts without serious readjustment. My discussion of Western ideologies of gender and feminist theories of sexual harassment with Muslim women has produced several positions incompatible with some assumptions of this paper. A central point is the view that harassment is a specific problem of Western industrial society. In theory, harassment would be unknown in an ideal Muslim society, where the complementary balance of gender roles and separate spheres of activity and responsibility would prevent the situation arising. Herbert (*Talking of Silence*, pp. 132–65) has made an interesting analysis of 'female-controlling practices' which provides a useful frame of reference for cross-cultural comparison of the forms of social control that affect women.

8. The summaries are composed from comments made by all respondents on a number of different occasions. On consulting with respondents, all agreed that the issues I have mentioned are those which they feel to be most important in their own cases. Six women describe the strategic errors they made in responding to their harassers as 'a major mistake', which intensified the harassment and made them feel partly responsible for the harassment itself.

9. In general the opinion that the wrong course of action had been adopted was based on one of two arguments. The first was that the harassment should have been ignored and would have stopped if this course of 'action' had been sustained. A change of tactics had exacerbated the harassment. The second was that a formal accusation should have been made without hesitation or advance warning on recognition of the harassing behaviour. The latter position appears to contradict the women's assertion that they would not accuse a perpetrator if harassed again. After questioning more than half the original respondents about this, it became apparent that they agree the ideal response to harassment is to make an immediate public accusation through formal channels. However, personally they would ignore future harassment rather than risk a repeat of past experience. Read (*Sexual Harassment at Work*) found that a majority of women who experience harassment at work prefer to leave their jobs rather than report the problem.

10. The accounts of harassment from men ignored career-related factors in theories about false accusations (also see note 17).

11. From our initial contact and at all subsequent meetings, respondents began each account of their experience by explaining that they had been wrongly accused of harassment. I was further surprised by the consistency of the written accounts I requested at a later stage of research. More than half opened with, 'It was all a terrible mistake'; the remainder concluded the opening sentence or paragraph with the phrase 'but the accusation was completely false'.

12. Fourteen respondents elaborated on reasons for their accusers' loss of interest. The most popular explanations of why the woman's sexual interest had declined were that she had felt insulted by the apparent lack of interest (five out of 14); she had become worried about how colleagues might react to the intended relationship (four out of 14); she was embarrassed by not having had her interest reciprocated (three out of 14); or she got bored waiting and had found a replacement (two out of 14).

13. The 'workplace scenario' was used in almost all the men's narratives of harassment, even in the accounts of the six men who had not been working with their accusers. The argument based on a view of 'the typical working relationship' was described as 'the classic example' or 'the usual situation' which leads to a mistaken accusation of harassment. The 'work example' was judged to be a good illustration of their explanation that harassment is 'sexual', is 'natural'.

14. The degree of consensus on this issue also suggests that the range of criteria employed in settling disputes needs closer scrutiny.

Twenty respondents had withdrawn an allegation of harassment when it became apparent that a resolution of the case would be made on the basis of personal sexually-related evidence. One woman commented:

> It was his word against mine, so how could they come to a decision without wanting to use details of my sex life as evidence of whether I should have felt harassed? If they couldn't prove I really was being harassed, they could at least label me 'sexually experienced' or 'virginal', and then decide that my interpretation of his behaviour as harassment was justified or not.

15. Almost two decades after Farley's study (*Sexual Shakedown*), her assertion that men view women workers as sexual objects rather than employees remains a wholly accurate conclusion in relation to these research findings. Also see S. G. Cole, 'Child Battery' in C. Guberman and M. Wolfe (eds), *No Safe Place: Violence against Women and Children* (Toronto: Women's Press, 1985); M. French, *Beyond Power: On Women, Men and Morals* (London: Sphere, 1986); Herbert, *Talking of Silence*.

16. This recalls the more general issue of complicity as expressed by Herbert (*Talking of Silence*, p. 25):

> So long as sexual harassment is considered sexually motivated, women and girls find it hard to understand it in the same way as they would a mugging. For a mugging is regarded as something which is outside their control but sexual harassment implies ... women's complicity.

17. Further evidence includes the absence of any mention of power-related issues in the detailed written accounts of the accused, such as the pattern of authority in a man's working relationship with his accuser, or a consideration of career-related motives for false accusations.

18. Popular public awareness of Complexity and Chaos Theory may be taken as evidence of the interest in universal governing systems and principles. It is possible to suggest that there is an implicit gendered association at work which relates to notions of 'order' and evokes the stereotypes of male order and female/womanly disorder.

19. Herbert, *Talking of Silence,* pp. 10–11.

20. Having preserved the anonymity of my offical research subjects, I feel that it would be unfair and unreasonable to connect named individuals to opinions which they expressed informally.

4

Offence is the Best Defence? – Pornography and Racial Violence

Gargi Bhattacharyya

Harassment is usually made possible by a power imbalance between groups – men can harass women, whites can harass blacks, straights can harass gays, because the harassed group suffers wider social disprivilege. The activity of harassment reiterates this skewed relation, puts the harassed party back in his or her place. His or her identity feels less negotiable and fluid and more painfully certain. Harassment is a way of ensuring people who are already having a bad time are painfully aware of their predicament. It serves as a reminder of local power relations, while reproducing the same patterns. We can think of harassment as a threatening restatement of the status quo. This might take place between individuals or institutions as a face-to-face encounter, or it might take the form of some more free-floating message. In some situations, words and pictures, marks on bits of paper, can feel very dangerous. This is what I want to think about here – what makes some kinds of representation threatening? And when? To whom? What would it take to feel safe?

In Britain in the early 1990s these questions reemerge in that nebulous and perhaps non-existent arena, the politics of 'race'. Europe is in the process of destroying and remaking itself in unrecognisable ways; as a by-product of this the far right of various locations, those who organise around an explicitly white supremacist or violently xenophobic agenda, is once again organised and respectable. Much as Britain resists its Europeanisation in most regards, there are indications that there is also a resurgence of organised racism in the UK too. In response to this a number of national anti-fascist organisations have been formed – the Socialist Workers Party has resurrected at least the name of the Anti-Nazi League, Militant back an organisation called Youth Against Racism in Europe, the higher profile Anti-Racist Alliance appeals to a broader left constituency and purports to represent black communities. Against this backdrop there have been various and frightening racist attacks and murders in areas where the far right (which in Britain consists of a number of interconnected organisations, all of whom seek to achieve a purified nation of white gentiles) has been organising. The murder of Stephen Lawrence in April 1993 in an area of southeast London which had seen at least three other racial killings in the previous two years has received unexpected (for racist attacks) national publicity because of fears that this attack is one frightening instance of wider trends. Protests against the murder have tended to focus on the presence of a local British National Party bookshop as a contributory factor – the dissemination of explicitly racist material in the area is seen to have increased racist violence. In this context it becomes difficult to argue with any degree of good conscience with the claim that racist attacks are part of the horrific everyday of contemporary Britain, and that this might be the case independently of the distribution of fascist publicity. When black boys are being stabbed in the street it is hard to focus your attention on the ambiguities of interpretation.[1]

Sometimes things seem uncertain – with the best will in the world, a right position does not become apparent. You know that there is evil in the world, but it doesn't seem clear what you should do or think about this. In Britain a black skin, a skin which is beige or sienna, mocha or chocolate, a skin in the range from high honey to deep black-brown, this skin can get you into trouble. Some physical characteristics can become an encumbrance in everyday life. A whole range of writing is available to convince the doubting of this.[2] I am already convinced of this: I believe that for some people racism makes the world a dangerous place. This danger makes black people vulnerable to harassment and threat on a racial basis. These bullyings by suggestion can work because of the wider context of racism, because the hurt is already there to be capitalised upon. I also believe that words and pictures can contribute to this pain. What feels uncertain is the sort of contribution this might be. I don't believe that the relationship between what people see and what people do is a straightforward one. I also don't believe that either seeing or doing are easily understood activities. But in the pit of my stomach, in some pre-educational residue or schooling in self-preservation, I know that some kinds of communication can make me hurt and frightened, that some representations can heighten the sense of racial vulnerability. My education lets me know that the body cannot be apart from culture, or even residually separate from schooling; but it is in the realm of physical manifestation that I am constituted as racialised and this is the realm in which I feel racial fear, however fictionally. Sometimes you can know the theory and still not feel it. I want to stress this point because it is an indication of why there are situations in which the most diligent scholar cannot make her argument stick. This resistance to analysis and education has to be recognised as more than just foolishness because it is an indication of what our analysis cannot encompass yet. The reader should bear this in mind when immersed in the comfortable familiarity of the reading which follows – try to think twice about the parts which seem most easily convincing, about the things you think you know already.

A whole range of theories argue that looking is about pleasure.[3] Words and pictures provide a space in which the observer can exercise some of her most pleasurable experiences of self.[4] Constructing meaning in relation to an object allows the practice of control and the articulation of desire. Objects which are staged to be read promise a chance both to see what you want and to pretend that you can get it. Making meaning is a way of feeling good, a method of expressing your areas of ineradicable powerlessness in an activity which demonstrates your power. This way of thinking allows us to appreciate that horror may be as enjoyable a genre as romance, despite the apparent disparities in their audience responses.[5] If we concentrate on what the reader does we can imagine that pleasure might derive from the *route* to meaning, from the activity rather than from the effect in itself (and what could the effect itself be? What identification of effect is not in fact a naming of the shape of interpretation?). This is one understanding of why ugly might be fun, of how you might take pleasure from looking at things even while recognising their unpleasant aspects.

What is argued by a whole range of other people is that some things are just ugly. Some words and pictures are unattractive and insulting, they degrade what they represent and create disrespect in those who look. These representations are dangerous and frightening no matter which way you look at them. No tricksy method of reading or highflown theory of interpretation can take away from this threat. Here ugly is offensive in ways which mean that it should never be fun. Only freaks would get their kicks like this. We can think of this as obscenity, as eliciting that mixed-up response of being at once transfixed and disgusted. In this framework the reader/observer is placed as the victim of her response. The obscene representation is the one which robs the reader of the pleasurable agency of interpretation – making meaning doesn't feel like the exercise of power here. These words and pictures bite you before you know what is happening.

Of course, predictably, there is an area of uncertainty between ugly fun and obscenity – which causes problems for people who are concerned about the rights of both enjoyers of ugly fun and victims of obscene threat. The law prohibiting incitement to racial hatred recognises this uncertainty, so that prosecution depends upon the likelihood of violence. This means that the harassment suffered by those who feel threatened by violence, whether or not it is particularly likely to occur at that point, cannot be registered by this law. What I want to think about here is the extent to which ideas of racist obscenity are informed by debates about the representation of sexuality, with this often meaning the depiction of women's bodies. The two arenas are not analogous, but there are points at which the arguments seem to seep into each other, particularly in discussions of the senses of threat experienced by harassed and terrorised groups.

THE RACE RELATIONS ACT 1976: ANTI-RACIST COMMONSENSE

Under the heading 'Incitement to Racial Hatred' the Race Relations Act 1976 amends the Public Order Act 1936 with the following insertion:

A person commits an offence if –

(a) he publishes or distributes written matter which is threatening, abusive or insulting;
or
(b) he uses in any public place or at any public meeting words which are threatening, abusive or insulting,
in a case where, having regard to all the circumstances, hatred is likely to be stirred up against any racial group in Great Britain by the matter or words in question.[6]

It is explained that 'written matter' includes any writing, sign or visible representation'.[7]

Although this section of the legislation has been notoriously difficult to make effective, the reasoning behind the prohibition has considerable currency.[8] In a society in which the perception of racial difference is a cause of tension and violence, some sorts of representation make this situation worse. This is undesirable for everyone, on the basis that it constitutes a threat to *public order*. The maintenance of a peaceable society depends upon the avoidance of this disruptive violence – what is being safeguarded is social stability rather than the welfare of minority groups. Some things should not be said because they cause trouble for everyone. I take this to be the reasoning behind a whole range of anti-racist commonsense. The point here is not that some groups of people are more sensitive to insult than others. The feelings of the already persecuted are not the issue. The response to obscenity is not the direct criterion of judgement in this scenario, although this framework of value comes into the identification of threat, abuse or insult. Instead, what is being judged is the likely effect of certain representations – if this is judged to be socially disruptive then the representation should be disallowed and its purveyor punished.

The 1976 Act revises a previous piece of legislation, the Race Relations Act of 1965. Under this earlier law, people could be prosecuted if they made representations which they intended to be racially threatening and which were likely to be so. To be prosecuted under this law you had to know what you were doing and really mean it. The perpetrator of the crime of incitement had to feel hatred and plan violence and, more than this, actively instil violent feelings in others. The revisions of the 1976 Act did away with this requirement that the prosecution should prove intent. The shift seems to be a recognition that the social meanings of representations are not determined by the intentions of their makers, and also an acknowledgement that the intentions of a speaker or writer may not be available to any observer, no matter how careful and informed his or her reading. In this, lawmaking seems to follow literary criticism and looks to a sociology of reception for the definition of meaning.[9] However, despite the development in the theory of interpretation implied here, the prohibition against inciting racial hatred still assumes that some meanings are unambiguous. Even though meaning is seen to be dependent on context, within this context the racism of some representations is assumed to be self-evident.

FEMINISM AND ANTI-CENSORSHIP

This implied certainty about some sorts of racist meaning distinguishes discussions of racist representation from discussions about pornography. Debates about pornography, particularly between feminists, have occupied large amounts of time and energy in thrashing out the difficulties of representation and the production of meaning.[10] While these issues remain far from resolved and continue to be the cause of much tension and animosity, this has meant that all sides have had to acknowledge that the meanings and effects of words and pictures are not self-evident. Anti-porn feminists argue that images which pretend to be enjoyable are in fact violent. Anti-censorship feminists respond by reinstating the agency of the viewer: pornography can't be equated with violence in any straightforward sense and might be enjoyable for some women. Anti-porn feminists come back with a feminist theory of false consciousness by which women who like porn are dupes of the system. Either way, the arguments are about interpretation.

Some feminist proponents of censorship point to British race relations legislation as a model to be emulated.[11] In this argument, pornography is to women what racist propaganda is to black and Jewish people. The pro-censorship lobby clearly has a stake in showing meaning to be stable and knowable – otherwise, how can you tell what to censor? However, the need to steal a theory of certain meaning from the highly imperfect legislation against incitement to racial hatred is an indication of how unavailable definite meanings are in the arena of sexual representation.

BEING CAREFUL ABOUT THE NON-ANALOGY BETWEEN RACE AND GENDER

The politically informed argument to make at this point is that race and gender are not analogous, and that racist representation is nothing like pornography.[12] Explicitly racist material admits its own racism and declares distaste for the racially different to be a rational and desirable response. In this genre depictions of the racialised are designed to excite disgust, not desire. The pleasure of the viewer is supposed to stem from an augmented sense of superiority rather than from a sexual turn-on.

The narratives around pictures-of-women pornography are not like this. The explicit narrative is of a desire without disdain, an appreciative state of arousal.[13] Whatever position we take on the possibilities of respect for women within mainstream pornography, this way of thinking is distinct from an explicit racism in which the refusal of respect is the organising principle. Debates around pornography have been conducted as battles about aesthetics, about the criteria of taste – the same sets of representations have been argued to produce both revulsion and good feeling: what is leisure to one person is sick to another. Issues of freedom of speech and morality have been subsumed under this notion of aesthetic value; offence has come to be seen as almost exclusively a matter of taste.[14] Defenders of pornography have attempted to reeducate the tastes of their opponents in order that the beautiful and pleasurable aspects of sexual representation can be appreciated – the argument is that there is a nice side to this if only people would see it.

Explicitly racist material, the stuff of propaganda and far-right newsletters, does not purport to have a nice side. Opponents require not a reschooling in the criteria of aesthetic judgement but to be convinced of the good sense of white supremacist thinking. Explicitly racist material seeks to confirm existing racism and to convert the doubting. What is pleasurable here is recognising ugly (foreign, black, Jewish) and

knowing yourself to be different from this – this material encourages
its audiences to feel white and proud. What is relished by the viewer is
a sense of superiority rather than a sense of lack. This kind of fun is only
available to some people. The 'ugly' aren't supposed to feel good about
seeing themselves like this.

Put this way, things seem clearcut. The complications of fun are over
here with pornography, and straightforward ugliness is over there with
racism. But what about that difficult overlap?

THINKING ABOUT THE CONNECTIONS BETWEEN RACE AND GENDER: THE EXOTIC

Recently I came across a magazine called *Asian Babes*.[15] In fact, 'came
across' is not quite the truth. Having been told of its existence by a friend,
I spent many months surreptitiously looking upwards as I walked past
the magazine racks of large newsagents. Unfortunately, I was too embarrassed to ask for it; not only because women are not supposed to buy
girlie mags, but also because requesting this publication seemed to
position me as too racialised a version of the narcissistic woman, obses-
sively seeking out mirrorings of my own image. To friends I could
explain my multiple and contradictory interests, but to shopkeepers I
still wanted to appear respectable. The allure of *Asian Babes* is structured
around allusions to precisely this type of veiling. The Asian babe is
outwardly demure while harbouring a hidden interest in the kinky
(what could be more perverse than scholarship for a young woman?)
– just wanting to have a look aligned me with the depiction of Asian
womanhood presented by the magazine. What I want to understand
is why this positioning felt and feels so peculiarly discomforting. Is this
a racist threat?

The magazine in my possession is in fact called *Hottest Asian Babes*
and purports to be a 'new best of special' first issue. I bought it in Leicester
in 1993, in a small newsagents which is part of a chain. Leicester has a
sizeable Asian population and is one of the most markedly Asian cities
in Britain. I presume that this plays a part in the magazine's distribution, on the assumption that it is aimed at either Asian men or at men
who see a lot (but still not enough) of Asian women. However, all of
this is speculation. I can only guess the intended audience of *Asian Babes*
by trying to categorise the multiple addressees of the magazine – a strategy
which is famously incapable of identifying actual audiences.

The magazine itself seems unclear about who it is addressing; its
markets seem not only multiple, but potentially incompatible. The
letters' page exhorts Asian 'boys and girls' from a variety of communities to contribute – 'Gujurati, Hindu Punjabi, Muslim, Sikh, Hindu,

Bengali': the roll-call of Asian diversity seems to be structured by a multi-cultural logic. Here is a promise to address the specificities of Asian identity in Britain, to give voice to all these ways of being Asian. The suggestion is that this is 'our' space, a chance to be young and British Asian and explicitly sexual and sexy. This possibility is extended to both 'boys and girls', and the theme of liberating Asian womanhood from the confinements of a constraining culture runs through the magazine.

This theme crosses over into another mode of address within the publication, that directed to the white viewer/reader who stands in the place of Western enlightenment in relation to the Asian woman shackled by Eastern traditions. The representations of Asianness purport to give voice to Asian experience *and* to make this depiction available to the outsider. The magazine plays the discourse of authenticity from both angles; on the one hand promising to reveal the secret truths of Asian sexuality in a way which is empowering to Asians, and on the other displaying this revelation as exotic spectacle to the white viewer who is privileged and titillated by unexpected access to this cultural difference. The linking fiction is the liberation of Asian women.

Visually the magazine seems to belong to the least sophisticated end of the tits-and-bits market. The pictures are lit harshly and unflatteringly, doing little justice to even the best-looking models. Costumes are private shop chic – polyester satin in red, white and black. One set of photos shows Kerry from Bradford posing in white suspender belt, black stockings and pale pink high heels on the formica surfaces of a fitted kitchen. Another has Dolly wearing black lacy underwear and plastic jewellery on a dralon sofa in what seems to be someone's front room. Some pictures are less obviously done at home: Lai Lai is shown in a sauna, complete with baby oil and a slightly softer focus, Ayisha in a dark and uncertain setting with gunbelts and other military hardware. However, about half of the spreads work around some notion of the girl next door. We see Suki at home, with her cat. Pages at a time are given over to the 'Shooting Gallery', supposedly displaying readers' wives and girlfriends. Whoever these women actually are, this celebration of the amateur is worth noting, particularly as the cheerful no-knickers-in-the-kitchen shot seems to disrupt many expectations about the stuff of straight male masturbatory fantasy. These women are not unattainable goddesses, and although they are young and firm and pretty, they are not blemish-free. Here the pornographic fantasy is not of the impossibly perfect woman (although some of the pictures are like this), but of everyday attractiveness without knickers. This is a standard gesture in men's magazines, both democratising in the suggestion that hot sex is available to everyone and unpleasant in the implication that (some) straight men view their sexual partners as trophies to be displayed.

What I am interested in is what happens to this gesture in the explicitly racialised context of *Asian Babes*. If we assume a largely Asian audience, then this is an example of a homosocial economy with an ethnic slant – in a context of racist persecution, Asian masculinity is bolstered by the representational exchange of Asian women. We might not have much, but at least we've got the girls.

If the magazine is not a community service, this scenario changes. If controlling the sexuality of Asian women is the last privilege of an Asian masculinity which is emasculated by racism in other areas (and this whole mythology of defensive barbarism is easily recognisable as part of popular narratives of Asianness in Britain), pictures of Asian women almost in their underwear take on a different significance. Here the sexuality on display figures as the last prize of a racialised community in retreat: outsiders can gawp at these crotches because our humiliation is so complete. It is possible to imagine a reading in which this spectacle serves as a ticket to transracial (as good as white?) manhood for Asian men. Pictures of Asian women could be offered as equivalents of the readily available depictions of white women, with the boys bonding by swapping pictures of 'their' women and remaking masculinity across racial divides. This might be happening – but I think that the status of Asians in contemporary Britain makes other stories more likely.

Popular racist and liberal mythologies vilify 'the' Asian family for being too patriarchal, too stifling. Even in the 1990s the horror story of the arranged marriage can provide an enjoyable excuse for media scandal and ethnic titillation. Lamentations about 'how badly they treat their women' lead smoothly into speculation about and denunciation of a whole array of the supposed cultural practices of these 'other' people. Asian women are regarded as downtrodden victims of menfolk who cannot make the transition to Western values. Making pictures of naked Asian women available to a general public is a slap in the face for Asian men who value the traditional as a certain version of femininity. I assume that the peculiar pleasures of *Asian Babes* occur in relation to this narrative, that the special frisson of the forbidden must come in part from breaking the taboos of a racialised community which takes pride in keeping some things private. In the context of 1990s Britain the desire to look at Asian babes is as much a response to Asianness as to babeness. I am convinced that this must be the case, that the contemporary swamp of racial meanings cannot be avoided, only negotiated. What remains uncertain is the sort of negotiation which is being made by a publication like *Asian Babes*.

In some senses the magazine extends the range of representations of Asians in Britain. It is potentially racist, but it is difficult to imagine a portrayal of the racialised which would not be vulnerable to recuperation by a racist narrative. Just say 'Paki' and you're there. Maybe extending the range is the only political gesture worth making in the realm of words and pictures. So why does *Asian Babes* still feel like racism to me? Is this a response to what I see or to where I live?

The stories, which intersperse the pictures and take the form of letters, seem to cover the range of British Asian stereotypes from white and Asian perspectives. Several are classic pornographic scenarios done out in ethnic drag. Here, with the modifying licence of summary, is a selection.

'My Very Own Dimple' tells the story of an east London draper with a soft spot for Dimple Kapadia (Bombay superstar and pin-up girl of the South Asian diaspora). Fortunately for him, he is seduced in his shop by a Dimple lookalike who is mad for his body. This is an Asian-only community story. It retells the familiar 'beautiful stranger who turns out to be on for it' narrative as an Asian-on-Asian story and marks desirability by reference to Hindi cinema. The virility of the Asian man is celebrated.

'Sex Hungry Asian Men' is supposedly written by a white woman in her twenties and of liberal tastes. She writes of an earlier wanton phase during which she would go with any Asian or Afro-Caribbean 'chap' for the asking. At this point she writes of her involvement with two Asian men. When each learns of the other's existence, they both come round to punish her. A threesome ensues, at her instigation, but despite its success cannot be repeated because one of the men doesn't like being naked in the company of other males. Although all the pictures are of Asian women, the pleasures of this and other stories rest on the notion that white women are hot for Asian men. Once again it is Asian masculinity which is flattered and confirmed (perhaps a little too anxiously?) as definitely heterosexual.

'My Gallant's Reward' is another community story, this time written from a woman's viewpoint. The woman describes herself as coming from Ilford, Essex, and she starts out telling an everyday story of Asian fear. She is carrying shopping home from the bus stop when she is attacked by local skinheads. She is rescued by the martial arts expertise of a chivalrous young Asian man. He bathes her wounds. She flaunts herself. He scolds her for being morally lax. Enthusiastic sex ensues. The story ends with her telling of their impending marriage, of which her parents approve because he is a chartered accountant.

'A Doctor in the House' is another white woman story in which the woman expresses surprise at being engaged to an Indian. She explains that while ill in hospital she met a young house doctor; they went out

on a series of dates, but he remained a perfect gentleman. Fed up with
this, she seduces him. Now they are getting married.

'My God, What a Body' introduces the first white man as teller of the
story and the first explicit acknowledgement of white racism. Geoff
describes himself as a white east Londoner who resented the influx of
Ugandan Asians into 'his' area. He then describes his transformation
from racist bigot to wishy-washy liberal as stemming from his lust for
the young Asian schoolteacher who lived across the road. Male heterosexual desire transforms the response to racial difference from irritation
and fear into sexual interest and titillation. The markers of another culture
stop being sources of anger and become points of added interest – the
attraction of her sari folds clinging to her bottom. This anti-racist
enlightenment cannot be translated to those who do not share his sexual
tastes. Geoff cannot woo his schoolteacher close to home for fear of
violent reprisals from the local racists. However, despite these hurdles,
they go on a date and enthusiastic sex ensues. We are told that this was
ten years ago and that they are now married. *Asian Babes* is congratu-
lated as an ultimate method of promoting racial harmony.

'Promiscuous Hippies' is about white hippy chicks in the East,
indulging in group sex with local Asian men. 'What Katie Did Next ...'
tells the story of a middle-aged Asian computer science teacher who is
seduced in the staff toilets by a buxom blonde student in her teens. The
'This is Your Wife' confessional page describes an Asian woman shedding
her sexual inhibitions with her white husband. 'Performing to Music'
has an Asian woman recounting her Diwali sexual adventures. 'Naughty
Parties' tells the story of a deserted Asian wife who comes out of her
shell at her white girlfriend's party, receiving cunnilingus from her friend's
husband and indulging in a bit of public lesbianism with the friend
herself. 'While the Cat's Away' reveals the secrets of bored Asian
housewives who seduce young workmen picked from the Yellow Pages
while their husbands are away on business.

Only one 'letter' has no story to tell. This is published under the heading
'It's About Time' and begins by complaining about British Asian support
for Saddam Hussein during the Gulf War. The piece then goes on to
congratulate the magazine for being the first to focus on the beauty of
Asian womanhood and argues that women are the most effective
antidote to racism. Resistance is anticipated from those in the community
who will see *Asian Babes* as an attempt to establish a new niche in the
pornography market, but the writer contends that this is a justifiable
cost if it results in a breaking down of barriers between the indigenous
British and Asian communities. This short letter, taking up only half a
page, is one of only two items in the magazine which offer no promise
of sexual excitement. The other is an advertisement for a personal

alarm, which I take to be another reference to the threat of racist attack and an indication that the magazine's advertisers expect a sizeable Asian readership.

Overall the writing in the magazine seems to tell a slightly different story from the pictures. I took the pictures to be fairly standard examples of the exotic within Britain, the double thrill of naked womanhood and naked blackness. Almost without thinking I assumed that the addressee was more powerful than the people pictured: for me these images were structured in relation to a gaze which was not only male but also white (and also class-marked, although I'm not yet able to decipher how this might work).[16] Yes, anyone could occupy the position of gazer, but for some people this would be a contortion rather than a comfort. In a defensive gesture I recouped the imagery of *Asian Babes* into a racist narrative myself, before it could be done to me. The meanings of these pictures seemed certain: they marked disrespect and indirectly contributed to the wider disparagement of Asians in Britain. In this context of known racism, all representations of Asianness were potentially harassing.

The words complicated matters. The explicit references to what it means to be Asian in contemporary Britain – the films you watch, the places you live, the violence you face – make this staging of the exotic very different. We can think of the exotic as the pornographic with race (however this is manifested). As with porn, the viewer is supposed to love the people depicted. This kind of pleasure must disassociate itself from upfront racisms if it is to be any fun. The peculiar buzz of the exotic relies upon its context remaining unspoken. Power disparity must be disguised as the mystery of difference. Naming the context of racism disrupts this pleasure. Everyone has to become more knowing. In *Asian Babes* the pictures invite you drool over brown flesh, while the words remind you that in Britain brown flesh brings its own trouble and pain. This racist imagery tells you about the racist arena in which it is made – which seems as close to an educative project as we're going to get. This doesn't take away my discomfort – *Asian Babes* can confirm every racist myth in the book if that is the predisposition of the reader – but if the alternative to discomfort is invisibility, then I'll learn to live with discomfort.

Looking at things which *might* be racist, which *might* incite further hatred, reminds me of where I am. I have to reassess sources of potential threat. This involves distinguishing between things which recall pain and things which can really hurt you, between the sensible and uncomfortable knowledges of self-preservation and the stuff that can really cause you damage. This distinction isn't clear. Being constantly reminded of your vulnerability might keep you as effectively terrorised as a physical attack, but only because physical attack is such a real and common possibility. You could only be free of this feeling of sometimes being hounded by words and pictures if you forgot what being black means in Britain. Given this, I don't think that changing the words and pictures is the answer.

Black people in Britain are under threat. So, what's new? This threat may come in part from reorganisation on the far right, but is more likely to come from the more dispersed forces of everyday British racism. The unhappy experience of harassment is part of this, a mode of victimisation which depends upon things being bad all over. I don't believe that there is a way of making words and pictures which can fix this, or can even make it feel better necessarily. I don't know whether words and pictures exacerbate a violent situation or not, but I do think that choosing silence and an illusion of safety over understanding means that things will never get better. The best that we can get from representations is some understanding of where we are, of what constitutes a threat. Feeling vulnerable is uncomfortable, but a reasonable response given the situation. Shutting your eyes might make you feel safe, yet, right now, feeling safe would be nothing but stupid. Better to learn to live with danger.

Notes and References

1. The idea that the young black man in the street is the metonym for the race or for the racialised has many drawbacks. Focusing upon street violence as a model of racism masculinises blackness and pushes the specificities of violence against black women to one side. However, I think it would be politically foolish not to give attention to the spectre of the murdered black boy when thinking about racist threat in contemporary Britain.
2. See, for example, Ashok Bhat, Roy Carr-Hill and Sushel Ohri (eds), *Britain's Black Population: A New Perspective* (Aldershot: Gower, 1988).
3. When this is theorised by Laura Mulvey in her highly influential analysis of visual pleasure – see Laura Mulvey, *Visual and Other Pleasures* (London: Macmillan, 1989) – the implication is that the viewer derives pleasure from looking at someone else's expense, usually that of women. Other writers have tried to think about the ways in which women also get pleasure from looking: see E. Deirdre Pribram (ed.), *Female Spectators: Looking at Film and Television* (London: Verso, 1988) and Caught Looking Inc., *Caught Looking: Feminism, Pornography & Censorship* (Seattle, Wash.: Real Comet Press, 1988) for two very different sorts of example.

4. With the experience of self, as always, formed through fantasy.
5. This is discussed in a range of writing about the genre of horror. See, for example, S.S. Prawer, *Caligari's Children: The Film as Tale of Terror* (New York: Da Capo, 1988); James B. Twitchell, *Dreadful Pleasures: An Anatomy of Modern Horror* (Oxford: Oxford University Press, 1985); Carol J. Clover, *Men, Women, and Chainsaws* (London: British Film Institute, 1992).
6. Part IX, s. 70 (2), Race Relations Act 1976 (London: HMSO).
7. Section 70 (6), Race Relations Act 1976.
8. Arguing that this law is inefficient, Feminists Against Censorship state that there have been no major prosecutions under the 'incitement to racial hatred' clauses since 1979, an indication of a more general political climate. See Gillian Rodgerson and Elizabeth Wilson (eds), for Feminists Against Censorship, *Pornography and Feminism: The Case against Censorship* (London: Lawrence and Wishart, 1991). For more detailed indications of why this law is difficult to enforce, see Joanna Oyediran, 'The United Kingdom's Compliance with Article 4 of the International Convention on the Elimination of All Forms of Racial Discrimination', in Sandra Coliver, Kevin Boyle and Frances D'Souza (eds), *Striking a Balance: Hate Speech, Freedom of Expression and Non-discrimination* (London: Article 19, International Centre against Censorship, 1992).
9. See Oyediran, 'The United Kingdom's Compliance with Article 4', for a helpful discussion of the development of laws against racist representations in Britain.
10. For some indications of the shapes of this debate, see Lynne Segal and Mary McIntosh (eds), *Sex Exposed: Sexuality and the Pornography Debate* (London: Virago, 1992).
11. The British-based Campaign Against Pornography and Censorship, which was formed in 1989, uses this model. For written examples of this argument, see Catherine Itzin (ed.), *Pornography, Women, Violence and Civil Liberties* (Oxford: Oxford University Press, 1992), Chapter 5: 'Pornography and Racism: Sexualizing Oppression and Inciting Hatred' by Aminatta Forna, and Chapter 26: 'Pornography and Civil Liberties: Freedom, Harm and Human Rights' by Catherine Itzin.
12. See Pratibha Parmar, 'Rage and Desire: Confronting Pornography', in Gail Chester and Julienne Dickey (eds), *Feminism and Censorship: The Current Debate* (Bridport: Prism, 1988), for a famous and persuasive instance of this argument.
13. I think this is what is demanded of anyone who wishes to succumb to the pleasures of pictures-of-women pornography, whether they are male or female, gay or straight. Other responses require a

resistance to the offered experience of delectation. Arguments which suggest that pictures depicting women as sexually available and responsive are expressions of disdain require the reader actively to refuse the immediate seductions of what they see.

14. See Ian Hunter, David Saunders and Duguld Williamson, *On Pornography, Literature, Sexuality and Obscenity Law* (London: Macmillan, 1993).

15. The concept of the babe is a US import, part of a mass-market fiction of the world of young heterosexual white men in the contemporary United States. This fiction is figured in part around a nostalgia for an earlier America in which, supposedly, whiteness, straightness and maleness were all more valued and powerful. This is in contrast to the contemporary situtation in which these boys are depicted as hopelessly awkward and endlessly frustrated. The popularity of this set of Americanisms thus becomes a celebration of failure, a reclaiming of the particular charmlessness of very young, straight, white men in the US. Using the term 'babe' as the articulation of your heterosexual desire can become a gesture of self-ridicule *as well as* being a reaffirmation of masculine privilege.

16. I'm impressed by Laura Kipnis' suggestive piece, '(Male) Desire and (Female) Disgust: Reading *Hustler*', in Lawrence Grossberg, Cary Nelson and Paula Treichler (eds), *Cultural Studies* (London: Routledge, 1992), and the idea that the affectation of 'low-class' taste in men's magazines might give voice to a range of political issues which cannot be encompassed by an analysis that concentrates wholly on gender.

Part II

Categories

5

Risk, Responsibility and
Sexual Harm

Ruth Jamieson

> The claims of justice and danger are rhetorical resources for all parties. On
> this fulcrum concepts of liability and tort are continuously at stake, always
> in the process of revision. (Mary Douglas)[1]

This chapter rethinks the ways in which rape and sexual harassment
have been constructed in legal discourse. Mary Douglas' work on risk
– notably her contention that the idea of risk may be used as a 'forensic
resource' by all parties involved in making or contesting claims of harm
– provides the point of departure for my analysis. The deployment of
the concept of risk may be said to be forensic when it pertains to law,
and also more generally when it is used rhetorically to attribute responsibility for harm. In applying Douglas' ideas to sexual harm, I will focus
on three related concerns. The first is the notion of risk as a social construction: how is risk both logically and discursively connected to ideas
of blame and responsibility – for example, in judicial or other attributions of blame to the victim? Secondly, I will look at the idea of risk
both explicitly in formal conceptions like 'negligence' and 'provocation', and implicitly in what Mary Douglas calls a 'forensic model of
the person'; that is, in the law's conception of the knowing and responsible individual. Finally, I will explore the possibility of using risk as a
rhetorical resource *for* women who are engaged in claiming legal redress
for sexual harm. Since the notion of risk is a social and gendered construction, it is contingent, mobile and elastic. So it is not inevitable that
risk always tells against women. I will also suggest that recent changes
to the legal discourse on sexual harm by, for example, the Canadian
Parliament or the European Commission, have foregrounded the
question of risk and responsibility, and that such reformulated legal
discourse may be used to frame the demand that *all* legal persons
should be held to a higher standard of mutual responsibility.

RISK AND BLAME IN LEGAL DISCOURSE

It is a commonplace of feminist writing on women's experience of harassment and sexual violence that women are, and perceive themselves to be, at risk of sexual victimisation, and that they routinely engage in avoidance strategies to minimise such risk.[2] Furthermore, when women's risk avoidance strategies fail, they are frequently deemed to be complicit in their own victimisation; for example in Menachem Amir's notion of 'victim-precipitated rape'.[3] Indeed, the judicial process itself often gives expression to other variants of victim blaming – such as remarks to the effect that a victim of rape had somehow 'asked for it', should have 'known what was coming', or had in some other way contributed to her own rape.[4] Judge Bertrand Richards (in Ipswich Crown Court, January 1982) attributed 'contributory negligence' to a woman who had been raped while hitch-hiking, and used it as a mitigating factor in sentencing her rapist (to a £2,000 fine).[5] Judge Richards' reasoning was supported by Sir Melford Stevenson, a retired High Court judge, who remarked that 'it is the height of imprudence for any girl to hitch-hike at night. That is plain, it isn't really worth stating. She is in the true sense asking for it.'[6] Despite the Lord Chancellor's comments to the effect that the 'imprudence' of the victim could not be used in mitigation, Thomas' work on sentencing suggests that imprudence construed as contributory negligence *does* influence rape sentencing where, for example, the victim had accepted a lift in a stranger's car or permitted any of the milder forms of sexual contact.[7] Following a similar line of logic, in 1988 the Employment Appeal Tribunal ruled that industrial tribunals which find that a woman has been sexually harassed may take into account her 'provocative style of dress while at work' when considering what compensation to award her.[8] Remarks like those made by Judge Richards may be thought by some commentators to represent 'bizarre decisions by maverick circuit court judges',[9] but, as I will argue later, they are made sufficiently regularly to form a significant element in the construction of rape and sexual harassment in the legal process, especially in the operation of the conventions governing 'relevance' or reasonableness. Women's fears of sexual harm and also their fears of the legal process itself must be situated in this context.

The 'rationality' or otherwise of women's fears of sexual harm and the precautions they take to avoid it have generally been evaluated either in relation to the 'reality' (that is, the statistical probability) of their risk of sexual harm,[10] or to the broader social reality of threat or danger within which the fear of sexual harm is constructed.[11] In contrast to those who have argued that, in the contemporary world, all citizens live with a generalised sense of risk and uncertainty, that the calculation of potential losses and gains in action is irrelevant in the dangerous world of 'late modernity',[12] I want to argue that analysis of specific risks involving the calculation of the probability and magnitude of potential outcomes has certainly not lost its salience *for law*. It appears primarily in tort law (the law of injury) in concepts like 'prudent foresight', 'foreseeability', 'recklessness' or 'negligence'. Such categories of responsibility (in the sense of blameworthiness) involve notions of risk avoidance; risk-seeking behaviour, on the other hand, comes under the criminal law category of 'provocation'. The point about these terms is not simply that they may be used as rhetorical resources by all parties contesting claims of harm, but that they are mobile conceptions which may move between the provinces of the law adjudicating different sexual harms. So while rape falls within the domain of criminal law, sexual harassment is treated as a civil injury. But both are articulated against a common discourse of sexual risk. Consequently, I want to argue that, rather than constituting different points on a continuum of (hetero)sexual violence, rape and sexual harassment are more accurately viewed as expressing *different* moments in the legal discourse of sexual risk.[13]

The Forensic Model of the Self

Whether it is used proactively to foresee harm, or retrospectively to attribute blame, the notion of risk presumes the same notion of cognition. John Locke was one of the earliest thinkers to postulate the cognitive and *judicial* necessity of 'the continuously conscious and responsible self' (which he christened 'person') for the making and testing of both claims and credibility. Locke described 'person' as 'a forensic term, appropriating actions and their merit; and so belongs only to intelligent agents capable of a law'.[14] This notion of agent responsibility is taken up by Mary Douglas as part of her analysis of risk and blame in Western culture. The prevailing model of the forensic self in contemporary (common law) legal discourse remains lodged within this paradigm of rational choice-making. It assumes a unitary, embodied, rational, self-interested and risk-averse individual capable of prudent foresight.[15] The law derives authority to hold wrongdoers responsible for their actions from its conception of the forensic person's *mental* capacity. Yet, at the same time, the law measures a person's credibility and agency by reading the signs of injury to her (or her alleged attacker's) *body*, taking those signs as corroborative evidence of a woman's resistance to rape.[16]

I turn now to a more detailed analysis of how discourses of risk construct the forensic person in rape trials and sexual harassment cases.

There are two closely related issues. The first concerns what constitutes 'reasonable risk-reading and risk-taking' on the part of the accused and the complainant, and whether and to what extent the standard care implied is the same for everyone. As I have already noted, getting through the day without sexual harm involves 'everyone in thinking *probabilistically* about risk in the field of their ordinary competence' (emphasis added).[17] Women engage in a 'commonsense' form of risk analysis which takes sexual danger as a given. Men, on the other hand, do not and are not expected to factor into their everyday conduct the possibility of their own sexual victimisation.[18] Defence counsels in rape trials frequently argue that the woman got it wrong. How could she *not* have read the man's intentions as sexual? Surely she knew that as a woman she was a sexual target? In response to this, I ask what would constitute reasonable risk-taking on the part of the woman, such that she would not be declared to have contributed to her own harm? And what, if any, awareness of the risk of causing sexual harm is required on the part of the man?

The contrast with the discourses that operate in sexual harassment hearings is instructive. Here the problem is whether the woman was 'unduly sensitive' in reading danger (injury or detriment) into the man's essentially harm*less* conduct. Both forms of sexual harm are ostensibly articulated against a common forensic model of the person – one that presumes the legal subject is a unitary, embodied and rational individual who is capable of prudent foresight. But each reveals a different face of risk. Rape and sexual harassment victims are constructed, respectively, as 'imprudent' in their disregard of sexual risk or as 'prudes' in their oversensitivity to it. Significantly, 'prude' is a term (with a long history) used to derogate women. Hence, complaints of sexual harm are commonly rebutted by being measured against a reasonable person's reading of the situation. The complainant is said to read danger or experience detriment where none was intended. The forensic retort to a charge of rape (which so often involves the argument that the woman has contributed to her own harm) is, once again, that the complainant's reading of risks is faulty. But this time it is because she disregards what a reasonable person (woman) would see – that in the world as it is she is *always* at risk of sexual harm.

Besides the notion of cognition (mental capacity), there is the second issue of intersubjectivity: in the legal context, the capacity to avert to the state of mind of the other. This is entailed in legal discourses of risk as they are expressed in notions such as care, foresight or recklessness. In cases of rape and sexual harassment, what notions of cognition and intersubjectivity are assumed to operate in the communication of desire and consent?

TAKING REASONABLE CARE

The law's recognition that people do and ought to engage in a 'common-sense' version of risk analysis is exemplified in the concept of negligence, which falls under the rubric of the law of tort. Risk also finds indirect expression in criminal law; for example, in adjudications of mistaken conduct, recklessness or provocation. Although my specific concern is with ways in which conceptions of risk are used in the legal discourses of rape and sexual harassment, I want first to investigate how risk is constructed in the concept of negligence, or contributory negligence in the law of tort. Generally, negligence means omitting to do something a reasonable person would do, or doing something a reasonable person would not do, which in consequence occasions some harm. The degree of negligence, carelessness or indifference is proportional to the magnitude of the risk taken. In other words, the legal subject (or 'person', which can include an institution or 'corporate body') has a duty to care whether his or her actions result in harm to others.

Salmond suggests a utilitarian conception of risk analysis is entailed in the duty to care:

> The risk depends, in its turn, on two things: first, the magnitude of the threatened evil, and second, the probability of it. The greater the evil is, and the nearer it is, the greater is the indifference or carelessness of him who creates the danger.[19]

Salmond then notes that the standard of care the law has adopted is one which, though it prohibits unreasonable carelessness, does not at the same time demand unreasonable (excessive) precautionary care.[20] Most importantly, for the purpose of this analysis, the standard of care is *not* a subjective one: it is determined by what is reasonable in the circumstances of particular cases as seen from the point of view of an 'ordinarily prudent man [sic]'.[21] The reasonableness of the particular conduct at issue will depend, Salmond argues, on the proportionate relationship between the risk of harm to which other persons are exposed and the 'object to be obtained by the activity in question'.[22] This calculation of risk, constructed retrospectively by courts and tribunals, is taken to constitute the legal fact upon which the liability to negligence is found.

What has risk as expressed in the concept of negligence got to do with rape or sexual harassment? Firstly, as I indicated earlier, the imputation of contributory negligence on the part of the victim has already crept into rape trials, as a means of excusing or diminishing the magnitude of the harm done.[23] Risk is here construed to mean an act or omission amounting to a want of care on the part of the complainant (the victim). This, together with the accused's own negligence, amounts to a proximate cause of the victim's injury. Secondly, the idea of risk presumes a capacity on the part of both parties to exercise prudent foresight; that presumption, in turn, is founded upon a particular, forensic model of the person – the law's 'reasonable man'. The importation of tort concepts of contributory negligence into rape trials has a parallel in the use of the criminal law concept of provocation and the relevance of previous sexual history to diminish the damage done to victims of sexual harassment. Here risk is expressed by the calculation of how much harm was suffered, a calculation which, in turn, depends on a notional value assigned to the character or feelings of the claimant prior to the injury. In the case of *Snowball* v. *Gardner Merchant Ltd. (1987)*, the Employment Appeal Tribunal stated that:

> Compensation for sexual harassment must relate to the *degree of detriment* and, in that context, there has to be an assessment of the injury to the woman's feelings, which must be looked at both objectively with reference to what any ordinary reasonable female employee would feel and subjectively with reference to her as an individual. [Emphasis added][24]

The Employment Appeal Tribunal ruled that evidence about the complainant's attitude to matters of sexual behaviour was admissible in determining a complaint of sexual harassment, reasoning that 'it is pertinent to inquire whether the complainant is unduly sensitive, or as in this case, ... is very unlikely to be upset by a degree of familiarity with a sexual connotation'.[25] This ruling appears to problematise a particular complainant's capacity to suffer (emotional) harm when measured against the standard of the ordinary reasonable (sexually decorous) woman employee. Thus legal discourses on sexual harm can be seen to code sexual risk in terms both of the legal subject's capacity to avoid harm *and* of her capacity to be harmed (for example, if she has transgressed culturally dominant sexual codes).

I want to focus now on the standard of reasonableness in respect of risk-avoidance which is expected of women in the legal discourse on rape. I have argued that part of the legal argument in rape cases turns on a woman's capacity and duty to perform a reasonable reading of danger, with her *capacity* to foresee harm being assumed to be no different to that possessed by the 'person' of legal discourse. This also supposes that there is a good enough fit between the forensic person's cognitive capacity and the reality of the practical world for that person to be expected to foresee the consequences of his or her own actions. However, foreseeing the consequences of one's own actions cannot be achieved without factoring in the probable actions of others. In speculating about the likely actions of others while reading risk, the person is *not* engaged in a direct apprehension of reality. In forming a judgement about the *likely* actions of others, a person has not only to draw upon the other's actual conduct but has also to decide what is relevant in that situation; for example, the race, sex, age, dress or demeanour of the other(s). What may be relevant to one actor at any given moment in time is not necessarily seen to be relevant by another. It is here that the social and gendered construction of risk is inescapable. Douglas notes how people draw upon specifically cultural repertoires of explanation – 'heuristics', in her terms – which they use to determine the riskiness for them (or for their children) of particular situations. So, for instance, we find ourselves telling our daughters that if a man in a car stops to ask for directions, they should never get within grabbing distance of him, or that they should never reveal to visitors to the front door or to people who phone that they are 'home alone'. What we are teaching our children and what they will learn for themselves is that they must take account of these categories of social difference because others do.

The Code of Practice annexed to the European Community's Recommendation on 'Protecting the Dignity of Women and Men at Work' explicitly mentions the fact that some specific groups are particularly vulnerable to sexual harassment. It cites the work of Michael Rubenstein, who documents the link between 'the risk of sexual harassment and the recipient's perceived vulnerability'.[26] The Code identifies

> divorced and separated women, young women and new entrants to the labour market and those with irregular or precarious employment contracts, women in non-traditional jobs, women with disabilities, lesbians and women from racial minorities

as being disproportionately at risk of sexual harassment at work, along with gay men and young men.[27] Ulrich Beck has suggested that people occupy different 'social risk positions' which are patterned by virtue of their gender, age, ethnicity or other social attributes.[28] I want to argue, however, that what I have said about the practices of women involved in what Stanko calls 'reading danger' (informed by an awareness of their own social risk positions)[29] is no less true, *epistemologically*, of the activities of men 'reading consent'. I now want to examine the way in which reading consent is constructed as risk in the legal discourses of rape and sexual harassment.

READING CONSENT, KNOWING THE DIFFERENCE

What constitutes reasonable care is not only a socially constructed standard, but a variable one. Taking ordinary care for their own safety involves women in an analysis of sexual risk which assumes a range of different power relations. Coercive male sexuality is ever and always a natural feature of these power relations, which women are expected to have both the capacity and the duty to take into account in their everyday lives. The vital assumption appears to be that women understand male subjectivity to the extent of knowing how their actions are likely to be construed by men. This is thought to enable them to calculate the probability of their own sexual victimisation in particular circumstances. What assumptions are made in law about men's capacity to read sexual risk situations? How is sexual risk constructed for men? In the discussion which follows I will deal at some length with the way in which sexual risk is inscribed in legal discourses on rape and then contrast this with how risk is marked in sexual harassment.

In English law, the legal definition of rape is based on the presumption that it is possible for the reasonable man to know whether or not a woman consents to sexual intercourse, or at least that he has the capacity to appreciate an obvious and serious risk that she may not be consenting. The question of whether she actually consents, and to what extent he appreciates either the fact or the possibility of her non-consent at the time of the offence, is settled retrospectively in the court's reconstruction of the rape event. The court reconstructs the alleged offence in order to determine whether both the man's conduct and state of mind (mental attitude) answer the legal definition of rape.

The House of Lords' decision in *Morgan* (1976) is often cited as the signal instance of a 'subjective' interpretation of *mens rea* (the mental element) in rape.[30] Prior to *Morgan*, it had been widely held that, in order to be excused, a mistake must be reasonable.[31] Under this doctrine, the reasonableness or otherwise of a particular mistake would be determined in reference to the 'objective' standard of what the ordinary prudent man would have known or foreseen in the same set of circumstances. However, in *Morgan* the accused's subjective (honest, but mistaken) belief in the woman's consent, even though unreasonable, was held to constitute a defence because the mental element required for rape – intent – was absent.

Many people construed the *Morgan* decision (dubbed 'the rapists' charter') to be abandoning the requirement for reasonableness in the formation of a belief in consent. The decision provoked a widespread public demand for a review of the law on rape. The Advisory Group on the Law of Rape (the Heilbron Committee) which was appointed for that purpose ultimately recommended the retention of *Morgan* principle.[32] Accordingly, the Sexual Offences (Amendment) Act 1976 reflected this 'subjective' interpretation of *mens rea*. It confirmed that the mental element of rape was intention and recklessness. Section One of the Act specifies that:

a man commits rape if
(a) he has unlawful sexual intercourse with a women who at the time of the intercourse does not consent to it; and
(b) at the time he *knows* that she does not consent to the intercourse or he is *reckless* as to whether she consents to it. [Emphasis added][33]

Establishing the *mens rea* of rape (knowing the woman does not consent to sexual intercourse or being reckless as to whether she does) involves a reconstruction of how the man 'read' the woman's consent. It has been argued that, in so far as liability for the offence of rape is determined on the basis of the man's subjective reading of consent, the law conceives of rape as 'a cognizable injury from the point of view of the reasonable rapist'.[34] It is worth noting here, by way of contrast, that in sexual harassment cases what was in the mind of the accused is of little moment. So, for example, in the case of *Strathclyde Regional Council* v. *Porcelli* the Court of Session ruled that s.1 (1) of the Sex Discrimination Act 1975 'is concerned with "treatment" and not with the motive or objective of the person responsible for it'.[35]

RECKLESSNESS

Showing that the accused was reckless as to whether the woman consented is sufficient to establish the *mens rea* of rape. But the courts' interpretation of what is meant by 'recklessness' as it applies to rape has varied. In *Pigg* (1982)[36] and then also in *Thomas* (1983),[37] the Court of Appeal held that an accused was reckless if it could be shown either (i) that 'he was indifferent and gave no thought to the possibility that the woman might not be consenting in circumstances where if any thought had been given to the matter it would have been obvious that there was a risk she was not', or (ii) that 'he was aware of the possibility she might not be consenting but nevertheless persisted regardless of whether she consented or not'.[38] Here the Court of Appeal applied the definition of recklessness propounded in *Caldwell*[39] and *Lawrence*[40] (both 1981) to the effect that recklessness consisted in a person's 'failure to direct his mind to the possibility of a risk, which would have been obvious to him if he had done so'.[41] This conception of recklessness presupposes that:

there is something in the circumstances that would have drawn the attention of an ordinary prudent individual to the possibility that his act was capable of causing the kind of harmful consequences that the section which creates the offence was intended to prevent and that the risk of those harmful consequences occurring was not so slight that an ordinary prudent individual would feel justified in treating them as negligible.[42]

In *Pigg* and *Thomas*, recklessness about the risk of sexual harm hinged on the accused's ability to foresee the consequences of his actions. Yet, in the later case of *Satnam and Kewal S* (1984),[43] the Court of Appeal ruled that in *Caldwell* recklessness (as to the consequences of one's actions) did not apply in rape. It reverted to the significantly more subjective view that recklessness in rape was to do with foresight 'as to the state of mind of the victim'. Hence both an accused who unreasonably believes in consent and one who simply fails to think about consent cannot be liable. Clearly, this represents a retreat from the implied duty to care about the consequences of one's actions implied in *Pigg* and *Thomas*. What this amounts to, according to Smith and Hogan, is that in order to establish recklessness in rape it must be shown that the accused was aware of the possibility that consent was absent, but went ahead regardless.[44]

The intersubjectivity entailed in this requirement for prudential foresight in rape is expressed in terms of risk and reasonableness. The model of the 'forensic person', which postulates the rational, centred and purposive legal subject, for whom other persons' concerns are marginal,[45] has now to accommodate greater intersubjectivity – at least to the extent that it is presumed the legal subject has some capacity for knowing the state of mind of the other. What reasonableness does *not* entail, however, is any general or positive requirement that the man needs to take the trouble to ask the woman whether she consents or not.[46] In the absence of any concomitant duty to care about the harmful consequences of one's actions in rape, the law's recognition of the defence of honest (but unreasonably held) belief in consent has the effect of condoning the man's 'easily avoided and self-serving mistake produced by the actor's indifference to the separate existence of another'.[47]

Given that the *mens rea* of rape is intention or recklessness in the commission of the offence, one would expect that the risk in rape for men would be constructed in terms of foreseeing the harm to the woman, or at least the risk of her non-consent. But the essentially retrospective character of the law's reading of risk enables the elision of two discrete issues. The issue of a man's liability in rape is often confounded with the separate issue of the risk of the woman 'crying rape'. This term, which in the thirteenth century meant a woman's naming of the offence and calling on the community for assistance by raising the hue and cry,[48] has recently been redeployed forensically to accuse the woman herself. Crying rape now connotes a woman's *ex post facto* ('the morning after') renaming of 'sex' as rape out of motives of spite, shame or regret, and her calling upon paternal authority for protection through her unwillingness to accept responsibility for the consequences of *her own* actions.[49] In press coverage of 'date rape' cases, the primary focus has generally been on the irresponsibility of the woman involved. Scant attention is paid to the irresponsibility of the man concerned, often with the effect of depicting the man as the hapless victim of sexual risk.

In contrast to the *mens rea* required in a criminal offence, the 'mental element' in sexual harassment (a civil wrong) concerns what lies in the mind of the complainant and not of the accused, since the 'essential characteristic' of harassment is that it is unwanted by the recipient. But it is not sufficient for the complainant 'honestly to believe' she was harassed. It must be demonstrated that she suffered some detriment or injury to her feelings, as measured against an 'objective standard' of reasonableness; that is, against the standard of what an ordinary reasonable woman would have felt if subjected to the same treatment.

The law of rape, on the other hand, is predicated on the assumption that the reasonable man must at least be capable of subjectively knowing the difference between a woman's consent or non-consent, even if he is from time to time mistaken. But the key point is that the possibility of knowing the difference is inextricably bound up with the ways in which sexuality is culturally constructed, and, in particular, with the ways in which ideas of sexual desire, sexual advances and sexual aggression are differentially signified and understood by men and women.[50] Given this kind of cultural field, the task of reading a woman's consent or refusal becomes an intrinsically confusing, perilous and taxing business for the man involved, especially as the 'normal' sexual behaviour of women is said culturally to be characterised by reluctance, vacillation, equivocation and conflicting desires. The culture may suggest that the man is expected to overcome these outward signs of non-consent with persistence and persuasion. Temkin suggests that from the male point of view, seduction and rape are the end-point of a continuum of non-consent which he must overcome, either by persuasion or by force.[51] It is clear, however, that men's judgement as to women's consent is to some extent situational; the American sociologist of male sexuality, Murray Davis, argues that there is a 'system of relevances' whereby the actor focuses on what is pertinent to understanding a particular interaction.[52] In those culturally given situations which provoke sexual arousal in men, there is what Davis calls 'a lascivious shift' in the system of relevances out of what Davis terms 'everyday reality' into 'erotic reality'. It is these erotic relevances which then proceed to inform men's reading of the interaction.

This shift in relevance frequently provides a 'commonsense' gloss for the legal adjudication of rape cases. So, for example, in the 1982 case at the Ipswich Crown Court which I referred to at the start of this chapter the trial judge attributed contributory negligence to a 17-year-old woman who had been raped while hitch-hiking, remarking that the circumstances of the case did not 'disclose any particular intention to rape this young lady, rather a lecherous hope that she would have sex with you'. But it is significant that in some cases of sexual harassment, there has also been recognition that harassers use categories of social difference for 'tactical' purposes, to denigrate and undermine the victim rather than for any strictly sexual pay-off. Thus, in *Strathclyde Regional Council* v. *Porcelli* Lord Emslie remarked that:

> Although in some cases it will be obvious that there is a sex related purpose in the mind of a person who indulges in unwanted and objectionable sexual overtures to a woman or exposes her to offensive sexual jokes or observations that is not this case ... It [the sexual harassment of Mrs Porcelli] was a particular kind of weapon, based on the sex of the victim, which ... would not have been used against an equally disliked man.[53]

In the first instance, the rape victim's want of care (contributory negligence) consisted in her failure to appreciate the sexual relevance *for the man* of the interaction which resulted in rape. In the second case, the accused men tried to rebut the claim they had sexually harassed the woman complainant by insisting on the sexual (erotic) *irrelevance* of their conduct. So in rape, the system of relevances which informs the accused's reading of consent determines what is read as significant and what is disregarded in retrospective adjudications of responsibility. What is regarded, denied or neutralised is the foreseeability of sexual harm. In sexual harassment, the focus is on the harm itself.

LACK OF CONSENT

My discussion so far has related to the man's reading of consent, as it is retrospectively constructed in court to establish whether the man had a criminal intention or whether he exhibited recklessness with respect to the consequences of his action for the woman concerned. But the issue of consent is also tried in another way: the legal 'fact' of the woman's lack of consent must also be established. The offence of rape is rarely witnessed; without witnesses, evidence about consent or lack of consent must come from the parties involved. Rape is also an offence which is defined as a departure from ordinary heterosexual behaviour by virtue, specifically and only, in respect of the woman's lack of consent. Two things follow from this. Firstly, situating rape within the paradigm of 'normal' heterosexual interaction or transaction carries with it the idea that pleasure can be experienced by both parties. In the absence of any witnesses who could contradict it, this straightforward equation of sexuality and pleasure often works to disqualify the testimony of the woman.[54] As a consequence, more stringent tests of credibility and corroboration are applied to the complainant's testimony. Secondly, determinations of what constitutes relevant evidence respecting the reasonableness of the man's reading of consent, or the legal fact of the woman's non-consent, draw much more heavily on 'commonsense' conceptions of rape and sexuality – that is, from the wider, heavily scripted and pornographic sexual culture – than the legal discourse admits it allows. The standard of relevance applied to the evidence in a rape trial (that is, to the fact-finding in a trial, and to the question of what the accused knew, thought about or intended) is a variable standard,[55] and one which is clearly embedded in that broader, culturally given 'commonsense'. Sexual risk is a social construction, which is read through 'powerful cultural lenses which amplify some risks and obscure and distort others'.[56] This 'commonsense' knowledge – and popularly recognised theories such as Freud's seduction theory – are elevated from the status of ideas or myths about male and female sexual motivations[57] to the status of legally admissible social *facts*, and deemed through the lens of relevance to be essential to understanding the whole case.[58]

'Commonsense' knowledge, of course, relates to what is 'moral, good, possible and appropriate', and its power derives from its claim to be 'natural, obvious and true'.[59] Hence Sir Melford Stevenson's assertion that the *fact* that a woman is in the 'true sense' negligent ('asking for it') if she hitch-hikes at night is 'so plain, it is not really worth stating', or Judge Raymond Dean's instruction to an Old Bailey jury that 'Just because a woman says no, she does not necessarily mean it.'[60] As Adler has observed in her own studies of rape trials, what constitutes relevant evidence is largely a matter of what seems relevant to a particular judge;[61] to that, I can only add that what appears to him to be relevant will be what he regards as 'natural, obvious and true'. Through this interplay of 'commonsense' and legal relevance, the sexual relations which are presupposed (and therefore apparently self-evident) in criminal court practice are also maintained and reproduced in reality.[62] As Madame Justice L'Heureux-Dubé noted in a recent rape case in the Supreme Court of Canada,[63] a judge's exercise of discretion on the admissibility of evidence pertaining to the complainant's previous sexual history, dress or reputation (on the grounds that it is relevant to the issue of consent) is peculiarly likely to draw upon stereotype and myth.[64]

Elsewhere in her writing on risk, Mary Douglas posits that there are three models of forensic explanation: the 'moralistic' model, which finds the cause of harm in an earlier transgression; the 'individual adversaries' model, which locates the cause of harm in an individual's having been outwitted or outmanoeuvred by an adversary; and a third style of blaming, which assigns fault to an outside enemy. Each forensic model involves a repertoire of possible causes from which a plausible explanation for harm is chosen. The choice of plausible causal narrative in turn entails a corresponding repertoire of obligatory actions to be performed by the offender or the community.[65] Douglas' typology of 'styles of blaming' explains what otherwise appears only to be a 'ragbag of ideas' about male and female sexuality and responsibility.[66] This 'ragbag of ideas' is regularly and routinely drawn upon in courtroom rhetoric, and specifically in the contested attributions of blame in cases of rape and sexual harassment.[67] Elements of all three models of forensic explanation may be marshalled in the retrospective search for a plausible account of particular instances of sexual harm. So, for example, the well-known requirement that a rape complainant's 'story' must be corroborated nearly always involves the rehearsal in court of conceptions of female sexuality and desire, drawn from repertoires of stereotype and myth. They locate the cause of harm in the moral failing of victims, which judges and jurists then declare to be relevant, admissible and true.[68] Elliott suggests that there are a number of special causes behind women 'lying' about rape, among which are revenge, guilt and shame about 'what was done in two minds and later repented', fear of parental censure and confusion of fantasy with reality.[69] The 'sound reason' for requiring corroboration of the woman's testimony, according to Glanville Williams, is that the woman may make deliberate false allegations because she suffers from

> sexual neurosis, fantasy, jealousy, spite or simply a refusal to admit she consented to an act of which she is now ashamed … experience shows that the complainant's evidence may be warped by psychological processes which are not evident to the eye of commonsense.[70]

These allegedly sound reasons for discounting the victim are gleaned from the explanatory repertoire of 'commonsense' discourse.

Probably the most important feature of this repertoire is the definition of 'real rape' as being an unforeseeable, sudden, violent attack by a stranger (the 'outside enemy'), involving an entirely and self-evidently blameless victim.[71] Similarly, sexual harassment is a 'real' harm only when sustained by a woman who has never transgressed the rules of sexual decorum. The repertoire is deployed in what Weedon calls the discursive field of law to construct, blame or excuse the legal subjects of rape and sexual harassment. The forensic use of these conceptions of sexual harm is elastic and variable, precisely because social rules 'seldom, if ever, take the form of categorical imperatives' but rather serve as 'qualified guides for action which are limited in their application according to particular times, places, persons and circumstances'.[72] Legislative discourses of intent in Western liberal democracies are usually couched in terms of equality of treatment and the prohibition of wrongs. In this sense they fulfil an educative purpose. However, in practice, because legal proscriptions are neither static nor absolute, it is possible to identify conceptions in the legal discourses – like those on sexual risk – which can be used as a forensic resource by women.

In problematising the motivation of a rape complainant, legal and 'commonsense' discourses also put at issue the capacity of a woman to witness her own harm, and the very credibility of the account she may want to offer. Moreover, in suggesting (as Glanville Williams does) that the issue of the woman's consent cannot be approached through 'commonsense', doubt is cast on the capacity of even the reasonable man to attend to the risk of the woman's non-consent. Since the standard of care required of any man accused of rape cannot be greater than that required of any reasonable man, and since the reasonable man is only required to read consent through the prism of this 'commonsense', then it follows that the 'commonsense' and legal discourses of risk undermine the foreseeability of risk in specific instances. The foreseeability of sexual harm, therefore, though socially variable in the sense of attending to social differences as contingencies in any individual case, is categorically invariable *in the sense that coercive male sexuality is taken to be a given feature of the overall social order, and the specific social encounters, within which people are called upon to account for their actions.*

My purpose in advancing an argument in this detail about the legal (and 'commonsense') discourses of rape is to try to show how the risk of sexual harm is allowed, in these particular legal discourses, to be more or less obvious to women victims, while permitted to be quite the opposite (opaque, difficult and excusable) for men who have been accused of 'taking advantage' of a non-consenting woman. It should be clear, at this stage, that these discourses also problematise *the possibility of intersubjectivity* among the forensic persons of law in respect of sexual harm, and subvert the duty, which is much celebrated elsewhere within the law, to have regard for the safety of others. The law evades the question of intersubjectivity, I would argue, by such reference to 'commonsense' knowledge, and in the way it frames women's desires and the expression of their consent to sexual relations. The explanatory repertoire associated with this 'commonsense' knowledge also contains causal narratives which attribute responsibility, or excuse conduct, in interactions resulting in rape – for example, via the identification of particular exchanges which could have unfortunately been taken by the man to imply the woman's consent. This depicts sexual harm in rape as the product of instances of miscommunication or mistakes, sometimes accompanied by the bemused acknowledgement that men and women inevitably view sexual events quite differently.[73] Distorted communication appears intrinsic to the contemporary construction and management of relations between the sexes, most markedly so in potentially sexual encounters.[74] By contrast, where rape *is* confirmed in a court case, these confusions are resolved. The responsibility for that rape is attributed on the basis of the complainant's having failed rationally to identify the risks entailed and/or of the accused having abandoned the caution that ought to accompany communication between the sexes in such a confusing world.

The position I want to develop here is not one that denies the power of such 'commonsense' discourses, particularly but not exclusively for men. I do want to recognise that there are situations in which men (and women) may become 'lecherously hopeful' and want to read consent into the responses to their actions. In contemporary legal discourse and practice, however, this recognition of sexual desire or interest is used, almost exclusively, as a way of interpreting and excusing the behaviour of men in situations which lead to rape or sexual harassment. The 'reasonableness' of the interpretation of a woman's level of interest by the 'lecherously hopeful' man is not measured against the woman's version of her own intent, but always against a standard as to what the 'ordinary reasonable man' would have done, believed or foreseen in a similar set of circumstances. The competing claims of sexual harm are adjudicated, constructed and applied by reference to an 'expansible' judicial repertoire, which is then deployed to attribute blame or to excuse.[75]

Where recklessness is sufficient to establish liability for rape, the adjudication of sexual harm and attribution of fault can be said to rest on a duty to care. The question then is, what is the standard of care required of the ordinary prudent man? My answer is that the duty to care – which in rape amounts to the requirement that the man avert to the *possibility* of the woman not consenting – ought to be treated as expansible, as in the tort law relating to negligence. Williams and Hepple, for example, observe that 'the grounds of action may be as various and manifold as human errancy; and the conception of the legal responsibility may develop in adaptation to altering social conditions and standards. The categories of negligence are *never closed'* [emphasis added].[76] The objective standard of conduct entailed in the duty to care about sexual harm is also expansible, I want to argue, in the direction of imposing a responsibility to respect the sexual autonomy of others.

ALL REASONABLE STEPS?

Carol Smart shares the pessimism of many feminists writing on law in her observation that 'the law cannot provide the solution to the sexual oppression it celebrates and sustains'.[77] However, recent reform of the law on sexual assault in Canada does suggest new possibilities. It shows that concepts such as 'reasonableness', which are routinely reiterated and reconstructed in the application of law to particular cases of sexual assault, may now potentially be rhetorically turned in on themselves to subvert the masculinist discourse of law.

In August 1991 the Supreme Court of Canada (in the appeal case of *R* v. *Seaboyer; R* v. *Gayme)* struck down the existing section 276 (the 'rape shield provision') of the Criminal Code on Sexual Assault, which prohibited the use of the victim's previous sexual history in certain circumstances, on the grounds that, because it potentially excluded evidence that could be relevant to the defence, it infringed the accused's right to a fair trial as guaranteed in the Canadian Charter of Rights and Freedoms. This prompted a reexamination of the law on sexual assault, resulting in amendments (passed on 15 June 1992) which narrow the ambit of judicial discretion in determining the admissibility of evidence about the complainant's previous sexual history, imposing the requirement that judges give detailed reasons for their decisions on this question. The amendments also define the type of conduct that constitutes consent,[78] and list situations in which consent will not be deemed possible.[79] The amended law codifies the existing common law, and clarifies and restricts the defence of mistaken belief in consent. Section 273.2 of the Canadian Criminal Code now states (a) that the accused may not claim that he (or she) believed the complainant consented to the sexual activity at issue where (i) the accused's belief arose from the accused's self-induced intoxication; or (ii) the accused's belief arose from the accused's own recklessness or wilful blindness; and (b) it also specifies that belief in consent will not be a defence *unless* the accused *took all reasonable steps* in the circumstances known to the accused at the time to ascertain that the complainant was consenting. As Kim Campbell, the then Canadian minister of justice, remarked in her address on the second reading of the bill (C-49), the effect of this amendment to the provision on the defence of honest mistaken belief is that 'the consent to sexual activity can no longer be assumed, presumed or "believed" unless reasonable steps have been taken to ascertain that consent has in fact been given. Commonsense and responsible conduct so demand.'[80] Requiring that reasonable *steps* be taken in securing consent represents a move towards what Gardner has described as a 'procedural', as distinct from an exclusively 'substantive', construal of honest mistake.[81] He regards the notion of 'care' as having considerable forensic potential for the development of liability where a man claims a defence of honest mistaken belief in consent. It is obviously interesting to speculate, in the age of AIDS, on the sources of the current legal interest in the duty to care in sexual encounters, but that is not the burden of this chapter.

CONCLUSION

I want to suggest that the 'all reasonable steps' requirement of the amended Canadian sexual assault law imposes a positive duty on all sexual actors to take account of the state of mind of the other person involved with respect to his or her consent.[82] In so doing, it opens out a rhetorical space for arguing that there must be a presumption of sexual self-determination for women as well as for men, which must be factored into establishing the reasonableness of any particular reading of consent.[83]

Article 2 of the Commission of the European Communities' 'Recommendation on the Protection of the Dignity of Women and Men at Work' calls for the development by all member states of 'positive measures designed to create a climate at work in which women and men respect one another's human integrity'.[84] This notion, that all legal persons (including corporate bodies) have a positive duty to avoid harm being caused to others, is reflected in a recent (1989) sexual harassment case (*Crane* v. *C Link Ltd*). Here an industrial tribunal found that employers can be 'vicariously liable' for sexual harassment by supervisors, whether they were aware of it or not, if they had taken no *positive steps* to prevent harassment occurring.[85]

This chapter recognises that the resort to law is not simply a discursive engagement with existing power relations – it is also a didactic one. Law's primary concern may be with attributions of blame, but it may also create the *possibility* of acceptance of mutual responsibility. In a recent paper, Braithwaite and Daly argue that the moral and reintegrative potential of law (for example, in 'confronting exploitative masculinity with pro-feminist voices') might be realised in a communitarian model of justice, but they do not say how the principles of sexual autonomy and mutual responsibility could become entrenched in the moral construction of the community.[86] While I agree that there is little to lose and much to gain by exploring alternatives to the adversarial adjudication of sexual harms, I think that there is also a compelling argument for insisting that feminists recognise the forensic potential of particular legal conceptions of risk, within the law as practised now, for establishing a duty of mutual responsibility in sexual conduct.

Notes and References

1. M. Douglas, *Risk and Blame: Essays in Cultural Theory* (London: Routledge, 1992), p. 25.
2. See the work of Elizabeth (Betsy) Stanko, 'When Precaution is Normal: A Feminist Critique of Crime Prevention', in L. Gelsthorpe and A. Morris (eds), *Feminist Perspectives in Criminology* (Milton Keynes: Open University Press, 1990), *Everyday Violence: How Men and Women Experience Sexual and Physical Danger* (London: Pandora, 1990), and 'Ordinary Fear: Women, Violence and Personal Safety', in P.B. Bart and E. Moran (eds) *Violence against Women: The Bloody Footprints* (London: Sage, 1993). See also M. Gordon and S. Riger, *The Female Fear* (London: Macmillan, 1988).
3. M. Amir, *Patterns of Forcible Rape* (Chicago: University of Chicago Press, 1971).
4. Z. Adler, *Rape on Trial* (London: Routledge, 1987); P. Pattullo, *Judging Women: A Study of Attitudes that Rule Our Legal System* (London: Rights for Women Unit, National Council for Civil Liberties, 1983); C. Smart, *Feminism and the Power of Law* (London: Routledge, 1989), and 'Penetrating Women's Bodies', in P. Abbott and C. Wallace (eds), *Gender, Power and Sexuality* (London: Macmillan, 1991); Stanko, 'When Precaution is Normal'; and J. Temkin, *Rape and the Legal Process* (London: Sweet and Maxwell, 1987).
5. The Lord Chancellor (Lord Hailsham) responded to the public outcry which followed Judge Richards' decision by saying that 'imprudence' on the part of the victim could not be a mitigating factor in sentencing.
6. Quoted in Adler, *Rape on Trial*, p. 20.
7. D.A. Thomas, *Principles of Sentencing* (London: Heinemann, 1979), pp. 113–14.
8. *Wileman* v. *Minilec Engineering Ltd* [1988] IRLR 144. In this case, a woman was awarded the sum of £50 for the injury to her feelings resulting from four and a half years of sexual harassment by a director of the company which employed her.

9. See Michael Zander, 'A New Class of Crime', *Guardian* (16 December 1982); and Melanie Phillips, 'The Benches Marked by Prejudice' *Guardian* (2 December 1988).

10. J. Hanmer and E. Stanko, 'Stripping away the Rhetoric of Protection: Violence to Women, Law and the State in Britain and the U.S.A.', *International Journal of the Sociology of Law*, 13 (1985), p. 369; J. Young, 'Risk of Crime and Fear of Crime: A Realist Critique of Survey-based Assumptions', in M. Maguire and J. Pointing (eds), *Victims of Crime: A New Deal?* (Milton Keynes: Open University Press, 1988); and Stanko, 'When Precaution is Normal,' and 'Ordinary Fear'.

11. R. Sparks, 'Reason and Unreason in "Left Realism": Some Problems in the Constitution of the Fear of Crime', in R. Matthews and J. Young (eds), *Issues in Realist Criminology* (London: Sage, 1992).

12. The term 'late modernity' is taken from A. Giddens, *Modernity and Self-identity: The Self and Society in the Late Modern Age* (Cambridge: Polity, 1991).

13. The argument that male violence ought to be regarded as a continuum has been made by S. Brownmiller, *Against Our Will: Men, Women and Rape* (London: Secker and Warburg, 1975); L. Kelly, *Surviving Sexual Violence* (Cambridge: Polity, 1988); C.A. MacKinnon, 'Feminism, Marxism, Method and the State: Toward Feminist Jurisprudence', *Signs* 8 (1983), pp. 635–58. For a more recent application of this perspective, see J. Halson, 'Young Women, Sexual Harassment and Heterosexuality: Violence, Power Relations and Mixed-Sex Schooling', in Abbott and Wallace, *Gender, Power and Sexuality*, pp. 97–113.

14. Quoted in Douglas, *Risk and Blame*, p. 218. See John Locke, *An Essay Concerning Human Understanding*, ed. P.N. Nidditch (Oxford: Clarendon, 1975), II, xxvii, p. 26.

15. Douglas, *Risk and Blame*, pp. 220, 228.

16. See G. Reekie and P. Wilson, 'Rape, Resistance and Women's Right to Self-defence', *Australia and New Zealand Journal of Criminology* 26 (1993), pp. 146–54; and Smart, 'Penetrating Women's Bodies'.

17. Douglas, *Risk and Blame*, p. 63.

18. M.B. King, 'Male Sexual Assault in the Community', in G.C. Mezey and M.B. King (eds), *Male Victims of Sexual Assault* (Oxford: Oxford University Press, 1992), p. 10. For a discussion of the sexual victimisation of men, see R. McMullen, *Male Rape: Breaking the Silence on the Last Taboo* (London: Gay Men's Press, 1990); and S. Garfield, 'When Man Rapes Man', *Independent on Sunday* (6 December 1992), p. 17.

19. J. Salmond, *Jurisprudence* (London: Sweet and Maxwell, 1937), p. 542.

20. Salmond, *Jurisprudence*, p. 543.
21. Salmond, *Jurisprudence*, p. 544.
22. Salmond, *Jurisprudence*, p. 544. As regards sexual risk, the presumption appears to be that intimacy, whether verbal or physical, is consensual unless it can be otherwise established or unless the offence is defined to preclude consent in specific instances (such as when the victim is below the age of consent, mentally incapacitated or unconscious).
23. There is no express reference to a woman's duty to care in the law of rape. Nonetheless, it appears to be considered relevant in determining the credibility of her testimony and the fact of her non-consent.
24. *Snowball* v. *Gardner Merchant Ltd* [1987] IRLR 397, at p. 398. The Employment Appeal Tribunal ruled that evidence as to the complainant's attitude to matters of sexual behaviour was relevant and admissible in determining a complain of sexual harassment, reasoning (at para. 11, p. 400) that 'it is pertinent to inquire whether the complainant is unduly sensitive, or as in this case … is very unlikely to be upset by a degree of familiarity with a sexual connotation.'
25. Sir Ralph Kilner-Brown, in *Snowball* v. *Gardner Merchant Ltd*, para. 11, p. 400.
26. Commission of the European Communities, 'Code of Practice on "Protecting the Dignity of Women and Men at Work"', Annex to the Recommendation of the European Commission, *Official Journal of the European Communities*, L49 (24 February 1992). See M. Rubenstein, 'The Dignity of Women at Work: A Report on the Problem of Sexual Harassment in the Member States of the European Communities', Part I (Brussels: Commission of the European Communities, 1988).
27. Commission of the European Communities, 'Code of Practice', p. 3.
28. U. Beck, *Risk Society: Towards a New Modernity* (London: Sage, 1992), p. 23.
29. Stanko, *Everyday Violence*, p. 8.
30. *DPP* v. *Morgan* (1976) A.C. 182. J.C. Smith and B. Hogan define *mens rea* as the 'mental attitude' of the accused with respect to the commission of the offence. They list four possible mental attitudes as being 'intention, recklessness, negligence and blameless inadvertence'. See their *Criminal Law*, 7th edition (London: Butterworths, 1992) p. 53.
31. In *R* v. *Tolson* ([1889] All E.R. Rep. 26 C.C.R.), the common law principle on governing the defence of 'mistake' was restated thus:

an honest and *reasonable* belief in the existence of circumstances which,
if true, would make an act for which a person is indicted an innocent
act, or proof that such a person had made an honest and reasonable
mistake, has always been held to be a good defence to a charge involving
mens rea. [Emphasis added]

32. 'Report of the Advisory Group on the Law of Rape', Cmnd. 6352
    (London: HMSO, 1975).
33. Until the House of Lords' amendment to the Criminal Justice Bill
    (11 July 1994) rape was narrowly defined in English law as non-
    consensual penile penetration of the vagina, and did not therefore
    apply either to other assaultive sexual acts or to sexual assaults on
    males. The extended definition of rape (which amends section one
    of the Sexual Offences Act 1956) will include anal and vaginal penet-
    ration of a person (woman or man) without consent.
34. MacKinnon, 'Feminism, Marxism, Method and the State', p. 654.
    It is arguable that sexual harassment is a 'cognisable injury' from
    the point of view of the reasonable (female) victim. In sexual
    harassment cases where injury to feelings is claimed, the sensibil-
    ities of the harassed woman are evaluated against the 'objective
    standard' of the ordinary reasonable woman who, it is implied,
    conducts herself entirely within the bounds of sexual decorum. It
    is more than a little ironic that the first successful case of sexual
    harassment brought by a man against another man was based on
    the argument that the victim suffered detriment in that he would
    have been treated differently (that is, *not* subjected to crude sexual
    banter and touching) if he were a woman. The male victim's sexual
    conduct and attitudes were not at issue in this case, clearly in part
    because he did not claim injury to feelings, but also, one suspects
    because he was a man. *Gates* v. *Alpha Steel* (21 June 1993), reported
    in The *Daily Mail* (22 June 1993), p. 23.
35. *Strathclyde Regional Council* v. *Porcelli* [1986] IRLR 134, at p. 137.
36. *R* v. *Pigg* [1982] 2 All E.R., 591, C.A.
37. *R* v. *Thomas* (1983) 77 Cr. App. R. 63.
38. Lord Lane in *R* v. *Pigg* [1982] 2 All E.R. 591, at p. 599.
39. *R* v. *Caldwell* [1981] 1 All E.R. 961; [1982] A.C. 341.
40. *R* v. *Lawrence* [1981] 1 All E.R. 974; [1982] A.C. 510.
41. *R* v. *Caldwell* [1982] A.C. 341. See Smith and Hogan, *Criminal Law*,
    p. 69.
42. Lord Diplock in *Lawrence* [1981] 1 All E.R. 974 at p. 982; [1982] A.C.
    510, at p. 526.
43. *R* v. *Satnam and Kewal S* (1984) 78 Cr. App. R. 149; 'Case and
    Comment: Rape', *Criminal Law Review* (1985) p. 236.
44. Smith and Hogan, *Criminal Law*, p. 458.

45. M. Barrett, 'Words and Things: Materialism and Method in Contemporary Feminist Analysis', in M. Barrett and A. Phillips, *Destabilizing Theory: Contemporary Feminist Debates* (Cambridge: Polity, 1992) p. 208.
46. Temkin, *Rape and the Legal Process*, p. 85.
47. T. Pickard, 'Culpable Mistakes and Rape: Relating Mens Rea to the Crime', *University of Toronto Law Journal* 75 (1980), p. 83.
48. In his discussion of rape (of virgins) Henry de Bracton specifies that a woman who has been raped 'must go at once and while the deed is newly done, with the hue and cry, to the neighbouring townships and there show the injury done her to men of good repute, the blood and her clothing stained with blood, and her torn garments'. Bracton (*c* 1250), in G.E. Woodbine (ed.) *On the Laws and Customs of England* (Cambridge, Mass.: Harvard University Press, 1968), vol. II, p. 415.
49. The notion of 'date rape', which is most often discussed in terms of miscommunication about the changing 'rules of (sexual) engagement', is especially prone to this construction. See media coverage of the Donnellan case, which was heard at the Old Bailey in October 1993; for example, Mary Braid, 'Feminism and the Students' Mating Game: Sorting out the Rules of Engagement', *Independent on Sunday* (17 October 1993). Katie Roiphe argues that the feminist campaign against date rape is a 'symptom of a more general anxiety about sex' which has been amplified over the past five years, partly in response to 'the added fear of AIDS'. She regards the concerns expressed by those she styles the 'rape-crisis feminists' as emanating not so much from a rape crisis as from 'a crisis in sexual identity'. Date rape is distinguished from real rape in this way by the positing of the miscommunication of desire and consent as the plausible causal explanation of the harm done. See K. Roiphe, *The Morning After: Sex, Fear and Feminism* (London: Hamish Hamilton, 1994), quoted in the *Guardian,* Women's Page (25 October 1993).
50. K. Bumiller, 'Fallen Angels: The Representation of Violence against Women in Legal Culture', in M. Fineman and N. Thomadsen (eds), *At the Boundaries of Law: Feminism and Legal Theory* (London: Routledge, Chapman and Hall, 1991) p. 107; and MacKinnon, 'Feminism, Marxism, Method and the State'.
51. Temkin, *Rape and the Legal Process*, p. 75.
52. M. Davis, *Smut: Erotic Reality, Obscene Ideology* (Chicago: University of Chicago Press, 1983) p. 12.
53. *Strathclyde Regional Council* v. *Porcelli*, at p. 137.
54. Adler, *Rape on Trial*; S. Estrich, *Real Rape* (Cambridge, Mass.: Harvard University Press, 1987); and Temkin, *Rape and the Legal Process*.

55. J. Temkin, 'The Limits of Reckless Rape', *Criminal Law Review* (1993), p. 5; H. Allen, 'One Law for All Reasonable Persons?', *International Journal of the Sociology of Law* 16 (1988), p. 424.

56. K. Dake, 'Myths of Nature: Culture and the Social Construction of Risk', *Journal of Social Issues* 48 (4) (1992), p. 33.

57. Temkin, 'The Limits of Reckless Rape', p. 6.

58. M. J. Mossman, 'Feminism and Legal Method: The Difference it Makes', in Fineman and Thomadsen, *At the Boundaries of Law*, p. 288.

59. C. Weedon, *Feminist Practice and Poststructuralist Theory* (Oxford: Blackwell, 1987), pp. 75–7.

60. *Guardian* (11 April 1990).

61. Z. Adler, 'The Relevance of Sexual History Evidence in Rape: Problems of Subjective Interpretation', *Criminal Law Review* (1985), p. 779.

62. C.A. MacKinnon, *Towards a Feminist Theory of the State* (Cambridge, Mass.: Harvard University Press, 1989), p. 127; K. Daly, 'Criminal Justice Ideologies and Practices in Different Voices: Some Feminist Questions about Justice', *International Journal of the Sociology of Law* 17 (1989), p. 2.

63. *R* v. *Seaboyer*; *R* v. *Gayme* [1991] S.C.C.; 83 D.L.R. (4th), p. 193 at 201.

64. L'Heureux-Dubé, J., observed that, like most myths and stereo-types, conceptions of women and sexual assault 'operate as a way, however flawed, of understanding the world and, like most such constructs, operate at a level of consciousness that makes it difficult to root them out and confront them directly … This baggage belongs to us all'. *R* v. *Seaboyer*; *R* v. *Gayme* [1991] 83 D.L.R. (4th), pp. 209, 213. See also J. Temkin, 'Sexual History Evidence – The Ravishment of Section 2', *Criminal Law Review* 5 (1993), pp. 5–7; and J.R. Schwendinger and H. Schwendinger, 'Rape Myths in Legal, Theoretical and Everyday Practice', *Crime and Social Justice* 1 (1974), pp. 18–26.

65. Douglas, *Risk and Blame*, p. 5.

66. Temkin, *Rape and the Legal Process*, p. 82.

67. K. Soothill, 'The Changing Face of Rape?', *British Journal of Criminology* 31 (4) (1991), pp. 383–92.

68. The mandatory requirement on judges to warn the jury that it is unsafe to convict on the uncorroborated evidence of the complainant will be abolished when the Criminal Justice and Public Order Bill becomes law in the autumn of 1994. Thereafter, the issue of such a warning will be discretionary.

69. D.W. Elliott, 'Rape Complainants' Sexual Experience with Third Parties', *Criminal Law Review* 4 (1984), p. 13.

70. Glanville Williams, quoted in B. Toner, *The Facts of Rape* (London: Hutchinson, 1977), p. 112.
71. On the question of 'commonsense' ideas about how the genuine rape victim should behave and their use in legal discourse, see Temkin, 'Sexual History Evidence', p. 7; and Bumiller, 'Fallen Angels', pp.95–7.
72. G.M. Sykes and D. Matza, 'Techniques of Neutralization: A Theory of Delinquency', *American Sociological Review* 22 (1957), p. 257.
73. P.B. Bart and P.H. O'Brien, *Stopping Rape: Successful Survival Strategies* (Oxford: Pergamon, 1985), p. 19.
74. Toner, *The Facts of Rape*, p. 50.
75. The term 'expansible' is used by G. Williams and B.A. Hepple in *Foundations of the Law of Tort* (London: Butterworths, 1976) p. 90.
76. Lord Macmillan, in *Donoghue* v. *Stevenson* [1932] A.C. at p. 619, quoted in Williams and Hepple, *Foundations*, pp. 90–1.
77. Smart, *Feminism and the Power of Law*, p. 49. Cf. MacKinnon, *Towards a Feminist Theory of the State*.
78. Defined in s. 273.1 (1) of the Criminal Code of Canada as 'the voluntary agreement of the complainant to engage in the sexual activity in question'.
79. Section 273.1 (2).
80. 'Notes for an Address by the Honourable Kim Campbell, Minister of Justice and Attorney General of Canada, on the Occasion of the Second Reading of Bill C-49, an Act to Amend the Criminal Code Respecting Sexual Assault', Ottawa, Ontario, 8 April 1992.
81. S. Gardner, 'Reckless and Inconsiderate Rape', *Criminal Law Review* 13 (1991) p. 177.
82. The Canadian Criminal Code recognises that the offence of sexual assault may be committed by both men and women on both men and women.
83. C. Boyle, 'Offences against Women', in J.S. Russell (ed.), *A Feminist Review of Criminal Law* (Ottawa: Canadian Advisory Council on the Status of Women, 1985); Temkin, *Rape and the Legal Process*. Another attempt to shift the meaning of non-consent away from evidence of physical resistance on the part of the victim has been the suggestion that consent ought to be defined as a 'performative act' which is 'absolute, positive and verbal'; see Reekie and Wilson, 'Rape, Resistance and Women's Right to Self-defence', p. 150. This conception of consent appears to have been adopted by Antioch College, Ohio, in an attempt to deter sexual offences on campus. The college – which also has some distinctive initiatives in other respects of student life – now has a policy on rape and sexual harassment which requires that 'verbal consent' should be obtained

with each new level of physical and/or sexual contact, or conduct in any given interaction, regardless of who initiated it. See Barbara R. Roessner, 'Sex by the Book', *Guardian* (30 September 1993).

84. Commission of the European Communities, 'Recommendation on the Protection of the Dignity of Women and Men at Work', p. 2.
85. Industrial Tribunal (South London, case no. 07017/89).
86. J. Braithwaite and K. Daly, 'Masculinities, Violence and Communitarian Control', in T. Newburn and E. Stanko (eds), *Just Boys Doing the Business: Men, Masculinity and Crime* (London: Routledge, 1994).

6

Anti-lesbian Harassment
Celia Kitzinger[1]

Claudia Brenner and her lover Rebecca were walking along a forest trail when a stranger met them on the path, identified them as lesbians, shot them eight times and left them for dead. Rebecca bled to death under a tree where she had run for shelter. Claudia survived with five bullet wounds.[2]

Kathleen Sarris appeared at a press conference as an 'out' lesbian. The next day she began receiving threatening telephone calls and letters, and two weeks later (after seeking help from the police, who told her there was nothing they could do) she was held captive in her office by a man who, for three hours, beat her with his fists, his gun, and his belt. He sexually molested and raped her, saying repeatedly throughout the assault that he was acting for God.[3]

The ex-boyfriend of Steph's woman lover threatened her, first with menacing behaviour and physical violence, and then blackmail. 'I got a letter from him which said that unless I gave this woman up, he would inform the school at which I was teaching that they were employing a "queer", and furthermore he would make charges of child molesting against me.' He went through with this threat and the Headmaster's response was such that Steph felt forced to resign from her job.[4]

Harassment of lesbians ranges from murder, rape, torture and other forms of physical attack through to defamation, intimidation, ostracism and verbal abuse. One comprehensive overview of anti-gay violence and victimisation in the United States of America found that up to 87 per cent of lesbians and gay men report having been verbally harassed, 27 per cent have been hit with objects, and between 10 per cent and 20 per cent have experienced vandalism. Over 75 per cent of the thousands of women and men studied expected to be the target of future harassment because of their sexual identity.[5]

CHOOSING OUR TERMS

The phrase 'anti-lesbian harassment' is only one of a whole lexicon of terms which have been invented to talk about our oppression. Others include 'heterosexism' (often favoured because it makes *hetero*sexuality the problem); 'homophobia' (in common use but much criticised for conveying an individualistic and psychologised idea of lesbian oppression);[6] 'homohatred'; 'queer-bashing', 'anti-gay violence' and 'anti-lesbianism'. The words we choose matter. As a radical lesbian feminist, I choose words which give lesbians maximum visibility, avoiding those which are commonly read as mostly or exclusively related to discrimination against gay men. I use the term 'anti-lesbian harassment' in this chapter because this is a book about harassment, but it is important to note at the outset that this serves to focus on particular forms of lesbian oppression at the expense of others. For example, the word 'harassment' (derived from a variant of the Old French *harer*, 'to set a dog on') [7] suggests a discrete incident, or a series of such incidents, directed at the person who is being harassed (name-calling, assault, vandalism). It less obviously refers simply to an offensive milieu (which is one reason why it took time and legal wrangling before pin-ups and centrefolds in the workplace were recognised as 'sexual harassment').[8] And it still sounds odd, implausible, extreme, for me to claim that I am 'harassed' by having to live in a society in which heterosexuality is everywhere flaunted – on advertising hoardings, on television screens, by the church wedding bells that ring out over my house most Saturdays and by the het couples walking unselfconsciously down the street entwined in each other's arms. 'Harassment' sounds odd, too, as a term to describe legal and policy discrimination; can I be 'harassed' by a law which prevents me from marrying a woman lover, or by my university superannuation scheme which pays pensions to widows and widowers, but not to the partners of lesbians? 'Harassment' primes one to see particular actions rather than the bias of a whole culture. Yet no analysis of lesbian oppression can be complete without an understanding both of discrete acts of harassment and of the heterosexist system within which they occur.

Similarly, 'harassment' sounds like something that 'happens'; it's quite hard to interpret the word to mean silences, absences, evasions. Yet when there is *no* anti-lesbian explosion from your parents because you have 'de-dyked' [9] your flat before their visit; when there is *no* physical assault after the evening at the bar because you predicted trouble and booked a taxi to get home; when you are *not* dismissed from work because you stayed in the closet; when you are *not* subjected to prurient or disgusted questions because you talked about your weekend activities in sentences that meticulously avoided the use of any pronouns ... when these non-events slip by as part of life's daily routine, has no anti-lesbianism really occurred? We might rather argue that anti-lesbianism has been functioning in its most effective and most deadly way. Lesbians are no longer being directly silenced and rendered invisible by heterosexuals: we are doing it to ourselves. The term 'harassment' cannot easily be read as encompassing these instances of self-censorship. Gay psychologist Anthony D'Augelli comments that, among the gay and lesbian students he surveyed, 'nearly half of them had made specific life changes to avoid harassment'.[10] An alternative perspective (obscured by the term 'harassment' itself) is that these students have made life-changes (including moving out of dorms, concealing books and magazines, inventing fiancé[e]s back home) *because* of harassment. In an oppressive heterosexist society it is not necessary, most of the time, to beat up lesbians, or to murder or torture us in order to ensure our silence and invisibility. Instead, a climate of terror is created in which lesbians 'voluntarily', and of our own free will, 'choose' to stay silent and invisible.

CONSTRUCTING ANTI-LESBIANISM AS A SOCIAL PROBLEM

Harassment, discrimination and violence against lesbians is not new. It is centuries old, and has often been legally endorsed or tolerated. The medieval witchburnings are perhaps the best known example: authorities and popular opinion linked witchcraft, heresy and lesbianism, and the phrase 'woman with woman' was often an accusation in witch trials.[11] Legal scholars cite many other instances of systematic and legalised lesbicide in Anglo-European patriarchy. The infamous 1260 Code of Orléans in France mandated that for the first two offences a lesbian would 'lose her member' and for the third offence she would be burned alive.[12] Mid-sixteenth-century Spanish and Italian jurists tailored the punishment to the nature of the activity: if she 'behaves corruptly with another woman only by rubbing' she is beaten, but if she 'introduces some wooden or glass instrument into the belly of another' she is put to death.[13] As the New World became colonised, European powers extended their laws prohibiting lesbianism (for example the Portuguese imposition of the death penalty for lesbians in Brazil in 1602).[14] Even when the law has not explicitly endorsed the beating and murder of lesbians, it has usually been found not to prosecute anti-lesbian violence with the same vigour with which it addresses crimes against 'normal' women.

There has probably always been individual resistance to anti-lesbian acts, but until the rise of the lesbian liberation movement in the late 1960s there was little possibility for collective resistance. More recently still, lesbians and gays have begun to document anti-lesbian incidents as part of a concerted effort to enlist social science research and public policymaking bodies in constructing such actions as a social problem. In the US, the first national study focusing exclusively on anti-gay violence was conducted by the National Gay and Lesbian Task Force in 1984, and research in this area has burgeoned since then. Such surveys attempt to define as a social problem experiences previously seen by many as an inevitable part of gay and lesbian life. Just as feminists defined as social problems (with legal and policy implications) issues like wife-battering, child sexual abuse, sexual harassment and rape in marriage, so the lesbian and gay movements have attempted to define harassment and discrimination against lesbians and gay men as a social problem with social causes and (at least potentially) social remedies.

In the UK this has led to the adoption of 'sexual orientation' clauses in some workplace anti-discrimination policies; while in the US anti-lesbian and anti-gay harassment (along with other newly labelled 'hate crimes') was brought to public attention through the adoption, in 1989, of the California Senate Bill 39. This requires that the state's Department of Justice 'acquire data to be used for statistical analysis concerning any crime or attempted crime which causes physical injury, or property damage, which is, or appears to be, motivated by the race, religion, sexual orientation, or ethnicity of the victim'.[15] Congressional hearings on 'hate crimes' have been held, and the 'Hate Crime Statistics Act' was passed in 1990. The term 'hate crimes' suffers from many of the problems identified earlier; for instance, lesbians are subsumed into a category with gay men (by use of the words 'sexual orientation'), so that we become invisible. The term also implies (as does 'anti-lesbian harassment') that the major – or only – forms of harassment are discrete incidents, not recognising that these occur within an anti-lesbian social context: this oppressive social context is thus obscured. Use of the word 'crime' also fails to capture the oppression of lesbians through legal tolerance of, indifference to or promotion of anti-lesbianism. Section 28 of the UK Local Government Act 1988, for example, which prohibits the 'promotion' of lesbian or gay lifestyles as 'pretended families', is an oppressive piece of legislation that is widely understood actively to endorse the removal of pro-gay literature from the shelves of public libraries, and the sacking of openly lesbian or gay teachers in schools.[16] The label 'hate crime' seems properly to refer to those acts which are against the law, rather than those which are legally endorsed, and hence obscures a key site of lesbian oppression. Nevertheless, the term 'hate crimes' incorporates the important idea that assault can sometimes be understood not as a random, opportunistic, or particularistic attack, but rather as the targeting of members of specific groups as symbols or representatives of that group: thus some forms of harassment not only harm their victims, but also send a message of intimidation and fear to entire communities.

I will now turn to existing literature in psychology, sociology and social policy to explore some of the conceptual difficulties which arise in the attempt to define anti-lesbianism harassment as a 'social problem'. As a feminist and a lesbian, I believe that all forms of anti-lesbianism are pervasive, offensive and damaging. Many cases of anti-lesbianism, such as the incidents with which this chapter opens, are unquestionably atrocious and horrifying attacks upon lesbians. Lesbians are also subjected daily to numerous incidents which are less clearcut and about which we wonder: 'Is that anti-lesbianism, or am I being oversensitive?'; 'How can I tell the difference between anti-lesbianism and racism?', and 'Did that happen because I'm a lesbian, or just because I'm a woman?' Lesbians who respond to incidents with questions like these are not in a good position to challenge the perpetrators. We are left unable to name our experience clearly and are therefore often unable to act. Those who have a vested interest in not recognising anti-lesbian harassment as a social problem may rely on and encourage this uncertainty.

In addressing the questions and uncertainties outlined above, it is important to recognise that there is no one 'true' definition of anti-lesbian harassment; rather we construct the meaning of anti-lesbian harassment as part of the process of defining anti-lesbianism as a social problem, and the definitions we choose have personal, social and political implications.

CONCEPTUAL DIFFICULTIES IN THE CONSTRUCTION OF SOCIAL PROBLEMS

The construction of new social problems is always contested, because it challenges the taken-for-granted reality of the 'perpetrators' (and often also that of the 'victims'). Those highlighting the problem are engaged in a contest over meanings and definitions. It is possible to identify five strategies often used in opposing the construction of a new social problem:

1. The frequency double-bind: those highlighting the social problem are quizzed as to the frequency with which the alleged problem (say, sexual harassment) occurs. If they produce low frequencies, their opponents claim that as the problem is rare, it isn't 'really' a problem. If they produce high frequencies, their opponents claim that as the alleged 'problem' apparently happens all the time, it can't really be very serious, but is just 'part of life'.[17]

2. The personal/political split: the alleged 'social problem' is relocated firmly in the arena of the personal and private; the state, it is claimed, has no place legislating private behaviour. Marital rape, date rape, sexual harassment, wife-battering and the physical punishment of children all attract such accusations.[18]

3. Victim-blaming: arguments used here include – women cause sexual harassment by dressing provocatively or behaving flirtatiously; child sexual abuse is caused by seductive Lolitas; wives cause themselves to be beaten up by nagging their husbands; and there isn't any rape in cultures where women don't say 'no'.[19]

4. Reversals: questions about the inverse of the 'social problem' are raised. In relation to child sexual abuse, for instance, activists may be accused of denying the existence of the sexually active and desiring child. In relation to sexual harassment, the possibility of sexual harassment of men by women becomes an issue.[20]

5. Boundary disputes: concern is expressed about defining the boundary between 'normal' and 'problem' behaviour. Where does 'office flirtation' end and sexual harassment begin? Does social awareness about child sexual abuse mean the end of bedtime cuddles between father and child? How clear is the demarcation between 'normal' sexual intercourse and 'date rape' or 'marital rape'?[21]

Such strategies are often used merely to mock, trivialise and – if possible – dismiss the new 'social problem'. For example, colleagues have told me that anti-lesbianism in an academic setting is relatively rare (they mean I have never been beaten up on campus); when I respond with descriptions of commonplace anti-lesbian comments and heterosexist assumptions, they tell me that such behaviour is the normal stuff of heterosexual interaction and cannot be labelled 'anti-lesbianism' (the frequency double-bind). I have often been told that what I do in bed is my own business – and not to flaunt it in the workplace (the personal/political split); if I insist on being so blatant, I must expect to attract hostile responses (victim-blaming). In classic 'reversal' mode, heterosexual women accuse me of silencing and alienating them by insisting on my lesbianism; while my definitions of what constitutes 'anti-lesbian' behaviour are routinely challenged (boundary disputes). Such arguments are often self-protective and self-interested ploys used by those who stand to gain by not recognising certain types of behaviour as problematic.

It is not surprising, therefore, that activists have frequently responded with little more than irritated restatements, or dogmatic definitions. Most men, according to the authors of a book on sexual harassment, know perfectly well what sexual harassment is: 'the confusion is transparent pretence ... sexual harassment is not that difficult to recognise. It is not, in the vast majority of cases, ambiguous behaviour.'[22] But these questions can also be serious issues of concern for feminists, questions which we need to address in analysing the dimensions of the social problem we are confronting and in considering how best to tackle it. There is no one 'right' answer as to *how* 'anti-lesbian harassment', 'sexual harassment', 'child sexual abuse' and so on should be defined. We should not allow ourselves to be forced into the position of trying to construct and defend watertight, once-and-for-all, 'accurate' definitions. Rather, our definitions are socially constructed to serve specific political ends. We can expand or contract our definitions with corresponding effects on the 'size' of the problem and on its apparent 'normality'. We can make decisions about where (and whether) we place the boundaries between 'problem' and 'normal' behaviour. We need to be able to think about the agency of 'victims' and to consider the way in which 'choices' are constructed under oppression. In other words, we need more than simply defensive responses to the arguments raised above; we also need to theorise them. If we discount the difficulties inherent in constructing definitions of social problems, we leave uncharted territory for our opponents to exploit. Moreover, we have a great deal to gain both theoretically and practically by leaving the safe realm of polemic to risk exploring the limits of our theories, the boundaries of our concepts. It is at those boundaries that we are most likely to develop new insights and novel challenges.

TAKING A DEFINITIONAL STAND

It is possible to argue that all forms of harassment done to a lesbian are 'anti-lesbian' harassment, because they are directed against a lesbian, who is and continues to be a lesbian while being harassed. This argument would insist that it is not possible (or not politically desirable) to differentiate between those occasions when a lesbian is harassed as a lesbian, and those occasions when she is harassed as whatever else she is – and when is she ever other than a lesbian?

The counter-argument points to forms of oppression other than anti-lesbianism (including those bundled together as part of the definition of 'hate crime': racism, anti-semitism, religious prejudice – and, we might add, classism, disableism and ageism). Sometimes such oppressions are more salient in causing a lesbian's harassment than is her lesbianism. Lesbians who share other oppressions report confusion as to how accurately to label their experience: 'When working in a white environment it's racism anyway. If they get to know that I'm a lesbian then I can't tell if it's anti-lesbianism or racism.'[23] It is the focus on the motives and intentions of the harassers that leads to these uncertainties and difficulties: do they hate you because you're black, or because you're lesbian? The answer (probably both) is ultimately unknowable. They may not tell you; they may be lying; or they may deceive themselves. In any event, it should not be necessary to rely on the oppressor's testimony to define what happened. An alternative is to shift the focus from the intentions of the harasser to the identity (or identities) of the person being harassed.

We are harassed as whole people: we don't ever stop being all of whom we are. When anti-semitic comments are made because of my surname, being lesbian may not be irrelevant: I have retained my 'maiden' name and my heterosexual sister, who took her husband's non-Jewish name, is not subjected to such comments. My friend who is subjected to racist taunts as she walks through a hostile neighbourhood late at night is certainly harassed because she is black, but the opportunity for the harassment arises as she returns home late at night from a lesbian bar. We do not experience our oppressions as fragmented according to discrete identity categories, nor should we have to label what happens to us as though it could be neatly categorised into mutually exclusive or competing oppressions.

The notion of anti-lesbianism which is separate and clearly distinguishable from any other form of oppression can only be a 'prototypical' white, middle-class, able-bodied, gentile concept of what anti-lesbianism is and how it works. *All* lesbians suffer from anti-lesbianism, although the form it takes varies depending on the race/ethnicity, class, age and disability status of the lesbian at whom it is directed. For example, the same man who, drawing on racial and class stereotypes of British women, taunts a middle-class white lesbian with frigidity or sexual inexperience, may assume that a working-class black lesbian is sexually promiscuous, has extensive experience of sex with men, and is continually ready and willing for sexual encounters. The black woman's experience is not anti-lesbianism *plus* racism, but anti-lesbianism *structured by* racism, or racism *structured by* anti-lesbianism. The emphasis she chooses to give this may depend on her audience and her intentions: with black heterosexual women, it may be necessary to speak of the former in order than they notice her oppression *as a lesbian*; with white lesbians, it may be necessary to speak of the latter, in order that they notice her oppression *as a black woman*. (If, on the other hand, she wants emotional support and empathetic understanding, she may choose to emphasise the oppression she shares with her audience.) The question 'Was it anti-lesbianism, or was it racism?' sets up a false dichotomy. There is no 'prototypical' lesbian, harassed 'purely' for her lesbianism, against which all other lesbians' oppression can be compared in order to determine the extent to which their victimisation can be said to be 'additional' to hers. Oppressions are not additive, but interactive.

Although on particular occasions and in specific contexts we may wish to insist on the primacy of one oppression or another, there is much to be gained by starting from the assumption that any incident of harassment, discrimination or oppression is directed at the whole person and can appropriately be labelled anti-lesbian *and* racist *and* disableist *and* ... whatever other aspects of our identity are routinely under attack. *Every* harassing incident directed against a black lesbian is both racist *and* anti-lesbian; *every* harassing incident directed against a disabled lesbian is both disableist *and* anti-lesbian. We don't have to pit oppressions one against another. Rather, by labelling what happens to us as inclusively as possible, we enable a shift of focus from the confusion of either/or to the awareness of both (or all) and how they interact.

(Homosexual) Woman *or* (Female) Homosexual

Definitions of 'hate crimes' do not include crimes motivated by woman-hatred. Rape, sexual harassment and other forms of sexual assault on women do not qualify as hate-motivated crimes unless the perpetrator can be shown to have attacked some aspect of the victim's identity other than her gender (such as her race, religion or sexual orientation). All lesbians are women [24] and share many aspects of women's general oppression under heteropatriarchy. Yet the need to describe something as a 'hate crime' or as an anti-gay assault requires that we dislocate our experience as 'women' from our experience as 'homosexuals'.

In much social science research, as in policy documents, anti-lesbian harassment must be classified as either 'sexism' (harassment of lesbian-as-woman) or as 'anti-gay' (harassment of lesbian-as-homosexual). Such conceptual divisions suggest that lesbians are harassed *either* because we are women *or* because we are homosexuals, and that any specific case of harassment properly belongs to one category or the other. Were we harassed as women (who happen to be lesbian, a fact which may or may not have been known or suspected by the assailant); or were we harassed as homosexuals (who happen to be female)? While lesbians differ in class, race, ethnicity, age and disability status, we share a common oppression as women. The attempt to 'separate out' one form of oppression from another breaks down completely when confronting the extent to which harassment is 'really' anti-lesbian versus anti-woman. Because all lesbians are women, the overlap of oppressions is complete.

By ignoring the fact that one is always a lesbian (even when being harassed as a woman) and always a woman (even when being harassed as a gay person), it is indeed possible to classify *some* incidents as either 'anti-woman' or 'anti-gay' – by focusing on the presumed motives of the harasser. When, for example, in conversation with a male colleague, I bent down to retrieve my appointment diary from my bag on the floor, and another male lecturer known only to my colleague called in passing, 'Hi Pete! I see you've got a woman on her knees! That's the way to keep them!', the incident seems to be 'anti-woman': my lesbianism (if he knew about it) was irrelevant to him – what I symbolised was a generic female. When, on another occasion, after applying for a job for which I was not shortlisted, a member of the selection committee told me that the head of department had flatly refused to consider an 'out' researcher on lesbian and gay issues, saying that 'it would make a laughing stock of the department', it seems not unreasonable to assume that he might have ridiculed a gay male researcher of homosexuality in the same way – in other words, that this is an 'anti-gay' incident. But many other incidents defy such classification. Is it 'sexism' or 'anti-lesbianism' which led a male colleague, walking with me, an 'out' lesbian, through a deserted wooded area of the campus towards the computing centre, to ask me whether I had a partner, adding that he had 'always wanted to go to bed with two lesbians'?

Lesbianism is perceived by many men primarily in terms of sex.[25] Pornographic depictions of pseudo-lesbian activity are commonplace.[26] Lesbians are portrayed as sex objects for men, who perform on each other the necessary 'foreplay' as preparation for the entry of the male and his penis. Consequently, many lesbians are sexually harassed not because they are women, but because they are lesbians.[27] Some forms of sexual harassment are specific to 'out' lesbians – men sometimes act on the assumption that we share a 'male gaze' when looking at women, and that we can be 'one of the boys' in enjoying pornographic pin-ups or ogling passing females; many lesbians find this humiliating and offensive.[28] Rape, too, may be directed not at a 'woman' but at a lesbian: all we need is a good fuck, or the right man. According to researchers of anti-lesbian violence, 'rapists often verbalise the view that lesbians are "open targets" and deserve punishment because they are not under the protection of a man'.[29] Anti-lesbian rape may also involve attempts by the rapist to degrade lesbian sexuality – one lesbian couple were forced at gunpoint to engage in sexual behaviour together, then raped.[30]

Men sometimes seem genuinely surprised to find – having taken pornography as literal truth – that they have offended us with their sexual incursions. One man who attempted to kiss me shortly after I told him I was a lesbian (as part of an academic discussion about our current research projects) was baffled by my outrage, clearly believing that in coming out as lesbian I had 'introduced sex into the conversation': that it was I, not he, who had opened up the topic of sex for public discussion, I who had started the 'salacious' exchange, I who had demonstrated a 'sexually liberated', 'swinging' attitude to sexuality – an attitude to which he was merely responding in kind. Where I understand the words 'I am a lesbian' to mean a statement of political choice, social identity, and personal commitment, as well as (in this context) having implications for the doing of research, he had understood my words as a sexual invitation. 'Coming out' is often perceived as 'coming on', or as 'playing hard to get'. In coming out as lesbians we're 'asking for it'. We 'bring upon ourselves' whatever forms of harassment are subsequently directed at us. We could, after all, have stayed in the closet.

The pressure to pass as heterosexual is itself an indication of oppression, and one which sets the scene for other forms of harassment – including, for the closeted lesbian, the threat of disclosure. Sexual harassment emphasises heterosexual norms of intimacy and behaviour, reminding the lesbian of her own 'outsider' status. For lesbians attempting to 'pass as straight', sexual harassment may have to be endured if they are not to run the risk of being accused of lesbianism. The indivisibility of oppression is apparent in that many lesbians find that what starts as (apparently) a clear case of 'anti-woman' harassment escalates to anti-lesbianism when they signal their unavailability:

> One respondent illustrated this pattern in her analysis of an incident that began with a man asking to see her breast as she walked by him on the street. She ignored the comment and walked on. He continued the harassment by saying 'Dyke'. She concluded, 'so the worst kind of woman that he can imagine, a woman that won't respond to him at all, must be a lesbian. Otherwise I would've been flattered that he wanted to see my breast.'[31]

Although both heterosexual and lesbian women are subjected to this sort of harassment, anti-lesbian insults carry a particular threat for lesbians: women confident in their heterosexual status may be able to ignore or challenge such insults, but for closeted lesbians there is the danger of being 'outed'.

Even if a woman is 'out' as a lesbian in her workplace, she may be engaged in a personal PR campaign in which she sets out to demonstrate the falsity of the stereotypes. Many lesbians, for example, are keen to show by their own behaviour that lesbians are not ugly man-haters, and may set out to dress in a way which men are likely to find attractive, to engage in a friendly manner with men, to demonstrate that they *could* catch a man if they wanted one – that their lesbianism isn't *faute de mieux*.[32] Lesbians engaged in this course of action sometimes find themselves less clear than heterosexuals as to what constitutes 'sexual harassment' and may be forced to tolerate considerably *more* harassment than do many heterosexual women.

The old-fashioned definition of a lesbian as a woman who chooses to engage sexually with women, and not with men,[33] means that for lesbians *all* sexual advances from men are unwanted, unreciprocated and unsolicited. In so far as 'sexual harassment' is defined as 'unreciprocated, unsolicited, unwanted male behaviour which has as its aim the reduction of a woman to a sex object',[34] lesbians can define *all* sexualised behaviour from men as 'sexual harassment'. The term 'sexual harassment' relies upon a distinction between desired and reciprocated heterosexual interaction and unwanted heterosexual interaction. Since as lesbians we want *none* of it, *all* of it can be labelled 'sexual harassment'. Typically, however, lesbians are not comfortable with this relabelling strategy, understanding that for heterosexual women distinctions between 'flirtation' and 'harassment' are important (albeit difficult to make clearly).[35] As lesbians, we are expected to see ourselves as a special 'minority' group who cannot expect our definitions, expectations and preferences to be understood or found acceptable by the heterosexual world.[36]

We are sexually harassed *because we are visible as lesbians* (and therefore a pornographic turn-on or a challenge) or we are sexually harassed *because we are not visible as lesbians*, assumed to be heterosexual or attempting to pass as heterosexual and therefore 'fair game'. The non-additive nature of lesbian oppression is clearly indicated in instances of sexual harassment. Our oppression as lesbians is not the same as the oppression of generic (presumed heterosexual) women, plus that of generic (assumed male) homosexuals.

Seeking Help, Choosing Allies, Fighting Back

In this chapter I have argued, firstly, that we are oppressed or harassed as 'whole people' and, secondly, that our oppression is specific to the 'whole people' that we are. This means that the label 'anti-lesbian harassment' is often not sufficient to describe our experience, because it singles out only one part of our identities. Equally, however, 'anti-lesbian harassment' is necessary as a term which describes a specific form of discrimination which cannot be deduced from adding the experience of being a 'woman' to the experience of being a 'gay person'.

Problems of definition always arise in the construction of any social problem, and 'anti-lesbianism' is no exception. The definitions we

apply to our experiences play an important role in determining our understanding of what is going on, and the range of possible reactions.
Definitions have implications for action. If we dismiss the catcalls, the
sexual innuendo, the anti-lesbian jokes as 'just part of life', refusing to
label them as 'harassment', we are unlikely to complain or to seek
remedies. If we label them *only* 'anti-lesbian harassment', we may be
losing other dimensions of these assaults – their attack on racial, class,
age, or disability characteristics.[37] If we label them *only* 'racist' or 'sexist'
(for example) we lose sight of the intersection of race, sex and so on in
constructing our lesbianism; and, conversely, of the role of our lesbianism
in constructing our racialised and gender-specific identities. We need
to pay close attention to all aspects of our oppression, and to develop
clearer understandings of their interrelationship, if we are to fight back
effectively.

The term 'anti-lesbian harassment' has drawbacks. It focuses attention
on only one aspect of the whole experience. Harassment in general tends
to be constructed as something which can be sliced up into 'pure'
exemplars of different oppressions – such that one can identify incidents
which are 'purely' racial harassment, 'purely' sexual harassment and so
on. The fiction that there is anti-lesbian harassment which is 'purely'
anti-lesbianism (uncontaminated by issues of race, class, sex and so forth)
actively prevents some lesbians from seeking help. Workers at various
of the organisations that have been set up to help lesbian and gay
crime victims[38] typically find that lesbians and people of colour are under-
represented in their client populations. A former coordinator of one such
group, Community United Against Violence, explains: 'Women who
are victimized often are not sure whether it was an anti-lesbian or anti-
woman attack. The issue of women not going to Community United
Against Violence is directly related to making that distinction.'[39] The
current program coordinator makes a parallel point in relation to people
of colour:

> the majority of people of color who report to us say that they find it difficult
> to separate the anti-gay or anti-lesbian element of the attack from the
> elements that are racial. The incidents seem to be motivated by both for a
> lot of people.[40]

In terms of seeking help, then – and 'help' in this context refers not
only to the provision of emotional or psychological support but also
to information about the legal options open to victims of 'hate crimes'
– insistence on a 'purist' definition of anti-lesbian harassment is
counterproductive. It makes it *less* likely that lesbians (especially black

lesbians or those with disabilities) will feel able to use the services on offer.[41]

But it would be a mistake to react by abandoning any notion of the specificity of 'anti-lesbianism'. It would be easy to shrug in bewilderment at the dizzy array of overlapping and multiple oppressions, and to resort to the use of 'harassment' as an undifferentiated category. 'I was harassed', you could say – leaving unspecified the particular nature of that experience. However, there are good political reasons for retaining, and for further developing, the notion of 'anti-lesbian harassment'. Firstly, it names an oppressed group and hence renders us (and our oppression) visible to those who might prefer not to see. Apparently inclusive language ('Everyone should be free from harassment of any kind') cannot achieve this. Just as the creators of the US Declaration of Independence somehow overlooked the fact that the inalienable rights and freedoms it purportedly guaranteed to all US citizens were denied to over half the population (women and slaves), so there is always the danger that oppressed groups will be excluded from rights and protections unless they are specifically included by name. A concrete illustration of the power of naming for lesbians and gay men comes from the extension, in May 1988, of Penn State University's policy defining sexual harassment of students specifically to include harassment based on sexual orientation:

> This was a change with practical consequences. Before this, without a mention of lesbians or gay men existing on campus and with no extension of policies about harassment to them, a R[esident] A[ssistant] could dismiss, instead of report, the ubiquitous 'fag' or 'dyke' joke. Following the change, the same joke became 'sexual harassment' and was covered by university sanctions ... The most important consequence of the amendment to the harassment policy was the long-overdue acknowledgement of the invisible minority, if only in terms of its need for protection from abuse ... Discussion about 'sexual orientation' now could become routine, and more and more academic and administrative leaders needed to use the 'L and G words'. The silence was broken. More words followed, and quickly. There was now a context in which the words could be said, and in which they had to be heard.[42]

One important reason for insisting on 'anti-lesbianism' as a conceptual category, then, is to signal our existence and our resistance.

A second key reason for wanting to retain the concept of 'anti-lesbian harassment' relates to the exigencies that structure the social movements and communities from which we would hope for social or political support. The practical reality is that, in many instances, to insist on our 'wholeness', to draw attention to our multiple oppressions, is to court disaster. 'Secondary victimisation'[43] is the term used by social scientists to designate the experience of further harassment occurring in the place where you have gone for help. When I tell a friend about an anti-lesbian experience and she retorts, 'Well, you shouldn't have been so blatant', that's secondary victimisation. When a lesbian takes her lover, cut and bruised after an attack on the street, to the hospital, and the medical staff separate the two women, phone parents or ex-husbands and refuse to impart information except to 'next of kin', that's secondary victimisation. Lesbians who, for whatever reasons, do not have access to lesbian organisations and communities, and who turn for help to other groups, are very likely to encounter secondary victimisation in the form of further anti-lesbianism.

Of course, many lesbians encounter secondary victimisation *within* lesbian groups as well. Lesbians with disabilities have written of the ableism of the women's and lesbian movements (as well as describing the sexism and anti-lesbianism of the disability movements).[44] Black lesbians have challenged the racism they are forced to confront in feminist and lesbian groups (as well as speaking out against the sexism and heterosexism of their black communities).[45] Jewish women have written of anti-semitism from lesbians and feminists (and of anti-lesbianism from Jewish sources),[46] while working-class lesbians describe the classism of lesbians and feminists (as well as the anti-lesbianism of their working-class communities).[47] The concept of 'racism' is crucially important for a black lesbian in a white lesbian group; so, too, the concept of 'anti-lesbianism' is crucial for her in a group of black heterosexual women.

Ironically it is precisely because of the indivisibility of oppressions that we must insist on identifying each oppression individually. Unless lesbian groups are forced to recognise and deal with anti-semitism, racism, classism, disableism and the like, lesbians who seek help from such groups will experience secondary victimisation from women who conceptualise 'anti-lesbianism' from a purely white, gentile, able-bodied, middle-class perspective. Similarly, unless the communities and movements concerned with other oppressions are forced to recognise their own anti-lesbianism, lesbians within those groups will be subject to secondary victimisation in parallel fashion. The only way of making *all* our communities safe for *all* lesbians is by drawing attention to anti-lesbianism in all its forms. We need the category 'anti-lesbian harassment' as a practical political tool in working towards this end.

Recognition of the specificity of 'anti-lesbian harassment' does not necessarily imply lesbian separatism. It need not prevent us from seeking help from non-lesbians (when they can give it), choosing allies wherever we find them and fighting back with whoever will help. We can make local and strategic decisions about our allegiances and our sources of support. There are many issues on which (for example) heterosexual and lesbian women can work together, because we are united in opposition to a joint enemy (for instance, the requirement of the Child Support Act that an unmarried woman claiming unemployment benefits disclose to the authorities the name of the father of her child[ren]; or the denial of artificial insemination facilities to unmarried women). At the same time, we need to be careful not to subordinate our concerns as lesbians to heterosexual women's issues. Early (heterosexual) feminist campaigns against sexual harassment involved hanging round on street corners whistling at men, displaying male pin-ups or reversing male pick-up behaviour.[48] While such activities proved a major irritant to their male targets, they also served to reinforce heterosexism and hence added to the oppression of lesbians. The failure of the feminist movement to treat heterosexism as seriously as sexism, and to understand how hetero-sexism works to reinforce and maintain the oppression of all women, continues to be a grave problem. Indeed, some heterosexual feminists have now become more concerned about preserving and celebrating heterosexual relationships than about dealing with sexual harassment or violence against women.[49] When feminists do write about harassment and violence against women, many (presumably heterosexual) authors include little or no discussion of lesbians' experiences of harassment.[50] Anti-lesbian harassment from heterosexual feminists is still common-place,[51] and as lesbians we need terms like 'anti-lesbianism' to name and challenge it.[52]

In sum, it is evident that 'anti-lesbian harassment' is not a transpar-ent or unproblematic term. It is important to recognise the role of language in constituting (rather than merely reflecting) experience, and to construct forms of talking about our oppression that are most likely to help in countering it. It does not seem helpful cavalierly to carve up harassment into discrete segments, each with its own labelled oppression; too often this results in some oppressions being ignored altogether, or their importance discounted as they fall to the bottom of a hierarchical ranking. Nor does it seem helpful to throw a blanket term over the whole complicated messy experience of harassment, obscuring the detail and complexity of our oppression. Both approaches offer ammunition to our enemies – those who would prefer not to notice, or not to engage with the social problems we are trying to highlight. Whose interests are served by dividing 'lesbian' from 'woman' from 'black' from 'having a disability'? Who gains when we are unable to name our oppression? Who benefits from our uncertainty and confusion? The approach I have advocated here is to name oppressions and to make them visible, while also exploring the interactions among them. The more sophisticated our analyses of harassment, the less likely we are to be silenced by oppressive strategies such as 'boundary disputes' or 'reversals'. The more sensitive we are to different forms of oppression, and to their intersections, the better we become at seeking appropriate help, choosing allies appropriate to our struggles and fighting back with the clearest idea of what it is we are fighting against, and how best to win.

Notes and References

1. I would like to thank Sue Wilkinson for her careful reading and helpful comments on an earlier version of this chapter.
2. Paraphrased from Claudia Brenner, 'Survivor's Story: Eight Bullets', in Gregory Herek and Kevin Berrill (eds), *Hate Crimes: Confronting Violence against Lesbians and Gay Men*, (London: Sage, 1992).
3. Paraphrased from Kathleen Sarris, 'Survivor's Story', in Herek and Berrill, *Hate Crimes*.
4. Steph, quoted in Nina Taylor (ed.), *All in a Day's Work: A Report on Anti-lesbian Discrimination in Employment and Unemployment in London*, (London: Lesbian Employment Rights, 1986), p. 74.
5. Kevin Berrill, 'Anti-gay Violence and Victimization in the United States: An Overview', in Herek and Berrill, *Hate Crimes*.
6. See, for example, Celia Kitzinger and Rachel Perkins, 'Watching Our Language' (Chapter 2), *Changing Our Minds: Lesbian Feminism and Psychology* (London: Onlywomen and New York: New York University Press, 1993).
7. *Collins Dictionary of the English Language*, 1979. Longman's synonym dictionary (1979) offers:

   1. raid, harry, beset, beleaguer, drive or press hard, terrorize, persecute, molest, oppress, afflict, victimize; 2. bother, pester, hector, bug, hassle, drive nuts or crazy or bananas, drive up the wall, hound, dog, nag, pick on, pick at, be or get on (s.o's) back, torment, taunt, bedevil, tease, tweak, mock, heckle, plague, trouble, fret, worry, bait, provoke, badger.

8. See Alison Thomas and Celia Kitzinger, '"It's Just Something that Happens": The Invisibility of Sexual Harassment in the Workplace', *Gender, Work and Organization: An International Journal* (1994).
9. A term used by some lesbians to refer to the removal of any evidence of their lesbianism; such evidence might include lesbian posters, books, music, newsletters or magazines, and/or the belongings of a female lover.

10. Anthony D'Augelli, 'Lesbians and Gay Men on Campus: Visibility, Empowerment, and Educational Leadership', *Peabody Journal of Education* 66 (3) (1989), pp. 124–41.

11. J.B. Russell, *Witchcraft in the Middle Ages* (Ithaca, NY: Cornell University Press), cited in Ruthann Robson, 'Legal Lesbicide', in Jill Radford and Diana Russell (eds), *Femicide: The Politics of Woman Killing* (Buckingham: Open University Press, 1992).

12. Lillian Faderman, *Surpassing the Love of Men: Romantic Friendship and Love between Women from the Renaissance to the Present Day* (New York: William Morrow, 1981), cited in Robson, 'Legal Lesbicide'.

13. J. Brown, *Immodest Acts* (Oxford: Oxford University Press, 1986), cited in Robson, 'Legal Lesbicide'.

14. D. Greenburg, *The Construction of Homosexuality* (Chicago: University of Chicago Press, 1988), cited in Robson, 'Legal Lesbicide'.

15. Richard Berk, Elizabeth Boyd and Karl Hamner, 'Thinking More Clearly about Hate-Motivated Crimes', in Herek and Berrill, *Hate Crimes*.

16. Further information about Section 28 can be found in Jill Earnshaw, 'Homosexuals and Transsexuals at Work: Legal Issues', in Marilyn Davidson and Jill Earnshaw (eds), *Vulnerable Workers: Psychosocial and Legal Issues*, (London: Wiley, 1991). Note that legal lesbicide has also been discussed earlier.

17. Thomas and Kitzinger, '"It's Just Something that Happens"'.

18. Celia Kitzinger, 'Depoliticising the Personal: A Feminist Slogan in Feminist Therapy', *Women's Studies International Forum* 16 (5) (1993), pp. 487–96.

19. For more on victim-blaming see Kitzinger and Perkins, *Changing Our Minds*.

20. Two common reversals are: (1) lesbians beat each other up (lesbian battering) and oppress each other (anti-lesbianism within lesbian communities); and (2) lesbians oppress heterosexual women. Both deserve discussion at more length than is available here. The former is certainly a serious problem, but should not be used to distract from heterosexual anti-lesbianism. The latter is a misreading of 'oppression'; see Marilyn Frye, 'Oppression', in Margaret Andersen and Patricia Hill Collins (eds), *Race, Class, and Gender: An Anthology*, (Belmont, Calif.: Wadsworth, 1992).

21. Cf. Nicola Gavey, 'Technologies and Effects of Heterosexual Coercion', in Sue Wilkinson and Celia Kitzinger (eds), *Heterosexuality: A 'Feminism & Psychology' Reader*, (London: Sage, 1993).

22. Billie Wright Dziech and Linda Weiner, *The Lecherous Professor: Sexual Harassment on Campus* (Boston, Mass.: Beacon Press, 1984), p. 18.

23. Cited in Taylor, *All in a Day's Work*, p. 25.

24. In order not to hold up the argument here, and for the sake of clarity of exposition, I'm deliberately overlooking some French feminists' arguments that lesbians are *not* women: cf. Monique Wittig, 'The Straight Mind', in Sarah Lucia Hoagland and Julia Penelope (eds), *For Lesbians Only: A Separatist Anthology*, (London: Onlywomen, 1988).

25. Many heterosexual women, too, conceptualise lesbianism as primarily a sexual activity. This sexualised view of lesbians leads to harassment from heterosexual women, for example:

> [My secretary] used to come into my room because we did a lot of dictation and stuff, but when she closed the door behind her to keep the noise out and then came out later, all the others would be nudging her and making gestures. They'd say things like, 'Aren't you brave going in there and having the door locked. Did she make a pass at you then?'
> In Taylor, *All in a Day's Work*

26. Jenny Kitzinger and Celia Kitzinger, 'Doing It: Representations of Lesbian Sex', in Gabriele Griffin (ed.), *Popular/izing Lesbian Texts* (London: Pluto, 1993).

27. This is a very common experience. Other similar examples are cited in Taylor, *All in a Day's Work*.

28. I have been offered pornography by men who expected me to join with them in admiring the images, and shown photographs of a yachting holiday with a bikini-clad girlfriend by a man who, as I lingered over one of the snaps, commented jocularly, 'You are meant to be looking at the boat, not the woman.'

29. Linda Garnets, Gregory Herek and Barrie Levy, 'Violence and Victimization of Lesbians and Gay Men: Mental Health Consequences', in Herek and Berrill, *Hate Crimes*, p. 213.

30. Garnets, Herek and Levy, 'Violence and Victimization of Lesbians and Gay Men: Mental Health Consequences'.

31. Beatrice von Schulthess, 'Violence in the Streets: Anti-Lesbian Assault and Harassment in San Francisco', in Herek and Berrill, *Hate Crimes*.

32. Ironically, concern about 'appropriate' gender role behaviour may be exacerbated for lesbians who are 'out' – 'There's this stereotype that all lesbians are big tough butch women in trousers and crew cuts,' said a librarian whose colleagues know she is lesbian, 'so I make a special effort to do my hair nicely, and wear quite feminine clothing, skirts and make-up, just to sort of say, "look, we're not all like that".' This is explored further in Celia Kitzinger, 'Lesbians and Gay Men in the Workplace' in Davidson and Earnshaw, *Vulnerable Workers*.

33. Definitions are never simply descriptive, and always rely on an implicit politics. This is the definition of 'lesbian' I choose, as a radical lesbian feminist, to signal my political allegiances. Liberals, humanitarians and non-radical feminists have offered a range of other definitions ('anyone who says she is', 'someone who *prefers* sex with women to sex with men', 'someone who primarily chooses sex with women, but may also have sex with men from time to time', and so on). See Celia Kitzinger, *The Social Construction of Lesbianism* (London: Sage, 1987) for a discussion and critique of liberal humanistic definitions of lesbianism; and Kitzinger and Perkins, *Changing Our Minds* for a discussion and critique of non-radical feminist psychological definitions of lesbianism. My use of the term 'old-fashioned' to characterise the radical feminist definition reflects the extent to which Queer Theory presents itself as the newest and most chic perspective on these issues. According to Queer Theory, the radical challenge to normative definitions of sex and gender comes not from lesbianism per se but from 'fucking with gender' – that is, by doing 'sex' (whether with women or with men) in such a way as to expose the fundamental unnaturalness of conventional definitions of 'male' and 'female'. Attempts to do this include portrayals of lesbians with penises, the celebration of sado-masochism, bisexuality, transvestism and transsexuality, and the reclamation of butch/femme roles. For more information on Queer Theory, see Cherry Smyth, *Lesbians Talk Queer Notions* (London: Scarlet, 1992). For a critique of Queer Theory, see Celia Kitzinger and Sue Wilkinson, 'Virgins and Queers', *Gender & Society* special issue on sexuality (1994).
34. Lisa Tuttle, *Encyclopaedia of Feminism* (London: Arrow, 1986).
35. Cf. Gavey, 'Technologies and Effects of Heterosexual Coercion' for a discussion of *women's* difficulties in telling the difference between sexual intercourse and rape; and Lloyd Vogelman, *The Sexual Face of Violence* (Johannesburg: Ravan, 1990) for a discussion of *men's* difficulties in telling the difference between sexual intercourse and rape.
36. See G. Green, M. Barnard, R. Barbour and J. Kitzinger, 'Who Wears the Trousers? Sexual Harassment in Research Settings', *Women's Studies International Forum* 16 (6) (1993), pp. 627–37.
37. White people have races and ethnicities too. Exploration of the role of 'whiteness' in constructing lesbian (or *any*) identities is minimal. I have not discussed 'whiteness' in this chapter because the chapter focuses on oppressed identities. See, however, Peggy McIntosh, 'White Privilege and Male Privilege: A Personal Account of Coming to See Correspondences through Work in Women's Studies', in

Andersen and Collins, (eds), *Race, Class, and Gender*, pp. 70–81; Deborah Jones, 'Looking in My Own Back Yard: The Search for White Feminist Theories of Racism for Aotearoa', in Rosemary Du Plessis (ed.), *Feminist Voices: Women's Studies Texts for Aotearoa/New Zealand* (Oxford: Oxford University Press, 1992); Helen (charles), 'Whiteness – The Relevance of Politically Colouring the "Non", in Hilary Hinds, Ann Phoenix and Jackie Stacey (eds), *Working Out: New Directions for Women's Studies*, (London: Falmer, 1992); Marilyn Frye, 'White Woman Feminist', in Marilyn Frye, *Willful Virgin: Essays in Feminism* (Freedom, Calif.: Crossing Press, 1992); Ruth Frankenberg, *White Woman, Race Matters: The Social Construction of Whiteness* (London: Routledge, and Minneapolis: University of Minnesota Press, 1993).

38. New York City, San Francisco and Boston all have such groups. See Herek and Berrill, *Hate Crimes*.
39. Lester Olmstead-Rose in 'The Community Response to Violence in San Francisco: An Interview with Wenny Kussuma, Lester Olmstead-Rose, and Jill Tregor', in *Hate Crimes*.
40. Jill Tregor, in 'The Community Response to Violence in San Francisco: An Interview with Wenny Kussuma, Lester Olmstead-Rose, and Jill Tregor', in Herek and Berrill, *Hate Crimes*.
41. Community United Against Violence is concerned about this problem, is actively engaged in outreach work to lesbians of all races and now has a multiracial, multiethnic staff, including people of all races, backgrounds, classes and ages, and people with disabilities.
42. D'Augelli, 'Lesbians and Gay Men on Campus'.
43. See, for example, Herek and Berrill, *Hate Crimes*. The term 'victim' has been the subject of some debate within feminism because it is seen as emphasising women's powerlessness rather than our resistance. The term 'survivors' (often used within a psychological framework) is a currently popular alternative. It is important to recognise, however, that some women do *not* 'survive' assaults upon them (they end up dead), and also that no woman is ever responsible for her victimhood. A (presumably unintended) negative effect of the vogue for 'survivorhood' has been an increasing tendency to blame women for being 'victims' rather than 'survivors' (see, for example, the New Age literature critiqued in Sue Wilkinson and Celia Kitzinger, '"Whose Breast Is It, Anyway?": A Feminist Consideration of Advice and "Treatment" for Breast Cancer', *Women's Studies International Forum*, 16 [2] [1993], pp. 229–38). An extended discussion of the use of the terms 'victim' and 'survivor' in the context of power and powerlessness can be found in Kitzinger and Perkins, *Changing Our Minds*, pp. 39–48.

44. See, for example, Kirsten Hearn, 'Oi! What about Us?' in Bob Cant and Susan Hemmings (eds), *Radical Records: Thirty Years of Lesbian and Gay History*, (London: Routledge, 1988); M. Sorella, 'Lies, Lies and More Lies', *Sinister Wisdom*, 35 (1988), pp. 58–71.

45. See, for example, Cheryl Clarke, 'The Failure to Transform: Homophobia in the Black Community', in Barbara Smith (ed.), *Home Girls: A Black Feminist Anthology*, (New York: Kitchen Table Women of Color Press, 1983).

46. For example, Evelyn Torton Beck, *Nice Jewish Girls: A Lesbian Anthology* (Watertown, Mass.: Persephone, 1982); Merril Mushroom, 'Merrill Mushroom is a Jew', *Common Lives, Lesbian Lives: A Lesbian Quarterly* 7 (1983), pp. 78–85.

47. See the special issue of *Lesbian Ethics* on class and classism (Spring, 1991, 4 [2]) and the special issue of *Sinister Wisdom* on lesbians and class (Winter 1991, 45).

48. Naomi Weisstein describes her involvement in such activities in the early 1970s in an interview quoted in Celia Kitzinger, 'Revisioning Weisstein, Revitalizing Feminism', *Feminism & Psychology: An International Journal*, 3 (2) (1993), pp. 189–94.

49. See, for example, Wendy Hollway's book review of Terry Pattinson, *Sexual Harassment … The Hidden Facts* (London: Futura, 1991) in *Feminism & Psychology* 2 (3) (1993), pp. 484–6; and Wendy Hollway, 'Theorising Heterosexuality: A Response', *Feminism & Psychology* 3 (3) (1994), pp. 412–17.

50. There is nothing at all on lesbians in Dzeich and Weiner, *The Lecherous Professor,* or in Nathalie Hadjifotiou, *Women and Harassment at Work* (London: Pluto, 1983). A few lesbians are contributors to anthologies (see for example Amber Coverdale Sumrall and Dena Taylor (eds), *Sexual Harassment: Women Speak Out* [Freedom, Calif.: Crossing Press, 1992]) or interview studies, (for instance, Elizabeth Stanko, *Everyday Violence: How Men and Women Experience Sexual and Physical Danger* [London: Pandora, 1990]), but the specifics of their experience *as lesbians,* and the relationship between their lesbianism and their experience of male violence, is barely touched on.

51. Anti-lesbian harassment from heterosexual feminists is common; the sexualisation of lesbianism is one mechanism through which anti-lesbian harassment from heterosexual women is expressed. For example:

> When I was a student I applied to do relief work at a Girl's Project in Camden … I asked a woman … if she would give me a reference (she was a feminist). She asked me about the project – all I had to do was go

in once or twice a month and do a night shift. The hostel had nine girls in it aged between 16 and 19, most of them had been in care. The woman was really worried about giving me a reference ... because I was going to be let loose in a hostel for young women and I was a lesbian!

(quoted in Taylor, *All in a Day's Work*)

52. It might also be helpful if heterosexual women could understand how anti-lesbianism damages *them*. As Radicalesbians said back in the late 1960s:

Lesbianism is the word, the label, the condition that holds women in line. When a woman hears this word tossed her way, she knows she is stepping out of line ... Lesbian is a label invented by the Man to throw at any woman who dares to be his equal, who dares to challenge his pre-rogatives (including that of all women as part of the exchange medium among men), who dares to assert the primacy of her own needs.

(Radicalesbians, *Woman-identified Woman* [pamphlet],
Somerville, Mass.: New England Free Press, 1969;
reprinted in Hoagland and Penelope, *For Lesbians Only*)

7

Sexual Harassment and Sexual Abuse: When Girls Become Women

Suzanne Raitt

It was my first afternoon working on my own at a refuge for battered women and their children. I was alone upstairs with two-year-old Lisa, a precocious and disarmingly cheerful child whose mother's boyfriend had threatened them with a knife. Lisa was building a house by piling soft cushions up against the sloping attic roof. They stood awkwardly, like leaning stones, and Lisa called to me to come in behind them. We had sometimes played going to sleep, and we lay down side by side and closed our eyes. We always peeped, and laughed; sometimes we hugged. This time Lisa was licking my cheek. I thought, how odd, she's almost trying to put her tongue in my mouth. I waited. Lisa kept leaning on my breasts with her hands. Then she straddled me and started to move slowly up and down, rubbing against my stomach with the seat of her little green trousers. She was staring at me, huge blank eyes, willing me to cooperate. I thought, 'Oh God, she's been watching her parents,' and her tiny fingers felt for my nipples. I sat up and told Lisa I didn't want to play any more. But that made her cry, and she started hitting me round the face, hurting me and trying to pull me back behind the cushions. I had to keep saying no, no. When Lisa went to the hospital, the doctor found evidence of vaginal trauma. She'd been sexually abused by some older boys who used to hang around her grandmother's house.

Across the years I remember most vividly of all Lisa's silence and her concentration. I remember the way she held my gaze and made me feel, in spite of her small size, that I was hers. Our mutual fear, and the weight of her silence, hold me still.

It is about silence, and the ways in which we speak, that I want to write here. Lisa led me to that as well. Usually she spoke incessantly, an incoherent stream in which if you listened hard you could distin-

148

guish one or two words. She was a child who longed to speak, but whose language had come into being distorted by her own urgency. Her body remembered and spoke for her, and then her experience was rephrased again by the doctor, her mother and the refuge workers. We can say with confidence that she was 'sexually abused'; we don't know whether we can legally call her abuse 'rape' because she could not say exactly what happened.

But what about what happened to me, minor though it was? It was certainly unwanted and unexpected sexual contact, but was it 'harassment'? Can a small child harass an adult? If Lisa had straddled an unwilling child, would it have been 'bullying', or 'abuse'? I ask these questions not because I expect to find answers that could possibly account for the complexity (or even the simplicity) of the situation, but to draw attention to the assumptions behind different categorisations of what Liz Kelly uncompromisingly calls 'sexual violence'.[1] Why is an unwanted male hand on an unwilling female body sometimes called 'sexual harassment' and sometimes called 'sexual abuse'? This chapter will explore these questions in the context of women's own naming of their experiences, as well as in the context of institutional and socio-logical definitions. The aim of my inquiry will be to find out what such namings tell us about our construction of related categories like 'woman' and 'girl', 'public' and 'private', 'workplace' and 'home', and, finally but most significantly, 'victim' and 'survivor'.

It is, of course, no accident that 'woman', 'public' and 'workplace' find themselves on one side of the divide, and 'girl', 'private' and 'home' on the other. An understanding of one of these concepts depends on an understanding of all the others. 'Woman' and the 'workplace' are almost always cited together in definitions of sexual harassment. Friedman, Boumil and Taylor give the following definition of sexual harassment, based on the 1977 Equal Employment Opportunities Commission (EEOC) guidelines in the US, where sexual harassment can be prosecuted as sex discrimination under Title VII of the 1964 Civil Rights Act:

Sexual harassment is by its very definition, offensive and unwelcome. More specifically, it is conduct or behaviour characterized by unwanted sexual advances made in the context of a relationship of unequal power or authority. The victims of sexual harassment are usually women who are subjected to verbal comments of a sexual nature, unconsented touching and requests for sexual favors. The perpetrators of sexual harassment are usually men who, by virtue of their superior positions of authority, are able to threaten the victim (or at least make her feel threatened) with the loss of her job or interfere with her performance on that job by intimidation and the creation of a hostile work environment.[2]

This is a classic 'workplace' definition, in which sexual harassment is seen as one of the hazards of paid employment for women. Sue Wise and Liz Stanley note that most definitions in the UK follow this pattern, largely because in Britain it was trade unions during the early 1980s who took the lead in research and action in this area.[3] Since sexual harassment was originally constructed within these parameters, most subsequent commentary also regards it as a phenomenon of women's working lives and of their employment outside the home.[4]

As an infringement of civil liberties, sexual harassment in these versions is always constructed as a social event. As Wise and Stanley say, 'what constitutes "sexual harassment" is a matter of social construction'.[5] Presumably they mean by this that 'sexual harassment' is produced at the intersection of a number of different public discourses: workplace legislation and guidelines, interpretations of physical and other evidence, testimonies in a court or a tribunal. Sue Read comments that since 'there is virtually nowhere a woman can go in public where she does not risk being subjected to sexual attentions', 'sexual harassment' must be elaborately constructed as a socio-sexual category exactly in order to exempt some forms of sexual attention from being understood in this way.[6] It is not simply sexually harassing behaviours, then, that extort 'female subservience', but the way in which the category itself has been constructed.[7] It tacitly assumes, for example, that women cannot be sexually harassed anywhere where they work without an 'employer' (in the home, for example), thereby denying that such work is 'work' at all. It assumes that women who are 'unemployed' cannot be harassed. Like rape legislation, it produces a woman's consent as a problematic category, not in her interests but in the defendant's. As Wise and Stanley imply, sexual harassment as a category relies not only on conservative ideologies about heterosexuality (the man 'advances', the woman 'responds'),[8] but also, I would suggest, on conservative notions of what constitutes the 'workplace' and the 'home', the 'public' and the 'private'. This construction also refuses to constitute as 'sexual' the harassment many women face on grounds of race, or lesbianism. The category 'sexual harassment' is constructed in ways that refuse women's experiences before they even get to court.

I am aware of the danger of deconstructive tactics such as these. Sexual harassment in the workplace is a major and damaging feature of almost all women's lives, and the possibility of legal action has empowered some women and protected many others. But it is also true that there are many women whose experiences of harassment are misrecognised, or ignored, in the workplace definition. I am arguing not for the abandonment of the category – far from it – but for an increased awareness of the often conservative ideologies through which it is constructed and enforced.

Sue Wise and Liz Stanley are two feminists who have offered a wider definition of sexual harassment, as a challenge to workplace definitions which, in their words, 'see sexual harassment as a particular type of behaviour ("sexual") which is done by a particular type of man ("atypical") in a particular place ("work")'. Wise and Stanley's definition emphasises the regularity and the mundanity of harassing behaviour: 'all sexual harassment behaviours are linked by the way they represent an unwanted and unsought intrusion by men into women's feelings, thoughts, behaviours, space, time, energies and bodies.'[9] The strength of this approach is that it abandons unhelpful conceptualisations of work and the public sphere in order to refocus attention on a woman's own space as it traverses the public and the private worlds: her mind and her body, uniquely her own and yet continually, and sometimes oppressively, constructed as available for public consumption. Their example of a day in the life of 'Wendy Average' stresses that Wendy is exposed to a range of harassments, from her husband refusing to get out of bed first to feed the cats, to being jostled by a man on a bus.[10] They object to the 'sexualisation' of sexual harassment: at what point, they ask, does 'sexism' become 'sexual', and therefore 'sexual harassment'?[11] Just like the 'workplace', the 'sexual' is too contested a category of experience for both women and men for it to be a reliable criterion for definition.

The problem with this expanded, 'minimalist' definition[12] is that it is legally unenforceable, exactly because it abandons all the conservative assumptions, in the 'workplace' definitions, about when and where women are public beings, both subject to social control and entitled to protection from it. In order to act publicly against the harassment of 'woman', 'woman' must first be produced as a social category; and this production, in a sexist society, will be accomplished in sexist terms, for it is as a product of sexism that the social is understood in the first place. 'Woman' is constructed in Wise and Stanley's definition as a self-enclosed space: as they say, 'we know ourselves to be whole, complete subjects, who are quite self-contained and quite capable.'[13] The flaw in this argument is that not only do many women not experience themselves as 'whole, complete subjects', often exactly because they have been sexually intruded on in some way, but also that public discourses such as the law similarly fail to recognise the subjecthood of women. Feminist history is full of women fighting for their social and legal construction as 'self-contained' and 'capable' (in relation to the Sex Discrimination Acts, for example). Wise and Stanley's move is a strategic one, since they seek to emphasise women's resistance to sexual harassment as much as their vulnerability to it ('survivor' is a key word here);[14] but there is a political strategy behind the opposite response as well. Exactly because 'women' are constructed and reconstructed, exactly because their subjectivities are never given and whole, those women who have been damaged (whose existence, of course, Wise and Stanley do not seek to deny) can change, and repair the damage. Jacqueline Rose's account of the relation between feminism and psychoanalysis, although undertaken for rather different ends, can help us here with its emphasis on the unconscious:

> The unconscious constantly reveals the 'failure' of identity. Because there is no continuity of psychic life, so there is no stability of sexual identity, no position for women (or for men) which is ever simply achieved. Nor does psychoanalysis see such 'failure' as a special-case inability or an individual deviancy from the norm.[15]

Psychoanalysis is a discourse which has been criticised for denying women's 'public reality' (see Masson for a discussion of Freud's 'suppression' of women's incest),[16] but it can also be seen as producing a vivid, if transposed, account of it. The ubiquity of women's experience of psychic difficulty and disintegration is analogous to, and in many cases caused by, the ubiquity of their sexual harassment and sexual abuse.

Feminist commentaries on sexual harassment, such as Wise and Stanley's or Kelly's, often concentrate on producing 'woman' as a social agent, active in resisting her own oppression. Written into the typical workplace definition which I quoted above from Friedman, Boumil and Taylor is an assumption that 'woman', as a social being, is always produced in subordination to 'man' (he has the power to harass only because he also has the power to hold out benefits in return, or to make the woman feel intimidated). Concealed behind the construction of sexual harassment as a form of intimidation is an assumption that women are already unequal in the workplace before the harassment even starts. Catharine MacKinnon argues that workplace definitions displace attention from one social hierarchy (gender) onto another (employer/employee), to occlude the prior structural oppression of women by men:

> Only when ordinary, everyday affection and flirtation come into the context of another hierarchy is it considered potentially an abuse of power. What is not considered to be a hierarchy is women and men — men on top and women on the bottom.[17]

Nonetheless an assumption of this hierarchy is implicit in definitions of workplace sexual harassment: allegations can only be made if it is believed that repeated and unwanted sexual advances from men to women are by their very nature a form of intimidation, which produce a 'hostile environment'. It is here that workplace definitions come very close to a radical feminist analysis of relations between men and women. Both feminist analyses and workplace definitions take for granted the enormous difficulty that women experience in withholding their consent to sex; both are predicated on the assumption that it is easy for men to coerce women sexually.

I would suggest, then, that it is in response to this uneasy high-lighting of women's social and sexual vulnerability that feminists like Sue Wise and Liz Stanley stress women's agency, their power to resist, their 'self-contained' quality. Another conclusion to be drawn from their analysis of the pervasiveness and banality of many forms of sexual harassment might be, however, that women's spirited resistance merely conceals their inability ever to consent in any meaningful way. Liz Kelly, during her survey of sexual violence, found that she had to construct two new categories of sexual violence, 'pressurized sex' and 'coercive sex', to cover all those situations in which a woman's consent has apparently been given, but in which she knows, in fact, that she has no choice.[18] MacKinnon highlights the same situation in a slightly different way:

> Ask a woman if she has ever been raped, and often she says, 'Well ... not really.' In that silence between the well and the not really, she just measured what happened to her against every rape case she ever heard about and decided she would lose in court.[19]

If the category of harassment depends on a woman's lack of consent, and if consent for women is so problematic as to be virtually meaningless (as in the above examples), then harassment as a category becomes mean-ingless; and so too, as disturbingly, does the notion that women can meaningfully resist. If we cannot effectively consent, we cannot effec-tively refuse, either. As MacKinnon puts it, 'because the inequality of the sexes is socially defined as the enjoyment of sexuality itself, gender inequality appears consensual.'[20]

All this seems miles away from most women's experience, of course. As Wise and Stanley point out:

> Treating men as always and forever, essentially and necessarily, enacters of sexual harassment not only flies in the face of experience, it is also immensely insulting to the large majority of women who choose to have men in their lives. Such women are not stupid and neither are they masochists; rather they have a sophisticated awareness of the subtleties of male behaviour. They know that men needn't be sexist, but can behave in sexist ways at some times and not at others.[21]

As Wise and Stanley put it, 'what women know'[22] is that sexual harassment is a frequent phenomenon, but that consensual heterosexual exchanges are at least as frequent. This more pragmatic approach, which relies on the evidence of individual experience rather than on the analysis of social structures, is I believe simply at odds with the thinking behind both a radical feminist analysis like MacKinnon's, and that behind workplace definitions of sexual harassment. Wise and Stanley state both that women's lives are a constant negotiation of sexually harassing behaviours, and that women freely choose to interact sexually with men. The impossibility of this position is demonstrated by the fact that Wendy Average, their prototype woman, does not consent to a single heterosexual exchange during the course of a typical day. In fact she spends most of her time and energy devising strategies to avoid heterosexual contact.

Workplace definitions of sexual harassment can be read, then, as a recognition that women and men are unequal, and that 'consent', in the workplace, is as problematic as it is anywhere else. The difference is that in the workplace, a social space, activities that are elsewhere constructed as private (that is, sexual activities) are transformed by the context into public behaviours, and therefore become subject to public scrutiny and control. In other words, in the workplace there is no private space (even a locked office after hours signifies a public identity), and gender becomes the sign not of an interior difference (psychological or biological) but of a different relation to the socioeconomic order. This particular understanding of gender seeps into feminist commentaries and surveys on sexual harassment as well: most commentators mention as one of the adverse effects of sexual harassment on women an inability to concentrate on their jobs, and diminished professional performance. Indeed Lin Farley goes so far as to suggest that the minority of women who enjoy behaviour that most women would experience as sexual harassment, enjoy it exactly because they have internalised an image of themselves as women, not workers.[23] The apparent recognition of structural inequality between men and women that we find in workplace definitions is not actually a recognition of women as females, but of workers who are potentially less productive than other workers in the institution. This is precisely the approach, ironically, that disadvantages women as potential employees and has kept women out of the labour market for years.

So how badly does sexual harassment affect women? What are its consequences for women as women, and as workers? Sue Read lists the following possible consequences of sexual harassment for women: nervousness, depression, emotional instability, discontent, fear, anger and an inability to concentrate.[24] She cites a 1982 survey by the Alfred Marks

Employment Bureau in the US, in which eight per cent of all employees reported suffering various forms of physical and depressive illness as a result of sexual harassment. Lin Farley notes that 'ego-functioning' is impaired by this, and that the women concerned suffer a loss of autonomy and control.[25] Constance Backhouse and Leah Cohen mention negative consequences ranging from anger and anxiety, to a 'deep sense of guilt', to stomach-aches, headaches and nausea, and finally to physical or psychological breakdown and hospitalisation.[26] Of course many millions of women are not affected nearly as severely as this, but all commentators agree that women are adversely affected to a greater or lesser degree. Backhouse and Cohen comment:

> Their ordeal is not as graphic as in rape and battering. Sexual harassment takes its toll in a long drawn-out battle of nerves, where the woman is generally the loser. She may lose not only her job, but her self-confidence and self-esteem.[27]

This emphasis on the potential enormity of the effect of sexual harassment on the vast numbers of women who experience it was a part of the movement in the late 1970s and early 1980s to get sexual harassment recognised as a major hazard in the workplace. More recent texts, such as those of Wise and Stanley and Kelly, tend to emphasise women's courage and capacity to 'survive'. But there is still an implicit recognition of the great psychological and physical harm that sexual harassment can do, a harm belied by its name – which implies that the behaviour is a mere irritant: persistent perhaps, but not dangerous.

Yet many definitions of sexual harassment do include sexual assault and rape, and it is at this point that the categorisation of sexual crimes becomes even more blurred. Backhouse and Cohen, Read and Farley note that sexually harassed women are sometimes raped.[28] Friedman, Boumil and Taylor observe that there is sometimes no firm line between sexual harassment and what they call 'date rape';[29] in other words, behaviour that is categorised as sexual harassment can sometimes include rape. At this point a criminal prosecution can be brought (as it cannot for sexual harassment), and the behaviour is reinterpreted as no longer harassment, but crime. Yet for the woman involved this may still be one horrific part of the 'long drawn-out battle of nerves' of which Backhouse and Cohen speak;[30] it still occurs in the context of the workplace and demonstrates a constellation of power relations which includes status, money, relative positions in the organisation, and gender. The legal interpretation of what has happened to the woman, however, leaves behind all the complex structures cited in the sexual harassment guidelines (employment and so on) and constructs the event as purely a matter of biology and of gendered bodies: penetration of the vagina by a penis. Any other relation which the man and the woman have to one another (apart from a blood relationship) is, in the legislation anyway, irrelevant (although, as we all know, if there has been a prior relationship, particularly one of marriage, it will be very hard to get a conviction). 'Woman' here, unlike in the sexual harassment guidelines, means simply 'vagina'. Rape, unlike sexual harassment, is not recognised as an effect of the social. Definitions of rape, unlike those of sexual harassment, refuse to recognise that there may have been hierarchies other than those of the body in place before the attack occurred. It is because of this that feminists have spent so much time seeking to convince the legal profession that rape is far more than a matter of an unwanted penis in a vagina, and that it expresses exactly the same inequalities as other sexually harassing behaviours. Like sexual harassment, rape is a social crime and a mechanism of social control. In Susan Brownmiller's words, 'from prehistoric times to the present, I believe, rape has played a critical function. It is nothing more or less than a conscious process of intimidation by which all men keep all women in a state of fear.'[31] We could say the same of sexual harassment.

It is at this point that we come back to Lisa. Carrie Herbert, discussing the sexual harassment of schoolgirls, comments, in apparent contradiction of my own argument, that 'sexual harassment is not usually a "public" affair.'[32] She means that most of the incidents of sexual harassment experienced by the girls she was working with took place discreetly, when the girl was alone with the perpetrator, and that they left no physical signs. This seems to deny my observation that definitions of sexual harassment construct the workplace as a space in which everything is public. But in fact it does not straightforwardly deny it; it simply draws our attention to the difference between 'woman' and 'girl'. As we have seen, 'woman' in sexual harassment guidelines signifies 'worker', someone in a particular position in the socioeconomic hierarchy: a function of the public world. 'Girl', on the other hand, suggests someone who does not yet have access to the public sphere; it is because of this, among other reasons, that many women find it so offensive to be called 'girls'. (When I was working at a refuge for incest survivors, we took 16 years to be the age at which you progressed from 'girl' to 'woman', since at 16 you were suddenly constructed as capable of a number of social acts: sexual consent, for example.) The harassment which happens to 'girls' can by definition never be public, since 'girl' is not a public category. Unlike an adult woman, a girl can never consent, even if she wants to, and there is no need to specify the particular conditions which produce her sexual harassment: she is always harassed by sex, and her sex is never a social event.

Yet adolescent girls, biologically somewhere between child and woman, are often seen to be on the borderline between harassment and abuse. It is particularly difficult to answer the question with which I began this paper (why is an unwanted male hand on an unwilling female body sometimes called 'sexual harassment' and sometimes called 'sexual abuse'?) in relation to 'girls'. Within the same book there is often a slippage between the two terms when it is teenagers who are under discussion. Carrie Herbert tries to tease out the distinctions between them, using the example of a man fondling a breast:

> If ... the perpetrator was a male teacher and the recipient a female student, this behaviour would be sexual abuse and could be dealt with through the social services or the police. Because the teacher is in a position of responsibility and is *in loco parentis*, it is especially serious, for he is abusing his position as an adult, a teacher and a guardian.
>   If both the recipient and the perpetrator were students and the behaviour came to the attention of the school management, it would most likely be dealt with as sexual harassment, and whilst the female student could press charges, the likelihood is that this would not be recommended because of the lack of witnesses, the age of the perpetrator, prolonging the case and detrimental effect on the recipient.[33]

Here the same action is 'abuse' when the perpetrator is a parental figure, and 'harassment' when the relationship between perpetrator and recipient is similar to that between co-workers: there is not necessarily any private, interiorised relation between them, and their exchanges are assumed to belong to the 'public' world of the school. But between the teacher and the student, the public/private boundary is blurred. The teacher is *in loco parentis*; structurally there is an intimate connection between the teacher and student which makes the girl vulnerable to the private crime of 'abuse', rather than the public one of harassment.

Lisa's insistence on silence and concealment are part of the way we understand abuse as distinct from harassment. The whole point of sexual harassment is that it is a public act, with quantifiable public consequences (a promotion, or an intimidating environment). Friedman, Boumil and Taylor point out that co-workers who have not been sexually harassed can bring a claim of unlawful discrimination if they feel someone else has been given a work-related benefit for sexual reasons.[34] But although sexual abuse within a family affects every member of it, child sexual abuse is constructed as a private crime. Beatrix Campbell, writing about the Cleveland sex abuse controversy,[35] comments:

> Because sexual crime has not been seen as the expression of a social relationship, we have been left with the politics of crime and punishment, from which we all retreat when we are faced with these realities of sexual abuse.[36]

Like rape, sexual abuse is seen to operate outside social hierarchies, behind the closed doors of the family home, and one of its most distressing violations is often said to be of the child's private feeling of trust.[37] As Wise and Stanley point out, child sexual abuse is constructed as an intrapsychic, rather than a social, event.[38] Analytic accounts assume that either the abusing adult, or the family, is dysfunctional, and they seek explanations for the tendency to abuse in the adult's own family history or present role in the family. As Elizabeth Ward points out, 'in the clinical literature, however, one finds no consideration of male-to-female power dynamics, and very little consideration of power as a factor at all.'[39] Sexual abuse is interpreted as a phenomenon of the family as an institution which resists the social, as well as mediating it. David Finkelhor in 1986 suggested that it was exactly that capacity of the family to turn in on itself that was responsible for child sexual abuse: the typical victim in Finkelhor's survey is lonely and isolated, probably living with a stepfather (who will not necessarily be the abuser), with a remote or over-severe mother and with few friends.[40] The point is not whether or not Finkelhor is right, but the way in which he has interpreted his findings to produce child sexual abuse as an asocial crime, which characteristically affects children whose public identities are marginal or insecure. Books like Finkelhor's construct child sexual abuse as a private event that occurs within the inner world of the family.

This construction of sexual abuse as an intrapsychic, rather than a social, event is implicit behind the self-construction of many women who experienced sexual abuse as a child. Beatrix Campbell notes that this is part of its appalling coerciveness:

> Often the child has a dynamic relationship with the abuser, cares for him, and in enduring the abuse takes care of him. To disentangle the child from all that isn't easy: you're facing the child with something about itself, about its participation in a relationship in which it had none of the power but all the responsibility.[41]

Campbell's approach suggests that the effect of child sexual abuse is not simply to refuse the social, but actually to produce a false illusion of a social self for the child, who finds herself constructed as a responsible and consenting adult long before such an identity is a real possibility. It is not so much that child sexual abuse is constructed as a phenomenon of the private sphere as that it enforces a false sociality, encouraging the child to develop a public and private self before the moment at which she is publicly recognised in that way.

The violent construction of the child's 'privacy' by the abuser, a construction which is synonymous with the abuse itself, is constantly alluded to by adult survivors of child sexual abuse. Some survivors have spoken of the way in which a false notion of privacy has structured their psyche into adult life. The process of recovery is the realignment of the public and the private selves. Sylvia Fraser, in her memoir of her incestuous abuse, *My Father's House*, describes the way in which she repressed the memory of her abuse so thoroughly that she became two personalities who did not communicate:

> Though we had split one personality between us, I was the majority shareholder. I went to school, made friends, gained experience, developing my part of the personality, while she remained morally and emotionally a child, functioning on instinct rather than on intelligence. She began as my creature, forced to do what I refused to do, yet because I blotted out her existence, she passed out of my control as completely as a figure in a dream.[42]

Many commentators note the frequency of forgettings such as Fraser's, and in amnesias like hers the social is mapped onto the psychic like a microcosmic reflection of the adult world.[43] The sexual develops as the unconscious of the social, just as the repressed memories of the abused child become the unconscious of the child who believes she has not been abused. It is the family as an institution which provides the bridge between the private and the public, in the same way that for a survivor like Fraser dreams mediate between the unconscious and the conscious selves. Perhaps privacy is never anything more than a familial dream, as a belief in the unconscious is never anything more than a psychoanalytic act of faith. Or we could put it another way round: the family is itself a dream, a way of trying to connect the intractable spaces of public and private experience.

Seen in this light, constructions of the family as an inviolable private space are defences against its dreamlike qualities, its unreality. Incest survivors carry this burden too, as Sylvia Fraser suggests about her other self: 'hers was the guilty face I sometimes glimpsed in my mirror, mocking all my daytime accomplishments, forcing me to reach for a counter-illusion: I was special in a good way. I was a fairytale princess.'[44] As public and private are realigned during the process of recovery, childhood memories and images of the family lose their spectral quality: 'now that my father's house has given up its secrets it has become an old friend, each room a scrapbook of my past, little changed but the flowers on the wallpaper.'[45] The house is no longer one of the dark shadows of the unconscious, but a familiar memory whose corners hold no secrets. In Fraser's book it is symbolic of her own psychic structure, whose repressions are gradually undone as the book (and her life) progresses, and which by the end no longer holds any significantly unfriendly surprises.

The experience of healing is often seen as the transition from a feeling of victimisation to one of victory; from being a 'victim' to being a 'survivor'. Liz Kelly comments that 'feminist activists need to pay far more attention to the language we use', and the deliberate use of the word 'survivor' to refer to those who have experienced sexual crime has been one of feminism's most significant contributions to the literature on sexual harassment and child sexual abuse.[46] Part of its importance lies in its recognition that not all women do survive such trauma;[47] and that those who do have come through a disaster which affects not just one, not just a few, but many women. Jacqueline Spring, in her account of her incest, writes of the painful transformation from 'being victim to being survivor' in the context of a shared recognition and renaming: 'With their help we have peeled ourselves painfully, wonderingly and then joyfully away from our old victim identity, we have rehearsed with them the testing of new outside relationships. We are the lucky ones, the survivors.'[48]

For Spring, as for Fraser, surviving is a renegotiation of private and public spaces which crucially depends on a revised understanding of the social and of intrasubjective relations. No longer burdened with the secret of a private crime, the survivor achieves an authentic privacy and a simultaneous sense of herself as an effective agent in the public world. The realisation that her therapist has a happy private life, that after one session she is going home to watch the Cup Final, fills Spring with an extraordinary joy: 'Eve cared about me. But Eve was not going home to worry about me. Far from it. She was going home to enjoy her life in her own way.'[49] It is her lack of responsibility for maintaining Eve's privacy which frees Spring to redevelop her own: 'what she was telling me was that she would look after herself. I had no responsibility for her. What she was telling me was I would, I could look after myself.'[50] The adult no longer has to carry the child's burden of producing and protecting the privacy of another, whether that other be abuser or therapist. Instead, as a 'survivor', she like the therapist is free to cross and recross the boundaries of private space, and to live simultaneously in the sexual and the social.[51]

For Spring, writing was a crucial mode of access to those boundaries.[52] The small but significant number of autobiographical or poetic accounts of child sexual abuse that I have been mentioning suggests that often part of surviving child sexual abuse is the need to tell, to recreate the experiences and make them public. The search for the right words, the right images, becomes the search for the lost self whose memories are buried in the unconscious. There is even a certain romance or beauty in the process of the search, a romance that Spring makes explicit: 'it grew increasingly sweet to be cared for so intensively and comprehensively by my therapist. Walking up the hill, I feel as if the pink petals of a rose in my breast are opening towards her.'[53] Survivors of sexual harassment, on the other hand, do not on the whole write extended autobiographical accounts of their harassment and their escape from it. Textbooks include case histories, but this is quite a different thing, without the sustained interiority that is characteristic of books like Fraser's or Spring's. Why is there this difference? For if sexual harassment is psychically disturbing in the ways I outlined in the first half of this chapter, we might expect to read as many narratives of recovery and self-definition in cases of sexual harassment as we do for child sexual abuse.

For the answer to this question we need to return to the kinds of argument suggested in the first part of the chapter. Sexual harassment, even while it may have profound implications for the inner life of the woman who experiences it, is defined and experienced as an exteriorisation of femaleness, a making public of the woman's sex and self. Child sexual abuse, on the other hand, as I have suggested, is one of the ways in which a violent patriarchal society produces its own privacy and constructs its own sexuality as a secret matter. The child finds it difficult to tell because confused beliefs about children's credibility and agency block their access to the public world. Even when the abuse is exposed and punished, more often than not it continues to be interpreted as the idiosyncratic response of one dysfunctional individual or family. The survivor's response is shaped and determined by the nature of the abuse she suffered, so that the woman who has been sexually harassed seeks to reconstruct herself as 'woman' and 'worker'; and the woman who was sexually abused as a child seeks to reinterpret her own interiority, her own 'womanliness'. Because of this, interpretations of sexual harassment, even feminist ones, obscure the private psychic impact of sexual harassment on women, and research into child sexual abuse often underestimates the significance of the social for the forms and consequences of this kind of sexual crime. Women and girls everywhere urgently need a rethinking of our notions of what the public and the private are, of their relations to one another, and of the categories of 'girl' and 'woman' themselves. For our understanding of sexual violence against women depends on our understanding of these concepts, and our understanding of sexual violence shapes our response to it. If Lisa's desperate silence has taught me anything, it has taught me that the sexual and the social are not predetermined categories which construct a safe and reliable relation to the world, but that they are in themselves dangerous models for thought, and even more dangerous spaces for experience.

Notes and References

1. Liz Kelly, *Surviving Sexual Violence* (Cambridge: Polity, 1988).
2. Joel Friedman, Marcia Boumil and Barbara Taylor, *Sexual Harassment: What It Is, What It Isn't, What It Does to You and What You Can Do about It* (Deerfield Beach, Fla.: Health Communications, 1992), p. vi.
3. Sue Wise and Liz Stanley, *Georgie Porgie: Sexual Harassment in Everyday Life* (London: Pandora, 1987), p. 30.
4. Constance Backhouse and Leah Cohen, *The Secret Oppression: Sexual Harassment of Working Women* (Toronto: Macmillan, 1978); Ann Sedley and Melissa Benn, *Sexual Harassment at Work* (London: National Council for Civil Liberties, 1982); Sue Read, *Sexual Harassment at Work* (Feltham: Hamlyn, 1982).
5. Wise and Stanley, *Georgie Porgie*, p. 204.
6. Read, *Sexual Harassment at Work*, p. 9.
7. Lin Farley, *Sexual Shakedown: The Sexual Harassment of Women on the Job* (New York: Warner, 1980) p. 33.
8. Wise and Stanley, *Georgie Porgie*, p. 43.
9. Both quotations are from Wise and Stanley, *Georgie Porgie*, p. 71.
10. Wise and Stanley, *Georgie Porgie*, pp. 116–20.
11. Wise and Stanley, *Georgie Porgie*, p. 43.
12. Wise and Stanley, *Georgie Porgie*, p. 71.
13. Wise and Stanley, *Georgie Porgie*, p. 82.
14. Wise and Stanley, *Georgie Porgie*, p. 67.
15. Jacqueline Rose, *Sexuality in the Field of Vision* (London: Verso, 1986), p. 91.
16. J.M. Masson, *The Assault on Truth: Freud's Suppression of the Seduction Theory* (Harmondsworth: Penguin, 1985).
17. Catharine A. MacKinnon, *Feminism Unmodified: Discourses on Life and Law* (Cambridge, Mass. and London: Harvard University Press, 1987), p. 89.
18. Kelly, *Surviving Sexual Violence*, p. 78.
19. MacKinnon, *Feminism Unmodified*, p. 105.
20. MacKinnon, *Feminism Unmodified*, p. 7.
21. Wise and Stanley, *Georgie Porgie*, p. 130.
22. Wise and Stanley, *Georgie Porgie*, p. 129.
23. Farley, *Sexual Shakedown*, pp. 42–3.

24. Read, *Sexual Harassment at Work*, p. 22.
25. Farley, *Sexual Shakedown*, p. 36.
26. Backhouse and Cohen, *The Secret Oppression*, pp. 45–6.
27. Backhouse and Cohen, *The Secret Oppression*, p. 50.
28. Backhouse and Cohen, *The Secret Oppression*, p. 38; Read, *Sexual Harassment at Work*, p. 28; Farley, *Sexual Shakedown*, p. 33.
29. Friedman, Boumil and Taylor, *Sexual Harassment*, p. 45.
30. Backhouse and Cohen, *The Secret Oppression*, p. 50.
31. Susan Brownmiller, *Against Our Will: Men, Women and Rape* (New York: Bantam, 1976), p. 5.
32. Carrie Herbert, *Talking of Silence: The Sexual Harassment of Schoolgirls* (London: Falmer, 1989), p. 33.
33. Carrie Herbert, *Sexual Harassment in Schools: A Guide for Teachers* (London: David Fulton, 1992), p. 74.
34. Friedman, Boumil and Taylor, *Sexual Harassment*, pp. 35–6.
35. In summer 1987, two paediatricians at Middlesborough General Hospital in Cleveland, Dr Marietta Higgs and Dr Geoffrey Wyatt, were suspended after they diagnosed 121 cases of suspected child sexual abuse between spring and early summer of that year. Their diagnoses relied partly on the controversial 'anal dilation' test. A judicial enquiry headed by Lord Elizabeth Butler-Sloss reported ambiguously in 1988.
36. Beatrix Campbell, *Unofficial Secrets: Child Sexual Abuse – The Cleveland Case* (London: Virago, 1988), p. 5.
37. See, for example, Jean Renvoize, *Innocence Destroyed: A Study of Child Sexual Abuse* (London: Routledge, 1993), p. 146.
38. Wise and Stanley, *Georgie Porgie*, pp. 199–200.
39. Elizabeth Ward, *Father–Daughter Rape* (London: Women's Press, 1984), p. 142.
40. David Finkelhor, *A Sourcebook on Child Sexual Abuse* (London: Sage, 1986), pp. 71–80.
41. Campbell, *Unofficial Secrets*, p. 9.
42. Sylvia Fraser, *My Father's House: A Memoir of Incest and of Healing* (London: Virago, 1987), p. 24.
43. See, for example, Renvoize, *Innocence Destroyed*, pp. 145 and 150; Kelly, *Surviving Sexual Violence*, pp. 143–4.
44. Fraser, *My Father's House*, p. 15.
45. Fraser, *My Father's House*, p. 234.
46. Kelly, *Surviving Sexual Violence*, p. 157.
47. See Toni A.H. McNaron and Yarrow Morgan (eds), *Voices in the Night: Women Speaking about Incest* (Pittsburgh and San Francisco: Cleis, 1982), pp. 166–7, for a discussion of these issues.

48. Jacqueline Spring, *Cry Hard and Swim: The Story of an Incest Survivor* (London: Virago, 1987), pp. 158–9.
49. Spring, *Cry Hard and Swim*, p. 75.
50. Spring, *Cry Hard and Swim*, p. 75.
51. See Louise Armstrong, 'Surviving the Incest Industry', *Trouble and Strife* 21 (Summer 1991), pp. 29–32. Armstrong objects to the 'institutionalisation of speaking out on incest' (p. 29), and comments that therapy's construction of the 'survivor' implies that incest is an illness from which the victim must heal, rather than a 'socially accepted violation' to which the most appropriate response is 'social change' and 'rage' (p. 30).
52. Spring, *Cry Hard and Swim*, pp. 96–7.
53. Spring, *Cry Hard and Swim*, p. 24.

Part III
Contexts

8

Seventy Times Seven?
Forgiveness and Sexual
Violence in Christian
Pastoral Care

Ros Hunt

And Jesus told them a parable to the effect that they ought always to pray and not lose heart. He said,

> In a certain city there was a judge who neither feared God nor regarded man; and there was a widow in that city who kept coming to him and saying, 'Vindicate me against my adversary.' For a while he refused; but afterward he said to himself, 'Though I neither fear God nor regard man, yet because this widow bothers me, I will vindicate her, or she will wear me out by her continual coming.' And the Lord said, 'Hear what the unrighteous judge says. And will not God vindicate his elect, who cry to him day and night? I tell you he will vindicate them speedily.'[1]

This parable told by Jesus is one that many who have suffered sexual harassment or sexual abuse have claimed for themselves. In particular they identify with those crying out to the unjust judge, whom they see as representative of a church hierarchy indifferent to their suffering. They, like the widow, demand justice. However deaf Christian churches[2] are to the justice of their case, those who have been harassed or abused nevertheless feel that their constant demand will eventually wear down the authorities until they are vindicated. God will hear the justice of their case; they are his elect; 'he will vindicate them speedily.'

The mainstream Christian churches have apparently failed to hear the cries of those who have been harassed or abused.[3] One indication of their failure to respond is that there are no official liturgies dealing with recovery from rape, abuse or harassment. Most churches have liturgies consisting usually of prayers and biblical readings to mark the passing of life events such as birth, marriage and death. As well as these, which are to be found in the prayer books that many church members own, other books are used as supplements, books of which usually only the clergy are aware. One example would be *The Pocket Ritual* used by Roman Catholics and some Anglicans, which contains prayers for all occasions, including such matters as the blessing of a home or a car. However, there are no prayers or liturgies for recovery from violence.

This gap has begun to be filled by women who have started writing their own prayers and rituals. Perhaps the earliest example was that of a rape exorcism service at a women's conference in Union Theological Seminary in New York in 1973.[4] Such liturgies were included in the Women Moving Church conference in 1981.[5] Soon examples of these liturgies were published, such as those to be found in *Womanchurch* by Rosemary Radford Reuther.[6] Other groups such as the Philadelphia Task Force on Religion and Women also produced liturgies, and as these materials became more widely disseminated other women's groups began writing services to answer their own particular needs.[7] Of course, liturgy is not confined to that to which church authorities have given a stamp of approval; as soon as prayers are used in a public context, they become liturgy. As yet the churches have taken no steps to incorporate such liturgies into prayer books. It is not clear from this whether the liturgy commissions and groups responsible for official formulation and publication are unaware both of the pastoral need for and the existence of unofficial liturgies, or whether they feel that it would be inappropriate to include them in prayer books. Perhaps the most useful prayers to be found in official liturgies are in the *Book of Occasional Offices of the Episcopal Church of the United States of America*, in which the healing service contains a prayer that asks God 'to drive away all sickness of body and spirit, and to give you that victory of life and peace which will enable you to serve you both now and evermore'. The *New Zealand Episcopal Prayer Book* includes a section of prayers for use in critical situations, for instance 'for people facing the loss of a limb or serious impairment'. Many of these prayers can be adapted, but it is the experience of those who work pastorally with those who have been harassed or abused that something more specific and direct is required. It is also the case, especially for those who have been sexually abused as children, that the word 'healing' is loaded and fraught with difficulty, particularly in a Christian context. The very existence of a prayer marked, for instance, 'for someone who has been abused' assures those who have been abused that their pain is legitimate, that their position is acknowledged and that similar things have been done to someone other than themselves.

Many of those who have experienced sexual violence find that the wording of official liturgies in common use not only does not answer their needs, but also contributes to their pain. For many, if their abusers were their fathers, emphasis on the imagery of God as Father is painful. There are many other biblical images of God which can be used – God is judge, king, landowner, potter, our rock, our fortress, our defence, our shield and so on – but official liturgies show a reluctance to use them. Many liturgies emphasise the sinfulness of human beings, and the faithful are exhorted to confess their sins in words such as, 'If we say we have no sin we deceive ourselves and the truth is not in us. But if we confess our sins, God who is faithful and just will forgive our sins and cleanse us from all unrighteousness.'[8] Those who have been abused or harassed are quick to see themselves as sinful, especially because they have frequently been told they are so by their perpetrators, and often by their clergy; they are eager and willing to take the blame for what has been done to them and think that confessing 'their' sin will perhaps make them feel better. Experience shows that this does not happen.

Texts which are difficult occur all the time. For instance, from the Church of England post-communion prayer, the line addressed to God, 'We offer you our souls and bodies to be a living sacrifice', is difficult for those who feel that for the duration of their childhood their souls and bodies were just that – a living sacrifice.[9] It is all very well to object that such an interpretation disregards the original context, but these words also have a contemporary context, which is harmful to those who have been abused.

Besides the absence or difficulties of liturgy in the mainstream churches in Britain, there are also no official church policies against harassment, or codes which make it clear that abuse is unprofessional.[10] Although we may disagree on just how useful policies are, or can be made to be, a commitment to establishing a policy does at least show an understanding that there is a problem which needs consideration. However clumsy and inadequate policies may turn out to be in practice, the formation of them can be a consciousness-raising exercise; the process of accepting there is an issue that has to be tackled, the attempt to define the problem, and the phrasing of policies to deal with the perceived problems and the use of them are in themselves a learning process. A publicised policy gives the ordinary churchgoer assurance that those in authority accept that such an act as sexual harassment might be committed, even by a member of the clergy, and that it is a serious issue worthy of time and attention. The very existence of a policy assures those who have been harassed or abused that something unacceptable has taken place, that the institutional church sees it as a breach of correct behaviour and that those who have suffered are not to blame for what has been done. From the ways in which reports of harassment and abuse are currently being handled, it appears that senior church

leaders feel that any accusations, even if substantiated, are best dealt
with as privately as possible and without involving criminal investiga-
tions by the police. Set procedures might at least help appropriate and
responsible action to be taken.

On the other hand, policies and procedures often do not succeed in
obtaining the desired result. Policies can distance those who write them
and whose responsibility it is to enforce them from those whom policies
are meant to empower, and this does not produce good pastoral care.
The way in which a code of practice has to be followed may well frame
a person's story in a way which she or he does not wish, or in a way
which is unhelpful to her or him. With an increasing number of cases
reported in the press, it is clear that churches in Britain, as in the United
States, will have to act to show that they are addressing the issues, in
order both to gain public credibility and to deal with pending legal suits.

In the United States, there are Roman Catholic dioceses that have been
refused insurance because there have been too many claims of compensation against abusing clergy.[11] The Roman Catholic church in the
United States expects to pay US $1 billion in court costs by the year 2000.[12]
There is a danger of some dioceses going bankrupt.[13] In the courts, where
churches have been deemed to have failed in their responsibility
adequately to train and supervise their ministers, cases are being found
against them.[14] It is worth noting that churches are being sued not for
acts of abuse by their ministers, but for an institutional failure to handle
cases of sexual harassment properly. In 1991 the Episcopal diocese of
Colorado was found liable for $1.2 million in damages for its mishan-
dling of a case of ministerial misconduct.[15] In the United States, the
Church Insurance Company is now one of the few insurance companies
that will insure against clergy sexual misconduct.[16] However, it will not
include such insurance in its basic multiperil policy; churches now have
to purchase separate coverage. In order to buy this insurance, churches
have to fulfil certain requirements. These include the introduction of
policies and procedural manuals (the insurance company is running
training days in various parts of the United States to show how this can
be done), provision of education on sexual misconduct, background
checks on employees, limitations on pastoral counselling, and stringent
reemployment procedures after an instance of sexual misconduct. There
are also guidelines on hiring and training personnel in children's and
youth ministry, while those seeking insurance are required to provide
four hours of training on child sexual abuse both to church employees
and to volunteers supervising youth ministry.[17]

Of course, it must be remembered that these cases are occurring in a
society which sees the law both as the first recourse and as an appropriate recourse. Up to now the law has not been the forum in which

people in Britain have chosen to work out such cases. This may change, however. Ecclesiastical Insurance, the English equivalent of the Church Insurance Company in the United States, does not insure against clergy misconduct. Meanwhile, it is interesting that insurance companies, those whose business is to know about risk limitation, consider education and training to be basic prerequisites for reducing the occurrence of clergy sexual misconduct.[18] Of course, the risk that the insurance company is trying to limit is not the risk to the injured party, but the risk to the church, the employers of those who commit the offence. It is, however, outrageous that it is financial factors which are pushing churches to institute training and policies on these issues, rather than awareness that the Christian faith calls for justice and that sexual harassment and sexual abuse are cases of profound injustice.

Justice is indeed a major claim of the Christian faith. Again and again the God of the Hebrew scriptures calls the chosen people to be a people of justice. God says, 'Rather, is this not the fast that I choose: to loose the bonds of wickedness, to undo the thongs of the yoke, to let the oppressed go free, and to break every yoke?'[19] Or, again, 'The Lord has told you what is good: and what does the Lord require of you but to do justice, and to love kindness, and to walk humbly with your God?'[20] This is the tenor of the life and teaching of Jesus throughout his earthly ministry. He seeks justice for those who are oppressed by society, and especially for those who experience discrimination and injustice at the hands of religious authorities. In the story of the healing of the woman bent double, Jesus heals a woman in the synagogue on the Sabbath day.[21] When the synagogue official complains that Jesus has transgressed the law by working on the Sabbath, Jesus points out that the law allows for an ox or donkey to be freed from its stall on the Sabbath in order for it to drink, so, equally, this human person should be freed from her illness. Similarly, Jesus heals a man with a withered hand on the Sabbath.[22] In this instance, he was being watched by the Pharisees to see if he would break the law. Jesus points out that it is acceptable for someone to rescue a sheep from a pit on the Sabbath, 'and a man is worth much more than a sheep'.[23] In both these stories, the Pharisees seek to maintain the authority of the Torah by sticking to the letter of the law. In contrast and in seeking after justice, Jesus considers that it is possible to transgress a strict interpretation of the law in order to assist someone in need.

We see then that institutional churches, insurance companies and those who have been harassed or abused all want the same results – the end of harassment and abuse – but for very different reasons. Where these reasons coincide, there is the possibility of productive and positive change. But where does that impetus for such change originate? The Church of England, for instance, fought very hard to be excluded from the Sex Discrimination Act 1975; women clergy are not entitled to maternity leave. It would seem unlikely that such an institution would take up a progressive position with regard to the sexual misconduct of clergy.

What is happening at the moment is woefully inadequate. When Roman Catholic priests are moved from parish to parish for no apparent reason and with no explanation, cover-ups may be be suspected. In many cases, nothing is done to restrict the areas of responsibility of such priests. Senior clergy are acting under the mistaken impression that they are serving their churches well by acting in this way. In fact the public reputation of their churches suffers because people feel that they have been deceived, more children and young people are abused, and frequently those who have been abused by members of the clergy become estranged from their churches. One leading bishop disagrees with this practice. On the institution of his diocesan policy on sexual abuse, the Roman Catholic bishop of Chicago said, 'I accept the clinical data which suggests that once it has been demonstrated that a priest is an abuser, he should never again return to parish ministry or any ministry which might place a child at risk.'[24]

For all the distinctiveness of what clergy are and do, certain aspects of their roles do overlap with other professionals, such as counsellors, social workers, doctors and therapists. They are one group among many to whom people look in times of crisis, as well as in the course of day-to-day living and working. These professionals all have a responsibility and a duty to act in an appropriate professional manner. In Britain at the moment, clergy are ambivalent about having a 'professional' status. Some, especially Church of England clergy, see a long history of the vicar as a professional man. At the same time, there is also a definite anti-professional model: a picture of a bumbling, unworldly, kindly old vicar who is harmless and humorous. Some clergy resist seeing themselves as professionals because the word has acquired negative associations – with yuppies, cold-heartedness, the greediness of big business and so on. But 'professional' also has positive connotations; it can mean that the clergyperson has specialist training in certain areas, and skills and experience that he or she has acquired, which can be used to benefit the member of the congregation who is consulting him or her.

In general, ministers see much more of some members of their congregations than most other professionals see their clients or patients. They will tend to spend much more time together, either on church committees and at meetings, or at social events. It is perfectly normal for a priest or minister to receive invitations to parishioners' homes or invitations to meals, and this is an appropriate part of his/her role. Added to this, it is often appropriate that clergy know the intimate details of their parishioners' lives; they care about them and pray for and with them.

Different denominations traditionally view their clergy in different ways. Some branches of Christianity, notably most Evangelicals and the Free Churches, emphasise the model of the church as family. These traditions imply that it is the duty of the minister to have emotional involvements with all members of the congregation regardless of age, as a father would properly have with his children. For Roman Catholics, one of the rationales for celibacy is that it enables the priest to have the same love and tenderness for all members of the parish, implying a rather deeper intimacy than would be proper in any other professional relationship.

It is clear from this that the distinctions between what is social and what is work are more blurred in the life of a minister than they are in most professions. It is part of the clergy's job to socialise with parishioners. It is therefore correspondingly more difficult for the clergyperson to see that he/she has professional boundaries to observe. Most clergy have personal friendships or relationships with members of their congregations; most have experienced sexual attraction to someone in the congregation, or have received sexual invitations from someone in their pastoral care, and many have crossed the professional boundary at some time or another. They have not considered the powerful position which they occupy in relation to their parishioners; the minister is the one with experience and training; he or she is the one being consulted; he or she is not in the midst of making a difficult personal decision, or in the throes of a crisis; the minister's role in the church is one of power with respect to the members of the congregation. Added to this, in each individual circumstance more power may lie with the minister through sex, age, colour, financial security, education and language skills. The minister should always be aware of this situation and, as the one with power, he or she is also the one responsible for maintaining appropriate boundaries.

The other professionals listed above may be said to have similar responsibilities to those of the clergy with respect to their use of power. However, for the minister there are added complications to deal with. For instance, there is the Christian assumption that all people are equal before God. This gives an impression of equality in the relationship between minister and parishioner which may hide the power relationship that really exists. Many clergy may well object here that they not only minister to their congregations, but that they are ministered to by their congregations as well. This is true; no one would deny that a teacher may well learn from his/her students, but that is not the primary reason for the relationship.[25] In the same way a minister or priest may well receive help and support from parishioners, but this is not the reason for the existence of the relationship. As with other professionals, the minister should not be seeking to have his or her personal needs met by parishioners.

Some would question whether it is entirely inappropriate for a minister to sexualise a relationship with someone in his/her pastoral care. It may be argued that it is perfectly permissable, for instance, for a minister to go out with someone from his/her congregation. If such a mutual desire for a relationship other than the professional one is found to exist, then this should be acknowledged, and the minister should cease being pastor or priest to that person while the other relationship is explored. A dual role of intimate friend and confessor or counsellor is inappropriate and should be avoided.

So what happens when a minister feels it appropriate to give a distressed parishioner a hug? Touch is important; we know that as human beings, in order to thrive, we need to be touched. In itself, touch is morally neutral, neither good nor bad. However, we all know when we receive touches that are comforting or feel good, and when we receive touches that make us uncomfortable or feel bad. The person giving the touch may have only good intentions, but the intention does not determine how that touch is received. There are too many unknowns. It does not take into account the way the receiver feels about touch generally, how she or he is feeling at that moment, her or his previous history of being touched or history of being abused, what her or his choice at that particular time is, and so on. Exactly the same action could be received in many different ways, depending on the situation and experience of the recipient. Thus a pastor can give what is meant as a supportive hug and is experienced as sexual harassment.[26]

If a clergyman does abuse or harass a member of his congregation intentionally, how does this differ from a similar situation where, say, a doctor harasses a patient or a therapist harasses a client? In many ways the situation seems very similar; a professional working from a more powerful position uses that position to take advantage of someone in a less powerful position. There may be confusion on the part of the person harassed; there may be the suggestion, stated or implied, that what has been done has been done for the good of the client or to help the patient. The client or patient, firm in the idea that the helping professional knows best, may consent to what has been done. The professional has authority; and the complainant may have made a mistake, may have misunderstood or may not be believed because of the offender's professional position.

In the situation where the offender is a minister or priest, these beliefs are, if anything, emphasised. It is more difficult for the person who has been abused or harassed to believe that the minister can possibly be doing anything wrong, and if that is so for the one who has been abused or harassed, it is also the case for anyone to whom she or he tries to disclose what has been done. The offender is protected from suspicion by the office of minister or priest and by the expectation of goodness and holiness that that position carries with it. The priest is seen in some traditions as representing God and mediating God's love and forgiveness, so the priest speaks and acts with God-given authority. In other traditions, the minister is one especially chosen by God to carry out God's preordained plan. In both cases the minister or priest is holy and it is difficult to challenge what is said or done by such individuals. Added to this are fears that any disclosure of what has been done will lead to the church or denomination having a lower public image, so loyalty to the group inhibits such a disclosure. Moreover, the one who has suffered harassment will see that any disclosure may well remove a source of spiritual nourishment and social support. Many ministers are able to carry out their work successfully because they have charismatic personalities. To make an accusation against someone who has such a personality is very difficult, especially when such a minister has a particular reputation for holiness.

When an accusation of sexual harassment is made, standard responses by professionals include statements that the accuser is mentally unstable and/or is obsessed with the professional concerned, and that the whole story is a fantasy. When the harasser is a clergyman, he has additional refutations available. The accuser is sinful, or even possessed by the devil and in urgent need of spiritual healing. What is certain is that one of the two parties concerned must be lying, and the implication is that as it is the minister or priest who has greater spiritual maturity, then it is the member of the congregation who is at fault. The greatest error that the minister or priest will admit to is an error of judgement.

Most clergy training does not address these problems. Subjects such as appropriate boundaries, the role of the cleric, and clerical power and responsibility are barely touched on. Training usually concentrates on academic matters at the expense of pastoral ones. This lack of discussion, or even acknowledgement that such issues exist, contributes to ignorance and the unthought-out crossing of professional boundaries.

It is not only in the field of professional ethics that clergy lack training, but in the whole realm of sexual harassment and sexual abuse. In a society where it is estimated that as many as one in four girls and one in seven boys will have experienced some sort of sexual abuse by the time they reach the age of 18, this is a great gap in pastoral training. Of course not everyone can be an expert in every field, but it is essential that pastors should have some basic knowledge of sexual violence and the effects which it can have on people, so that when they are approached on this subject they do not do additional harm. It may well be appropriate for them to refer parishioners to some more experienced organisation, but they should at least have some awareness of the issues raised by sexual harassment and sexual abuse, and the additional problems that may exist for a Christian in dealing with what has been done to her or him.

Let us take the case of a priest of the Church of England who has a charismatic personality and a reputation for great spirituality. Because of this, he has many young people coming to him for training in a life of prayer. Some of the young men share his house and follow his suggestions to improve their spiritual life. He begins to tell one or two that they have particular gifts in this area, and that if they follow his teaching they have the potential to be very holy indeed. He then starts introducing them to penitential practices, with which he helps and from which he gains sexual satisfaction. They are perhaps surprised at the form of some of the things which he insists are necessary for their spiritual growth but, since he is such a holy man, and seen as such by the rest of the church, they think that he must be right and so they submit to him. This continues for many years as young men join and leave his household. Those who have been singled out for his especial favours move on confused and upset by their experiences. They are unable to tell others for a variety of reasons; they are not entirely sure who else has received such attentions; they after all did consent to what was done to them; the man who has taught them continues to receive the approval of the church and to gain preferment, although rumours of what has happened in his house are rife. The church authority does not check up on this priest. When one young man finally approaches the police and the priest is charged, others come forward to confirm what he has been doing. He accepts a police caution and resigns.[27] The story reaches the press, and on the resignation of the priest the church authorities express regret that such a fine man who has done so much good work should suffer such accusations, saying what a loss he will be to the church. Nothing is said publicly that what he has done is wrong and abusive; no regret is expressed about what the young men have suffered; and the priest in his resignation statement to the press does not even apologise for what he has done. Contrast this with the real situation of Archbishop Alphonsus Penney of Newfoundland, who heard reports of child sexual abuse by religious for 15 years and did nothing. When the case finally came to light and was reported in the press, he resigned, saying to the abused youngsters:

We are a sinful Church ... Our anger, our pain, our anguish, our shame and our vulnerability are clear to the whole world ... We are sorry for the times you were not believed, were not supported or were ostracised in any way by the community. For every word and action that has deepened your pain, we are profoundly sorry.[28]

Returning to the hypothetical case of the Anglican vicar, how does this make the young men who suffered abuse at his hands feel? They are apparently not believed; the church offers them little in the way of support and indeed its apparent indifference to them compounds the abuse they have already suffered. They are effectively silenced from telling their stories elsewhere because of the church's apparent disbelief or unconcern. How does this fit in with the faith which they have been trying to follow, and the teaching about a God who loves all people and loves justice? They are alienated from the support of others in the church, feel that they perhaps are in some way to blame, or have been stupid, and have no way of seeing that they were the victims of abusive behaviour with which the church has colluded. The church has colluded because it has failed to protect the vulnerable; it has not inspected the way in which the priest led his life, although well aware of the way in which his house was run. It has allowed one man to have immense power and total responsibility for many young lives without providing any framework of accountability. It has failed to act on previous complaints other than to censure the man privately. When the press reports an incident, the church's statements are all concerned with supporting the priest in question, with no mention of what those whom he has abused have suffered.

There are endless horror stories that can be told. A woman goes to her priest and tells him that for years her older brother has been sexually abusing her. He listens and responds by telling her that she should go to confession so that she can confess her sins of impurity. Nothing is said about his sin; the implication is that the priest considers it is somehow her fault that her brother abused her.[29] Another woman who is helping to organise a study day on sexual abuse and the church puts up a poster in her church; her vicar promptly asks her, in public, if she has been abused. A woman from a Free Church tradition is told by her pastor that she is not recovering from the rape she has suffered because she is blocking the healing that God wants to give her; again, somehow it is her fault! A pastor who has had intercourse with a 17-year-old member of his congregation tells his colleagues that it wasn't his fault because she was very provocative and asked for his special attentions. His colleagues hear this and blame the young woman for what the pastor has done. The consequence is that she is unable to return to her own

church; when she tries to go to another church in the same neighbourhood she is looked upon with suspicion by the pastor of that
church, and seen as someone who is likely to cause trouble.

A Methodist woman goes to her minister to discuss her marriage, which
has run into difficulties. In the privacy of his study, he makes comments
on her figure and dress and begins to fondle her. When he tries to kiss
her, she leaves and complains to his superiors. She is blamed for what
he has done and ends up having to leave that congregation. Yet another
woman goes to her vicar because she wants to talk about being sexually
abused by her father when she was a child. She is not actually blamed
for what has been done to her, but he questions if perhaps she didn't
do something to encourage him. Or perhaps her memory is not entirely
accurate and the passage of time means that she misremembers what
happened. Her father, after all, is a fine upstanding member of the
community and has been a church warden for many years. Another
woman who was abused as a child by a group of people, which included
the curate, goes to see his bishop to complain about what was done to
her. He suggests that she should simply go and see the perpetrator and
discuss it with him.

In many of these cases it seems impossible for ministers to act with
such insensitivity. Surely, one would think, such instances must be rare
or isolated? One has only to talk to Christian survivors of sexual abuse
and those who have been sexually harassed by their clergy to realise
that these stories are normative. For people who confide in their clergy
to receive such reactions compounds their guilt, shame, distress and other
negative feelings about themselves. They often feel that they have been
abused again by the church to whom they have turned for help when
they are dealt with in such ways.

Another major factor against the disclosure of abuse by a minister or
priest is that the teaching of the Christian churches has always emphasised
forgiveness. Someone who has been harassed or abused is likely to
think that even if a minister has acted wrongly or unprofessionally, that
she/he should be trying to forgive him. It is what her/his Christian faith
requires of her/him. Such a prevalent view comes from an inadequate
teaching of what forgiveness is, or should be. Most clergy would agree
with this, but if this is said, then it becomes the woman's fault for misunderstanding and the responsibility once again becomes hers; she
has misinterpreted the nature of forgiveness. This entirely sidesteps the
fact that forgiveness is a much discussed theme in Christian circles;
ministers and priests have preached on it, hymns are sung, prayers are
said, lessons are read about it. Moreover, the churches have taught what
forgiveness is through tradition and through stories, lives and examples
held up to be followed. Similarly, if women say that they find the

image they have of God is frightening or violent, they are told they have a mistaken concept of God. This may be true, but these 'mistaken ideas' are predominantly learned in church.

One way in which faith is taught and informed is through the lives and actions of the saints. They are held up as examples to be followed. We do not see as frequently as we once did the children's books of lives of the saints, although they are still to be found in religious bookshops and on church bookstalls. The most popular in Roman Catholic or Anglo-Catholic churches were those that divided saints' stories into gendered collections such as *The Boys' Book of Saints* and *The Girls' Book of Saints*. Each book told the story of those saints whom children were supposed to emulate. Maria Goretti was a favourite subject of the books for girls. The story of the canonisation of Maria Goretti in the twentieth century is perhaps one of the most unhelpful to women who have suffered or been threatened with male sexual violence. This is in fact a story of a sexual attack, with previous sexual harassment, and one of the few stories in the martyrology that deals with this sort of subject. For the girls and women who read these stories and were expected to live as Maria Goretti did, defending their virginity at all costs, there were few other discourses to draw upon – and this continues to be the most readily available. A recent study of child sexual abuse within Christian families, *Christianity and Incest*, includes interviews with ten Christian women who are survivors of sexual abuse. Two of them cite the story of Maria Goretti as a childhood memory of an example to follow.[30]

At the age of twelve, Maria was attacked by one of her family's lodgers who, although he claimed insanity as a defence, was found by the courts to be responsible for his actions. For some time he pestered her for sexual favours and then, having set up a situation where they would be alone in the house together, he threatened to stab her if she did not allow him to have intercourse with her. She resisted and he stabbed her repeatedly. She died of her wounds the next day, having forgiven him for what he had done. When she was canonised in 1950 and made the patron of Catholic youth, Pope Pius XII said of her that 'sustained by divine grace and the response of the firm resolution of her will, she laid down her life and preserved her glorious virginity'.[31] In her canonisation articles it was said, 'In her, holy mother Church also honours innumerable others who in similar circumstances preferred death to dishonour.'[32] What is the Roman Catholic church saying to women if it teaches that God would prefer a twelve-year-old girl to be dead rather than to lose her virginity? What message is given to women about their worth if the church considers it more praiseworthy for them to allow themselves to be stabbed to death rather than submit to rape? What does this say to women who have not given up their lives in defence of their 'honour'?

It is also interesting to note that, in the case of Maria Goretti, the pre-conditions for declaring someone a martyr were changed. Until her case, a martyr had to die bearing witness to an article of the Christian faith. Since virginity is not an article of the Christian faith, a new category was invented – bearing witness to the Christian way of life. It was Maria's responsibility to 'preserve her virtue' and remain 'pure and unsullied'.[33] The church then holds up the virtue of this young woman forgiving her would-be rapist as an example. One of the pamphlets telling Maria's story explains that the priest who came to give her the last rites reminded her that Jesus on the cross forgave his murderers.[34] It goes on to say, 'She seemed to reflect. Her eyes rested upon the crucifix upon the wall. Then with the voice expressive of her generous soul, she explained: "I, too, pardon him. I, too, wish that he come some day and join me in heaven".'[35] This is in fact the muddling of two parts of the Passion story as told by St Luke. Christ did not forgive those who put Him to death, but commended them to His father, 'Father, forgive them; for they know not what they do.'[36] In speaking with the two robbers who were crucified with Him, Jesus says to one of them, 'Truly, I say to you, today you will be with me in Paradise.'[37] There is no obvious reason for this confusion other than it fits the point the pamphlet writer is trying to make; he presumably is attempting to prepare the ground for what he knows to come afterwards – the conversion and release of Maria's murderer.

Alexander Serenelli was captured and sentenced to 30 years' hard labour for the murder of Maria Goretti. At first he denied that he had committed the crime, then he tried to plead insanity. As Godfrey Poage puts it:

> For the first eight years of imprisonment he was reported to be an ugly and difficult prisoner. Then in 1910, according to testimony he gave, he had a dream. He said he dreamed of Maria who was gathering lilies in a field. She turned to him and the lilies became radiant and she gave them to him. Mr. Serenelli said it was that dream that convinced him that he was forgiven. He became a model prisoner and was finally freed by an amnesty twenty-seven years after the murder.[38]

On Christmas Eve 1937 he asked the forgiveness of Maria's mother, Assunta Goretti. 'Maria forgave you, Alexander,' she answered, 'so how could I possibly refuse?'[39] The story continues that the next day, Christmas Day, mother and murderer received communion together. Both were also present at Maria's beatification and canonisation. In the process towards canonisation, among other objections, the devil's advocate[40] objected that Maria hesitated before pardoning her assassin, that she may have provoked him and that she should have disclosed earlier the fact that Serenelli was harassing her – the implication being that she had been enjoying his attentions. It is interesting that the issues of her forgiveness and its timing delayed the process of canonisation.

For Christians, the life that must be imitated above all others is the life of Jesus Christ. This too may be a difficult example, for superficially we have here a man who, depending on the tradition and the atonement theology adopted by particular denominations, is either given up to death by his father or allows himself to be hurt with the approval of his father, and remains submissive to his father's will, whatever that demands. The Canadian theologians Brown and Parker put it thus:

> When a theology identifies love with suffering, what resources will its culture offer ... And when parents have an image of a God righteously demanding the total obedience of 'his' son – even obedience to death – what will prevent the parent from engaging in divinely sanctioned child abuse? The image of God the Father demanding and carrying out the suffering and death of his own son has sustained a culture of abuse and led to the abandonment of victims of abuse and oppression. Until this image is shattered it will be almost impossible to create a just society.[41]

This is a difficult image to deal with, especially for those abused by their fathers and those abused well into their adulthood, but many have consoled themselves with the idea that the abuse must be God's will for them, and that Jesus did God's will whatever the cost. Again ministers might object that here is a theological misunderstanding, as indeed there is, but by doing this ministers deny their share of responsibility for inadequate teaching that has allowed such ideas and misunderstandings to grow and thrive. If the effects of sexual harassment and abuse were addressed in clergy training, they might be better able to preach and teach about the vexed question of suffering.

At lunchtime on Thursday 6 March 1986, Jill Saward was viciously raped in her own home. Her father, the Reverend Michael Saward, Vicar of St Mary's, Ealing, and her boyfriend, David Kerr, were badly beaten. This much-reported case became known as the Ealing Vicarage rape case. It is interesting partly because of the controversy that surrounded the question of forgiveness and the sentencing of the intruders and rapists. Shortly after these crimes were committed, the vicar announced publicly to the press that he had not only forgiven the men in question for what they had done to him, but had also forgiven them for what they had done to his daughter. One questions his right to be forgiving them for his daughter's rape, unless he considered her virginity to be his property. His forgiveness comes out of his authoritarian position as father and priest, and in this case not only does not allow the young woman room for her own emotions but exerts moral blackmail on her to forgive her rapists as swiftly as possible. In her book *Rape, My Story*, Jill Saward does say on several occasions that she has indeed forgiven the men.[42] She explains why. She had had a previous experience of a family friend making a pass at her. He had apologised and asked her for forgiveness, and although she grunted that she did, she kept bitterness and resentment in her heart and was rude or ignored him whenever he visited her house. She writes that she eventually realised what she was doing, went to him, and asked him to forgive her for her bad behaviour. When she had done this, she says, she let go of her anger and found that she was no longer being harmed by her own feelings. She apparently wishes to be able to forgive her rapists because that way she expects to feel better herself. She thinks that what is going wrong in the process is her. Again it is her responsibility – the same sort of responsibility that many women who have suffered rape, harassment or abuse take on themselves.

Jill Saward also writes that in some ways she found it more difficult to forgive the judge who sentenced the three men. He gave the first man five years for burglary and five years for rape, buggery and indecent assault; he gave the second man five years for burglary and three years for rape. The articles stolen were a few trinkets and a rented video, and it is not surprising she found it outrageous that her own suffering was put on (or below) a par with these things. This was especially difficult because, when the judge was sentencing the men, he implied that he was able to give them lighter sentences because she had been able to forgive them.

We can see from these examples that the Christian teaching on forgiveness causes much confusion for Christian survivors of harassment and abuse. Forgiveness is a word used to mean many different things. We hear it most commonly in the phrase 'forgive and forget'. As Marie Fortune reminds us, in terms of sexual abuse within the Christian community this is usually said to the person who has been abused to mean 'You forgive, so that we can forget.'[43] Forgiveness is not about forgetting what was done; in the case of rape or sexual abuse, it simply cannot be forgotten. It may fade in importance, it may become so that it is no longer at the forefront of the abused person's mind all the time, but it becomes part of that person's life experience, absorbed into that which makes her or him the person that she or he is. The experience can never be forgotten. Forgiveness is also used to mean that the offence that has been done is somehow no longer seen as an offence, that it does not matter any more. This is not possible or appropriate. If an action is wrong or sinful, then it remains a wrong or sinful act. It does not suddenly become not a sin because someone has repented. If there is true repentence, then that sin is not counted against the sinner any more, but the actual act is still a sin. Sexual abuse and sexual harassment will always of their nature be sinful acts; they diminish the personhood of the perpetrator and the person sinned against; they harm the community in which the sin is performed and they damage the wider community. At the deepest level they are offences against God, because by their very nature these sins damage creatures made in God's own image and beloved of God.

Forgiveness is possible when the offence no longer binds the person who has been abused.[44] It is a gift of God's grace, and comes at the end of the healing process. It cannot be hurried, it cannot be demanded. In order for it to happen, there has to be a situation of justice.

Reconciliation between the abuser and the abused is something else that is often demanded. For this to happen there has to be true repentance on the part of the abuser. Many abusers seek forgiveness from God, by going to sacramental confession or by telling what they have done to a pastor and seeking his or her prayers. The abuser may experience genuine sorrow for what he has done; he may have a true desire to be at peace with himself, with his neighbour and with God. These responses in themselves do not constitute repentance. In the Hebrew bible, the Hebrew word for repentance is *shub,* which means the action of turning around; in the New Testament, the Greek word for repentence is *metanoia,* meaning a fundamental reversal of a pattern of life. Thus to repent is to change one's way of life, both in thought and deed. Reconciliation is only possible if the abuser truly repents and the abused has reached a stage where she or he is able to forgive.[45]

The needs of those who have been abused sexually, physically, emotionally, spiritually or psychologically should not be underestimated. For those within the Christian community (by this I mean all those who profess the Christian faith and who belong to a worshipping group of some description), it is extremely important that justice is done and that it is seen to be done within the community, both for the sake of the community itself and for the individual concerned.[46] One pattern of action, recommended by the Rev. Marie Fortune and endorsed by those who have suffered sexual violence, is as follows:

1. Truth-telling. Individuals who have been abused need to tell their stories as they perceive them. Whatever the results of this truth-telling exercise, it is in the interests of the physical, emotional, spiritual and psychological health of the abused that space is made for this to happen.
2. Truth-hearing. Victims/survivors need the truth to be heard by others in the community and need to receive an acknowledgement that this is indeed the truth. This should not be a passive receiving

of information, but an active one. Others of the community should be saying, 'I hear you,' 'I believe you,' 'It's not your fault,' 'It was wrong of him to do that,' and so on.

It is possible that the rest of the community may have difficulty in believing. Denial of an event is a common human reaction; we see it around us all the time, as in the face of death. In the case of sexual abuse, there is often denial, perhaps because what we are being asked to believe is so nasty, or because the person who has abused is otherwise seen as a good or spiritual person, or is renowned for his or her wonderful work. It is important to remember that we are complex beings and therefore complex judgements are possible. If someone who abuses is otherwise a holy person, it does not mean that the abuse becomes acceptable.

Genuine truth-hearing is accompanied by appropriate actions. It will not do for the community to say, 'I hear and believe you,' and then fail to take appropriate action with regard to the complaint.

3. Compassion. This means that those who have suffered at the hands of an abuser need others to realise the extent of their suffering. This does not mean taking on their anger, fear, indignation or other feelings, for if that happens those who have been abused are robbed of their feelings. They may then feel that they have to care for the rest of the community, or individuals within it, instead of being able to continue their own important emotional process. What compassion requires is that the community is prepared to hear both what is said and the silences, and to try to comprehend the depths of suffering that has been involved for the abused. This is especially difficult, because our natural reaction as listeners is to 'fix it' or 'make it better'. That way we feel the victim/survivor suffers less, and we as listeners and part of the community suffer less. We have acted to try and improve the situation; we have offered something. The problem with this approach is that it cuts short justice, and neither justice nor healing is served.

4. Protection of the vulnerable. It is often this desire to protect the vulnerable that finally makes those who have been abused come forward to tell their stories. They can see no other way of preventing similar abuse being perpetrated on others. For victims/survivors, it may be of utmost importance that no one else has to go through the same horrific experiences as they did. Within the Christian community in this country at the present time, the immediate reaction seems to be to cover up; we do not want to wash our dirty linen in public. We have already had difficulties perhaps in believing what we have been told, and now we have to act appropriately with regard to it. It is important to remember that the community is not

a court of law. In most cases, the community turns to the law court as a model for action, but the law isn't necessarily the most appropriate model. Our justice-making should be rooted in scripture. There does not have to be a trial with proof; if there is a reasonable suspicion, the Christian community has to act appropriately to protect the vulnerable.

5. Accountability. There has to be accountability for the abuser. This is painful for the perpetrator, because he must come face to face with the reality of what he has done. However it is vital, for without it there can be no real repentence. In one group of twenty-seven men who had been convicted of offences of incest, twenty-five of them professed Christianity. In every case, before they had been reported to the police and convicted, each had gone to their minister or priest and confessed what they were doing. In each case, they were prayed over, absolved or forgiven according to their particular tradition, and were sent home where they continued to abuse until they were found out and reported via some other channel. These men reported that these actions, presumably performed in their best interests by their clergy, were very harmful for them. It kept them from being accountable for what they were doing and enabled them to continue doing it. The responsibility for their actions had been removed from them; grace and forgiveness had been achieved too cheaply.[47] This is a powerful witness. The clergy they had consulted for various reasons had cut short a necessary process. It would have been appropriate for the minister or priest in each case to have supported the perpetrator in reporting himself to the authorities, so enabling justice and healing to begin.

6. Restitution. This is both a symbolic act and a practical necessity. If there has been true repentence on the part of the perpetrator, there will automatically be restitution. The perpetrator will be asking what he can do to try and make amends. It is possible that the perpetrator will not have reached this stage of repentence in his own journey, but the church must take it on immediately. Symbolically the church needs to act out that it believes the complainant. It needs to apologise on behalf of the perpetrator, because after all it has some responsibility for allowing the situation to exist. Thus the church acknowledges the wrong done, enacts belief and takes steps to prevent it happening again.

Those who have been abused also need help in very practical ways, for instance with money to pay for counselling. It is also quite likely that those who have been abused have lost employment or accommodation as a result. It is appropriate that the church takes on the restitution of these losses, and thus also enacts its belief.

7. Vindication. This is the final stage. Those who have been abused are set free. The abuser no longer has power over them or others. The church has listened, heard and acted aright. The unjust judge has given right judgement; those who have been abused are set free to get on with their lives.

This is one pattern for what might happen within a church community. In any given situation, it may not be possible for all these things to happen. Only those who have suffered can say how much has been achieved. However, if justice has been achieved, then the situation in which it is possible for forgiveness to take place has been created.

It can be seen from this that the mainstream Christian churches in this country have a long way to go in their handling of clergy sexual misconduct, sexual harassment and sexual abuse. In Britain, people may not be so ready to sue their churches for negligence as they are in the United States, but the increasing numbers of cases show that similar problems do exist in the UK. The women's movement has in the last 20 years given women and men the courage and the vocabulary to speak of domestic violence. The same is true of sexual harassment and abuse. There is no reason to suppose that in Britain we will not see the same increase in the reporting of clergy sexual misconduct as has happened in the United States. The bishops, moderators and other senior church leaders do not seem to realise what is likely to happen. Clergy need to be trained in issues of sexual abuse and sexual harassment in order to have an understanding of the gravity of these offences. They also need education to enable them to realise the power of their own position, and the implications that that position has for others. It is time that churches recognised that here are ethical issues which urgently need to be addressed, and that their calling as Christians includes a call to make justice.[48]

Notes and References

1. Luke 18: 1–8. (All biblical quotes in this chapter are from the Revised Standard Version.)
2. In this chapter, I use 'Christian churches' or 'the church' to refer to the major denominational churches in Britain, except where the context is clearly that of a particular denomination.
3. In this chapter, I discuss harassment and abuse together, because although they can involve different kinds of behaviours, helping people through the effects of them involves similar pastoral responses.

4. Private correspondence with WATER – Women's Alliance for Theology, Ethics and Ritual, Silver Spring, Maryland, USA.
5. Private correspondence with WATER.
6. Rosemary Radford Reuther, *Womanchurch: Theology and Practice of Feminist Liturgical Communities* (San Francisco: Harper and Row, 1985).
7. Various unpublished liturgies by Women in Theology, Christian Survivors of Sexual Abuse and Dr June Boyce-Tillman, to name but a few.
8. An introductory sentence, before the general confession in Evening Prayer, in the *Book of Common Prayer*, quoted from 1 John 1: 8.
9. *Alternative Service Book*, 1980. Post-communion prayer, Rite A.
10. At the moment there appears to be no consensus on the use of language with regard to policies or codes of practice. For instance, the United Church of Canada has produced a document containing a theological statement, policy definitions and procedures entitled *Sexual Abuse (Sexual Harassment, Sexual Exploitation, Pastoral Sexual Misconduct, Sexual Assault) and Child Abuse (1993)*. The Roman Catholic Diocese of Chicago has published *Clerical Sexual Misconduct with Minors: Policies for Education, Prevention, Assistance to Victims and Procedures for Determination of Fitness for Ministry (1992)*.
11. *Clergy Misconduct: Sexual Abuse in the Ministerial Relationship* (Seattle: Center for the Prevention of Sexual and Domestic Violence), section VI, p. 99.
12. *Clergy Misconduct*, section VI, p. 78.
13. *Clergy Misconduct*, section VI, p. 99.
14. David Skidmore, 'Parishes Face Limits to Insuring for Sex Abuse', *Episcopal Life* (one of the newspapers of the Episcopal Church of the United States of America), April 1993.
15. Skidmore, 'Parishes Face Limits to Insuring for Sex Abuse'.
16. Letter from the Church Insurance Company (CIC) to all episcopal parishes, 7 April 1993.
17. Letter from the Church Insurance Company.
18. Again, there is no generally accepted terminology in use. Phrases such as 'ministerial misconduct', 'clergy misconduct' and 'sexual misconduct' are all in common use. The Center for the Prevention of Sexual and Domestic Violence in Seattle makes very clear and useful distinctions between these terms – taking 'clergy misconduct' to include, for instance, falsifying tax returns – but these have not been adopted.
19. Isaiah 58:6.
20. Micah 6:8.
21. Luke 20:10–17.

22. Matt. 12:9–13.
23. Matt. 12:12.
24. Press conference, Chicago, 1 October 1992.
25. *Clergy Misconduct*, section III, p. 12.
26. *Clergy Misconduct*, section III, p. 39.
27. An acceptance of a police caution is an admission of guilt.
28. Hilary Cashman, *Christianity and Child Sexual Abuse* (London: SPCK, 1993), p. 66.
29. Private conversation with Margaret Kennedy of Christian Survivors of Sexual Abuse (CSSA).
30. Annie Imbens and Ineke Jonker, *Christianity and Incest* (Tunbridge Wells: Burns and Oates, 1992), p. 223.
31. *The Divine Office*, vol. III: *Office of Readings*, 6 July, St Maria Goretti, Virgin and Martyr.
32. Quoted by David Farmer under Maria Goretti in *The Oxford Dictionary of Christian Saints* (Oxford: Oxford University Press, 1982), p. 176.
33. *The Divine Office*, as in note 31.
34. Godfrey Poage, CP, *In Garments All Red: The Story of Maria Goretti* (Washington, DC: Ave Maria Institute, 1971).
35. Poage, *In Garments All Red*, p. 65.
36. Luke 23:34.
37. Luke 23:43.
38. Poage, *In Garments All Red*, p. 72.
39. Poage, *In Garments All Red*, p. 17.
40. The devil's advocate is the person who during the process of beatification and canonisation is employed by the church to make objections to the life and actions of the person under consideration, and to argue against their canonisation.
41. J.C. Brown and R. Parker, 'For God So Loved the World?' in J.C. Brown and C.R. Bohn (eds) *Christianity, Patriarchy and Abuse* (New York: Pilgrim Press, 1990), p. 9.
42. Jill Saward, *Rape: My Story* (London: Pan, 1991), p. 148.
43. 'Forgiveness, The Last Step', a workshop given by Marie Fortune at the binational conference 'Called to Make Justice', Chicago, May 1993.
44. Luke 13:13.
45. Marie Fortune, *Sexual Violence: The Unmentionable Sin* (New York: Pilgrim Press, 1983).
46. I would like to thank Marie Fortune for permission to use this outline from her workshop 'Forgiveness, The Last Step', and also for all her help and inspiration in this field.
47. Jeremiah 6:13–15, quoted in *Clergy Misconduct,* section VI, p. 102.
48. 'Called to Make Justice', Chicago, May 1993.

9

The Lecherous Professor Revisited: Plato, Pedagogy and the Scene of Harassment

Diane Purkiss

In 1984 a study of sexual harassment in the academy was published; its title was *The Lecherous Professor*.[1] I want to begin to rethink the way feminism has addressed the problem of harassment by examining the meanings of this title, and what it can tell us about what we can and cannot say about harassment in the academic workplace.[2] At first glance it seems taxonomic: the lecherous professor as a special species of professor, like the long-winged fly or poststructuralist criticism. Taxonomic gestures can create discomfort, not because all professors are lecherous but because the move can let the rest of the professoriate off the hook: if the lecherous professor is a special species cut off from other professors by his lechery, and he can be dealt with by forensic proceedings, then he can simply be exiled from his professorship, separating finally and forever lechery and the profession; everyone else can then carry on as before. Anyone who has ever tried to do this will know how difficult it is, partly because the quasi-legal procedures of a harassment case are often read as a *choice* between affirming the professional or professorial status of the accused, and affirming his lechery; if the former is to be defended, the latter cannot be conceded, and so we find more or less dreadful anecdotes about senior academics judging harassment cases and asserting that the careers of promising or brilliant men must not be ruined by vindictive women. The title of *The Lecherous Professor* plays into the hands of such rhetoricians by insisting on the separability and opposition between the professor and his lechery. It exposes a weakness in the quasi-legal rhetoric of harassment, which names certain behaviours as a crime. This naming is indispensable, but it has the effect of arguing implicitly that harassment is aberrant, deviant, abnormal; abnormal to the profession, to professors. What this often means *in practice* is that the accused has only to show that he is not

189

professionally deviant to convince others that he is not a harasser. The idea of the normality of the accused and his resemblance to a set of professional norms can be used – speciously – to rebut any charges of inappropriate behaviour, for how can a pillar of the profession be equated with that which is deviant from it? Separating the professor from his lechery by coding it as deviant from professionalism can be unhelpful juridically, and it is also unhelpful to the victim.

Following on these reflections about representing the professor and his lechery as easily separable and even opposed, the word 'lechery' requires attention. 'Lechery' commonly signifies excessive or inappropriate desire; according to the OED, the word derives from the Old French word *lichiere,* meaning debauchery or gluttony, which has also given birth to modern French *lecher* (to lick) and to the now-obsolete English word 'liquorish'. To be lecherous is to devour, to lick; it is an oral crime, a crime of the mouth, rather than the eyes. The etymology reveals the lecher as a Kleinian infant, seeking to devour or consume the object of its warring passions. To be lecherous is to seek the obliteration of the desired object.[3] This buried meaning is significant for harassment, as shall be demonstrated in due course. But in other respects, the connotations of 'lechery' are unhelpful. There is a chime of church-bells about the word, an aroma of 'puritanical' distaste for the excess of sex. The word has an obsolete popular cognate: in my mother's day, 'letch' was a woman's code-word (though a fairly explicit one) for a man who might also be known as 'the office pest' or NSIT (Not Safe In Taxis). This recalls an older women's language for marking out and thus attempting to handle the problem of harassment, but it also recalls a world in which women's *only* ways of managing that problem were by euphemisms and evasions, by circumscribing their own activities in order to 'evade the clutches' of the lecher. I use this Victorian language deliberately because 'lecherous' does have a melodramatic sound, suggesting women in flight from green-fanged male sexuality. Women are portrayed in these narratives as powerless undesiring subjects fleeing from desiring ones. As well as separating desire from the professor, the term lechery separates it from women, so dislike of harassment predicates itself on dislike of sex. Patently, this is not an empowering model for women in the 1990s; if dislike of harassment is made to depend on women's supposed purity, harassment cases will become tests of women's purity, and women will be denied the status of desiring subjects entitled to say yes or no.

Nonetheless, the term 'lechery' does reflect something important, albeit in a confused way. It reflects a perfectly legitimate, perfectly genuine fear of the invasiveness and pervasiveness of misused male power. However, that male power attaches not to private lechery, but to the disregarded noun 'professor'. It is the apparently uncontroversial, unweighted term which carries the charge of power and therefore the charge of fear. The power of the *professor* is the problem; by coupling it with the more loaded term 'lecherous', Dziech and Weiner have concealed this. For it would not matter as much or in the same way if the lecherous one were not a professor; it is the coupling of lechery and professorship which constitutes the problem of harassment. Harassment occurs only when a public position of power becomes a means to demand sexual consent.[4] Locating the problem in private male sexuality may have been motivated by an understandable wish to simplify the problem, or it may be an attempt to reassure those professors who do not see themselves as lecherous that the idea of sexual harassment poses no threat to them.

Another way to read the division between lechery and the professor is to see 'professor' as a scene where the crime of lechery is committed. That is, lechery is portrayed as something which comes from outside the professional setting, an unwonted intruder. This interpretation of the title *The Lecherous Professor* is heavily borne out by the text of the book, which struggles to explain outbreaks of professorial lechery with reference to psychological models of childhood; that is, the only academic scene considered is the scene of the professor's schooldays. Dziech and Weiner are not analysing lecherous professors, but lechery; hence the recourse to psychological models. Their hypotheses have the effect of rendering the professor's lechery as increasingly a stranger to his professorship; desire and actions are decontextualised, assumed to be generated within the professor or outside the academy in his childhood or adolescence. In this way, the title of Dziech and Weiner's study reflects the connotations of the term 'sexual harassment' itself. By naming harassment as a crime, feminist rhetoric partakes of a discourse of crime which points backwards to the private self and circumstances of the criminal for a causal explanation. The milieu is not analysed and hence not blamed: indeed, its normality can be affirmed by portraying lechery as an alien invader. If successfully represented as such, that invader can be pushed out into the outside from which it came, in an act of scapegoating which allows the evil to be carried away and the space of professorship and professionalism purified.

However, the very notion that lechery can be expelled to purify the academy implies that lechery is a construction of the academy; the idea that the harasser's lechery is separable from his professorship locates it within his professorship. This can be illustrated by thinking about not merely lechery but professorship, and its cognates profession, professionalism, professing. These cognates often contain a chime of church-bells too; to profess is to vow, and this is still the term which nuns and other religious orders use for the final vows which will seal them from the world. One popular image for the academy is the image of a monastery, partly because the historical origins of the universities in Britain lie in monasticism. This is reinforced by the architecture of quadrangles and courts which characterise Oxbridge and the American Ivy League; the courts have the effect of seeming to seal the academy's walls from the outside world. The space of the monastery explicitly implies the exclusion of desire and sexuality, and the female body as object of desire. But these connotations differ sharply from the connotations of professionalism, professional conduct and so forth which are also cognate with the term professor. These cognates appear to connect the academic to the world, or at least to other professions. As Bruce Robbins points out, the professional is usually figured in popular culture as the possessor of a store of expertise. The professional is the one presumed to know, but the price of that knowledge is the adoption of a public role from which the personal is excluded in favour of unambiguous objectivity.[5] Curiously, this actually ties up with the monastic connotations of 'profess' in that both terms exclude the personal and make the professor and his lechery seem inconceivable together.

These topics are not exactly novel, since there have been numerous theory-inspired studies of the academic profession recently, many of them in response to hysterical outbursts about ideological indoctrination and political correctness from the American right. What interests me about this shouting-match – one can scarcely call it a dialogue, since neither party responds in detail to the other's statements – is that while the academy's right-wing critics are paranoically concerned with academic pedagogy, left-liberal defenders scarcely mention the classroom at all, despite the obvious political imperative to address the right's criticisms.[6] There may be many reasons for this silence; the most obvious is Jonathan Culler's suggestion that the right assumes that the function of the humanities is the transmission of cultural artefacts to a new generation, while the left repudiates this aim. But Culler is disturbingly jaunty about what the *left* values; he cheerfully suggests that its concern is simply with research and peer standing.[7] This may explain why most defenders of the academy look inwards to an academic readership rather than outwards to the general reader. The profession does equate success with research, conference attendance, publications and fame among peers, rather than with being a good teacher.[8] To say this is not to side with right-wing critics who see neglect of the classroom as the root of all evil.[9] It is not neglect of the classroom as a place to attend that is worrying, but an unwillingness to think about its operations when not actually inhabiting it. This is a weakness of the right as well; the right's collective fantasy of academic pedagogy as a cross between dependent fandom on the students' part and a kind of Foucauldian panopticon on the teachers' part is precisely the kind of pedagogy which needs examination and reconstruction. Nonetheless, the right is correct to point out that the equation of academic success with activities outside the classroom means that the classroom doesn't get talked about much. The development of a set of professional norms which do not 'cover' activities in the lecture-hall fosters the split between the identity of the professor and the identity of the lecher which I have been discussing. In effect, not talking about the classroom, not bringing it into a public sphere of debate and discussion, has the effect of privatising it, making it a space of no concern, an untheorised space of blankness on the map of professional identity. This is worrying because it has the effect of decontextualising the events of sexual harassment, of separating them from their academic context.

Far from enabling academics to examine their activities more carefully, the right's attacks have frustrated such moves by throwing everyone onto the defensive. The right's attacks on the academy take the form of arguing that students are being 'indoctrinated' or 'brainwashed' by lefty teachers into accepting certain 'PC' versions of events. The favoured example in America is the left's revelation that Thomas Jefferson was a slave-owner; right-wing critics deplore the way this can be used to detach students from the cherished values of the Declaration of Independence. This example creates an opposition between 'classroom indoctrination' and the fresh breezes of free speech.[10] This is embarrassing for the left, since it is a simplistic inversion of a familiar left-wing argument of the 1960s. The left used to argue that the universities were the site of indoctrination, failing to give Jefferson's slaves the kind of authoritative voice which they granted to Jefferson. It was this set of beliefs which inspired many of us to alter curricula in the ways the right now finds so disastrous. This makes it difficult to argue now that classrooms are not *really* sites of indoctrination, because we are now in charge of them and we grant our students plenty of free speech and *never* make them feel less entitled to speak even if they are paid-up members of the Ku Klux Klan.[11] Of course, it is easy to respond by deconstructing the opposition between indoctrination and free speech: is free speech an idea or practice into which one can be indoctrinated? If one can be indoctrinated out of it, surely one can be indoctrinated (back) into it? If it is just another object of indoctrination, how can it be the opposite of indoctrination? And if the academic left is so powerful, how is it that most students aren't Marxists or even feminists? Unfortunately, these reflections leave the awkward question of how power operates in the classroom unaddressed.

These might be some causes of the failure to rethink pedagogy; what is the result? Although curricula have changed, the classroom has stayed the same. Academics now teach Harriet Jacobs, Jacques Derrida, homoerotic representation in Shakespeare; but these 'new' things are taught in fundamentally the same ways in which Dickens, James and moral seriousness used to be taught. The tutorial, the essay, the seminar and the examination persist, as do notions of what constitutes a 'good' essay, exam or seminar, though the allowable *content* has changed after some conspicuous public struggles. By an unofficial tradeoff, feminism and postructuralism have been allowed into the academy provided they accept academic pedagogical and professional structures.[12] The only time these structures are ever seriously debated within the academy is as part of cost-cutting exercises. What is bizarre about this state of affairs is that research has shown these structures disadvantage women students and teachers alike. It has long been known that in a mixed seminar women students will talk less than men, will have less impact on the course of the discussion, will be taken less seriously, will receive fewer detailed comments on their observations.[13] Nobody needs a survey to see that a system of final examinations is disadvantageous to women with family responsibilities; it has also been argued that it disadvantages women students because they are less confident. The essay, too, can be difficult for the diffident, since it requires a rhetoric of dogmatic certainty. Mastery of discourse means a studied avoidance of 'colloquialisms', a category almost solely defined by the academic guardians of discourse, and a production of smoothness, evenness and narrowness rather than range, diversity and eclecticism. The goal is tight control rather than wide interest. What impresses academics in written work is the mystified but somehow recognisable 'brilliant insight', which must be cast in objective rhetoric to seem like truth. The hazy but holy criteria for 'quality' are never discussed or examined systematically, and what local discussion of teaching there has been in theoretical circles invariably excludes marking. Academics who agree about little else will often agree about the general quality of a student's work, so there seems to be nothing to discuss. In the academy there has been no debate of these issues at all since the early 1970s. It begins to look as if the silence around pedagogy has some significance; as if pedagogy, by becoming what is taken for granted, unquestioned, undiscussed, unassailed, is actually what constitutes the identity of the professor.

The first step in thinking through the classroom is to begin to think about what we are doing in the classroom and how we came to be doing it. Let us suppose, then, that I am teaching one of Fredric Jameson's essays on utopias and dystopias in mass culture.[14] This might be how I would define a particular seminar to myself in preparing it. I have made the text available to the students; in class, I will assume they have read it, though I also know that some of them won't have done so. But I make the assumption all the same, because my construction of the 'discussion' depends crucially on the notional egalitarianism of shared reading. By all reading Jameson, we are somehow all alike; even if in practice we have all read it differently, these differences arise from a notional sharing. The photocopied article is a level playing field. This is a specious but useful fantasy which allows us to evade dealing with the issues of power; it is specious because I as tutor have not only read that one piece by Jameson several times, but also several of Jameson's books, accounts of Jameson by other theorists and the works of at least some of the theorists whom Jameson cites or rewrites.[15] As a result of this reading, I do not find Jameson's text difficult; I am in a privileged position in relation to it. How do I use that privilege, and how does it operate in the pedagogical context?

My job is to transmit that privilege to the students, assuming they do not have it already. I can do this 'straightforwardly' by giving them a lecture which is an account of Jameson that they can substitute for the labour of arriving at their own reading. I can disguise this transaction by splitting up my lecture into comments, leading questions, responses to questions or comments, which preserve the courteous illusion of democracy. Whichever I choose, the goal of my proceeding is the same; I am trying to make the students resemble me, resemble or mimic my mastery of Jameson. I am in effect casting them as my disciples.[16] Whether I seduce them into the role with charisma, *enthousiasmos* or the illusion of democracy, or force it on them with a naked display of power, the result is the same. They are supposed to imitate me more and more closely, and the ones who imitate me most assiduously are the ones seen as the 'best' students. By imitation, I don't mean that they are going to dress like me (though I have seen this happen) or impersonate me vocally (though I do note that my students pick up my verbal tics). What I mean is that the students are supposed to imitate my mastery of Jameson.

Now, what most tutors mean by a 'good' seminar will be one in which some of the students have mastered Jameson sufficiently to be able to talk back to the tutor, one in which a 'general discussion' of Jameson and the issues he raises ensues. This is the ideal because (respectably) it looks more democratic to those of us uncomfortable with mastery and it is taken as a sign that the students have learned something; we might entertain legitimate hopes that they will be more critical of visions of the future hereafter, or that they are now well placed to handle the fractured discourses of More's *Utopia*. Discussion also counts as a sign that everyone is playing the imitation game. The tutor is positioned as the one who talks. It follows that the most subversive thing a student can do is remain silent, though some students see silence in seminars as a painful disempowerment, and often develop strong feelings of envy and loathing for more articulate classmates. This is because they know full well that talking in a seminar signifies power; they may withhold their speech from a desire not to play the game, or from an acute fear that their words will give them away as imperfect imitations, insufficiently knowing. As I write these words, I am conscious of a desire to insist that I of course would not look down on a student who committed a grammatical solecism or who didn't know what surplus value was. Up to a point these protestations might be true. But the point is that as the tutor I do represent to the students somebody who can decide their futures, somebody who can admit them to the club of the knowing or slam the door in their faces. Protesting that there is no such club or that the rules of the club are laughable rings hollow in the hierarchical institution and culture which surrounds us all.[17]

Some teachers might well object that they do not wish their students to imitate them, that they welcome disagreement up to and including substantial political or moral differences. But acts of disagreement do not escape the imitation game and its logic, and assuming that they do confuses free speech with absolute freedom. For if a student disagrees with Jameson, on what grounds does she do it? If she says, for example, that she sees Jameson's conception of postmodernity as a globalisation of an aesthetic which applies only to the New Class in the Western world and covers over the geographical, historical and cultural divisions which organise late capitalist power-relations, she is demonstrating precisely the mastery of Jameson's discourse which has been taught to her. Indeed, the teacher may be pleased with her in part because her outburst denotes success in the task of imitation; she has succeeded so well that she is now competent enough to argue with the teacher on academic ground. The more she disagrees with the teacher, the more closely she replicates academic authority. But what if a student says that Jameson is wrong because both the bible and Nostradamus predict an apocalypse in 1998, and the shooting of John F. Kennedy was the first sign of this apocalypse since he was shot by an international conspiracy of Satanists whose identity Jameson is concealing because he is a communist? (This really happened in one of my classes.) Should one ask the student to obey a few academic rules, to provide some evidence for her claims, for example? Should she be allowed to change the course of the discussion? The fact is that within a seminar there *are* unwritten and unexamined rules about what counts as valid; the object of going to the seminar is indeed in part to learn these rules. The rules are administered by the tutor, and the first rule is that students must imitate the tutor.

Now, this model is not the only one and it ignores several important facts. The students do not of course come to the classroom naked; they are always already part and product of a more general culture, in which the dominant discourses are not Spenser and Jameson but film, TV and music. In this sense, many teachers in the humanities probably think that students are too well armoured against them rather than too vulnerable to their power. However, one of the effects of the increasing estrangement of students from print culture is that their resistance to the tutor's point of view is weakened; because they are uncomfortable with high culture, they are more dependent on the teacher's explication of it, less able to refute him or her.[18] Moreover, tutor and students can alike go away and forget or reject what was said. Though in practice the imperatives of filling sheets of paper in essay or exam makes this more difficult for the students, they may not be at all interested in the tutor's views *except* as ways of completing assessed work; that is, they may dutifully write sheet after sheet on the horrors of world capitalism before going out to vote Tory. It is important to acknowledge the students' power to reject (in the end) much of what they are told; it is also important to acknowledge that such a rejection will most often be secret, evasive, silent rather than openly discussed, if only because most students do not have the rhetorical or cultural competence to dispute a tutor's reading of Jameson or Milton and win. Imitation can be simply a game, a piece of Renaissance self-fashioning, a role adopted in the classroom and abandoned at the door, but this just acknowledges the existence of the power structures I have been discussing.

A male colleague once told me proudly (and a little defensively) that he had had an open and frank discussion with his female students, who had objected to the fact that the seminar syllabus contained no women. In the end, he said, they had all agreed that those who wanted to work on women could do so, but outside the seminar, that is in their own time. When I spoke to the women students concerned, they had a different story to tell. 'I tried to get him to include some women's writing,' one of them told me, 'but he's so much more articulate and clever than I am that in the end I just didn't know what to say to his arguments.' They disliked him intensely for refusing to take their opinions seriously, but had no intention of 'making fools of themselves' and risking his displeasure by saying so to him. The point is not about 'free speech' but about discourse: my colleague plainly believed that he had persuaded the women to change their minds, while actually they had only changed their words. They simply felt unable to muster sufficient discursive skill to go on discussing the issue with him. This anecdote shows that interaction with students is often supposed by academics to be more open, more plural and more democratically free than it appears to the students, who are frequently conscious that they are caught in a power-saturated set of discourses to which they must defer.

But what gives the discourses of my colleague their power? I want to begin by looking at the structure of pedagogy in Plato's dialogues, since the dialogue form of ancient philosophy is still the founding text of pedagogy. As there is a positive babble of argument and disciplinary contestation about Plato within classics and philosophy, with all sides making more or less explicit truth-claims for their readings, it is impossible to pinpoint a single authentic scholarly or classicised Plato from which my reading may diverge. I am not making a comparable truth-claim for my attempt to insert Plato into a discussion on pedagogy. Rather, I want to look at the figure of 'Plato' as he moves through academic discourses of self-fashioning and self-constitution, trying to catch and examine the fleeting, elusive traces of the academy and the academic myths encoded in the body of texts we call 'Plato': 'Plato' as the intellectual or philosophical father created by the son to fill his needs, 'Plato' as the academy's fantasy about itself, 'Plato' as the academy's myth of origins. At the same time, 'Plato' can never be finally divided from Plato, for it is in attempts to construct Plato that we eventually track down his shadow 'Plato'.

After all, the very word 'academy' is the name for the place where Plato taught; the crucial phrase 'the groves of academe' is still used (albeit jocularly) to describe academic space.[19] The Academy of Plato was situated outside the walls of Athens, symbolically separated from the city on which it sought to reflect. The phrase 'groves of academe', which makes this separation explicit, comes from Horace's *Epistles*.[20] It was picked up by Milton in *Paradise Regained* and used to describe the Platonic academy itself: 'See there the olive grove of Academe/Plato's retirement, where the Attic bird/Trills her thick-warbled notes the summer long.'[21] Earlier I mentioned the image of the university as monastery; the monastery translates the classical academy into the Judaeo-Christian context, since monasteries are envisaged as separate from the world and also as containers and reproducers of high culture in their libraries and *scriptoria*. A glance at the geography of British plate-glass universities reveals the pervasiveness of this classical–Christian notion of separation; most are constructed outside the town centre, and characteristically they are designed as a series of buildings surrounded by parkland. The parkland signifies the academy's separation from the public spaces of *polis* and *agora*. This design is testimony to a vision of the university as an enclosed world which replicates but also draws itself away from the public world of the *polis*. This can be understood more readily if we turn to the appropriation of the physical sight (or site) of the university by a writer who made heavy investments in a right-wing notion of pedagogy. Matthew Arnold was the creator of a school of literary criticism which understands education as power and revels in the fact. When Arnold describes Oxford, his own *alma mater*, he does so in a poem which is explicitly both classical and pastoral. The speaker is standing on Iffley downs, where he sees 'that sweet city with her dreaming spires'. This line has become so famous as a description of Oxford that its very prominence in the construction of the space of the British university seems to ask for some consideration. Although Arnold calls Oxford a city, he emphasises its remoteness by locating it in a pastoral setting. The essence of the university is its division from other things, even from the speaker; it can be glimpsed only as an isolated phenomenon. The adjective 'dreaming' disassociates the spires from the kind of activity which normally characterises a city, activity which is purposive and utilitarian; instead, the reader is invited to see the spires as leisured, both above and beyond the urban realm.[22] After this image, it is not surprising to find that Arnold, along with other Victorians, explicitly invokes Platonism in his vision of the ideal university: 'we in Oxford, brought up amidst its beauty and sweetness, have not failed to seize one truth: that beauty and sweetness are essential characters of human perfection.'[23]

I want to look now at another kind of fantasy about what might be contained in the academy, a fantasy about love and especially about love in the classroom which also partakes of the myth of 'Plato'. The text here is a reported polemic against feminist attempts to ban sexual relations, whether consensual or not, between faculty and students; the speaker is William Kerrigan, a psychoanalytic critic and Milton specialist who has become the most visible and quotable opponent of such bans. Here is Kerrigan's disquisition on pedagogy:

> Teaching, considered in its full metaphorical reach, is among the major scenarios of Western eroticism. Teachers in the classroom try to make their ideas not just clear but beautiful. Students receive these ideas, and try to make them their own – to give them a novel beauty distinctly theirs. This ideological gift-giving, chaste in the classroom, can pass over into sexuality of the most powerful sort. Even arguing, as one knows from Shakespearean comedy, can assume the rhythms of foreplay.[24]

Kerrigan's discourse seems extraordinarily blind to its own suppressions and assumptions. For whom is teaching a great erotic scene? Do all participants in the scene of the classroom see it thus? The key to the whole nonsensical metaphor is the slippage in the second sentence from eroticism to metaphors of ideal beauty, and the way this is conflated with oratorical skill. It is this slippage which legitimates the dubiousness of the remainder and which marks Kerrigan's investment in the figure of 'Plato', for there is a decidedly Platonic ring about his assertion of the beauty and sweetness of ideas. As a result of this move, the student can be figured by Kerrigan as the container in whom the teacher's ideas will be placed. This inscribes the student in the now-familiar imitation game of learning, in which the erotic can be discerned merely because of the primal, infantile male fantasy that eroticism consists only of dominance and submission, gift and reception. The implicit phallocentrism of the metaphor of the gift is thinly disguised by the notional mutuality of gift-giving, since Kerrigan has already suggested that only the teacher's beautiful words are of real value. This phallocentrism has particular implications for both female students and female teachers.

Kerrigan's notion that erotic desire is somehow related to the desire for beautiful ideas and beautiful words is a Platonic notion. Plato, of course, makes more rigorous distinctions between levels of desire; for him, Kerrigan's collapse of desire for beauty into desire for sex with a beautiful person would be a lapse from the good. Nonetheless, Kerrigan's fantasy of eroticised pedagogy is an appropriation of Plato's rhetoric. We can see how this works by turning to Plato's dialogue *Phaedrus* via an earlier dialogue, *Charmides*, which explicitly locates philosophic desire via an eroticised scene of teaching. There is a revelation of Charmides' beauty and desirability from Critias, followed by a revelation of his beauty through direct description of him and indirect description of the effect he has on the men assembled in the gymnasium. Finally, Charmides sits down beside Socrates to learn a remedy for headaches. Socrates represents himself as overwhelmed by what he manages to see:

> When Critias told him I was the man who knew of the remedy, he gave me a look that is impossible to describe and made ready to ask me something. Everyone in the wrestling school swarmed all round us. That was the moment, my noble friend, when I saw what was inside his cloak. I was on fire, I lost my head.[25]

Similarly, Phaedrus is keeping a love-treasure inside his cloak in *Phaedrus*. The love-treasure is a speech by Lysias, the democratic orator, and the opening of the dialogue is a flirtation in which Socrates has to 'overcome' Phaedrus' coy reluctance to read him the speech. This opening dialogue about the speech of Lysias is a dialogue of seduction, turning on the processes of withholding and revelation. Phaedrus begins by mentioning Lysias, and Socrates gradually uncovers the fact that Phaedrus had heard his speech; more questions elicit the fact that the speech is about love (*eros*) and that Phaedrus' passion for the speech would have led him to study it till sunrise. This process of uncovering takes on increasingly eroticised implications, though the object of desire is the speech itself, until Socrates is describing himself as the lover (*erastes*) of speeches. He then figures Phaedrus as a coy beloved or *eromenos*; he refuses to speak the speech even though there is nothing he wants more. This eroticised play takes a comic turn when Socrates performs his customary manoeuvre of looking under a young man's cloak, though on this occasion it is the speech-roll which he discovers as the object of his desire and not the young man's body.

This kind of playful, exaggerated, even camp flirtation is characteristic of the Socratic dialogues; love of wisdom (*philosophia*) is routinely represented in them in terms of erotic or sexual drives, even though it is also a transcendence of them. The openings of dialogues particularly tend to figure a playful physical *eros* which will be displaced into a desire for wisdom as the dialogue unfolds. Another early dialogue, *Lysis*, begins with a discussion of how best to pursue a desired *paidika*, while Socrates opens *Protagoras* by teasing the listener with the intelligence that he has met someone more beautiful and desirable than Alcibiades; this turns out to be the elderly sophist Protagoras. The pleasure of philosophy – its teaching and learning – is always set up in relation to erotic desire, as that which contains and elevates itself above that desire. These erotic dramas are not extraneous to the dialogues in which they appear; they *are* the dialogue, and the philosophy cannot be abstracted from its metaphoric architecture. It is obvious from Kerrigan's moves that Platonism keeps insidiously recycling and representing the rhetoric of eroticism at the moment when it invests most heavily in the beauty of apparently disembodied ideas. It is this metaphoric architecture of Platonism which is appropriated by Kerrigan to form the basis for a fantasy about the eroticisation of the classroom. Instead of seducing to philosophy by means of eros, Kerrigan proposes seducing to eros by means of philosophy. This is reminiscent of the much-vaunted pedagogue of the film *Dead Poets Society*, with his reassurance that poetry is a great way to get girls. There, however, the scene of desire is private, physically removed from the classroom, whereas for Kerrigan the classroom itself is the scene of seduction.

In *Phaedrus*, 'interest' in the speech is described in terms of private, bodily desires. The text which has taken possession of Phaedrus, and which Phaedrus uses to seduce Socrates into conversation, is a text of seduction. Lysias' speech is designed to lure an erotic object into becoming the speaker's beloved. To counter its power, Socrates offers two speeches designed to seduce Phaedrus away from his passion for the words of Lysias, towards Socrates himself as teacher.[26]

This eroticisation of the word – hearing it, reading it, speaking it, inventing it – is closely examined in Jacques Derrida's reading of

Phaedrus' representation of the acts of transmitting *logos*, or rather his reading of the way *Phaedrus* constitutes the *logos* as that which can be transmitted and replicated by that philosophical community which defines itself as orthodox. Derrida argues that central to the transmissions of the philosophical text is the notion of philosophy – or truth – as authorised by the privileged relationship between articulate teacher and receptive student. This is not to deny that in a dialogue more than one person talks, but this can disguise a hierarchy of speakers; in *Phaedrus*, both Lysias' speech and the words of Phaedrus serve as pretexts for Socratic utterances, along with Socrates' own pseudo-speeches, constantly revised by Socrates himself. The pattern thus established, Derrida argues, is a form of patrilineal inheritance in which the father controls the son and shapes him into a replica of himself who will in turn narcissistically carry the father's authority and identity onwards.[27]

This philosophical myth of what Derrida calls insemination is developed by Hegel but is present in vestigial form in *Phaedrus* itself, in the myth of Thamus. Thamus is an Egyptian king who receives a visitor, the god Theuth who invented writing, geometry and numbers. He offers Thamus writing as a gift, but Thamus turns it down, citing a number of reasons which represent writing as a semblance or similitude of truth, not truth itself. Thamus continues:

> To your students you give an impression of wisdom, not the reality of it; having heard much, in the absence of teaching, they will appear to know much when in fact they know nothing, and they will be difficult to get along with, because they have acquired the appearance of wisdom instead of wisdom itself.
>
> (275b)

Derrida comments that the king, the father of speech, here asserts his authority over the father of writing.[28] Writing gets between teacher and pupil, or between father and son, breaking the ties of paternal self-replication and filial obedience which ensure the passage of truth from one generation to the next. For it is only by respecting the authority of the teacher, and not the authority acquired from other men's books, that the pupil can arrive at genuine wisdom. 'Logos is a son, then, a son that would be destroyed in his very presence without the present attendance of his father. His father who speaks for him and answers for him.'[29] Sameness guarantees truth, social stability and continuity.

Derrida is interested only in the way writing is constituted by these metaphors and myths, but as Page du Bois has pointed out, there is a degree of overlap between the eroticisation or seduction of the philosophic student and the representation of the paternal self-replication of the philosophic teacher.[30] And Derrida himself points out that Plato's representation of philosophic paternity is explicitly gendered when he writes that: 'it is all about father and sons, about bastards unaided by any public assistance, about glorious, legitimate sons, about inheritance, sperm, sterility. Nothing is said of the mother.'[31]

Du Bois argues that the implicit and explicit homoerotics of *Phaedrus* seem to centre on relations between men, relations which exclude women from true *eros* or desire for the *logos* and thus from philosophic truth. This implies the repression of the mother as figure, since the male self-replication central to pedagogical logic cannot be male and autotelic unless the mother is forgotten. In other Socratic dialogues the repression of the mother takes the form of the trope of teacher as midwife; for example, in *Theaetetus* Socrates figures himself as midwife to the birth of ideas.[32] This trope is picked up and used as part of an extended piece of academic fantasy by Allan Bloom.[33] Bloom presents himself throughout the volume as a diligent imitator of Plato, but of course his notion of 'Plato' is highly idiosyncratic and plainly shaped by his polemical project.[34] 'Midwifery', Bloom writes, 'describes teaching ... the birth of a robust child, independent of the midwife, is the teacher's true joy, a pleasure far more effective in motivating him than any disinterested moral duty would be'.[35] Here it seems that Bloom is disavowing a 'sophistical' project of student indoctrination, favouring instead the idea of assisting at an autotelic self-construction. Although it is hard to say exactly what the child is here – there seems to be a slippage between the notion of child as idea and the notion of child as student – the point is that Bloom in adopting this analogy is willing to take on a feminine role at the cost of displacing another woman. But despite the apparent abrogation of control implied in Bloom's renunciation of the roles of mother and father here, Bloom's wish to replicate himself in his students soon surfaces elsewhere. One of his most dreary strategies is to compare modern students with himself as an undergraduate, and to become aggrieved if they differ from him. The fact that 'they' like MTV while he likes Mozart is a source of grief and an occasion for banal sexology.[36] 'They' refuse to acknowledge the superiority of the 'traditions' that Mozart represents to the wicked and corrupting influences of sex, drugs, rock and roll, and women's writing. The entire volume is a lament for deviant sonship (daughters do not figure very largely in Bloom's schema) to which the image of the diligent Socratic midwife is opposed. This midwife self-image is opposed to the feminised mother-figures of feminist academics and rock drag queens, who have interfered in the reproductive process to shape their sons otherwise.

The repression of the mother is indeed essential if the erotic and paternal metaphors of the *Phaedrus* dialogue are to coalesce around a logic of replication. For example, when Socrates is describing a proper garden, one in which the *logos* can flourish self-replicatingly:

> when a man makes use of the science of dialectic, and taking a fitting soul plants and sows in it words accompanied by knowledge, which are able to help themselves and the man who planted them, and are not without fruit but contain a seed (*sperma*) from which others grow in other soils, capable of rendering it for ever immortal, and making the one who had it as happy as it is possible for a man to be.
>
> (276a–7a)

Here erotic metaphors of penetration following seduction coalesce with paternal metaphors of insemination and self-replication. By seducing the philosophic *eromenos*, the philosopher is able to inseminate him with his own seed (*sperma*) or words (*logoi*). These seed-words are transmitted intact, so that the *eromenos* becomes not merely the beloved but the son of his father-instructor, coming in time to resemble his father and to replicate his identity. That identity can in turn be passed on intact to future generations, making its begetter's name immortal. But for the metaphors of seduction and paternity to come together, the *eromenos* must be both the receptacle and nurturer of the seed (that is, the mother) and its ultimate destination (the son). The entire analogy depends on the exclusion of the mother from the philosophic space, and hence from truth.

I am not suggesting crudely that professors will attempt literally to inseminate their (male) pupils because their philosophic authority depends on doing so metaphorically; refutations of the influence of Plato on myths of academic self-fashioning rely too heavily on the assumption that the homophobia of the academy is proof of its immunity from fantasy about Plato.[37] We can draw two conclusions here. Firstly, this notion of teaching depends on a carefully managed articulation of the scene of learning in which the erotic and the intellectual are well mixed together and in which erotic desire metaphorises, constructs and is displaced into paternal desire. Secondly, the operations of this model depend crucially on the violent repression of the figure of the mother and the silencing or obliteration of women. As configured in *Phaedrus*, teaching is hom(m)osocial: an affair of male sameness. Given Derrida's examination of the pervasive influence of this Platonic model of eroticised paternity and seduction in today's philosophical pedagogy, what happens when women enter this scene of self-replication? One of Dziech and Weiner's respondents shows what happens; the female body is assumed to be incompatible with the space of ideas:

There she stands. A beautiful woman. Above her neck she is talking about the most abstruse subject. From the neck down her body is saying something altogether different. She wears good clothes. They show her body off to good advantage. And she acts as though she were completely unconscious of it. She acts as though she were a man, like the dog who thinks he is a human being. Sometimes it strikes me almost as freakish, this split between the way she talks and the way she looks. The two don't go together.[38]

This male academic figures the female body as object of desire and the female subject as repository or producer of knowledge as incompatible. The knowledge is figured as disembodied ('abstruse'); both talk and body, even clothes, are assumed to be communicative, offering messages which somehow cannot be sustained together. The speaker does not know why the 'split' strikes him as 'freakish'; he assumes that it will strike everyone that way, that his sense of an incompatibility between the female body and the abstruse message will be obvious to all. That he may be right is established by the frequency of this trope in campus novels.[39]

This question of difference is addressed by Michele Le Doeuff in 'Women and Philosophy'.[40] Le Doeuff argues that women are not excluded from philosophy at all, but rather are constrained within it to the occupation of positions seen as inauthentic and lacking in authority. Women have been excluded from occupying *institutionally* authoritative positions, and have been confined to operating within a personal and usually passionate relation to a particular philosopher. One might think of Heloise and Abelard, Elisabeth and Descartes, de Beauvoir and Sartre.[41] More recently, one might think of Paul de Man and his female disciples.[42] At first sight it might look as though these passionate relations between master and pupil replicate rather precisely the logic of the *Phaedrus*, with the woman in the role of *eromenos*, the beloved to be instructed. We might 'read' these relationships as expressions of the erotic transference which for Plato is an intrinsic part of the transmission of the *logos*. Le Doeuff praises Plato for recognising this element in philosophical relations, which she seems to take as realistic. But there are two crucial differences between the *Phaedrus* model and the male–female model. Firstly, the element of displacement has vanished; instead of a series of textualised erotic seductions and fantasies, we have an actual emotional or even physical relationship. Secondly, and for Le Doeuff this is crucial, woman's exclusion from institutions means that no third term mediates between her and her teacher–father; their relation is never transcended. However, there may be more to solving the problem than getting a few women into philosophy departments, since there is an obvious danger that in getting in they may either be

forced to replicate the father or be unable to represent his power.[43] Le
Doeuff tackles the latter dilemma in her more recent *Hipparchia's Choice*,
which opens with a hilarious account of a *viva* in which the candidate's
thesis is obliquely stigmatised when one examiner announces that all
the greatest Kant experts have beards.[44] Though Le Doeuff does not
discuss this, the woman disciple can never really represent the son of
her philosopher–father; that is, by virtue of her gender itself, she cannot
be a father (and the mother has no place in the paradigm). Metaphorically,
she can (so to speak) receive seed, but she cannot inseminate others;
'she' cannot be a father–philosopher. More generally, 'she' cannot be
any kind of authoritative father at all, so 'she' cannot make her own
father immortal.

How, then, does she look to her philosopher–father, to whom she
must represent that which his self-replication must repress? Perhaps
woman in the seminar can come to represent loss or lack, the incapacity
of femininity to inseminate. She is empty, and by contrast he is full;
she is weak and he is strong. This may sound reassuring, a way of
upholding masculine authority against the more evidently parricidal
threats posed by potential sons. But at the same time the woman is a
threat; she represents his own fears of lack of mastery, fullness, potency.
Finally, by virtue of her inability to perpetuate his institutional status,
to make him immortal, to assure his place in the public realm, she
represents the private sphere, the complement of the male sphere
which he must own. In this context, we can see his *literal* desire for her
in two ways: as a reaction to fear of her/his lack, an assertion of mastery
over what he fears he has failed to master, and as an attempt to thrust
her out of her threateningly improper place and into the proper sphere
of private and contained discipleship; or as a refusal to displace desire
into acknowledging her potential authority, as an attempt not to
inseminate her with the *logos* by (literally) inseminating her. The fact
that harassment (of one sort or another) almost always involves driving
the student away from the class may not be an 'unfortunate' side-
effect; it may be precisely the point.

I know of an academic who fills the entire class time with lengthy
stories of his sexual practices and preferences. His seminars are usually
inhabited mostly by women because he advertises them as gender
studies seminars. Of those who remarked on this man's practices, the
vast majority were actually complaining that the seminars did not
prepare them for exams. An accidental side-effect, or the symbolic key
to the situation? So we return in the end to the opposition between
lechery and professionalism; the professor's lechery is a way of refusing
to grant professional status to *women*. That is, lechery can be a way of
blocking or refusing to acknowledge the possibility that women may

be intellectual sons, intellectual *eromenoi*. And that is one reason it hurts women so much: it is an explicit denial of women's right to cultural authority.

The notion that discipleship in pedagogy is no longer problematic in a postfeminist world is much abroad, but a glance at the much-hyped work of Camille Paglia belies this optimistic appraisal. Paglia invests heavily in a rhetoric of academic discipleship instantly recognisable from Le Doeuff's analysis. In her hortatory memoir of Milton Kessler, who taught her as an undergraduate, Kessler is supposed to serve as an example to the degenerate young of today. These are a few of the ways she describes him:

> Great teachers live their subject. The subject teaches itself through them. It uses them and in return charges them with elemental energy.
>
> Kessler would weave in and out of his class his own passing thoughts, reminiscences, disasters. His classic formulation: 'I think of ...' It echoes in my mind, I use it in my book.
>
> Kessler freely showed emotion. Once, in class, he suddenly exploded with rage at some boys in the back row. He accused them of 'peeking', of peeping Tomism. 'Get out: it's *obscene!*' He meant, I assume, that they were sneering cynics, keeping themselves apart from the class.[45]

To this day, Paglia doesn't know what Kessler meant, but she is ready to endorse it just the same. That is discipleship, and so is her eager imitation of teacher's verbal tics. What is curious is that elsewhere Paglia's principal criticism of the Ivy League is its toadyism; this apparent contradiction can be resolved once one recognises that her notion of discipleship is overtly religious, and involves the abnegation of the self.[46] By contrast, the toadies Paglia stigmatises are the wrong kind of disciples, followers of false prophets, seekers of advancement. It's Socrates versus the Sophists again. Paglia's own imitations and sycophancies cannot be separated from her notion that a Great Teacher somehow represents something else – the subject, elemental energy – into which she plugs. I read Paglia's work because an older colleague told me that she had the answers for my generation; I was curious to see what he meant. The piece he actually referred me to was a piece on poststructuralists-under-the-bed which has nothing to say about pedagogy, but Paglia's worshipful endorsement of Kessler is plainly related to her disdain for those who would deny authentic self-presence and meaning.

The existence of these texts suggests that the left has not yet resolved the problems of replication, insemination and sonship, with their resultant figuration of women as sexual objects rather than subjects. Indeed, the rhetoric of sonship has been incorporated into the left's practices in research, publication and endless attempts at career advancement. There is a great deal of truth in Paglia's remarks about disciple-ship in the Ivy League (and her remarks apply equally well to Oxbridge). One reason everyone warmed to theories which emphasised the dominative power of discourse was because they themselves were inside a system where these ideas certainly held good. Oral toadying, however, is less significant in the groves of academe than a rhetoric of citation whereby citing an authority is supposed to grant authority to one's own discourse. This rhetoric can of course extend beyond citation and into various kinds of discursive imitation, from adoption of neologisms to wholesale replication of stylistic tricks. At some points in the 1980s the entire discipline of literary criticism seemed to be divided into schools or workshops, like Renaissance art (in this respect, at least), each one with its founding father, and one could tell from the moment one picked a book up whether it was school of Lacan, school of Greenblatt, or whatever.[47] Books often came with an endorsement from someone more senior considered to be the 'father' or 'mother' of whatever 'school' of criticism the book represented. If academic discourse in the 1990s seems more flexible and combinatory, this in no way diminishes the rhetoric of authority and the circulation of citation. Authority in the classroom, in the undergraduate essay, is also constituted this way. A colleague once suggested to me that the ideal admissions candidate would confess to a liking for Rilke, Philip K. Dick and Barthes.

In this system, what of the woman lecturer: if she cannot or has never been seen as a son, can she ever be seen as a father? Does she want to be seen as a father, and if not how can she present herself? Thousands of women lecturers know: their students (male and female) do not see them as authoritative fathers who control the *logos*, but as nurturative mothers. The fact that this may not be the way the woman sees herself is irrelevant.[48] One of the effects of taking up this role is a professional clash of norms: you get no promotional credit at any institution with which I have been involved for spending days carefully nursing students through emotional and intellectual crises. And as anyone who's been one of fewer than three women in a department knows, *all* the students come for help to the women. Women don't want to turn away the needy, because it's nice to be needed. But what about that paper, the one that has to be given next week? Doing it at midnight again?[49] Often women who manage to juggle all these demands get no credit from the students, because they (and many colleagues) see this as the outpouring of natural, feminine maternity. Male colleagues who are nurturing, on the other hand, are seen as giving up time reserved for research, and get some credit for it. However, women who refuse to be nurturing, especially those who refuse to nurture women students and female colleagues, are often seen as 'unnaturally' hard and competitive, even as anti-feminist or lacking in solidarity. Nor are they granted the authority of the father, if they should happen to want it; occasionally one sees some feminist academics successfully appropriate this space of paternity, but it is perhaps momentary, and a little chilling too.

We will solve nothing if we act out the paternal roles: whether we choose to be mothers or fathers. If the former, we leave men free to be Big Daddy and we confirm everyone's gender expectations; if the latter, we leave everything as it was and somewhere in the building some other woman is probably carrying the maternal can for us, as well as the little matter of subtending a system which constructs the desire of the harasser as its 'natural' outcome. Everyone dislikes essays which say at the end 'here is the problem: we must rethink X or Y' and then leave that work for others. It seems appropriate to canvass some of the remedies that have been suggested to me for this disease, including some I've tried myself.

In the absence of any serious discourse on pedagogy, the field has been invaded by an army of management-speakers wielding the dreadful discourses of encounter groups, human resource management and dianetics.[50] One might take as an example a well-intentioned book called *57 Things to Do in Seminars*. Titles again; the way this one is phrased ironically recalls *365 Things for Kids to Do on a Wet Day*. Its central rhetoric is of 'keeping the students amused' and 'making seminars fun'. Many of its suggestions involve making shapes out of the students, such as pyramids and circles, as if the students were raw material like PlayDoh and teaching itself a kind of game with amusement as its prime purpose. All this reproduces the notion that teaching is not serious *because* it is maternal: that is, the minute we move away from the father's insemination of his disciples, the only other culturally sanctioned models available are deeply feminised via figures of childminding and child-amusement. It can be no coincidence that pedagogy is a devalued branch of practice *and* that it is feminised. In this respect feminists have actually been even more guilty than others: a recent anthology of feminist critical 'autobiographies' revealed that many saw the academy as their chance to escape from the underpaid, undervalued, feminised space of teaching; they all remarked on this as if unaware that teaching is what they spend their time doing.[51] What is worrying is that *57 Things to Do in Seminars* and the other texts of this kind currently circulating are often presented as the solution to the problem of overly hierarchised teaching: if Plato is the problem, PlayDoh is the solution. In fact, however, this discourse does nothing to undercut gender stereotyping; it plunges us straight back into the dilemma of Big Daddy and Nurturing Mummy which I outlined above. Moreover, many students – and perhaps especially women students – also see university as their chance to escape from school and may not be pleased if we abandon our mission to differentiate them from the 'uncultured masses' without degrees; in human terms, envisaging students as children to be 'amused' sounds (to say the least) patronising.

These reflections lead me to reproduce Celia Kitzinger's remark that 'touchy-feely' therapy teaching is a harasser's charter, since it brings the personal and the confessional into the classroom and legitimates them.[52] Furthermore, I suspect that I have sometimes retreated into personalised teaching because I felt so uncomfortable in the position of the all-knowing father; unable to assume that authority or to gain acknowledgement of it from others, I felt less uncomfortable with the fantasy of a nurturing mother, although I am not very nurturative. Some of my students correctly perceived this as something of a masquerade, perhaps recognising that I retained the authoritative power of the father to admit them to or exclude them from high culture. Under my skirts, I was wearing a phallus. There is another problem too; what am I teaching my students if I refuse to exude authority? Am I teaching them that authority is a male perogative?

So where now? Hazy efforts to replace Daddy with Mummy have not been productive, and yet I still can't quite bring myself to go into reverse and become a father-figure. The 'old' system is also a harassers' charter, a misogynists' charter and the principal reason that women are not taken seriously in the academy, as teachers and students. I am in search of another model, and I turn now to a proposal made by Gargi Bhattacharyya.[53] Pointing out that the universities have spent a lot of energy in defensive rhetoric, fictively claiming to preserve a separation from the marketplace which does not really exist, she asked whether closing the gap between academe and the *agora* might offer something to us, something that might save us from the horns of the dilemma on which we are currently impaled. To rephrase her argument, she was suggesting that it may not be a calamity if the universities lose their isolation from the workplace which for most people constitutes 'the real world'. For if we left the pastoral groves of academe and instead recon-figured them as the open *agora*, a space of buying and selling and yelling, a public space, would eroticised insemination still be the hidden motivator of all our actions? The Platonic model is conceptually dependent on its spatial location; we don't assume any transcenden-tal transference between shop assistants and their merchandise, or between plumbers and the S-bend. We should reimagine the academy, then, as a noisy, *public* place in which professorship means being both a maker and a stallholder. We should represent seminars, tutorials and symposia as workshops, in which professors and students alike work to shape a variety of commodities, of which the student might be *one*. This does not have to imply a careless, dehumanising transaction if we think of ourselves and our students *together* occupying the place of a crafter, shaping the object of the craft to the highest possible smoothness and gloss. Perhaps this self-image might allow us to acknowledge our power and authority without embarrassment; perhaps it might allow us to see ourselves and our students as co-*workers*, with greater and lesser skill and diverse tasks, aiming together to produce a good, marketable, valuable commodity; this, after all, is what they expect of us. We might debate among ourselves and with them just what kind of shaping adds value, but the basic model need not be touched by this. Perhaps this model would make the relations between academic hierarchies and power structures more explicit; perhaps it would turn students' unions into a reality? Perhaps there might be open rebellion?

What would have to happen for this model to come into being? The following, among other things:

1. Teaching would have to be separated from assessment; the tutor should *never* be the customer as well. As I discovered (at Oxford of all places), this allows student and tutor to unite against the examiners (provided of course the tutor doesn't identify with them and isn't identified with them). It fosters the notion of co-working and it also removes a great deal of tutors' power (no more 'lay-for-an-A').
2. Teachers should never be able to decide who they will or won't teach, which means that admissions (general or local) must also be taken out of their hands and put into the hands of administrators. Teachers should try to help shape whoever turns up.
3. Seminars, lectures and tutorials should be evidently open and available to anyone (faculty, student, member of the public) who wants to attend. People should be able to wander through, to drift in and out. Ideally there should be a background of noise. A pub or city street café would be the ideal setting. Perhaps food and drink should be involved, so that everyone can displace lechery into them, like de Sade in prison.
4. Courses should *never* be taught solely by one person, nor should seminar groups be assigned one tutor for a whole term; everyone should swap, rather often. This would disrupt transference and also (pragmatically) open harassers to the scrutiny of others. Harassment would become a collective and more visible problem. Moreover, students should not be permitted to work with any individual for two semesters/terms consecutively, or for more than two terms *in toto*. In theory, swapping often might cut teaching preparation time: X teaches all the seminars in the week in which we do *Macbeth*, while Y teaches them all in the week in which we do *Othello*.

5. The abolition of tutorials as a principal means of teaching; they promote transference and insemination and are far too private. Lectures are preferable. The range of public discourses could be widened to include new technology; lectures and tutorials on computer networks, which are not much like a grove.

6. An idea from Gerald Graff: instead of covering over academic differences, we should make them the mainstay of our teaching.[54] There should be far fewer monovocal discourses; faculty members should openly debate with other faculty members instead of merely representing their opponents' views to students. As well as teaching students how to defend an argument, this would also deconstruct the notion that any faculty member is automatically authoritative. Students should be encouraged to join in and to hold their own debates. For those less invested in oratorical skill (a category which might include some women) there might be written debates that are nevertheless public and open, perhaps on gigantic pieces of butcher's paper in the corridors. There might be several of these on different themes running concurrently.

7. Essays and exam essays should not be the sole kinds of texts produced by students in literature courses; both are intrinsically private and neither ever circulates publicly. For assessment, they should produce public (though not necessarily oral) discourses, including speeches, tirades, poems, stories told orally, poems, plays, parties, films, newspaper articles, reviews, magazines, posters, polemics. These should be made available in corridors for anyone to read, buy or comment on. Students should be urged to reply at length to each other's efforts. In some disciplines, a return to straightforward multiple-choice factual exams might be combined with this, if a test of memory is considered important.

Not only would these changes disrupt paternalism and question the workings of authority, they would also offer the possibility of enhancing women's oral and rhetorical skills. I do not wish to suggest that harassment is due to a failure to answer back, but rather to suggest that women's oral disempowerment as students does not offer them the verbal skills and confidence they need to argue against harassers or anyone else who unreasonably obstructs their path. Feminist academics are failing women students if we fail to do all we can to increase their power in and over the spoken word. Currently, there is a real risk of producing the kind of feminist student who can summarise Irigaray on paper, but who can't defend feminist views against the most imbecilic assault by male students or professors.

All these suggestions require massive and probably unpopular institutional change, and already I can see only too clearly how many could be adapted to the maintenance of the existing state of affairs. I can also see how the idea of students as commodities might lead to the dreariest and most Gradgrindian forms of classroom oppression, and how the notion of students as commodities might come to overlap with the notion of women as sexual commodities. If you share these doubts, or if you think the whole plan 'impractical' (unlike the current silken smooth running of our degree programmes, naturally), I have an alternative, fringe suggestion involving Irigarayan mimicry.

Whether you are a man or a woman, try this remedy. Get hold of a huge pair of glasses. Shave the top of your head or wear a stocking cap. Wear a false beard. Wear huge fake brogues made of styrofoam, tweeds and a waistcoat. Imitate the voice of an Oxford don when you speak. Don't forget to lisp. And don't forget your leather phallus.

Notes and References

1. Billie Wright Dziech and Linda Weiner, *The Lecherous Professor: Sexual Harassment on Campus*, 2nd edition (Urbana: University of Illinois Press, 1990; 1st edition Boston, Mass.: Beacon, 1984). This is an American survey; as far as I am aware there has been no comparable book-length study for the UK.
2. In addressing harassment's production in and by the academy, I am attempting to particularise what has historically been seen as general; I do not mean my arguments to hold good for other contexts, whether professional or not, but I hope that others might begin the task of thinking about how different hierarchies and self-constructions might produce similarly oppressive results.
3. Desire is often displaced into one form of orality or another; Sade grew immensely obese when in prison.
4. In saying this, I mean to distinguish sharply between this narrow definition of sexual harassment, and the widening of the term to include so-called peer harassment, where no power-relations other than those of gender are involved. There is no space here to debate the fraught questions raised by this expansion of the term in detail, but it is probably evident that I subscribe to the narrower definition.
5. Bruce Robbins, *Secular Vocations: Intellectuals, Professionalism, Culture* (London: Verso, 1993), Chapter 1.
6. For some typical responses, see Andrew Ross, *No Respect: Intellectuals and Popular Culture* (London: Routledge, 1989), which does not mention the classroom as a site for intellectuals or for popular

culture; Gerald Graff, *Professing Literature* (Baltimore: Johns Hopkins University Press, 1989), which confines itself to curricula, and his 'Preaching to the Converted', in Susan Gubar and Jonathan Kamholtz (eds) *English Inside and Out: The Places of Literary Criticism* (London: Routledge, 1993), pp. 109–21, which confines itself to publications; the feminist autobiographies in Gayle Greene and Coppelia Kahn (eds), *Changing Subjects: The Making of Feminist Literary Criticism* (London: Routledge, 1993), which make few mentions of their own practices as teachers while discoursing lengthily on their experiences as undergraduates; and the essays on Shakespeare in Lesley Aers and Nigel Wheale (eds) *Shakespeare in the Changing Curriculum* (London: Routledge, 1992), where only the school-teachers consider pedagogy in any detail.

7. Jonathan Culler, 'The Humanities Tomorrow', in Culler, *Framing the Sign: Criticism and Its Institutions* (Oxford: Blackwell, 1988), pp. 41–57.

8. Two exceptions to the left's lack of interest in pedagogy are Barbara Johnson's 'The Pedagogical Imperative', in Johnson, *A World of Difference* (Baltimore: Johns Hopkins University Press, 1987), and Diana Fuss' 'Essentialism in the Classroom', in Fuss, *Essentially Speaking* (London: Routledge, 1990).

9. See, for example Camille Paglia, 'Junk Bonds and Corporate Raiders: Academe in the Hour of the Wolf' and 'The MIT Lecture: Crisis in the American Universities', in Paglia, *Sex, Art and American Culture* (London: Viking, 1992), pp. 170–248 and 249–98; Allan Bloom, *The Closing of the American Mind* (Harmondsworth: Penguin, 1987); E.D. Hirsch, *Cultural Literacy* (Boston, Mass.: Houghton Mifflin, 1987).

10. See Roger Kimball, *Tenured Radicals: How Politics Has Corrupted Our Higher Education* (New York: Harper, 1990); Dinesh D'Souza, *Illiberal Education: The Politics of Race and Sex on Campus* (New York: Vintage, 1992).

11. For an unconvincing assertion of the latter proposition, see Judith Gardiner, 'Radical Optimism, Maternal Materialism, and Teaching Literature' in Greene and Kahn, *Changing Subjects,* pp. 83–95.

12. For a brilliant discussion of these issues, see Jane Gallop, Marianne Hirsch and Nancy K. Miller, 'Criticizing Feminist Criticism', in Marianne Hirsch and Evelyn Fox Keller (eds) *Conflicts in Feminism* (London: Routledge, 1990), pp. 349–69; see also Jane Gallop, 'The Institutionalization of Feminist Criticism', in Gubar and Kamholtz, *English Inside and Out,* pp. 61–7.

13. For the earliest study of these well-known phenomena, see Michelle Stanworth, *Gender and Schooling: A Study of Sexual Divisions in the*

Classroom (London: Hutchinson, 1981); these findings are well known to the general public, and some women choose to send their duaghters to single-sex schools as a result. The fact that they have not even been considered in universities is a scandal.

14. I choose a theorist rather than a literary text as an exemplum in the hope of heading off certain anxieties of the right about students' and teachers' competence with Great Art.

15. These differences become even more marked if a literary text is the object of study, which is one reason that theory is easier to teach than Yeats, Joyce or Chaucer.

16. All of this would be even truer if I were trying to teach the students something more indefinite, like 'aesthetic appreciation' or 'making the poetry of X available to them'. For an analysis of how such aesthetic standards are learned, see Jonathan Dollimore and Alan Sinfield, *Political Shakespeare* (Manchester: Manchester University Press, 1985).

17. This discussion is crucially indebted to Pierre Bourdieu's review of the operations of the French *écoles* in his *Homo Academicus* (Oxford: Blackwell, 1988.) See also Susan Stanford Friedman, 'Authority in the Feminist Classroom: A Contradiction in Terms?', in Margo Culley and Catherine Portuges (eds), *Gendered Subjects: The Dynamics of Feminist Teaching* (London: Routledge and Kegan Paul, 1982).

18. For a discussion of this point, see Katha Pollitt, 'Canon to the Right of Me ...', *Nation*, 23 September 1991. Pollit suggests that some of the heat and dust about curricula are generated by the well-founded belief that whatever is selected will be the only thing the students will read.

19. Compare Paglia's use of the term 'academe' for the academy in her 'Junk Bonds and Corporate Raiders: Academe in the Hour of the Wolf'. My impression is that the term is applied particularly to the humanities.

20. 'Atque inter silvas Academi quaerere verum' – 'and seek for truth in the groves of Academe', Horace, *Epistles*, II.ii.45.

21. Milton, *Paradise Regained*, Book IV, ll. 244–6. Satan is speaking to Christ, and the image of retirement created here is not intended to be unambiguously positive.

22. Similar pastoral evocations of Oxford abound. Perhaps the best known is Evelyn Waugh's *Brideshead Revisited*; the first book of the novel, which alone concerns Oxford, is entitled 'Et in Arcadia Ego'. One might also mention the metaphor of the Oxbridge garden, which is often central to such figurations. These images were given added impetus by two world wars, in which the universities were apt to be figured as unreal alternatives to the anti-pastoral of war;

it goes without saying that such configurations were almost exclusively masculine. See Paul Fussell, *The Great War and Modern Memory* (Oxford: Oxford University Press, 1975), Chapter 7.

23. Matthew Arnold, *Culture and Anarchy*, Chapter 5, cited in Richard Jenkyns, *The Victorians and the Ancient Greeks* (Oxford: Blackwell, 1980), p. 248; see also Oscar Wilde's comparison in *The Critic as Artist* (1890) between the Platonic notion of education in beauty and the beauty of Oxford (in *The Artist as Critic: Critical Writings of Oscar Wilde*, ed. Richard Ellman [London: W.H. Allen, 1970], p. 252); and see also Walter Pater's notorious expansion of this theme in *Plato and Platonism* (London: Macmillan, 1909; 1st edition 1893).

24. William Kerrigan, 'Students and Lechers', *Observer Magazine,* Sunday 3 October 1993, pp. 22–3. Note the recurrence of the term 'lecher' in the title of the article. I am grateful to Alison Gill for drawing this text to my attention.

25. Plato, *Charmides*, 155 c–d, in *Plato: Early Socratic Dialogues*, ed. and trans. Donald Watt (Harmondsworth: Penguin, 1987).

26. For further discussion of the significance of the opening of the *Phaedrus*, see Anne Carson, *Eros the Bittersweet* (Princeton, NJ: Princeton University Press, 1986), especially p. 123. See also David Halperin, 'Plato and Erotic Reciprocity', *Classical Antiquity* 5 (1986), pp. 60–80. On homoerotic play in Plato, see Kenneth Dover, *Greek Homosexuality* (London: Duckworth, 1978); John J. Winkler, *The Constraints of Desire: The Anthropology of Sex and Gender in Ancient Greece* (London: Routledge, 1990).

27. Jacques Derrida, *Dissemination*, trans. and intro. Barbara Johnson, (London: Athlone, 1981), p. 133. Derrida is primarily interested in this as a metaphor for text–son and author–father, but this too can be seen as a pedagogical relation. The place of books in pedagogy deserves more consideration than I am able to give it here.

28. Derrida, *Dissemination*, p. 102.

29. Derrida, *Dissemination*, p. 77.

30. Page du Bois, *Sowing the Body: Psychoanalysis and Ancient Representations of Women* (Chicago: University of Chicago Press, 1988), pp. 170 ff.

31. Derrida, *Dissemination*, p. 143.

32. *Theaetetus*, 148e–151d; on thought as labour, see *Symposium*, 206c–e, *Republic*, 490b, *Phaedrus*, 278a–b; and on this image of the autotelic 'birth' of thought which is truth and sonship and which displaces the mother, see my doctoral dissertation, 'Gender, Power and the Body: Some Figurations of Femininity in Milton and Seventeenth-century Women's Writing' (University of Oxford, 1991), Section II, Chapters 4 and 5. It might be argued that there is yet another

potential model for pedagogy encoded in the Platonic corpus in the person of Diotima, who is said to be Socrates' teacher in the *Symposium*. Whether figured as knowing *hetaira* or inspired priestess-*anima*, the whole point about Diotima is that she is a figure in a male dialogue, a fantasy of femininity who can be made to speak in place of patriarchy and for her own exclusion from that of which she speaks. As Luce Irigaray puts it, 'She is not there. She herself does not speak.' The figure Diotima resembles is Athene, whose birth from a father's thigh literally displaces the mother, who has been obliterated and absorbed by the devouring father. For a more optimistic reading of Diotima, see David Halperin, 'Why is Diotima a Woman?', in Halperin, *One Hundred Years of Homosexuality* (London: Routledge, 1990), pp. 113–52; and see also Luce Irigaray, 'Sorcerer Love: A Reading of Diotima's Speech, Plato's *Symposium*', in Nancy Fraser and Sandra Lee Bartky (eds), *Revaluing French Feminism: Critical Essays on Difference, Agency and Culture*, (Bloomington: Indiana University Press, 1992), pp. 364–76. On Athene, see, among others, Marcel Detienne and Jean-Pierre Vernant, *Cunning Intelligence in Greek Society*, trans. Janet Lloyd (Chicago: Chicago University Press, 1974), pp. 55 ff; and Nicole Loraux, *The Children of Athena: Athenian Ideas about Citizenship and the Division between the Sexes*, trans. Caroline Levine (Princeton, NJ: Princeton University Press, 1993). On the representation of female teachers in terms of Greek myths of female autonomy, see Tennyson's *The Princess*; and on its political dubiousness see Mary Lefkowitz, *Women in Greek Myth* (London: Duckworth, 1986), Chapter 1.

33. Bloom, *Closing of the American Mind*. Bloom also translated Plato's *Republic* in 1968, with an extended interpretive essay arguing (among other things) that Plato's critique of the ills of democracy was correct, and that Plato was only joking when he advocated the inclusion of women in the guardian class in Book V.

34. In this Bloom is also locating himself in a tradition of inspirational teachers; both Jowett and Cory were compared to Socrates by pupils (Jenkyns, *Victorians and Ancient Greeks*, pp. 248–9), and during the Victorian and Edwardian periods public schoolmasters also routinely likened themselves to Socrates. 'Socrates was jolly to young fellows, and told them heavenly stories about the gods', opines a house-master in the school story *David Blaize*, cited in Peter Parker, *The Old Lie: The Great War and Public Schools* (London: Macmillan, 1990), p. 122.

35. Bloom, *Closing of the American Mind*, p. 20.

36. Bloom's observation seems as shaky as his analysis; many of my students (American as well as British) like classical music, as I did

when I was at university in the early 1980s. This raises the possibility that Bloom is also investing in seeing his students as more rebellious than they actually are. For this neoconservative rhetoric, see Richard Rich, 'Somewhere off the Coast of Academia,' in Lennard Davis and M. Bella Mirabella (eds), *Left Politics and the Literary Profession* (New York: Columbia University Press, 1990), p. 293.

37. For this line of defence, see Natalie Harris Bluestone's commentary in *Women and the Ideal Society: Plato's Republic and Modern Myths of Gender* (Oxford: Berg, 1987), pp. 140–3. Bluestone is critiquing Jean Baker Elshtain's denunciation of the sexual politics of the *Symposium* in her *Public Man, Private Woman* (Princeton, NJ: Princeton University Press, 1981). My argument here is not the same as Elshtain's, since for her Plato's understanding of gender is flawed because it rules out a feminine specificity which I do not believe exists. Rather, I am suggesting that Plato's texts form a pretext for a certain kind of misogynist fantasy about the disappearance or disavowal of the feminine *as conceived in patriarchy*.
38. Dziech and Weiner, *The Lecherous Professor* p. 152.
39. In David Lodge's *Small World,* for example, a beautiful young woman called Angelica specialises in romance narrative and gives a paper on deferral and invagination at a conference. The 'joke' is that in the academic audience only one man recognises the 'incongruity' of listening to a beautiful woman using words like invagination without becoming aroused. David Lodge, *Small World* (Harmondsworth: Penguin, 1984), pp. 322–3.
40. Also published in French under the title 'Cheveux longs, idées courts' (Long hair, short ideas). Michele Le Doeuff, 'Women and Philosophy', in Toril Moi (ed.), *French Feminist Thought: A Reader* (Oxford: Blackwell, 1988), pp. 181–209.
41. This is not to suggest that any of these women were completely pliable; Heloise at least resisted Abelard's instruction, sometimes violently, while de Beauvoir's writings can be read as a series of tricks and ruses which reassert her supremacy. For a fascinating discussion of Edith Wharton and discipleship which argues for the ruses of the woman in accepting a masochistic position and then trying to subvert it, see Louise J. Kaplan, *Female Perversions* (Harmondsworth: Penguin, 1993), pp. 206–8, 226–9.
42. This is not to imply that de Man's disciples were having affairs with him, a matter about which I have no knowledge or interest; personal and passionate do not necessarily mean actively sexual.
43. For a discussion of Le Doeuff's theory and this question see Elizabeth Grosz, *Sexual Subversions: Three French Feminists* (Sydney: Allen and Unwin, 1989), Section 3; and Meaghan Morris, 'Operative Reasoning;

Reading Michele le Doeuff' in Morris, *The Pirate's Fiancée: Feminism, Reading, Postmodernism* (London: Verso, 1988), pp. 71–102.
44. Michele Le Doeuff, *Hipparchia's Choice* (Oxford: Blackwell, 1992).
45. Paglia, 'Milton Kessler, A Memoir', in *Sex, Art and American Culture*, pp. 126, 127, 129.
46. For Paglia's criticism of toadying, see 'The MIT Lecture', in *Sex, Art and American Culture*, p. 298; she refers to 'a Paul de Man toady' at this point who is plainly Barbara Johnson, though Paglia does not name her.
47. This is not to suggest that feminists did not interrogate the logic of fathers, sons and daughters with regard to theory; for the best known of these interrogations, see Jane Gallop, *Feminism and Psychoanalysis: The Daughter's Seduction* (London: Macmillan, 1983).
48. See Friedman, 'Authority in the Feminist Classroom', p. 206.
49. Carolyn Porter, 'Getting Gendered', in Greene and Kahn, *Changing Subjects*, pp. 168–79.
50. Dianetics: the psychobabble of scientology, which involves a process called 'clearing' that is heavily reliant on confessionalism. Like many cults, dianetics recruits a lot through management seminars.
51. Greene and Kahn, *Changing Subjects*; see especially Porter, 'Getting Gendered', pp. 171–3, but most of the autobiographies mention this obliquely or directly.
52. Celia Kitzinger, discussion, Colloquium on Sexual Harassment, Cambridge, autumn 1992.
53. Gargi Bhattacharyya, 'Becoming the "Race Lady" in the British University', Women in Context Lecture Series, University of East Anglia, spring 1993; see also her contribution to this volume (Chapter 4).
54. Gerald Graff, *Beyond the Culture Wars: How Teaching the Conflicts Can Revitalize American Education* (New York: Norton, 1992).

10

Sexual Harassment in India: A Case Study of Eve-teasing in Historical Perspective[1]

Padma Anagol-McGinn

This chapter explores the complexities of a specific type of sexual harassment in India known by the popular and officially recognised name of Eve-teasing.[2] The first official definition was produced by the government of the Union territory of New Delhi in its Prohibition of Eve-teasing Act of 1984. This defines Eve-teasing as:

> When a man by words either spoken or by signs and or by visible represen-
> tation or by gesture does any act in public space, or signs, recites or utters
> any indecent words or song or ballad in any public place to the annoyance
> of any women ...[3]

In reality, however, women are subjected not only to remarks, songs and gestures laden with sexual innuendo but also to actual physical molestation of the person, signified by the grabbing of breasts and buttocks, tugging women's braids, jostling against them (although this is made out to be accidental), or spitting on their faces or clothes. The Law Commission of India, does not recognise Eve-teasing as acts of 'assault' but as 'indecent gestures'.[4] It has further suggested that such incidents require no new penal law, as Eve-teasing is 'amply covered by Section 509 of the Indian Penal Code'.[5] The seriousness of the offence of Eve-teasing is not acknowledged by the Indian Penal Code, precisely because it does not recognise Eve-teasing as 'assault'. My contention is that it does embody certain elements of assault but falls short of rape.[6] Eve-teasing is invariably committed by men on women. It is also invariably conducted in public places such as bus-stops; in trains and buses; on pavements, college campuses, cinemas (cinema-halls in India have a seating capacity ranging from 500 to 1,200); and in shopping areas in full view of pedestrians and crowds.

Eve-teasing is now a cognisable and non-bailable crime in some states of India.[7] Large billboards appear in cities carrying the message: 'Do not Eve-tease. It's a crime.' Why does the Indian government feel the need to publicise Eve-teasing as a crime? Was it ever a socially acceptable custom in India? To when can we trace the rise of this phenomenon? By providing a historical context, we can come to understand the processes behind this problem and also offer solutions to it.

The term is of Anglo-Indian derivation. 'Eve' indicates a Christian and 'white' discourse and as such embodies elements of transgression, danger and the notion of unruly female sexuality. It is very likely that the term was familiarised by British judges and journalists over cases of Eve-teasing that appeared in courts. This indicates that Eve-teasing as we recognise it in its present-day garb originated in India's colonial past; beyond that, its roots lie in the rites and rituals of certain Hindu carnivals which can be traced to Indian antiquity. Certain festivals, which are still in vogue, are characterised by a breakdown of sexual taboos between the sexes. One of the most popular of these festivals is the *Holi*, celebrated all over northern India and in western India where it is known under a different name – the *Shimga*. Men, women and children dress in fine clothes, gather in groups, visit neighbours and friends and spray each other with water-sprinklers. The water is coloured with dyes, creating a riot of colours and making it difficult to recognise anyone. This carnival validates the acts of hugging and kissing and forcibly sprinkling and dousing one another in coloured water. By midday, most of the revellers are inebriated with drinks and food mixed with *bhang* (cannabis).

This carnival gives a special licence to disorderly behaviour for both men and women.[8] Men are allowed to play the dominant role: they chase women – the norm is to chase willing rather than unwilling women – grab them and douse them with water. Women are allowed a complex behaviour in this rite. They can be unruly in public, break dress and behaviour codes (expressed in loud laughter and free physical movements) and respond to the flirtatious attention of men. A woman can rid herself of unwanted attention in smaller village communities where large extended families will help her, tied as they are by kinship relations.[9] Notions of family 'honour' also allow a degree of protection to women in village communities, which acts as a deterrent to harassers.

These carnivals probably originated as a 'valve' to let off steam in an otherwise sexually repressed society. What is significant, however, is the degree of autonomy the woman is able to exercise in such situations. She can realise hidden fantasies by responding to a preferred choice, or she can thwart the unwanted attention of men. In contemporary India, carnival behaviour has been recontextualised by Eve-teasing. In contemporary Eve-teasing, the public location of the act provides continuity with carnivals. But other factors differ. Firstly, the teeming millions of Indian cities give anonymity a sinister role. Carnival behaviour in cities allows men to force women to acknowledge their presence in unpleasant ways, and anonymity adds to a woman's insecurity. Women's objections today are not to *Holi* but to unknown men trying to play *Holi* with them.[10] Secondly, carnival behaviour may go some way to explain the apathy of crowds even when a harassed woman pleads for intervention. This is especially true if the Eve-teaser limits himself to singing an amorous love-song. The street mentality is that such a harasser is a 'mischief-monger'. In other words, he is probably 'love-stricken' and therefore 'harmless'.[11]

The changes of carnival behaviour in modern urban culture and its legitimation in crowd mentalities seems to me to be a crucial factor in understanding how Eve-teasing humiliates women. In carnivals, the presiding code is the ultimate will or 'consent' of the woman. In Eve-teasing, the notion of 'consent' does not exist. No woman agrees to be Eve-teased. It is forced upon her. It then seems fairly obvious that the only way pressure can be brought upon the Indian judiciary to legalise a separate penalty for Eve-teasing is to recognise it as 'assault' and without 'consent'. As the law stands today, Eve-teasing is treated as a minor offence punishable under the general category of Section 509 of the Indian Penal Code. One of the primary principles by which rape is defined as assault is the non-consent of the victim. Likewise, Eve-teasing ought to be recognised as an act involving the non-consent of the woman, rather than seeing it in terms of obscenity (indecent gestures) or as an act that threatens to 'insult the modesty of a woman'.

It has been suggested that certain licentious behaviours were accorded equally to both sexes in Indian carnivals, marriages and rituals. However, later a perceptible change occurred in Indian and state attitudes towards these special licences. What was once regarded as a welcome social release fell into disfavour and was condemned in the late nineteenth century. Recently, social and cultural historians have argued that the emergence of a small though significant Indian élite trained in Western education during the nineteenth century began to perceive certain Indian customs as repugnant.[12] This explanation is not entirely acceptable in the specific case of why the *Holi* festival was condemned.

Vernacular newspaper reports of the time[13] show that Western educated Indians were objecting to the changes they perceived in how the festival was celebrated in cities. Two changes they wrote about were the use of 'indecent expressions' and 'indecent songs and words', and acts of forcibly dousing with coloured water unwary passers-by, especially females, who were complete strangers to the revellers.[14] The objection was not made, for example, if a member of the Marwadi (Hindu mercantile class) sprayed another female member of his own community, whom in all probability he knew, but when he transgressed the familiar boundaries of his communal space and stepped outside to claim the same familiarity with a woman who was a total stranger. The factor of anonymity in a bustling city seems to have played a part in the changing nature of the festival. Equally significant is one journalist's observation that 'Such a thing was not observed during previous years.'[15] The shift in the connotations of *Holi* from 'acceptable' to 'unacceptable' was therefore linked to the alterations in male behaviour patterns in urban areas. The use of 'indecent words and songs' is also an indicator of how certain elements of the phenomenon of Eve-teasing was being manifested in the changing nature of the carnival.

Eve-teasing is not only associated with changes in carnival behaviour and attitudes to it, but is also due to changes brought by the impact of colonialism. The first recorded instances of Eve-teasing in its present-day form can be traced to the mid nineteenth century. While the term 'Eve-teasing' is not used in any of the sources I have come across in this period, the details of the phenomenon are within the contemporary definition of the term. For example, in 1883 a vernacular newspaper of Bombay described the manner in which women walking in public streets were treated:

> for sometime past a number of Parsi miscreants have met every evening between 7 and 9 o' clock in that part of the Bazar Gate Street which lies between the corner of the Manakji Shet's Agyari Lane and Bamanji Wadia's fountain and gibe at the Parsi ladies who happen to pass by that way. These *budmashes* [rogues or rascals] sometimes address indecent words to the ladies and sometimes waylay them. It is requested that the D.C.P. [District Commissioner of Police] take notice of this.[16]

Another newspaper in a south Indian town described an incident that is reminiscent of Eve-teasing. This reporter stated:

> In Gadag there is a well called Gobbardi. Some bad characters gather round it at 5 PM when women of the town come to fetch water and these bad characters sing obscene songs in their presence and insult them in various ways. The police have been informed but they have done nothing so far.[17]

Yet another Marathi newspaper reported that:

> several respectable residents of Memonwada complain that many bad characters collect at 4 o'clock every afternoon and sit till eleven at night on the corners of Chh'as Mohola [a suburban residential area]. They annoy the women who pass along these roads, and use indecent expressions. This

conduct is likely to give rise to a serious row one of these days. It behoves the police, therefore, to prohibit them from assembling.[18]

English and vernacular newspapers in colonial India carried reports on harassment of women quite regularly throughout the late nineteenth century. The novelty of this phenomenon is emphasised by the fact that the press considered it worth reporting at a time when nationalist activity and anti-imperialist resistance were dominating the news. The incidents reported in newspapers reveal several significant factors. Firstly, Eve-teasing appeared to be endemic in many parts of colonial India, if one can take press reports to be a representative and accurate source. Secondly, all reported incidents happened to take place in urban centres such as Bombay, Ahmadabad, Sholapur, Pune, Karachi and Kolhapur, which indicates the phenomenon was a problem plaguing cities and large towns. And all reports of Eve-teasing were accompanied by a plea for police intervention, revealing that some Indians at least took the problem seriously and believed the state should do so too.

Power relationships and racial tensions between the coloniser and the colonised, and the related public performance of the respective dominating and subordinated groups, are intricately linked to the forms in which Eve-teasing manifested itself during the late nineteenth century. Kenneth Ballhatchet, who has studied British attitudes to sexual behaviour across the boundaries of race and class, has shown how British authorities provided Indian women as prostitutes for British soldiers but actively discouraged officials from having Indian women as mistresses or wives. This contradiction in British policy, he argues, was shaped by the belief that maintenance of social distance between ruling and ruled was necessary for the preservation of authority.[19] Racism as an official ideology manifested itself in intricate ways; besides the behaviour Ballhatchet has described, it also included placing obstacles in the way of competing Indians who tried to enter the prestigious Indian civil service, and preventing them from trying Europeans facing criminal charges. Racialised elements of Eve-teasing were clearly evident in the day-to-day interaction of Europeans with the indigenous population. When sexual assaults took place which involved European men and Indian women, emotional responses were often raised to fever-pitch. Such incidents were perceived by Indians as British attempts to control Indian female sexuality and to deal a psychological blow to their own masculinity.[20]

At the lower levels of the British administration, among guards, soldiers and clerks, elaborate forms of domination were practised on the colonised, and systematically on the weakest subjects – Indian women. Newspapers reported many instances of British soldiers, railway guards and ticket collectors harassing Indian women.[21] Even when women ventured to file complaints, alarming numbers were reported as being ignored; when cases did reach the courts, the assailants were usually acquitted.[22]

An incident which brings out the 'public transcript'[23] of the ruling race, and which caused a major uproar in western India in the 1880s, was the *Pachumba* case. In November 1886 around 15 Hindu women were travelling on a steamer called *Pachumba* from Karachi to Bombay. Some European soldiers who were passengers on the same ship hooted at the women and, on failing to get a response, grabbed and kissed them forcibly. On reaching Bombay, the women complained to their families. This event then became more public with the full force of the Hindu communities of Bombay petitioning, performing plays and displaying posters and cartoons on the subject.[24] Many meetings were held in which influential élites gathered a subscription to file a law-suit. The jury, made up entirely of Europeans, acquitted the soldiers despite the testimony of two dozen women that the soldiers 'were in high spirits regarding the Jubilee celebrations of the Queen'.[25] This particular incident demonstrates that Eve-teasing in the colonial context was a public performance on the part of the power-holders, a claim to an inherent superiority as well as a demand of unconditional deference and submission from their subordinates. The fact that no one could help these women on the steamer shows how, in public places, colonised men were unable to assert themselves. It also demonstrates how, at a symbolic level, 'women' are used as 'signs' in the struggle of domination and subordination between rulers and ruled in colonial settings.

When complaints were lodged by women from 'respectable' backgrounds or influential Indian families, the government did make some efforts to curb the practice. One such example of government intervention is the case of a Parsi woman from Bombay who was assaulted by a European guard while travelling in a train. Following her complaint, the guard was transferred from passenger to goods train services and his wages were reduced.[26] This was a deterrent measure, but when complaints by women increased and were publicised through the vernacular press, the government decided to make some more permanent changes. One factor in the increase in Eve-teasing was the greater physical mobility of women, visible in railway travel. So alterations were made: railway services were improved in 1896 and rail travel was made safer for women by more segregation. The Bombay Railway authorities, for instance, employed Eurasian women to issue, examine and receive tickets from female passengers in segregated compartments.[27]

I have so far analysed incidents of Eve-teasing by Europeans on Indian women, which does not mean that Indian men did not practise the same on European women. George Orwell has written sensitively about his experiences in Burma, where he served as a police officer in the early part of the twentieth century. In his essay 'Shooting an Elephant', he writes:

> I was sub-divisional police officer of the town [Moulmein, in Lower Burma], and in an aimless, petty kind of way anti-European feeling was very bitter. No one had the guts to raise a riot, but if a European woman went through the bazaars alone somebody would probably spit betel juice over her dress. As a police officer I was an obvious target and was baited whenever it seemed safe to do so. When a nimble Burman tripped me up on the football field and the referee (another Burman) looked the other way, the crowd yelled with hideous laughter. This happened more than once. In the end, the sneering yellow faces of young men that met me everywhere, the insults hooted after me when I was at a safe distance, got badly on my nerves.[28]

The act of spitting betel-nut juice on the dress of the European woman has been interpreted by James Scott as an indication of Burmese contempt for British rule.[29] In Scott's view, subordinate groups can only express a 'hidden' transcript in covert ways, as open defiance would bring down the wrath of authority. In this case, the Burman took advantage of the anonymity of the crowd to drive home a message, that 'Europeans are not wanted here', while ensuring that the identity of the messenger remained screened.

This particular instance of Eve-teasing matches my own experience. While travelling in a crowded Delhi Transport Corporation bus in 1985, a man chewing a *paan* (tobacco leaf with lime and betel-nut) spat on me, leaving a bright red stain on my white blouse. My initial reaction was one of shock, anger and an acute sense of humiliation. What revealed that this had been premeditated was that the man completed the act just as the bus had come to a halt at a set of traffic lights. When I got up to give him chase, he jumped out and vanished into the crowds.

The act itself was identical to the one described by Orwell in the Burma of the 1930s. But the context was radically different: in the second case we were in post-independent India and the element of race was not the same – both the harasser and the harassed were Indian. In the Burmese case, the act was clearly expressing European and non-European racial tensions. In the second case, I believe that my harasser had more than one message to deliver. He was probably saying, 'You should not be wearing these clothes' (I was dressed in a skirt and a sleeveless blouse). The degree of differentiation between Eastern and Western sexuality and morality in the Indian consciousness is deeply embedded, with the former equated with spirituality and the latter with depravity.[30]

Stereotypes of Western moral values which are racist in content and tone are sustained by the awesome Indian commercial cinema industry.[31] And, in the immediate case of my messenger, his protest was definitely against his perception of my 'Westernisation' – although I feel this was not the only message. The others were: 'You ought not to be seen in public'; or simply 'You deserve only contempt' (the act of spitting traditionally signifies contempt in India). Analysis of my own experience of Eve-teasing leads me to believe that it expresses both power and racialised relationships between the sexes.

From colonial to present-day India, Eve-teasing has become increasingly associated with urban locations. Cities and large towns have certain characteristics that facilitate this form of sexual harassment. Successive migrations from the rural hinterland to industrial centres during the late nineteenth and early part of the twentieth centuries created the cities of Bombay and Calcutta. The imperial cities attracted immigrants in search of jobs and education, or trade and business ventures. Urbanisation was also increased by technology such as railways and coastal steamers.

However, colonial urbanisation was accompanied by certain peculiarities. Studies of migrations of the rural poor to urban centres reveal imbalances in urbanisation processes. The recruitment patterns of migrant labour in Bombay's mills during the 1920s reveal that male labourers from partly agricultural backgrounds usually left their wives and children behind to tend to their fields. Labourers who came from non-agricultural backgrounds, on the other hand, were forced to leave their families in the villages against their will, due to the low wages they earned as mill-hands. Either way, there was an imbalance in male–female ratios in large cities at the turn of the century, with males outnumbering females.

Gail Pearson calls Bombay of the 1920s a 'disproportionately male city'.[32] She has calculated that the ratio of women to men was approximately one to two. Her study of Bombay is complemented by the work of other historians who have studied the patterns of labour migration in the colonial cities of Kanpur and Calcutta.[33] While the social effects of such an imbalance on urban life, especially in regard to women, have yet to be studied, most historians agree that social tensions existed in congested industrial areas as a result of this disproportion in urban population. Gail Pearson, however, contends that 'middle class household women of the "respectable classes" were protected from this social tension'.[34] Her point can be called into question: accounts of middle-class Indian women in the late nineteenth and early twentieth centuries show that they were 'protected' only if they remained within the safety of their own homes.

Nineteenth-century India produced several major socio-religious reform movements, as a result of either cultural dislocation or cultural interaction with the West. Whether transitional (arising from indigenous forms of socio-religious dissent, with little influence from the West), or acculturative (originating within the colonial milieu and as products of cultural interaction with the West), these movements sought to transform Indian society by questioning the status quo.[35] Central to their programme for India's regeneration was redefining the role and position of women. Their proposed reforms included granting women the right to education, removing the ban on the remarriage of widows, and relieving widows from the restrictions of ritual pollution and enforced seclusion. The Indian Women's Movement of the late nineteenth century grew out of the mainstream reform movements.

The first generation of educated Indian women was also the first to experience the consequences of reforms particularly those put into motion during the 1860s and 1870s. The content of their education was identifiably Western. Their first steps in the public world were greeted with hostility. If the attitude of conservative Indians in the nineteenth century towards educating women was outright opposition, that of colonial state and Indian male reformers was ambivalent enthusiasm.[36] Segregated schools staffed only by female teachers, the location of these establishments and the provision of closed horse-drawn carriages for young girls travelling from school reflected the anxiety of educationists to protect 'respectable' girls from the real threats of the outside world.[37] As a number of historians working on this period have pointed out, it was only the most courageous and committed young women who could pursue higher education in the nineteenth century.

Autobiographies and biographies of the first- and second-generation female intelligentsia reveal that their quest for education often led them to encounter Eve-teasers. Anandibai Joshee, the first female doctor of Bombay Presidency, who chose to do her medical degree in the United States during the 1880s, justified her action in a public speech she delivered in Serampore (Bengal). She described the horrific harassment she faced while at school in Bombay:

> Passers-by, whenever they saw me going to school, gathered round me; some of them made fun of me and convulsed themselves with laughter; others more respectable in appearance made ridiculous remarks and did not feel ashamed to throw pebbles at me. Banias [merchants] and Tambulies [betel leaf and nut sellers] spitted [sic] at the sight of me and made gestures too obscene to describe.[38]

She justified going to a foreign country for a degree on the grounds that, in India, 'male doctors who take up the classes are conservative and to a certain degree jealous. Besides they take up a female class, rather to feast their eyes on the fair sex than to educate them.'[39] This statement shows that male doctors harboured professional jealousy, which they expressed by ogling women. Anandibai's experiences were common to women who sought higher education in the nineteenth century.

It appears that the objection to Anandibai's appearance on the streets was due to the fact that she was committing a forbidden act: seeking education, which religious Hindu texts forbade. Her harassers were not simply objecting to her presence in public but to the purpose of her presence. Had Anandibai proceeded to visit a temple, go on a pilgrimage or attend to her washing in the bathing ghats, she would have been unnoticed. But there were indicators – boots, stockings, books – that were signs of attending school. To the Indian public these marked a person who had adopted Europeanised dress and values. The various ways in which her teasers harassed her make for interesting analysis. Nineteenth-century discourse on educated women's sexuality held that learning made a woman independent and morally loose, like white women, and therefore dangerous.[40] The message in the indecent gestures made to Anandibai by the men on the road was that they perceived her to be a prostitute. The act of spitting also indicated utter contempt for her choice of non-Indian forms of dress and conduct. The message of these Eve-teasers was not just to 'get off the streets' but to remain at home and be an obedient, good and submissive wife.

More traumatic than the unmarried woman's quest for education was the situation of young Hindu widows. In the nineteenth century, widowhood meant a 'living death' to women. Due to the Hindu custom of early marriage, women were often widowed as early as nine or ten years of age. Since the touch and sight of a widow were considered impure and inauspicious, widows were condemned to austere lifestyles marked by fasts, sparse meals and a menial status within the household.[41] Marks of widowhood ranged from shaven heads, wearing only white or red coarse cotton sarees, and the obligation to avoid being seen or touched by members of high castes. Besides the worst kinds of degradation heaped on such a woman, she was unable to hope for a better life because of a ban on widow remarriage. Nineteenth-century reform movements took up the cause of Hindu widows, and soon widow homes and schools were established. By the middle of the twentieth century, nursing had increasingly become a profession for Hindu widows.

Widows were targets of sexual harassment within the home. Accounts left by them implicate close relations in this, sometimes one as close as a father-in-law or an uncle.[42] A widow's social status and lack of power also made her vulnerable to harassment from male servants. However,

I am focusing on the harassment she faced once she decided to seek a professional education or a public role. More than other women, widows often faced hostility from traditionalists when they ventured outside their homes. They were subjected to outright staring, abusive remarks, and sneering and jeering in public places. While firsthand information on this kind of harassment is still scarce, the following account written by an observer is revealing. Indirabai Deodhar, a welfare worker, attended a prize distribution ceremony of a social welfare organisation which ran several schools for widows in the 1920s. She noticed the peculiar behaviour of the spectators when a widow won a prize:

> Among the prize winners was a widow who had passed the examination in Nursing with flying colours. When her name was announced, she stepped on the stage. She was dressed in the traditional garb of the widows of those days – a simple dark red saree with the 'pallu' [end of the saree] tightly drawn over her 'clean shaven' head. As the widow stepped on the stage, the students and others crowding the galleries started hooting and stamping. They whistled and jeered.[43]

The incident ended dramatically when the chief guest chastised the college students for ridiculing the widow. In this particular incident, the widow was clearly still conforming to expected dress codes, as her tonsured head and garb indicate. The ridicule was directed at transgression of that social code which demanded she should not be independent, but instead should be subservient and should not leave her home.

Indian women in the nineteenth century who were sexually harassed in public places, whether unmarried, married or widowed, were often women who had broken with tradition by seeking public roles. In the case of Anandibai Joshee, her harassers intimidated her in such a threatening way that, had she been a less courageous woman, she would have abandoned her higher education plans completely. Obviously this was the desired goal of her harassers.

I have traced the evolution of Eve-teasing over a span of 100 years and suggested several possibilities for its origins. I do not, however, think that it has a single and straightforward explanation. The peculiarities of urbanisation in colonial India were a contributory factor to the increase of Eve-teasing in cities. It is suggested that the changing nature of Indian carnivals and its participants has blurred distinctions between purely carnival behaviour and that of the Eve-teaser. This lack of clarity often leads to unsympathetic and unresponsive crowds who simply witness sexual harassment on the streets, buses or trains.

Analysis of specific cases in the nineteenth century suggests that Eve-teasing directed a series of messages to the harassed women. These messages indicate the presence of racial tensions, power relations and fear of female sexuality. European men's harassment of Indian women shows clearly how roles of domination and subordination are assumed by ruling and ruled groups in the colonial context. On the other hand, when Indian women faced Eve-teasing from their male counterparts, this revealed Indian men's anxiety about Europeanised Indian women and underlined racial tensions. Eve-teasing as practised by Indian men on Indian women in the late nineteenth century and the early twentieth century seems to have been linked partly to the changing power relations between the sexes, as manifested by women's entry into the public sphere in its widest sense.

Notes and References

1. I am grateful to Seetha Anagol for her assistance in the preparation of this chapter.
2. Eve-teasing is quite distinct from other kinds of sexual harassment; for instance, harassment in the workplace. It is characterised by a great degree of visibility, a public location and spectators.
3. Delhi Prohibition of Eve-Teasing Act 1984.
4. *Law Commission of India, Eighty-fourth Report*, Section on 'Rape and Allied Offences', paragraphs 2.32 to 2.34 (New Delhi: Government of India, 1980), pp. 11–12.
5. Section 509 reads:

   > Word, gesture or act intended to insult the modesty of a woman. Whoever, intending to insult the modesty of any woman, utters any word makes any sound or gesture, or exhibits any object, intending that such word or sound shall be heard, or that such gesture or object shall be seen, by such woman, or intrudes upon the privacy of such woman, shall be punished with simple imprisonment for a term which may extend to one year, or with fine, or with both.
   >
   > *Manual of Criminal Laws, India, 1993* (New Delhi: Government of India, 1993), Chapter XXII, p. 128.

6. Certain women's organisations in India are also concerned with the peculiarities of Eve-teasing. They have agitated for a separate law whereby 'the law could penalise such behaviour in public places or on public transport vehicles particularly'. (*Law Commission of India, Eighty-fourth Report*, Section on 'Rape and Allied Offences', pp. 13–15.)
7. State Governments' recognition of Eve-teasing as a crime has largely depended on the agitations conducted by women's organisations, coverage by the local press, and public awareness and pressure.

8. These behaviour patterns are analogous to those at some of the medieval carnivals in France, although sexual inversion is missing in the Indian context. See Natalie Zemon Davis, *Society and Culture in Early Modern France* (Oxford: Blackwell, 1987), especially Chapter V, 'Women on Top', pp. 124–51.

9. The intricate relationship between kinship ties and women's lives, especially in regard to issues of abortion and infanticide in late nineteenth-century India, are traced in Padma Anagol-McGinn, 'Women's Consciousness and Assertion in Colonial India: Gender, Politics and Social Reform in Maharashtra, c.1870–c.1920', unpublished PhD thesis (University of London, 1994).

10. In 1981 female students at St Stephen's College protested on the day of *Holi* when around 60 armed ruffians from outside the college broke their way in and harassed them. See Deepti Priya, 'Challenging a Masculinist Culture: Women's Protest in St Stephen's College', *Manushi* 28 (1985), pp. 32–5.

11. This explanation was offered by other commuters to a friend of mine. Courtesy of Cynthia Noronha.

12. The most representative is Charles Heimsath, *Indian Nationalism and Hindu Social Reform* (Princeton, NJ: Princeton University Press, 1964), especially the introduction.

13. Many of the vernacular newspapers cited in this article are no longer available. However, in the nineteenth century the British government employed 'oriental' translators to transliterate in order to gauge the feelings of the masses. The Vernacular Newspaper Reports cited here are published summaries of different vernacular newspapers of nineteenth-century India and they cover rural as well as urban news.

14. Residential areas in the colonial period were based strictly on communal lines. That is, the various Hindu, Jain, Muslim and Parsi communities lived in segregated areas, probably to accommodate the strong pollution principles of the various communities.

15. *The Gujarati*, in *Vernacular Newspaper Reports* (hereafter VNR), week ending (hereafter w.e.) 3 April 1886, India Office Library, London.

16. *Jame-Jamshed* (VNR), w.e. 4 August 1883.

17. *Rasik Ranjani* (VNR), w.e. 26 June 1888.

18. *Kaside Mumbai* (VNR), w.e. 4 August 1879.

19. Kenneth Ballhatchet, *Race, Sex and Class under the Raj: Imperial Attitudes and Policies and their Critics, 1793–1905* (London: Weidenfeld and Nicolson, 1980).

20. Indian legal experts had no active role in a trial which involved a European assaulting an Indian. If an Indian assaulted a European, he generally incurred a harsh penalty. For a discussion on 'white

racism', see Sumit Sarkar, *Modern India, 1885–1947*, 2nd edition (London: Macmillan, 1989), pp. 22–4.

21. *Pune Vaibhav* (VNR), w.e. 2 April 1887; *Gujarat Mitra* (VNR), w.e. 29 January 1887.

22. *Praja Hitapatra* (VNR), w.e. 29 January 1887.

23. I have found James Scott's concepts of 'public' and 'hidden' transcripts particularly useful. In his elaboration of the theory of power relations in a colonial context, 'public transcript' refers to the 'open interaction between subordinates and those who dominate them'. James C. Scott, *Domination and the Arts of Resistance* (New Haven, Conn.: Yale University Press, 1990), p. 2.

24. *Akbare Sodagar* (VNR), w.e. 6 November 1886.

25. *Bodh Sudhakar* (VNR), w.e. 12 February 1887.

26. A summary of the entire proceedings in this case is in *Bombay Judicial Proceedings*, vol. P/1591, no. 3335, 1880 (Bombay: Maharashtra State Records Office).

27. *Bombay Samachar* (VNR), 11 February 1882, and also in *Satya Mitra* (VNR), 15 February 1896.

28. George Orwell, *Collected Essays* (London: Heinemann, 1961) p. 15.

29. Scott, *Domination and the Arts of Resistance*, pp. 14–15.

30. Binary oppositions such as East and West, which embody racial tensions, are colonial products in India. Nineteenth-century Indian intellectuals such as Swami Vivekananda and Dayanand Saraswati wrote on cultural differences between the East and West. For an analysis of their views, see Ashis Nandy, 'The Psychology of Colonialism', in Nandy, *The Intimate Enemy: Loss and Recovery of Self under Colonialism* (New Delhi: Oxford University Press, 1991), pp. 1–64.

31. The stereotype of the saree-clad, demure, submissive and obedient Indian woman and the smoking, drinking and miniskirt-clad educated Indian woman who eventually wrecks a good home is a recurrent theme in Indian films. The Indian feminist journal *Manushi* regularly reviewed these films during the 1970s and 1980s.

32. Gail Pearson, 'Women in Public Life in Bombay City with Special Reference to the Civil Disobedience Movement', unpublished PhD thesis (Jawaharlal Nehru University, New Delhi, 1979), p. 14.

33. Statistical evidence for the jute industry in Bengal in 1912 shows that the male:female ratio was approximately 4:1; see Dipesh Chakrabarty, *Rethinking Working-Class History, Bengal, 1890–1940* (Delhi: Oxford University Press, 1989), p. 10. For the Kanpur textile industry, see Chitra Joshi, 'Kanpur Textile Labour: Some Structural Features of Formative Years', *Economic and Political Weekly* (special number, November 1981), p. 1827.

34. Pearson, 'Women in Public Life', p. 14.
35. A great deal has been written on the intellectual history of nineteenth-century India. See, for instance, Kenneth W. Jones, *Socio-Religious Reform Movements in British India*, The New Cambridge History of India, vol.1, Part III (Cambridge: Cambridge University Press, 1989).
36. The British government in India and the reformers were equally anxious to control the movement for higher education for women in order to ensure that the latter were trained to be 'good wives and good mothers' rather than for vocational ends. See Anagol-McGinn, 'Women's Consciousness and Assertion', especially Chapter V.
37. Anagol-McGinn, 'Women's Consciousness and Assertion', especially Chapter V.
38. Anandibai Joshee, *A Speech by a Hindu Lady* (Bombay, unknown publisher, 1883), pp. 7–8.
39. Joshee, *A Speech by a Hindu Lady*, p. 6.
40. Several historians who have worked on the entry of nineteenth-century Bengali women into the 'public sphere' have made similar observations. See Meredith Borthwick, *The Changing Role of Women in Bengal, 1849–1905* (Princeton, NJ: Princeton University Press, 1984).
41. For an erudite study of the impact of Hindu ideology on the conduct of a orthodox Hindu woman as seen through an eighteenth-century text, see Julia Leslie, *The Perfect Wife: The Orthodox Hindu Woman According to the Stridharmapaddhati of Tryambakayajvan* (New Delhi: Oxford University Press, 1989), pp. 89–97, 303–4.
42. Often such harassment led to a widow conceiving an illegitimate child, and then to infanticide. The result was usually her excommunication from her caste and village, which meant a social death.
43. Indirabai Deodhar, 'This I Remember', *The Poona Seva Sadan Society, 1909–1969, Diamond Jubilee Souvenir* (Pune: Seva Sadan Press, 1970), p. 27.

11

In and Out of View: Visual Representation and Sexual Harassment

Jane Beckett[1]

Sexual harassment is to do with men exercising power over women in the workplace ... [it] involves repeated, unreciprocated and unwelcome comments, looks, jokes, suggestions or physical contact that might threaten a woman's job security or create a stressful or intimidating working environment.

(Ann Sedley and Melissa Benn)[2]

Sexual harassment also appeared neither incidental nor tangential to women's inequality but a crucial expression of it, a central dynamic in it.

(Catharine MacKinnon)[3]

[The] narrative takes on its own impetus as it were, so that one begins to see reality as non-narrated. One begins to say that it's not a narrative, it's the way things are.

(Gayatri Chakravorty Spivak)[4]

Sexual harassment has been part of the feminist project since the 1970s, when it was put firmly on the political agenda in the United States. The quotations above from Catharine MacKinnon and Ann Sedley and Melissa Benn disclose it as a process by which men enact social control over women in the workplace. These and subsequent accounts have argued for the necessity of forming legislative procedures to combat and erase workplace harassment.[5] Sexual harassment has come to be understood contradictorily as either 'aberrant' or 'natural' masculine behaviours which maintain and legitimise women in subordinate roles. But the central dynamic of sexual harassment has also been understood as maintaining power.

Sexual harassment is difficult to define. There is little common agreement about its boundaries and whether certain kinds of behaviour can be understood to constitute harassment. Stanley and Wise argue that its occurrence is, more often than not, a matter of the recipient's interpretation of the intent or motive behind a behaviour which is often not unequivocally 'sexual harassment'.[6] Two issues are at stake in these accounts. The first is the identification of sexual harassment in terms of behaviours such as those outlined by Sedley and Benn, and constantly referred to in feminist accounts of sexual harassment. Secondly, the issue of power seems crucial in developing feminist-centred accounts. This turns on the imperative that women refuse to be the objects and victims of sexual harassment, both by invoking the power of the law in forging legislative procedures and codes of practice, and by directly addressing the issue of power in practice. In the United States Senate hearings involving Anita Hill and Clarence Thomas in November 1991, the 'points of the vector' of power, as Toni Morrison has potently commented, were:

all the plateaus of power and powerlessness: white men, black men, black women, white women, interracial couples; those with a traditionally conservative agenda, and those representing neo-conservative conversions; citizens with radical and progressive programmes.[7]

As the Hill–Thomas hearings demonstrated, sexual harassment is intimately imbricated in the workings of power, caught up with narratives of race, sexuality, gender and class.

State legislation and practice form part of the discourses in which sexuality has been reread since the 1980s. Discussion of sexual harassment necessarily foregrounds the formation of sexed and gendered identities. Although usually referenced as exclusively heterosexual, the location of sexual harassment in a broader discursive field opens out different forms of sexuality and different power relations. The Hill–Thomas hearings expanded the debate, not least in the problems of acknowledging the existence of sexual harassment and defining it. In this case various strategies were put into play to deny that sexual harassment existed or, alternatively, to claim that feminist policing disallows affectionate joking in the workplace. Current feminist debate has engaged with contestations over sexually harassing behaviours, male violence and date rape. The uniformity of women's experience in sexual harassment has been questioned. Legal cases brought by men claiming harassment from women, a scenario popularised in Michael Crichton's novel *Disclosure*,[8] have recently challenged harassment as something solely directed by men against women. But does this pose dangers to the understanding of sexual harassment as a feminist project? Are the political imperatives of a feminist address to sexual harassment debilitated by universalising practices that deny or pluralise the specificity of women's experiences?

I want to examine some of the ways in which harassment has been read, and look specifically at the ways in which visual images define and are defined by accounts of sexual harassment. How far do visual images cloak and mask, support and relocate readings of harassment? In foregrounding the visual, I am aware that I am already working on the screen of sexual harassment, in the institutional practices of art school training in which women are often harassed, denigrated and marginalised. It could be argued that women are trapped by protocols of art practice which have little relevance to them.[9] But I shall show that women have participated productively with drawings for feminist publications, trade union literature and daily newspapers. Their images are highly political in the sense that they aim to engage women in political struggle and to bring about social change. Visual images have been widely used to represent sexual harassment; however, distinctions must be made between those which appear in the media and popular culture and those which circulate in the arena of high culture, since these different institutional sites produce different effects. In so far as they address the issue of sexual harassment, visual images of women and men participate in the ordering and regulation of sexualities in terms of aberrant and normative behaviours. Women artists have worked against the grain of dominant Western representations of women, disputing the immutability of these images, exposing their frailties and reworking their meanings. In the discussion which follows, my attention is primarily focused on work produced in the 1980s and 1990s which builds upon debates around the changing position and experience of women produced within the political geography of the new right.[10]

Searching for something to read recently in a hospital waiting area, I saw on a table a pile of newspapers and 'women's' magazines. Above them, pinned on a noticeboard, were two leaflets – 'Dealing with Sexual Harassment' and 'Practical Ways to Crack Crime: The Family Guide'.[11] Between them, these publications cover women's employment conditions and practices, addressing women as workers, consumers and carers in positions of authority and control, and in positions of powerlessness and seeking redress. The first of these, a Transport and General Workers Union (TGWU) leaflet for members and trade union representatives, sets out definitions of sexual harassment and offers guidelines for complaint procedures. In both publications, however, the visual element raises questions about the current boundaries of sexual harassment: it depicts locations, characterises its forms of behaviour, the unequal power relations and the naturalising narratives which encode and convey them.

Sexual harassment has a historical dimension, and the TGWU leaflet opens by calling it 'an old problem with a new name'. This claim bears traces of two issues. The first is the question of what are the boundaries which contain what has been discussed as sexual harassment, and the second is the parallel implication that what is currently understood as sexual harassment may be built on deeply engrained historical connotations. The difficulty of identifying what women have in common, if indeed it can be said that there is a common element to experiences of sexual harassment, is part of both these issues.[12]

Photographic images, particularly in newspapers, function as bearers of truth. Placed in conjunction with drawings, cartoons, advertisements and written text (whose different typesizes can disrupt, underpin or relocate accompanying images), they offer varying meanings and readings of the world for and to others. They position subjects within categories of class, race and gender and within narratives which become naturalised. They make available and prefer certain narratives to others. But the representation of women in the media is not a static site of power and control.

Portrayals of Asian women in the media, as Pratibha Parmar argues, demonstrate the instability of such representation. These overlap with '"taken-for-granted" images of Asian people formed well before the 1950s and 1960s when Asian migration to Britain was in any way significant'.[13] The modes of discussion of Asian women, she points out, are fuelled by economic conditions which oscillate across expansion and recession and cluster around concepts of them as 'victims' who have fewer civil rights and different cultural conceptions of marriage, who are 'sexualised' as the exotic other. Parmar traces the archaeology of these images back to the colonial past, showing how the sexual harassment of black women is fuelled and compounded by racism. This has profound effects on black women's daily experiences in Britian.

During the 1980s challenges to these representations were made by British women of colour through self-representation and self-definition in photography and art. 'Convenience not Love', a three-panelled silkscreen and collage made by Chila Kumari Burman, puts institutionalised racial and sexual harassment on display.[14] The central panel is ordered in three rows, at the centre of which are three (Asian?) passports, surrounded by images of Asian women, drawn from the media. The right-hand panel connotes British identity by a passport, an image of John Bull, a Union Jack and a set of official seals. The sexual and racial harassment of women as they pass through British customs are foregrounded in this piece. The passport, the official form of identity and nationality, connotes inclusion and exclusion and, as Parmar argues, is also locked into the colonial past. There is now considerable literature on the ways in which visual images are imbricated in colonising texts, addressing how women's bodies have been represented as indices of power, control and sexuality through images of mutilation, sexual abuse and rape.[15] Violent as the images are, they have been taken up in recent art by women. 'First Missionary Position' by Sonia Boyce, and a body of work by the Native American artist Jaune Quick-to-see-Smith and Robyn Kahukiwa of New Zealand, turn the representations of colonial violence and of women as the sign of colonisation into a powerful pictorial and political rhetoric.[16]

Central to accounts of sexual harassment since the 1970s is the identification of the workplace as the locus of such harassment. In Britain, the characterisation of certain forms of behaviour as harassing partnered assumptions about conduct in the workplace (initially understood as 'the office'). These concepts polarise into categories of normal and abnormal forms of masculine behaviour towards women. The passage I cited from Sedley and Benn's *Sexual Harassment at Work* suggests that two conditions underlie these characterisations: a set of ordered workplace relations within which equality between men and women could be possible, and the existence of threats to that order. Set against the latter is 'reciprocal romantic and flirtatious behaviour'.[17] A recent publication issued by Women Against Sexual Harassment (WASH) defines sexual harassment as: 'unwanted and unreciprocated behaviour of a sexual nature. It is NOT about fun and friendship, but is unwelcome behaviour at work leading to unacceptable employment practice.'[18] The distinction made between 'fun and friendship' on one side and 'unacceptable and unreciprocated' on the other is important here, and recurs throughout the workplace literature.

But sexual harassment is not merely codified in binary oppositions between normal and abnormal masculine behaviours. The heterosexual bias of discussions of harassment is itself a form of sexual harassment in occluding other sexualities and the complex articulations of power and structured inequalities. As MacKinnon has noted, these are 'neither incidental nor tangential to women's inequality, but a critical expression of it, a central dynamic in it'.[19] As one strategy for making evident these complexities, visual imagery has been taken for granted as illustrative of the written accompanying texts on sexual harassment, but it in fact takes both parallel and divergent positions with respect to it.

WORKPLACE NARRATIVES

In the 1980s women turned to part-time employment, and had recourse to a set of new laws against sexual harassment. Section 63 of the Sex Discrimination Act 1975, which gave industrial tribunals the power to hear complaints about discrimination at work, was reinforced by the

Plate 1: The world turned upside down

European Commission's code of practice for the elimination of discrimination and for the promotion of equal opportunities at work.
This was enshrined in the 1990 EC Resolution 'On the Protection of
the Dignity of Women and Men at Work'. Visual images are also subject
to these changing terms and conditions, and are productive of them
too.

The period within which sexual harassment has emerged as a highly
charged political issue for women has also been profoundly affected by
economic policies which have oscillated between expansionist rhetoric
and recession-led restraints. In the mid-1990s there are now more
women at work than ever before, and in some parts of the UK more
women are employed than men.[20] Recession economics have dictated
cuts in fulltime employment filled by men in favour of part-time,
lower-paid jobs filled by women. Together with changes in marriage
and divorce patterns, women's position in the workforce is now redefined
as an issue of survival and independence.

In a sharp and wittily observed critique of the workplace as the locus
of sexual harassment, a cartoon drawn by Posy Simmonds and published
in the *Guardian* in 1987 plays with the naturalised narrative of men filling
dominant managerial office roles, stripping bare the ideological formation
in a 'world turned upside down' (see Plate 1). Posy Simmonds' drawing
plays with those images which have structured the representation of
sexual harassment in the written texts – the overtly sexual languages,
jokes, unwelcome touching, the problematic domain of public spaces
and the reinstatement in an inferior position of the secretarial tasks
'Ronnie' carries out for his boss 'Miss Pye'. As the narrative unfolds, Ronnie
moves through different workspaces, all filled with women. He runs
menial tasks, is squashed into a lift by women in business suits who
leer at him, and is shouted at in the street by tough women working
on a construction site. The cartoon shows how predominant business
practices are founded on sexual harassment. These are the activities so
painfully recorded in experiential and anecdotal accounts of harassment,
and represented in the trade union and legislative literature. In the cartoon
the repeated inscription of inferior status, signified in the menial tasks
Ronnie performs, are reinforced by demeaning sexualised language,
couched as joking and fun, by which he is addressed.

Some tasks, such as buying cigarettes or crossing into the leisure
space of the pub, extend harassment out of the worksite. They stretch
the boundaries of the workspace, extending the dynamics of power and
control beyond it. A recent MORI poll on sexual harassment carried out
for the BBC found that views on what constitutes the limits of the
workplace marked the biggest difference between the women and men
interviewed. The main site of contention, it found, was over 'expecting

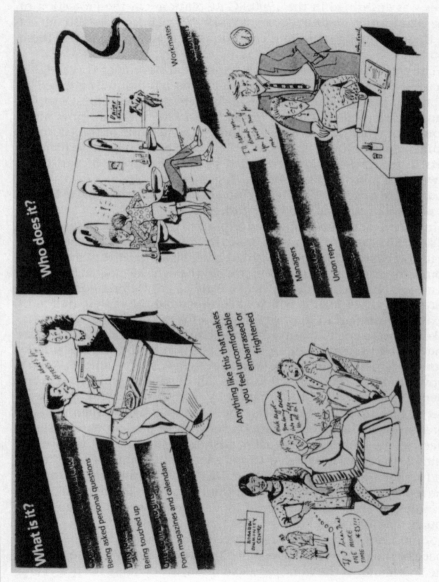

Plate 2: Sexual harassment. What is it? Who does it?

women to get the coffee or run errands', both activities seen by women as legitimately lying outside the workspace.[21] These activities were furthermore tied to women's constant inscription into domesticity and, by implication, inferiority. It is this narrative which is exposed by its role reversal in the Posy Simmonds' cartoon. In the last frame of the narrative 'Miss Pye', the young executive, is unmasked, returned to her role as young secretary and familiarly addressed as 'Lizzy' by her male boss whose name is significantly never given. The familiarised 'Ronnie' is obliterated in the reinstated normalised power structures of prevailing office narratives.

The cartoon lays bare relationships of power in diverse sites – from the exchanged comments across the workspaces to the stereotypical representations of construction site workers and masculine behaviours in pubs. All the drawings in this strip make visible the interrelationship of sexuality and space. In the concluding frame, this is figured by the boss oppressively leaning over the woman at her desk and into her space. This figure recurs in other drawings, such as those produced by Helen Kozich for a trade union handout (see Plate 2).[22] The office vignette of 'the boss' lurching over the typing figure, offering her a drink when she's finished his work, deploys the same codes. Represented in Helen Kozich's drawings are different workspaces – the cafeteria, the hairdresser, the community centre and the office space – in which are foregrounded potential harassers: workmates, managers, union representatives and customers. The various spaces and diverse forms of harassment traverse race, class and gender.

During the 1980s writings on sexual harassment were ordered around concepts of sexual difference and issues of inequality. By focusing on difference or inequality sets of common elements came to be identified as sexually harassing behaviours. By contrast, MacKinnon argued that the understanding of women's situation as a structural issue of 'enforced inferiority' demanded radical alteration.[23] It is this second line of argument which has given support to codes of practice, concerns with equal opportunity in employment and legislative procedures and lawmaking.

HARASSMENT AND EQUALITY

In the MORI poll already cited, twice as many women as men attributed men's resentment of women for taking their jobs as a motivating reason for sexual harassment. The focus on equality of opportunity in trade union literature and the European Commission report emphasises the

Plate 3: Construction workers at a site in the City of London wolf-whistling at a pedestrian

equality of workplace opportunity as fundamental to understanding and eliminating sexual harassment.

But do the employment expectations and conditions of women in the UK in the 1990s have a different dynamic? And how far do these changes mean redefining sexual harassment? Discourses of equality and job mobility are formulated against current media accounts of the relocation and inequality of women in the workforce, in terms of pay, job opportunities, possibilities of advancement. Various trade union strategies and procedures have emerged during the late 1980s and early 1990s to reinforce and refine UK legislation. The codes of practice and proposed action within the trade union movement and in company procedures have been articulated around clusters of terms such as 'equal opportunity', 'income inequalities', 'dignity at work', 'formal complaint procedures', 'managerial training' and the ubiquitous notion of 'glass ceilings'.

Representations in the news media of women who have fought successful harassment cases frequently focus on an image of a single woman. In the *Independent* (10 October 1993), a report on the way the TGWU deals with wolf-whistling positions a woman alone against four men (see Plate 3). The same newspaper's report of a successful industrial tribunal hearing of sexual harassment against a female bricklayer is accompanied by a photograph of the smiling, seated figure of a woman (the *Independent*, 7 January 1993). The caption to the photograph places her against her male 'workmates': 'No one man broke ranks. They were all pretty gutless.' The visual strategies here isolate women, setting them against groups of male power, in contrast to the written texts which usually represent common experiences among women. Women artists have represented the isolating, frightening experience of harassment. In a TGWU leaflet of 1993 a drawing by Sophie Grillet depicts a woman with her head in a bag and a co-worker asking the smirking boss, 'Why do you think Jane seems so unconfident these days?' In another drawing in the same leaflet, a think-bubble above a group of women reveals that they are all thinking: 'Who can I tell that I'm being sexually harassed? I feel so isolated' (see Plate 4).

Feminist strategies have reversed the concept of isolation so that women collectively represent a body of resistance. They have also unsettled and destabilised the image of the silent victim by moving to an image of the feminine body empowered and articulate. In trade union and equal opportunities literature, visual images directly show women workers refusing the harassing behaviours of male figures – for example, 'I'm taking a note of that remark, Mister' in 'Just Joking', TGWU leaflet of 1993; or 'Enough assez finito OK', the collective speech in the National Council for Civil Liberties (NCCL) booklet of 1982 which

Plate 4: Who can I tell that I'm being sexually harassed?

moves beyond the personal experience to a body of support. The drawing in the 1993 TGWU leaflet shows two opposing figures, a large burly male and a small woman, and carries the injunction, 'You think you're big, Mister, but We're bigger!' The 'we' in this phrase reinforces the collectivity of resistance. Christine Roche's drawing for the cover of Sedley and Benn's book depicts four women and one man collectively refusing harassing forms in their declaration, 'We don't find it flattering, cute, funny or sexy. We find it boring, stupid, degrading and threatening and we're doing something about it.' Again, Angela Martin's postcards for WASH draw on a collectivity not confined to a heterosexual definition. 'Sexual harassment? "Not in our workplace"' represents the diversity of harassment in terms of race, different abilities, classes and sexualities (see Plate 5). Another, the 'Why the hell should we' postcard, juxtaposes a lone woman in the left panel whose claim to cope with sexual harassment is powerfully refuted by a group of six women in the right-hand panel. The conjuring of a collective strength in the use of 'we' and 'our' in the speech-bubbles reinforces the visual representation of women as a group, as a resistant and refusing body. These drawings from the 1990s open out some of the concepts fundamental

Plate 5: Sexual harassment? 'Not in our workplace'

to the early definitions of sexual harassment to include the dimension of race, diverse inequalities and masculine experiences of harassment.

Demands for equal opportunities have produced a plethora of policies across British institutions and institutional practices. The interrelation between equal opportunities policies and sexual harassment at the instititutional level is evident in literature from trade unions, educational institutions, youth policy documents of local councils and Department of Employment documents. It is central to the drafts of a code of conduct for the prevention of sexual harassment by the Equal Opportunities Unit of the European Commission.[24] While equal opportunities is hot news, affecting the language in which job advertisements are couched and personnel departments of large organisations, nevertheless postive action with respect to women in employment is still an unfamiliar concept to many employers, trade unionists and women employees. This is despite ten years of equal opportunities policies. Paddy Stamp pointed out in *Spare Rib* in 1987 that 'Employment organisations like all British institutions carry with them a long history of sexism, racism and discriminatory practices, and the introduction of equal opportunity practices therefore means changing the rules by which the entire organisation operates.'[25] Moira Gatens' argument that concepts of equality are premised either on liberal individualism or on economic determinism – both are rooted in a form of humanism assuming fundamental universalities – suggests that going down the equality path bypasses the consideration of 'the ways in which power differently *constitutes* particular kinds of body and empowers them to perform particular kinds of task, thus constructing specific kinds of subject'.[26]

Workspace narratives, usually understood as taking place outside the home, carry with them clusters of images in which masculinity is encoded as dominant. Visual images participate in the broader categories in which unequal power relations are encoded, reinforcing and under-pinning workplace practices. Secretaries and clerical staff, for example, are frequently represented as sitting taking notes from a standing male boss; nurses take instruction from a white-coated doctor; women students take instruction from male lecturers. As Hélène Cixous and Catherine Clément have argued:

the political economy of the masculine and of the feminine is organised by different requirements and constraints, which, when socialised and meta-phorised, produce signs, relationships of power, relationships of production and an entire system of cultural inscription readable as masculine and feminine.[27]

Cixous and Clément's argument locates the signs of masculinity and femininity as differently encoded within relationships of power and cultural inscription. Men are rarely represented as nurses or cleaners, nor women as doctors, professors or scientists. The spatial arrangements of workspace – the location of office desks, screens and so on – position masculinity as psychically, socially, sexually and culturally powerful. Different workspaces differently structure forms of harassing subjectivities, but there are nevertheless gendered coded spaces.

By the mid-1990s, the focus on harassment understood as exclusive to the workspace appears limited. Workplace definitions ignore the home as a worksite and as a place of sexual harassment.

SPACE AND FATAL ATTRACTIONS

The relocation of women at work in the 1980s has been the subject of recent discussion.[28] As several writers have acknowledged, the emphasis on 'deregulation' as a key aspect of the Thatcher government's policies placed women both in part-time employment and within the Thatcherite 'enterprise culture'. The latter especially seemed to offer unique opportunities to women in the workplace to participate in the culture of success, and to enter the job market in new managerial roles or by starting their own businesses.[29] In her analysis of the attractions to women of 'enterprise culture', Janet Newman comments that it appeared to offer ways of bypassing traditional routes and the limited possibilities open to women in more conventional occupations. She cautions, however, that enterprise promotions were primarily addressed to white women, obscuring and ignoring the contemporary exploitation of black women's labour in the new economic patterns. The focus of her argument on this new pattern of work is an address to 'the ideological themes of mobility, opportunity and self-help ... presented to women in a manner which makes light of the structural inequalities which they face at work'.[30]

Enterprise culture addressed women in a seductive and pervasive discourse across film, fiction, television, women's magazines and self-help books.[31] Equality in the workplace and equivalence of opportunity were again the main themes; contained within an overarching discourse of individualism, they tidily folded in any troubling issues of difference and inequality. The stress on individual attainment ignored the inequalities of opportunity open to women in the workplace. 'Deregulation', furthermore, meant decline of trade union membership, and increases in part-time employment, contract labour and work conditions outside trade union negotiation. The underside of these shifts was the marginalisation of the equal opportunity and sexual harassment codes then being formulated within the trade union movement.

Representations of these supposed new opportunities for women use codes about success/failure, sexually normative/deviant, acceptable/ aberrant behaviours. The discourse of success in enterprise culture is subtly structured and specifically gendered, so that, as Gayatri Chakravorty Spivak has so convincingly argued, 'one begins to say it's not a narrative, it's the way things are'.[32] While successful masculinity is encoded in terms of adventure, successful femininity is by contrast coded in terms of appearance, dress and style and as exclusively heterosexual. Power-dressing, apparently signifying these changes, became one of the most circulated images of achieving femininity in the 1980s.

Visual images were crucial in the formation of a discourse of the successful, entrepreneurial woman. The stress on 'the feminine' permeated 1980s magazines and texts addressed to the new professional woman. Indeed the Posy Simmonds' cartoon (Plate 1) lay precisely, if contra-dictorily, within this discourse: successful women managerial staff do not in general employ men as secretaries. Janet Newman pinpointed the key concept in the representation of enterprise woman as her sin-gularity: 'Power is offered to women as individuals on condition that they reject the notion of the need for women to articulate demand at a collective level.'[33] In contrast, as we have seen, contemporary images in trade union literature frequently work in the contrary direction towards collectivity.

The closing frame of the Posy Simmonds cartoon follows one of the most persistent themes in the representation of sexual harassment. The woman office-worker is represented with a typewriter or personal computer receiving information from male managerial staff. The cramped space of the typing table acts as signifier of the unequal relations played out around it. As previously indicated, the male figure usually stands looming over the seated, hunched and bent figure of the woman, increasing the sense of contained and oppressive space. Contrasts in the gendering of spaces within workplaces cannot be explored fully here, but the narratives of adventure, action and, perhaps above all, mobility of the masculine space, signficantly carried out onto the street in Posy Simmonds' cartoon, are defined in opposition to the stasis of the contained and controlled feminine spaces in the workplace. In reality, the spatial ordering of workspaces does not operate with such rigid binary oppositions: it is important to point to the binary opposition at play in the visual imagery, although in Simmonds' cartoon women are located, if only temporarily, in managerial as well as secretarial roles. While some workspaces make mobile, active and controlling spaces available to women, the conventions at play in these drawings invoke gendered and uneasy workspaces.

Visual images connote active looking primarily as a masculine pre-rogative.[34] In the Posy Simmonds cartoon, interior and exterior spaces are all charged as different sites of looking. In a recent National Union of Journalists (NUJ) Equality Council sexual harassment brochure (see Plate 6), the workplace is perceived as unstable, driven by masculin-ity's active gaze, graphically formulated in the male workers' grins, fantasy-bubbles and a phallic arrow drawn from the eye of the layout artist to the *Playboy* calendar on the wall. In Helen Kozich's drawings (Plate 2) the speech – 'What's for afters then?', a male punter asks the café checkout woman; 'Hiah angel – you bring colour into my life', two men fling at a black woman worker in a community centre – verbalises the hidden fantasies carried into the active accompanying masculine look. Workspaces in these images are traversed by the masculine gaze, codifying official and feminist definitions of sexual harassment as 'looking and staring at a person's body' (WASH), 'leering looks' (TGWU), 'unreciprocated and unwelcome comments, looks, jokes' (NCCL).

- **What is it?**
- **Why is it a trade union issue?**
- **How do we prevent it?**
- **What can we do about it?**

Plate 6: What is it?

However, an active masculine look can be undercut and destabilised. Much workplace imagery represents women strategising to avoid being subject to the male gaze. In the NUJ brochure (Plate 6), a woman worker is actively engaged in looking at the equal opportunity codes of practice which replace the pin-up calendar on the wall. Or women actively refuse the look, as on the cover of the TGWU brochure (Plate 2), where women carry a 'hands off' notice. Helen Kozich's drawings also engage the female spectator: the community centre worker looks to the female reader, refusing the 'Hiah angel' called out by the two men.

PICTURING BODIES

Central to sexual harassment debates is the visual imaging of the masculine body in ways which make it intermesh with accounts of harassing behaviour. These sometimes use caricature, as in the NUJ brochure drawing (Plate 6), to destabilise masculinity's power-base by a joking mode. Femininity can be permitted to slip from a controlling masculine gaze. A woman, on the right of the drawing, reads an NUJ equality code of practice notice; behind her one of the male workers puts out a groping hand, but her active reading of the notice offers her a means of dealing with this potential harassment. It is not merely a strategy of avoidance but also an assertion of workplace rights. Although there are many images which specifically address men as harassers, the viewer, here addressed as female, is interpellated by these commonplace representations against which the harassing masculinities are deflected as caricature. Women are invited to locate themselves temporarily as subjects of harassment, but then to relocate the reading in positive terms. Most trade union literature cartoons work in this way.

The structure of the drawing in the NUJ brochure juxtaposes women as subject of sexual harassment and visual representation as harassing. Women's everyday office routines, represented on the right-hand side of the drawing, are polarised against the passive, naked representations of women in pin-up calendars on the wall on the left-hand side, in which the female body is sexualised and contrasted with the clothed women on the right.

Drawing attention to how the naked female body inscribes desire has linked the feminist address of sexual harassment, feminist art practices and feminist theory during the past two decades. Western culture is saturated with narratives of nakedness and, as Lynda Nead has recently pointed out, 'feminist art history has not yet produced a wide ranging examination of the meanings, values and assumptions that have been and continue to be propagated by the female nude within patriarchal culture'.[35] Recent sexual harassment literature and feminist art practices and theory have, however, sought to put these issues on the agenda. Nead's own work has looked at relationships between high and popular cultural representations of the female nude, and at the complex relations between art and pornography. While her discussion of the cultural distinctions between high art and pornography is relevant to feminist critiques of representations of nakedness in sexual harassment, the broader argument she presents is contradictory. Relevant to the discussion here are two factors: representations seen and understood as unacceptable; and questions of access and the siting of these images.

Sexual harassment literature refers throughout to the display of sexually explicit material such as promotional calendars, pin-up photographs and magazines. The implictions here are, firstly, that this material offends in and of itself, and secondly, that it motivates sexually harassing behaviour. The boundaries of the body and its meanings are at stake. On the former reading, the naked bodies of pin-ups and calendars are connected to the pornography debates: Nead's metaphor of an incontinent outpouring of pornography onto city streets has resonance here. The reciprocal definitions and exchanges between pin-up calendars, advertising and pornography have received considerable attention in recent feminist literature.[36] These discussions have led to three areas: women's magazines and advertising; debates on censorship, obscenity and pornography; and issues of pleasure and desire for women.[37] Sexual harassment has only been referenced implicitly. While images from the media and soft-core pornography seem to represent common ground, and to some extent fuel and intensify one another, it is also important to bear in mind their differences. Trade union material operates on a different terrain from that of cartoons and photographic representations in broadsheet newspapers.[38] The visual material may have contradictory meanings and effects for different groups of viewers/readers.

In the drawing for the NUJ brochure (Plate 6), the screen reading 'I'm watching you too' engages with this, as a rhetorical response to the multiplicity of sights at which the men are actively looking. 'I'm watching you too', while acknowledging the temporary position of women as subject to the erotic gazes of the men, also asserts through a combination of text and repositions of images certain strategies of empowerment. The implied displacement of subject positions in 'I'm ... you too', like Posy Simmonds' cartoon and speech-bubbles in other trade union literature, destabilises the image of woman as victim. It replaces it with an empowered subject position for the woman reader, simultaneously but only temporarily understood as witness. This is carried through in a dual strategy in which masculinity is represented as ridiculous, for example in the NUJ brochure seen as a toad squatting on a box of matches (a tinder box?), while women assert control signified in the same drawing in the rhetoric of identity – 'I' – who also watches from a different position, and in the women who turn their backs to the sexualisation of the office space and offer a different reading in the codes for equal practice pinned up on the wall. These strategies therefore displace any readings of woman as victim, in representation in the pin-up calendars and in sexually harassing behaviours, and instead instate self-respect and empowerment. Sedley and Benn suggest that pin-ups 'directly undermine an individual woman's view of herself and her ability to do the job'.[39] Women's drawings in trade union literature address the double sense of representation of woman, in her subjective experience as the object of harassment and as the object of the visual image deployed in further harassment. In the drawing for the NUJ Equality Council sexual harassment brochure, we are in the terrain of contested meanings over women's bodies. The office space is represented as a field of conflicting fantasies. The women read the men as toads, not princes, and scrutinise equality notices, while the men project their fantasies of sexual encounters on holiday onto women in the office, or stare at *Playboy* calendars and pin-ups.

Feminist art and theory has attempted during the past decade to deconstruct and destabilise meanings. Of course different meanings cannot be guaranteed, as Nead points out, and the risks are particularly acute in relocating readings of the female nude. But the work of women artists reproduced in the sexual harassment publications is significant in that it is held by and works within the constraints of their institutional procedures and discourses. This visual imagery can build on trade union codes and practices and intervene in the debate on sexual harassment; at the same time it can work towards broader relocations of images of the female nude.

A drawing by Christine Roche for ACTTION Against Sexual Harassment works from such a base (see Plate 7).[40] A seated man at a desk, in a photographic workroom surrounded by girlie calendars and pictures, says over his shoulder, 'Some girls just have what it TAKES, sweetheart ...' The energetic woman behind him tearing down the pictures from the wall, turns his comment into a sharp relpy: 'Right on – sweetbreads.' Here Christine Roche reverses the active agency of masculinity, seating the man passively, while the women, who clearly has 'what it TAKES', actively tears down the naked female body, seen in the pin-ups on the wall. Access to a masculine reading of the pin-up as sexuality, power and pleasure is denied and closed, and in its place a reading of feminine pleasures is jubilantly asserted.

Plate 7: Right on – sweetbreads

Across the sexual harassment literature, pin-up posters and calendars have been said to contribute to the power of affecting behaviours in the workplace. What underpins these claims is the understanding that the representation of the naked female body, which in the workplace narratives is the prerogative of the male gaze, replicates and reinforces power relationships. In a major work of 1978, entitled 'Rape' (see Plate 8), Margaret Harrison contested this public display of the female body and its attendant codes of masculinity. Across the upper band of the four which structure the painting are reproductions of famous images from high culture.[41] In each the body of a woman, sometimes naked, sometimes clothed, signifies masculine agency and sexuality – in aesthetic choice, as romantic chivalry and rejection. The implicit link between high cultural representations of women and male violence are explored by the juxtaposition of newspaper cuttings which report rape alongside razors, knives, broken bottles and scissors. These instruments of violence threaten any tranquil, romantic or aesthetic readings of the images above them, and locate fine art within the register of violence and abuse. The underlying violences, actual and psychic, of the fine art images are powerfully brought home in the cuttings and texts which thread between these contrasting images, reporting rape trials, and the repeated refrain of the myth that 'women ask for it'. The confrontation in Margaret Harrison's work between areas of visual representation normally understood to be discrete serves not only to unveil the shock and violence of the subject matter of the painting but also to uncover the narrative form of art, newspaper reports and advertising, which naturalise rape, sexual harassment and abuse.

Plate 8: Rape

The 1993–4 'A Zero Tolerance' poster campaigns on bus-shelters and street-hoardings in Edinburgh and London confronted the link between masculinity, violent assault and rape. On the street-hoarding posters, a photographic image is juxtaposed with text. The very ordinariness of the images, which show different kinds of women at home, baby-sitting, or at parties, is underpinned by the imagery of part of the text which is then ruptured in its conclusion. The romantic fantasy in the text – 'He gave her flowers, chocolates', and an accompanying glimpse of a party, the focus of which is a smiling suited man – is shattered by the way in which the text continues, ' … and multiple bruising'. The pleasures presented in the text and image displace readings of women as victims, or even witnesses to violence and rape, by shifting the focus from women's to men's bodies. Not only is the assailant foregrounded, but voyeuristic pleasure in violence or women's subordination is also denied. At the bottom of the posters, statistics and facts of violence against women and children are given.

HOME TRUTHS

Violence in the domestic environment has been the focus of consid-erable feminist analysis during the past 20 years. The broad discursive formations of 'the family', constantly circulated in state policies, in the media, in family photographs and in law, have been critically scruti-nised. The constant fracturing and reordering of familial ideology has been examined by several feminist academics. In an interesting discussion of the effects of the policies of the Thatcher governments on women, Franklin, Lury and Stacey have addressed the ways in which a discourse of familism was threaded through Thatcherism. Noting that the pervasive rhetoric of the family rarely had a specifically gendered address, they concluded that the silence about the condition of women in the domestic environment was necessary to the idealisation of the family:

> The sexual division of labour, women's unpaid work, processes involving repro-duction, not to mention domestic and sexual violence, indeed all the aspects of the family politicised by feminists over the past twenty years, were made invisible or individualised within this discourse.[42]

But this familial discourse was not unitary: it was fractured around race and class. Moreover, sexual harassment within the family is little discussed but is nevertheless part of familial relations. The central theme in women's experience of masculine violence, Hanmer and Saunders report, is powerlessness.[43]

Plate 9: Mr-close-friend-of-the-family pays a visit whilst everyone else is out

The problem with representing violence is that not only does it reinforce women's sense of powerlessness by imaging them as victims and men as aggressors and assailants, but it can also offer voyeuristic pleasure. The 'Zero Tolerance' London poster campaign which foregrounded domestic violence refused any such images, while the texts confronted assailants. The campaign is part of a broad feminist address to the ways in which violence serves to control and restrict women and children, and reinforces and reproduces male power. Building across one another's work, women artists have subtly explored the home as a location of encounters of sexual harassment and violence, and themes of vulnerability and fear. Sonia Boyce recalls her art school foundation year encounter with Margaret Harrison thus: 'She taught us that even rape can be a subject for our canvasses – sexual abuse, abuse of trust, abuse of power, an every day occurrence, a highly political act.'[44]

The experience of sexual harassment in the home, and the intensity of fear and isolation, are represented in Boyce's 1986 'Mr-close-friend-of-the-family pays a visit whilst everyone else is out' (see Plate 9). Represented only by the upper part of his body and an outstretched hand, 'Mr-close-friend' fills two thirds of the pictorial space. The harassed woman withdraws to the left but looks directly at the viewer. The image vividly represents the difficulties which have been registered by women in categorising as violent the behaviour of family or friends. Analysing responses to a survey which was carried out in Leeds on women's attitudes and experiences of violence, Hanmer and Saunders noted in 1984 that women found difficulty in defining behaviours of persons known to them. In Boyce's image, the woman seems caught into the drawn 'frame' on which numerous images of hands connote unwelcome and threatening touching. The woman interpellates the viewer, exposing this behaviour as unacceptable and threatening, demanding a response. The title of the work, written round the visual images, places 'pays a visit' above the central empty space of the picture, reinforcing the loneliness and fear of the woman's situation.

The home is also the locus of children's socialisation. In a drawing reproduced in Sedley and Benn's *Sexual Harassment at Work*, Christine Roche explores the home as a place where particular values are engendered (see Plate 10). Her drawing examines the ways in which visual culture is part of the socialisation of male identities. Seated in a comfy armchair, looking at a 'Page Three' nude, a man castigates his son playing behind him. This represents the harassment invasively in the home. The comfy chair represents masculine presence and ease at home against woman's absence at work – the invisibility of housework and/or women's double burden of work at home and outside the home; and in the erosion of women's leisure time from work.[45] In presenting masculinity in

Plate 10: Grow up son

formation, Roche represents it as a site of contradiction in the child's repeated refrain suppressed by his father who nevertheless looks at precisely those images which he is preventing his child from naming. She powerfully suggests that adult social pressures demand adherence to particular ways of seeing, feeling and acting.

Family issues are also addressed in leaflets such as 'Practical Ways to Crack Crime: The Family Guide', part of a government package on crime prevention. Linking in with other leaflets on practical ways to crack crime, this brochure emphasises awareness of dangerous situations and preventative forms of behaviour that the citizen can adopt towards person and property. The second page of the guide, flagged 'Your Family', juxtaposes an image of a woman walking alone in a dark street against a text which addresses women 'at home' and outlines street safety measures. This text uses definitions of violent crimes which locate women as the object of those crimes and designate both the home and the street as dangerous sites of possible attack from strangers. Men are problematically positioned in this text as aggressor and as defender. Sexual harassment is implicit in both text and illustrations.

Hanmer and Saunders have foregrounded the difficulties in defining violent crimes in terms of differences between reported experiences and violence as defined by the criminal justice system. Definitions of sexual harassment and abuse carry the same problematics. Three major characteristics of violent behaviour which Hanmer identifies have relevance to a discussion of sexual harassment: that physical assault is overwhelmingly carried out by men, that within the family men are more likely to assault women and that 25 per cent of all recorded violent crime is wife assault.[46] It is clear from this that women are much more likely to be assaulted by men know to them than unknown to them. 'The Family Guide' locates assault and violence against women either as outside the home or in a stranger's attack on the home. The interface between violence and sexual harassment in the home is far from clear, but the London 'Zero Tolerance' campaign is a move to connect harassment, violence and the representations of women rather more sharply.

STREET PRESENCE

Men are more likely to inhabit public spaces than women. A recent Norfolk crime prevention leaflet stresses the power dynamics of men's presence in public spaces.[47] On the cover is a drawing of a dark street down which a woman walks alone, shadowed by the figure of a man a few paces behind her. While the text advises on strategies of avoidance against attack, the images imply danger. Public spaces are presented as dangerous to women. Sexual harassment, the leaflet implies, is the intimidation of women in the public domain which may lead to crimes of violence. The stress in such leaflets is on abnormal heterosexual behaviours and harassments. What remains invisible and unspoken are racial harassment or homosexual intimidation.

Representations of the street commonly work with the image of a dark city space in which a woman walks alone, shadowed by either a single man lurking behind her or by prowling cars. In July 1993 *New Woman* magazine published the results of a survey and campaign against harassment, in which it listed commonplace comments made by men to women in the street, ranging from 'Cheer up, luv, it'll never happen,' to 'Hello gorgeous.'[48] The analysis revealed that women placed harassment in the public domain on a scale ranging from 'being called out to ... and wolf whistles' to being 'touched, attacked or raped by a stranger'. Men included in the survey were only asked if they had engaged in this behaviour.

'Smiling' masks sexual harassment by encoding it in jocular or friendly languages. A silkscreen print by Chila Kumari Burman entitled 'The smile you send out' recodes the smile in a complexly nuanced set of images. Clearly the relationship between a differently located reading and a politics of representation is complex in this work, articulated as it is around race and class. The pictorial space is divided into squares, some of which are further subdivided and each of which contains and frames many faces of Asian women, some serious, some smiling, some laughing. The rich colours of the print, in vibrant reds, blues and greens, add to and reinforce the multiplicity of the images. The whole piece offers a multitude of shifting, changing images of women, simultaneously refusing the injunction to smile as men demand, closing down that narrative and asserting in its place a differently coded set of smiling faces. The title of the piece refuses the interpellation – 'Give us a smile, darlin'' – and frames our reading in constantly repositioning the smiling women's faces in the shifting images across the work.

A much reproduced cartoon by Ros Asquith also depicts this unwanted, unsolicited, overfamiliar form of harassment and at the same time constructs clear resistance to it. A lounging, casually dressed man, one hand on hip, the other in his pocket, leers at a passing woman, saying, 'Cheer up, Darling. It may never happen.' Her response, 'It just has', appears in a thought-bubble. In this drawing the harassing interpellation is turned back against the harasser. This strategy was also used by the American performer and artist Laurie Anderson, who in 1979 recorded in a sequence of photographs the images of men who had just made similar remarks to her in the street (see Plate 11). In these images the men's faces register along a scale from astonishment to anger and aggression. By stripping bare the ideological constraints and exposing the moment of harassment, the dominant production of values is disrupted and disturbed. The street spaces are resignified by women's representation of women on the street, as in 'Reclaim the Night' marches and anti-pornography demonstrations. Direct address to dominant media values has been articulated by many women's groups in street demonstrations. In 1986 the women's newspaper *Outwrite* featured several street demonstrations against what were perceived to be sexually harassing representations of women in visual culture. For example, it was reported that women members of the NUJ picketed the offices of the *Sunday Sport* protesting against the imagery in that paper.[49]

Plate 11: Object, Objection, Objectivity.

These are important rereadings and reorderings of women's street presence. Across women's newspapers and magazines during the 1980s, protests against sexual harassment and presentation of images of women on the street circulated differently coded representations to women readers. The report in *Outwrite* (November 1986) of the accusation of police sexual harassment of women pickets at the non-stop picket outside the South African Embassy in Trafalgar Square, London, was taken up in the national press. In this report the narrative was focused around the legitimacy of this picket and the vulnerability of the women against the enforcement of law. This placed sexual harassment, as reportedly carried out by the enforcers of the law at street level, within polarised value systems which included women/men, harassment/law and order and had to be read off against the foregrounding of sexual harassment as subject to the law.

A Saab advertisement which appeared in the media in the autumn of 1993 sets in play again a narrative of the street (see Plate 12). It is structured to be read in a continuity with the contents of the papers in which it appeared (such as the *Guardian*, October 1993). There are three column blocks of text broken up by three images, which cross two columns of text and underpin the narrative of the copy, but also set up other narratives and other referents in their imagery. All this is set beneath a banner 'headline' which reads 'THE NEW SAAB 900 WILL FOLLOW YOU HOME IN THE DARK (SO NO ONE ELSE WILL)'. The text set in brackets appears over the first image of a woman standing beside a car in a darkened street. The woman, carrying a briefcase, has long straight blonde hair and is dressed in a sober suit. She looks to the left of the frame, towards the darkened part of the image, while the car headlights pick out an empty doorway to her right. Readers are positioned, like spectators at the cinema, both looking at what she sees – the darkened street – and what she does not see – the doorway. Beside this photograph, and following directly the line of her gaze, the text evokes the recent levels of street violence, 'You no longer have to be a woman to approach the journey from the car to the house with some trepidation. But fear not...' The text then continues by stressing the technological advances of the new Saab, which allow a temporary use of headlights to light the front door, clearly visible in all three photographs. The narrative of the text, driven around technical specification and price, is temporarily interrupted to pose the rhetorical question, 'But you might ask, is it any fun?'

On the face of it, this is a straightforward advertisement setting out, along with the technical specificities and price, the user-friendly – to women – extras of a new car. But the narrative covers several other texts, pretexts on which it is built and which it partly masks and screens. There

THE NEW SAAB 900 WILL FOLLOW YOU HOME IN THE DARK.
(SO NO ONE ELSE WILL.)

The level of street violence rises yearly.

You no longer have to be a woman to approach the journey from the car to the house with some trepidation.

But fear not ... for the engineers at Saab have dreamt up a way to light your way.

When parking the new Saab 900, you turn off the lights in the usual way, then give the light stalk a final tug.

This turns the headlights back on

Across all engine options, the new 900 concentrates on delivering the acceleration from 40 to 60° needed for safe overtaking.

So, the new 900 is a technologically-advanced car. But, you might ask, is it any fun?

A 50% torsionally stiffer body says yes.

Front-wheel drive says yes.

Fourth-generation ABS fitted as standard says yes.

And a possible top speed of 140mph (in the V6) says yes.

for a pre-set 30 seconds.

Time enough for you to lock the car and unlock the house.

Without the suspicion of a back-ward glance.

Intelligent use of the very latest technology is a hallmark of the new Saab 900.

To reduce glare on long night drives, the dashboard of the new 900 includes an ingenious Black Panel button.

Press it and all dashboard lights except the speedo are cut.

And, on the 900SE model, glass capable of absorbing up to 50% of radiated heat fills every window.

(There are enough over-heated drivers on the roads.)

If you're in the market for a car in the £15,995 to £21,795 bracket, by all means toy with the Audi 80, the BMW 3-series and the C-Class Mercedes.

But test drive the new 900. We think you'll agree that this Saab has the Germans on the run.

For further information on the new Saab 900 range, starting price £15,995, write to Saab Information Centre, Freepost WC4524, London WC2H 9BR. Or phone 0800 626556.

Name _____ Address _____

Postcode _____

Present car make & model _____ Year of reg _____ Age if under 18 _____

**THE NEW 900.
VERY SAAB.**

SAAB

Plate 12: Advertisement for the SAAB 900

is the obvious understructure of violence and threat, the intimidation of the street for women, even as they are excluded as the prime group addressed. The text marks this subtext with phrases such as 'follow you home in the dark – so no one else will', 'without the suspicion of a backward glance' and words such as 'violence' and 'trepidation'. The interrelation of text and images here articulate a particular ideological frame – the terrain of harassment, violence and rape. This is territory familiar from television, notably in the *Prime Suspect* television series of the early 1990s,[50] in repeated police statements and crime prevention brochures about the 'safety' of the streets, and in local authority street lighting policies. It is represented in visual imagery by women. This is the street pictured by Rachel Field in a painting (1988), in which two lorry drivers catcall out of the driver's cab. The violence of the harassment is signified by the heavy goods lorry lumbering up the dark street, in which two walking women appear small, vulnerable and isolated. In another painting, 'Heroes' (1991), Field again references the sense of intense isolation and fear of two women standing in a desolate landscape, surrounded by falling corrugated iron fences and confronted by four construction workers (see Plate 13). Two stand aggressively facing the two women, while two others, in an open shed, are contained against the isolation of the women. On the walls behind them are 'girlie' pin-ups and on the ground, lying open, a tabloid 'Page Three' image. The two women stand not only apart from the men in the pictorial space, but are represented on a smaller scale, in the distance and distanced. Their bodies are coded, attired differently from the exposed nakedness of the graphic images and photographs in the paper. Field, like Roche, is directly addressing the socialisation of masculinity as violent and as ordered around images of naked women.

Consider a recent discussion of the representation of the body in the news media. An article in the *Sun* (14 April 1992), set under the headline 'Busty Madonna "insults" builders', reported that a Madonna poster entitled 'Protect your assets – Madonna does', issued by the British Safety Council, had been banned by the Union of Construction Allied Trades and Technicians (UCATT) from building sites. In the text, part of the broader narrative of the tabloid papers in which the sexual availability of women is stressed, 'raunchy' is the sign of femininity, reinforced in the crude graphic image of Madonna on the poster and reproduced to accompany the article, while masculinity is encoded as working brick-layers. Madonna's clothing is stressed: she is seen in the reproduction as 'wearing her famous cone-shaped bra'. This is highly fetishistic, drawing a scopophilic gaze to the fragmented female body and to clothing.[51] In October 1993 the general secretary of the TGWU urged building site workers to silence their wolf whistles and leery comments.

Plate 13: Heroes.

The text and accompanying photograph in the *Independent* (23 October 1993), which reported this announcement, reveal only too clearly the general tropes at play across all these images, a narrativity that encompasses, contains and dislocates a complex of discourses about sexual attitudes, gender roles, gender differences and social experience. Beneath a headline 'Sex pests on the scaffolding silenced by their union', the accompanying photography clearly posed, entirely undermines the argument of the TGWU secretary. Four men, hands in pockets, two in hard hats, all lean forward to peer after a woman moving off to the right, pictured against the bare wall and dressed like the woman in the Saab advertisement, in a suit, carrying a briefcase (see Plate 3). Their dress – jeans, trainers, donkey jackets, hard hats – signifies complex meanings. It is this version of street harassment which is inverted in the cartoon by Posy Simmonds discussed earlier, when 'Ronnie' goes out onto the street where leering women lounge in informal clothing – jeans, boots and trainers – while 'Ronnie' moves to the right of the frame, eyes downcast (Plate 1). But the placing of the photograph and multivocality of text engages diverse positionings. If, as noted by the *Independent* reporter, male speakers claim that it is all good fun, and 'makes a girl feel better', women repudiate such attention and counter, 'It's worse back at the office, to be honest'.

CONCLUSION

Looking at the visual representation of sexual harassment has a particular currency and urgency in contemporary feminist politics. The package of images on offer in my hospital waiting area, of women's magazines, newspapers, trade union literature and police leaflets, are part of the broader terrain on which sexual harassment has been seen to operate. Sexual harassment is often predicated on claims to commonality of experience across women claims which in the 1990s have been contested.

The images discussed in this chapter, their pictorial organisation and spatial arrangement, together with the timing and placement of advertisements in national newspapers, are markers on the surfaces of broader narrative formations which, to extend Gayatri Chakravorty Spivak's argument, construct, form and articulate diverse interlocking narratives within which realities are situated and come to be understood as 'the way things are'. The narratives of sexual harassment thread their way through a complex of social narratives within which certain phrases, categories and positions articulate their power. The discourses of sexual harassment do their work because they are embedded in beliefs that this is the way things are; through their very invisibility they traverse often contradictory situations. Productive readings of visual images enable the viewer/reader to take up a position to combat and refuse harassment, as well as working within and operating on discursive formations of sexuality. In combating sexual harassment, images by women have made visible the very contradictions in the narratives in which sexual harassment glides unseen, providing a range of images of resistance and refusal, portrayals of fear and isolation, definitions of harassing conduct and situations. As I have argued, images of women are deeply implicated in sexual harassment. By contesting the prevailing regimes of looking and of visual representation of women, feminist strategies can alert women to the problems they face, and to their potential solutions.

Notes and References

1. Women Against Sexual Harassment (WASH) is an important resource to women in understanding and combating sexual harassment. I would particularly like to acknowledge the invaluable assistance of Paulette Keating of WASH and the help of the Women Artists' Slide Library: both made me welcome, found invaluable material and gave support. Discussions with Joanne Pilsbury and Deborah Cherry have also been invaluable.
2. Ann Sedley and Melissa Benn, *Sexual Harassment at Work* (London: National Council for Civil Liberties, 1982), p. 6.
3. Catharine A. MacKinnon, *Sexual Harassment of Working Women: A Case of Sex Discrimination* (New Haven, Conn.: Yale University Press, 1979), p. x.
4. Gayatri Chakravorty Spivak, *The Post-Colonial Critic: Interviews, Strategies, Dialogues* (London: Routledge, 1990), p. 19.
5. The formation of the discourse of sexual harassment in the UK is discussed in Sue Wise and Liz Stanley, *Georgie Porgie: Sexual Harassment in Everyday Life* (London: Pandora, 1987), especially pp. 30–8; and in E. Stanko, *Intimate Intrusions* (London: Routledge and Kegan Paul, 1985).
6. Wise and Stanley, *Georgie Porgie*, p. 53.
7. Toni Morrison (ed.), *Race-ing Justice, En-gendering Power: Essays on Anita Hill, Clarence Thomas, and the Construction of Social Reality* (London: Chatto and Windus, 1993), p. ix.
8. Michael Crichton, *Disclosure* (London: Century, 1994).
9. For some discussion of this issue, see Leah Kharibean, 'Survival in the Arts Survey', *Women's Art Magazine* 38 (January/February 1991), pp. 12–14; and Nicholette Goff, 'Access for Women into Art', *Women's Art Magazine* 42 (September/October 1991), pp. 4–5.

10. Tessa van Tusscher, 'Feminist Perspectives on the New Right', in J. Evans, J. Hills, K. Hunt, E. Meehand, T. van Tusscher, U. Vogel and G. Wylen (eds), *Feminism and Political Theory* (London: Sage, 1986), pp. 66–84.

11. Transport and General Workers Union, *Dealing with Sexual Harassment* (London: T and G Publications, 1993); and *Practical Ways to Crack Crime: The Family Guide* (Sudbury: Home Office, 1993). For a discussion of women's magazines, see Janice Winship, *Inside Women's Magazines* (London: Pandora, 1987); and R.J. Ballaster, M. Beetham, E. Frazer, S. Hebron (eds), *Women's Worlds: Ideology, Femininity and the Woman's Magazine* (London: Macmillan, 1990).

12. Teresa de Lauretis, 'Upping the Anti (sic) in Feminist Theory' in S. During (ed.), *The Cultural Studies Reader* (London: Routledge, 1993), pp. 74–89.

13. Pratibha Parmar, 'Hateful Contraries: Images of Asian Women in the Media', *Ten* 8 (16), pp. 72–8; reprinted in R. Betterton (ed.), *Looking On: Images of Femininity in the Visual Arts and Media* (London: Pandora, 1987), pp. 93–104.

14. Artist's collection; exhibited in 'Along the Lines of Resistance', Cooper Gallery, Barnsley, 1988.

15. See, for example, Mercedes Lopez-Baralt, 'From Looking to Seeing: The Image as Text and the Author as Artist', in Lopez-Baralt, *Guaman Poma de Ayala: The Colonial Art of an Andean Author* (New York, publisher unknown 1992), pp. 14–31; and Barnadette Bucher, *Icon and Conquest: A Structural Analysis of the Illustrations of de Bry's Great Voyages* (Chicago: University of Chicago Press, 1981). Lopez-Baralt discusses the seventeenth-century manuscript of the Peruvian Indian, Felipe Guaman Poma de Ayala. Her detailed and complex reading of the text and 398 interrelated drawings is concerned with the instatement of the colonial regime of the Spanish invaders; as she argues, 'Everything that has to do with exaggeration, excess, caricature, disproportion, violence and sex tied to violence is shocking in the drawings of the *Nueva coronica*.' Bucher's thoughtful and horrifying discussion of the illustrations to de Bry's texts traverses sixteenth-century European modes of classifying nature, and is concerned with the ways in which the representations of women are caught into cosmologies, Protestant doctrines and colonising sexualities.

16. M. Sulter, *Columbus Drowning* (Rochdale: Rochdale Art Gallery, 1992).

17. Sedley and Benn, *Sexual Harassment*, p. 7.

18. Women Against Sexual Harassment, *Sexual Harassment of Women in the Workplace: A Guide to Legal Action* (London: WASH, October 1990), p. 9.

RETHINKING SEXUAL HARASSMENT

19. MacKinnon, *Sexual Harassment*, p. xi.
20. In 1990 there were 11,785 million women employed, compared to 9,517 million 25 years earlier; almost half of these are in part-time employment.
21. MORI poll conducted for the BBC, spring 1993; WASH archives.
22. WASH archives.
23. MacKinnon, *Sexual Harassment*, p. 7.
24. The European Commision called on member states to 'take action to promote awareness that conduct of a sexual nature, or other conduct based on sex affecting the dignity of women and men at work, including the conduct of superiors and colleagues, is unacceptable ...' (Commision of European Communities: c (91) 2625 Brussels, 27 xi 1991, Recommendation, Article 1; WASH archives. This Recommendation was accompanied by a code of practice which advised member states of best practice, and called on them to implement the code in their workplaces.
25. Paddy Stamp, 'The Uphill Battle for Equal Opportunities', *Spare Rib* 178 (May 1978), pp. 35–8. However, as her accompanying cartoons so graphically represent, much of this remains at the level of cosmetic languages. In one of the cartoons the broom cupboard is designated office space for the Equal Opportunities officer, while in another the secretary is renamed by the manager 'trainee technician', altering, not changing, the rules of discrimination. For a more detailed analysis, see Paddy Stamp and Sadie Roberts, *Positive Action: Changing the Workplace for Women* (London: National Council for Civil Liberties, 1987).
26. Moira Gatens, 'Bodies, Power, Difference', in M. Barrett and A. Phillips (eds), *Destabilising Theory: Contemporary Feminist Debates* (Cambridge: Polity, 1992), pp. 120–37.
27. Hélène Cixous and Catherine Clément, *The Newly Born Woman,* trans. Betsy Wing (Manchester: Manchester University Press, 1986), pp. 80–1.
28. M. MacNeill, 'Making and Not Making the Difference: The Gender Politics of Thatcherism', in S. Franklin, C. Lury and J. Stacey (eds) *Off Centre: Feminism and Cultural Studies* (London: HarperCollins, 1991), pp. 221–40; A. Coyle, *Redundant Women* (London: Women's Press, 1983) and 'Continuity and Change: Women in Paid Work', in A. Coyle and L. Skinner (eds), *Women and Work: Positive Action for Change* (London: Macmillan, 1988), pp. 1–12.
29. Janice Newman, 'Enterprising Women: Images of Success', in Franklin, Lury and Stacey, *Off Centre*, pp. 241–59.
30. Newman, 'Enterprising Women', p. 254.

31. Estella Tincknell, 'Enterprise Fictions: Women of Substance', in Franklin, Lury and Stacey, *Off Centre*, pp. 260–73; and Newman, 'Enterprising Women', pp. 260–73.

32. Spivak, *The Post-Colonial Critic*, p. 19.

33. Newman, 'Enterprising Women', p. 254.

34. L. Mulvey, 'Visual Pleasure and Narrative Cinema', *Screen* 16 (1) (1975), reprinted in Mulvey, *Visual and Other Pleasures* (London: Macmillan, 1989); S. Moore, 'Here's Looking at You Kid', in L. Gamman and M. Marshment (eds), *The Female Gaze: Women as Viewers of Popular Culture* (London: Women's Press, 1988), pp. 44–59.

35. Lynda Nead, *The Female Nude* (London: Routledge, 1992), pp. 1–2.

36. Nead, *The Female Nude*. For a different discussion of the interrelation of high and popular cultural forms and sexual harassment, see Carol Duncan, 'The Moma's Hot Mamas', in Duncan, *The Aesthetics of Power* (Cambridge: Cambridge University Press, 1993). Marilyn French makes explicit the connection between sexual harassment and high culture in a section entitled 'War against Women in Art' in French, *The Women's Room* (London: Hamish Hamilton, 1992), pp. 165–7.

37. Ros Coward, 'Sexual Violence and Sexuality', *Feminist Review* 11 (summer 1982), pp. 9–22; Patricia Holland gives a divergent analysis in 'The Page Three Girl Speaks to Women, Too', *Screen* 24 (3) (1983), reprinted in Betterton (ed.), *Looking On,* pp. 105–19; See also Nead, *The Female Nude*.

38. For a discussion of women in the media, see H. Baehr (ed.), *Women and Media* (London: Pergamon, 1978); K. Davies, J. Dickey and T. Stratford (eds), *Out of Focus: Writings of Women and the Media* (London: Women's Press, 1987); Ros Coward, 'Underneath We're Angry', *Time Out* 567 (12 February–1 March 1981), pp. 5–7; G. Pollock, 'Missing Women: Rethinking Early Thoughts on Images of Women', in C. Squiers (ed.), *The Critical Image* (London: Lawrence and Wishart, 1990), pp. 202–19; Alison Young, *Femininity in Dissent* (London: Routledge, 1990). See also Mulvey, 'Visual Pleasure and Narrative Cinema'; M.A. Doane, *The Desire to Desire: The Woman's Film of the 1940s* (London: Macmillan, 1987); Rosalind Coward, *Female Desire: Women's Sexuality Today* (London: Paladin, 1982). For a discussion of women's magazines, see note 11 above.

39. Sedley and Benn, *Sexual Harassment*, p. 7; they discuss specific cases on pp. 14–15.

40. ACTTION drawing in Trade Union Resource Centre and Youth Employment and Training Resource Unit, *Combating Sexual Harassment* (Birmingham, 1991), p. 8.

41. Including P.P. Rubens, 'Three Graces' (National Gallery, London); J.P. Ingres, 'Ruggiero Rescuing Angelica' (National Gallery, London); D.G. Rossetti, 'St George and Princess Sabra' (Tate Gallery, London); E. Manet, 'Déjeuner sur l'Herbe' (Louvre, Paris).
42. Franklin, Lury and Stacey, *Off Centre*, pp. 39–40. Also see, for example, R.E. Dobash and R. Dobash, *Violence against Wives: A Case against the Patriarchy* (New York: Free Press, 1980); J. Hanmer and S. Saunders, *Well-Founded Fear: A Community Study of Violence to Women* (London: Hutchinson, 1984); J. Hanmer, J. Radford and E. Stanko (eds), *Women, Policing and Male Violence* (London: Routledge, 1989).
43. Hanmer and Saunders, *Well-Founded Fear*.
44. Catalogue 'Sonia Boyce' (London: Air Gallery, 1986).
45. For a discussion of harassment in the home see Wise and Stanley, *Georgie Porgie*, pp. 4 ff.
46. Hanmer and Saunders, *Well-Founded Fear*.
47. Norfolk Constabulary and Positive Steps Campaign, *Woman Alone* (Norwich, 1993).
48. 'New Woman Campaign: Real Men Don't Harass Women', *New Woman*, July 1993 (WASH archives).
49. Reported in *Outwrite*, issues 47 and 52 (July and November 1986).
50. For a discussion of the imagery of the street in *Prime Suspect* (first series 1991), see J. Beckett and D. Cherry, 'Fashioning the City', in L. Walker (ed.), *Cracks in the Pavement* (London: Sorella, 1993), pp. 5–11.
51. On fetishism, see Mulvey, 'Visual Pleasure'; and Lorraine Gamman and Merja Makinen, *Female Fetishism: A New Look* (London: Lawrence and Wishart, 1994). Working dress, particularly that of female nurses and policewomen, is often the focus for harassment: in a survey of working conditions of nurses, it was reported in the *Daily Telegraph* (29 September 1993) that 'almost 70 per cent have been sexually assaulted or harassed in the course of their duties' (WASH archives).

Select Bibliography

Abrams, K. 'Hearing the Call of Stories', *California Law Review* 79 (1991) 971–1052.

Adler, Z. 'The Relevance of Sexual History Evidence in Rape: Problems of Subjective Interpretation', *Criminal Law Review* (1985) 769–80.

—— *Rape on Trial* (London: Routledge, 1987).

Aers, L. and Wheale, N. (eds) *Shakespeare in the Changing Curriculum* (London: Routledge, 1992).

Aggarwal, A. *Sexual Harassment in the Workplace* (Toronto: Butterworths, 1987).

Allen, H. 'One Law for All Reasonable Persons?', *International Journal of the Sociology of Law* 16 (1988) 419–32.

Alliance against Sexual Coercion. 'Organizing against Sexual Harassment', *Radical America* 15 (1981) 17–34.

Amir, M. *Patterns of Forcible Rape* (Chicago: University of Chicago Press, 1971).

Anderson, M. and Collins, H. (eds) *Race, Class, and Gender: An Anthology* (Belmont, Calif.: Wadsworth, 1992).

Ardener, S. (ed.) *Perceiving Women* (London: Dent, 1975).

Armstrong, L. *Kiss Daddy Goodnight: A Speak-out on Incest* (New York: Pocket Books, 1978).

Bachman, R., Paternoster, R. and Ward, S. 'The Rationality of Sexual Offending: Testing a Deterrence/Rational Choice Conception of Sexual Assault', *Law and Society Review* 26 (1992) 343–72.

Backhouse, C. and Cohen, L. *The Secret Oppression: Sexual Harassment of Working Women* (Toronto: Macmillan, 1978).

—— *Sexual Harassment on the Job* (Englewood Cliffs, NJ: Prentice-Hall, 1981).

Ballaster, R., Beetham, M., Frazer, E. and Hebron, S. (eds) *Women's Worlds: Ideology, Femininity and the Woman's Magazine* (London: Macmillan, 1990).

Ballhatchet, K. *Race, Sex and Class under the Raj: Imperial Attitudes and Policies and their Critics, 1793–1905* (London: Weidenfeld and Nicolson, 1980).

Barrett, M. and Phillips, A. *Destabilizing Theory: Contemporary Feminist Debates* (Cambridge: Polity, 1992).

Bart, P.B. and Moran, E. (eds) *Violence against Women: The Bloody Footprints* (London: Sage, 1993).

Bart, P.B. and O' Brien, P.H. *Stopping Rape: Successful Survival Strategies* (Oxford: Pergamon, 1985).

Beck, E.T. *Nice Jewish Girls: A Lesbian Anthology* (Watertown, Mass.: Persephone, 1982).

Beck, U. *Risk Society: Towards a New Modernity* (London: Sage, 1992).

Benn, M. 'Isn't Sexual Harassment Really about Masculinity?', *Spare Rib* 156 (July 1985) 6–8.

Bennett, W.L. and Feldman, M. *Reconstructing Reality in the Courtroom* (New Brunswick, NJ: Rutgers University Press, 1981).

Benson, D.J. and Thomson, G.E. 'Sexual Harassment on a University Campus: The Confluence of Authority Relations, Sexual Interest and Gender Stratification', *Social Problems* 29 (1982) 236–51.

Betterton, R. (ed.) *Looking On: Images of Femininity in the Visual Arts and Media* (London: Pandora, 1987).

Bloom, A. *The Closing of the American Mind* (Harmondsworth: Penguin, 1987).

Bluestone, N.H. *Women and the Ideal Society: Plato's Republic and Modern Myths of Gender* (Oxford: Berg, 1987).

Borthwick, M. *The Changing Role of Women in Bengal, 1849–1905* (Princeton, NJ: Princeton University Press, 1984).

Bourdieu, P. *Distinction: A Social Critique of the Judgement of Taste* (Oxford: Blackwell, 1985).

—— *Homo Academicus* (Oxford: Blackwell, 1988).

Bowman, C.G. 'Street Harassment and the Informal Ghettoization of Women', *Harvard Law Review* 106 (1993), 517–80.

Boyle, C. 'Offences against Women', in Russell, J.S. (ed.) *A Feminist Review of Criminal Law* (Ottawa: Canadian Advisory Council on the Status of Women, 1985).

Brandenberg, J.B. 'Sexual Harassment in the University: Guidelines for Establishing a Grievance Procedure', *Signs* 8 (1982) 320–36.

Brewer, M.B. and Berk, R.A. (eds) *Beyond Nine to Five: Sexual Harassment on the Job. Journal of Social Issues* (special issue) 38 (4) (1982).

Bright, S. *Susie Bright's Sexual Reality: A Virtual Sex World Reader* (Pittsburgh, Penn.: Cleis, 1992).

Brodsky, G. and Day, S. *Canadian Charter Equality for Women: One Step Forward or Two Steps Back?* (Ottawa: Canadian Advisory Council on the Status of Women, 1989).

Brown, J. *Immodest Acts* (Oxford: Oxford University Press, 1986).

Brown, J.C. and Parker, R. 'For God so Loved the World?' in J.C. Brown and C.R. Bohn (eds) *Christianity, Patriarchy and Abuse* (New York: Pilgrim Press, 1990).

Brownmiller, S. *Against Our Will: Men, Women and Rape* (London: Secker and Warburg, 1975 and New York: Bantam, 1976).

Bularzik, M. 'Sexual Harassment at the Workplace: Historical Notes', *Radical America* 12 (1978) 25–43.

Bumiller, K. 'Fallen Angels: The Representation of Violence against Women in Legal Culture' in Fineman, M. and Thomadsen, N. (eds) *At the Boundaries of Law: Feminism and Legal Theory* (London: Routledge, Chapman and Hall, 1991).

Butler, S. *Conspiracy of Silence: The Trauma of Incest* (San Francisco: Volcano Press, 1978).

Cahn, N.R. 'The Looseness of Legal Language: The Reasonable Woman Standard in Theory and in Practice', *Cornell Law Review* 77 (1992) 1398–1446.

Caignon, D. and Groves, G. *Her Wits about Her: Self-Defence Success Stories by Women* (London: Women's Press, 1989).

Califia, P. *Macho Sluts* (Boston, Mass.: Alyson, 1988).

Cameron, D. *Feminism and Linguistic Theory* (London: Macmillan, 1985).

Campbell, B. *Unofficial Secrets: Child Sexual Abuse – The Cleveland Case* (London: Virago, 1988).

Caputi, J. *The Age of Sex Crime* (London: Women's Press, 1987).

Carson, A. *Eros the Bittersweet* (Princeton, NJ: Princeton University Press, 1986).

Cashman, H. *Christianity and Child Sexual Abuse* (London: SPCK, 1993).

Caught Looking Inc. *Caught Looking: Feminism, Pornography & Censorship* (Seattle, Wash.: Real Comet Press, 1988).

Chakrabarty, D. *Rethinking Working-Class History: Bengal, 1890-1940* (Delhi: Oxford University Press, 1989).

Chester, G. and Dickey, J. (eds) *Feminism and Censorship: The Current Debate* (Bridport: Prism, 1988).

Cixous, H. and Clément, C. *The Newly-Born Woman* trans. Betsy Wing (Manchester: Manchester University Press, 1986).

Clark, A. *Women's Silence, Men's Violence: Sexual Assault in England 1770–1845* (London: Pandora, 1987).

Clarke, C. 'The Failure to Transform: Homophobia in the Black Community' in Smith, B. (ed.) *Home Girls: A Black Feminist Anthology* (New York: Kitchen Table Women of Color Press, 1983).

Clover, C.J. *Men, Women, and Chainsaws* (London: British Film Institute, 1992).

Cole, E.K. (ed.) *Sexual Harassment on Campus: A Legal Compendium* (Washington, DC: National Association of College and University Attorneys, 1990) .

Coles, F.S. 'Forced to Quit: Sexual Harassment Complaints and Agency Response', *Sex Roles* 14 (1986) 81–95.

Coliver, S., Boyle, K. and D' Souza, F. *Striking A Balance: Hate Speech, Freedom of Expression and Non-discrimination* (London: Article 19, International Centre against Censorship, 1992).

Commission of the European Communities, Commission Recommendation of 27 November 1991 on the Protection of the Dignity of Women and Men at Work, *Official Journal of the European Communities* L49 (24 February 1992).

Conaghan, J. 'Harassment and the Law of Torts', *Feminist Legal Studies* 1 (2) (1993) 189–97.

Coward, R. *Female Desire: Women's Sexuality Today* (London: Paladin, 1982).

—— 'Sexual Violence and Sexuality', *Feminist Review* 11 (summer 1982) 9–22.

Cowley, D. 'The Retreat from Morgan', *Criminal Law Review* 4 (1982), 197–256.

Coyle, A. *Redundant Women* (London: Women's Press, 1983).

—— and Skinner, L. (eds) *Women and Work: Positive Action for Change* (London: Macmillan, 1988).

Cretney, S.M. and Masson, J.M., 5th edition, *Principles of Family Law* (London: Sweet and Maxwell, 1990).

Crichton, M. *Disclosure* (London: Century, 1994).

Culler, J. *Framing the Sign: Criticism and Its Institutions* (Oxford: Blackwell, 1988).

Culley, M. and Portuges, C. *Gendered Subjects: The Dynamics of Feminist Teaching* (London: Routledge and Kegan Paul, 1982).

Cunningham, C.D. 'A Tale of Two Clients', *Michigan Law Review* 87 (1989) 2459-94.

—— 'The Lawyer as Translator, Representation as Text: Towards an Ethnography of Legal Discourse', *Cornell Law Review* 77 (1992) 1298–387.

Dake, K. 'Myths of Nature: Culture and the Social Construction of Risk', *Journal of Social Issues* 48 (4) (1992) 21–37.

Daly, K. 'Criminal Justice Ideologies and Practices in Different Voices: Some Feminist Questions about Justice', *International Journal of the Sociology of Law* 17 (1989) 1–18.

D' Augelli, A. 'Lesbians and Gay Men on Campus: Visibility, Empowerment, and Educational Leadership', *Peabody Journal of Education* 66 (3) (1989) 124–41.

Davidson, M. and Earnshaw, J. *Vulnerable Workers: Psychosocial and Legal Issues* (London: Wiley, 1991).

Davies, K., Dickey, J. and Stratford, T. (eds) *Out of Focus: Writings of Women and the Media* (London: Women's Press, 1987).

Davis, L. and Mirabella, M.B. (eds) *Left Politics and the Literary Profession* (New York: Columbia University Press, 1990).

Davis, M.S. *Smut: Erotic Reality, Obscene Ideology* (Chicago: University of Chicago Press, 1983).

Davis, N.Z. *Society and Culture in Early Modern France* (Oxford: Blackwell, 1987).

De Costa-Willis, M., Martin, R. and Bell, R.P. *Erotique Noire, Black Erotica* (London: Doubleday, 1992).

Derrida, J. *Dissemination*, trans. and intro. Barbara Johnson (London: Athlone, 1981).

Detienne, M. and Vernant, J-P. *Cunning Intelligence in Greek Society*, trans. J. Lloyd (Chicago: Chicago University Press, 1974).

Dobash, R. E. and Dobash, R. *Violence against Wives: A Case against the Patriarchy* (New York: Free Press, 1980).

Dollimore, J. and Sinfield, A. *Political Shakespeare* (Manchester: Manchester University Press, 1985).

Douglas, M. *Risk and Blame: Essays in Cultural Theory* (London: Routledge, 1992).

Dover, K. *Greek Homosexuality* (London: Duckworth, 1978).

D' Souza, D. *Illiberal Education: The Politics of Race and Sex on Campus* (New York: Vintage, 1992).

du Bois, P. *Sowing the Body: Psychoanalysis and Ancient Representations of Women* (Chicago: University of Chicago Press, 1988).

Duncan, C. *The Aesthetics of Power* (Cambridge: Cambridge University Press, 1993).

Du Plessis, R. (ed.) *Feminist Voices: Women's Studies Texts for Aotearoa/New Zealand* (Oxford: Oxford University Press, 1992).

Dworkin, R. *Taking Rights Seriously* (London: Duckworth, 1977).

Dzeich, B.W. and Weiner, L. *The Lecherous Professor: Sexual Harassment on Campus* (Boston, Mass.: Beacon, 1984; 2nd edition Urbana: University of Illinois Press, 1990).

Edwards, S. (ed.). *Gender, Sex and the Law* (Beckenham: Croom Helm, 1985).

Elliott, D.W. 'Rape Complainants' Sexual Experience with Third Parties', *Criminal Law Review* 4 (1984) 4–14.

Equal Opportunities Commission (EOC) 'What the Courts Say about Sexual Harassment', Employment Division of the EOC (Manchester, no date).

Estrich, S. *Real Rape* (Cambridge, Mass.: Harvard University Press, 1987).

Evans, D.T. *Sexual Citizenship: The Material Construction of Sexualities* (London: Routledge, 1993).

Faderman, L. *Surpassing the Love of Men: Romantic Friendship and Love between Women from the Renaissance to the Present Day* (New York: William Morrow, 1981).

Faludi, S. *Backlash: The Undeclared War against Women* (London: Chatto and Windus, 1991).

Farley, L. *Sexual Shakedown: The Sexual Harassment of Women on the Job* (New York: Warner, 1980).

Feminists against Censorship. *Pornography and Feminism: The Case against Censorship* (London: Lawrence and Wishart, 1991).

Fineman, M. and Thomadsen, N. (eds) *At the Boundaries of Law: Feminism and Legal Theory* (London: Routledge, Chapman and Hall, 1991).

Finkelhor, D. *Child Sexual Abuse: New Theory and Research* (New York: Free Press, 1984).

—— *A Sourcebook on Child Sexual Abuse* (London: Sage, 1986).

Fortune, M. *Sexual Violence: The Unmentionable Sin* (New York: Pilgrim Press, 1983).

Fox-Genovese, E. *Feminism without Illusions: A Critique of Individualism* (Chapel Hill, NC: University of North Carolina Press, 1991).

Frankenberg, R. *White Woman, Race Matters: The Social Construction of Whiteness* (London: Routledge, and Minneapolis: University of Minnesota Press, 1993).

Franklin, S., Lury, C. and Stacey, J. (eds) *Off Centre: Feminism and Cultural Studies* (London: HarperCollins, 1991).

Fraser, N. and Bartky, S.L. (eds) *Revaluing French Feminism: Critical Essays on Difference, Agency and Culture* (Bloomington: Indiana University Press, 1992).

Fraser, S. *My Father's House: A Memoir of Incest and of Healing* (London: Virago, 1987).

French, M. *Beyond Power: On Women, Men and Morals* (London: Sphere, 1986).

Friedman, J. Boumil, M. and Taylor, B. *Sexual Harassment: What It Is, What It Isn't, What It Does to You and What You Can Do about It* (Deerfield Beach, Fla.: Health Communications, 1992).

Frye, M. 'Oppression' in Andersen, M. and Hill Collins, P. (eds) *Race, Class, and Gender: An Anthology* (Belmont, Calif.: Wadsworth, 1992).

—— 'White Woman Feminist' in Frye, M. (ed.) *Wilful Virgin: Essays in Feminism* (Freedom, Calif.: Crossing Press, 1992).

Fuller, L. 'Positivism and Fidelity to Law – A Reply to Professor Hart', *Harvard Law Review* 71 (1958) 630–72.

Fuss, D. *Essentially Speaking* (London: Routledge, 1990).

Gallop, J. *Feminism and Psychoanalysis: The Daughter's Seduction* (London: Macmillan, 1983).

Gamman, L. and Marshment, M. (eds) *The Female Gaze: Women as Viewers of Popular Culture* (London: Women's Press, 1988).

Gardner, S. 'Reckless and Inconsiderate Rape', *Criminal Law Review* 13 (1991) 172–9.

Gavey, N. 'Technologies and Effects of Heterosexual Coercion' in Wilkinson, S. and Kitzinger, C.(eds) *Heterosexuality: A Feminism & Psychology Reader* (London: Sage, 1993).

Gibson, S. 'The Structure of the Veil', *Modern Law Review* 52 (3) (1989) 420–40.

—— 'Bellum Pax Rursum', *Journal of Legal History* 12 (2) (1991) 148–54.

Giddens, A. *Modernity and Self-Identity: The Self and Society in the Late Modern Age* (Cambridge: Polity, 1991).

Gordon, L. 'The Politics of Sexual Harassment', *Radical America* 15 (1981) 7–14.

—— *Heroes of Their Own Lives: The Politics and History of Family Violence* (London: Virago, 1988).

Gordon, M. and Riger, S. *The Female Fear* (London: Macmillan, 1988).

Gottfredson, M.R. *Victims of Crime: The Dimensions of Risk*, Home Office Research Study no. 81 (London: HMSO, 1984).

Graff, G. *Professing Literature* (Baltimore, Md.: Johns Hopkins University Press, 1989).

Greed, C. *Surveying Sisters: Women in a Traditional Male Profession* (London: Routledge, 1991).

Green, G., Barnard, M., Barbour, R. and Kitzinger, J. 'Who Wears the Trousers? Sexual Harassment in Research Settings', *Women's Studies International Forum* 16 (6) (1993) 627–37.

Greenburg, D. *The Construction of Homosexuality* (Chicago: University of Chicago Press, 1988).

Greene, G. and Kahn, C. (eds) *Changing Subjects: The Making of Feminist Literary Criticism* (London: Routledge, 1993).

Grosz, E. *Sexual Subversions: Three French Feminists* (Sydney: Allen and Unwin, 1989).

Gubar, S. and Kamholtz, J. (eds) *English Inside and Out: The Places of Literary Criticism* (London: Routledge, 1993).

Guberman, C. and Wolfe, M. (eds) *No Safe Place: Violence Against Women and Children* (Toronto: Women's Press, 1985).

Gutek, B. A. *Sex and the Workplace: The Impact of Sexual Behavior and Harassment on Women, Men, and Organizations* (San Francisco and London: Jossey-Bass, 1985).

Hadjifotiou, N. *Women and Harassment at Work* (London: Pluto, 1983).

Halperin, D. 'Plato and Erotic Reciprocity', *Classical Antiquity* 5 (1986) 60–80.

—— (ed.) *One Hundred Years of Homosexuality* (London: Routledge, 1990).

Hanmer, J. and Maynard, M. (eds) *Women, Violence and Social Control* (London: Macmillan, 1987).

Hanmer, J. and Saunders, S. *Well Founded Fear: A Community Study of Violence to Women* (London: Hutchinson, 1984).

Hanmer, J., Radford, J. and Stanko, E. (eds) *Women, Policing and Male Violence* (London: Routledge, 1989).

Hanmer, J. and Stanko, E. 'Stripping away the Rhetoric of Protection: Violence to Women, Law and the State in Britain and the U.S.A.', *International Journal of the Sociology of Law* 13 (1985) 357–74.

Hart, H. 'Positivism and the Separation of Law and Morals', *Harvard Law Review* 71 (1958) 593–629.

—— *The Concept of Law* (Oxford: Oxford University Press, 1961).

Hearn, J. *Men in the Public Eye: The Construction and Deconstruction of Public Men and Public Patriarchies* (London: Routledge, 1992).

—— and Parkin, W. *'Sex' at 'Work': The Power and Paradox of Organisation Sexuality* (Brighton: Harvester Wheatsheaf, and New York: St Martin's, 1987).

Hearn, J., Sheppard, D., Tancred-Sheriff, P. and Burrell, G. (eds) *The Sexuality of Organisation* (London: Sage, 1989).

Hearn, K. 'Oi! What about Us?' in Cant, B. and Hemmings, S. (eds) *Radical Records: Thirty Years of Lesbian and Gay History* (London: Routledge, 1988).

Hemming, H. 'Sexual Harassment in Britain', *Equal Opportunities International* 4 (1985) 5–9.

Herbert, C. *Talking of Silence: The Sexual Harassment of Schoolgirls* (London: Falmer, 1989).

—— *Sexual Harassment in Schools: A Guide for Teachers* (London: David Fulton, 1992).

Herek, G. and Berrill, K. (eds) *Hate Crimes: Confronting Violence against Lesbians and Gay Men* (London: Sage, 1992).

Hey, V. *Patriarchy and Pub Culture* (London: Tavistock, 1986).

Hinds, H., Phoenix, A. and Stacey, J. (eds) *Working Out: New Directions for Women's Studies* (London: Falmer, 1992).

Hirsch, E.D. *Cultural Literacy* (Boston, Mass.: Houghton-Mifflin, 1987).

Hirsch, M. and Keller, E.F. (eds) *Conflicts in Feminism* (London: Routledge, 1990).

Hoagland, S.L. and Penelope, J. (eds) *For Lesbians Only: A Separatist Anthology* (London: Onlywomen, 1988).

Högbacka, R., Kandolin, I., Haavio-Maanila, E. and Kauppinen-Toropainen, K. *Sexual Harassment*. Ministry of Social Affairs and

Health, Finland, Series E: Abstracts 1 (Helsinki: Valtion Painatuskeskus, 1987).

Hollway, W. 'Review of Terry Pattinson *Sexual Harassment ... The Hidden Facts'* (London: Futura, 1991) in *Feminism & Psychology* 2 (3) (1993) 484–6.

Hunter, I., Saunders, D. and Williamson, D. *On Pornography, Literature, Sexuality and Obscenity Law* (London: Macmillan, 1993).

Imbens, A. and Jonker, I. *Christianity and Incest* (Tunbridge Wells: Burns and Oates, 1992).

Incomes Data Services (IDS) 'Sexual Harassment', Employment Law Problems, *IDS Brief* 439 (February 1991), 8–11.

—— 'Harassment at Work: The Legal Issues', *IDS Study* 513 (September 1992), 9–11.

—— 'Recent Developments on Sexual Harassment', *IDS European Report* 375 (March 1993), 17–19.

Itzin, C. *Pornography, Women, Violence and Civil Liberties* (Oxford: Oxford University Press, 1992).

Jackson, B. *Law, Fact, and Narrative Coherence* (Liverpool: Deborah Charles, 1988).

Jenkyns, R. *The Victorians and the Ancient Greeks* (Oxford: Blackwell, 1980).

Jensen, I. and Gutek, B. 'Attributions and Assignment of Responsibility for Sexual Harassment', *Journal of Social Issues* 38 (1982) 121–36.

Johnson, B. *A World of Difference* (Baltimore, Md.: Johns Hopkins University Press, 1987).

Jones, K. W. *Socio-Religious Reform Movements in British India*, The New Cambridge History of India, vol. I, Part III (Cambridge: Cambridge University Press, 1989).

Joshee, A. *A Speech by a Hindu Lady* (Bombay: no publisher, 1883).

Juliano, A. C. 'Did She Ask for It?: The "Unwelcome" Requirement in Sexual Harassment Cases', *Cornell Law Review* 77 (1992) 1558–92.

Kadue, D. 'Fact Sheet on Sexual Harassment', *Bulletin to Management* 43, Part II (Washington, DC: Bureau of National Affairs, 29 October 1992).

Kaplan, L.J. *Female Perversions* (Harmondsworth: Penguin, 1993).

Kelly, L. *Surviving Sexual Violence* (Cambridge: Polity, 1988).

Kerrigan, W. 'Students and Lechers', *Observer Magazine*, Sunday 3 October 1993.

Kimball, R. *Tenured Radicals: How Politics Has Corrupted Our Higher Education* (New York: Harper, 1990).

Kipnis, L. '(Male) Desire and (Female) Disgust: Reading *Hustler'*, in Grossberg, L., Nelson, C. and Treichler, P.A. (eds) *Cultural Studies* (London: Routledge, 1992) 373–91.

Kitzinger, C. *The Social Construction of Lesbianism* (London: Sage, 1987).

—— 'Depoliticizing the Personal: A Feminist Slogan in Feminist Therapy', *Women's Studies International Forum* 16 (5) (1993) 487–96.

—— 'Revisioning Weisstein, Revitalizing Feminism', *Feminism & Psychology: An International Journal* 3 (2) (1993) 189–94.

—— and Perkins, R. *Changing Our Minds: Lesbian Feminism and Psychology* (London: Onlywomen, and New York: New York University Press, 1993).

Kitzinger, C. and Wilkinson, S. 'Virgins and Queers', *Gender & Society* special issue on sexuality (1994).

Kitzinger, J. and Kitzinger, C. 'Doing It: Representations of Lesbian Sex' in Griffin, G. (ed.) *Popular/izing Lesbian Texts* (London: Pluto, 1993).

Le Doeuff, M. 'Women and Philosophy', in Moi, T. (ed.) *French Feminist Thought: A Reader* (Oxford: Blackwell, 1988).

—— *Hipparchia's Choice* (Oxford: Blackwell, 1992).

Lefkowitz, M. *Women in Greek Myth* (London: Duckworth, 1986).

Leslie, J. *The Perfect Wife: The Orthodox Hindu Woman according to the Stridharmapaddhati of Tryambakayajvan* (New Delhi: Oxford University Press, 1989).

Lloyd, C. and Walmsley, R. *Changes in Rape Offences and Sentencing*, Home Office Research Study 105 (London: HMSO, 1989).

Llewellyn, K. 'The Normative, the Legal, and the Law-Jobs: The Problem of Justice Method', *Yale Law Journal* 49 (1940) 1355–400.

Lopez, G. 'Lay Lawyering', *UCLA Law Review* 32 (1984) 1–60.

Loraux, N. *The Children of Athena: Athenian Ideas about Citizenship and the Division between the Sexes,* trans. C. Levine (Princeton, NJ: Princeton University Press, 1993).

Lott, B., Reilly, M. and Howard, D. 'Sexual Assault and Harassment: A Campus Community Case Study', *Signs* 8 (1982) 296–319.

McCormack, A. 'The Sexual Harassment of Students by Teachers – The Case of Students in Science', *Sex Roles* 13 (1985) 21–32.

McEwan, D. (ed.) *Women Experiencing Church: A Documentation of Alienation* (Leominster: Gracewing, 1991).

MacKinnon, C. A. *Sexual Harassment of Working Women: A Case of Sex Discrimination* (New Haven, Conn.: Yale University Press, 1979).

—— 'Feminism, Marxism, Method and the State: Toward Feminist Jurisprudence', *Signs* 8 (1983) 635–58.

—— *Feminism Unmodified: Discourses on Life and Law* (Cambridge, Mass.: Harvard University Press, 1987).

—— *Towards a Feminist Theory of the State* (Cambridge, Mass.: Harvard University Press, 1989).

—— 'Crimes of War, Crimes of Peace', in Shute, S. and Hurley, S. (eds) *On Human Rights: The Oxford Amnesty Lectures 1993* (New York: Basic Books, 1993) 83–109.

McNaron, T.A.H. and Morgan, Y. (eds) *Voices in the Night: Women Speaking about Incest* (Pittsburgh and San Francisco: Cleis, 1982).

Malmuth, N.M. 'Rape Proclivity among Males', *Journal of Social Issues* 37 (4) (1981) 138–57.

Masson, J.M. *The Assault on Truth: Freud's Suppression of the Seduction Theory* (Harmondsworth: Penguin, 1985).

Mernissi, F. *Doing Daily Battle* (London: Zed, 1984).

Mezey, G.C. and King, M.B. (eds) *Male Victims of Sexual Assault* (Oxford: Oxford University Press, 1992).

Minson, J.P. *Questions of Conduct: Sexual Harassment, Citizenship, Government* (London: Macmillan, 1993).

Mnookin, R.H. and Kornhauser, L. 'Bargaining in the Shadow of the Law: The Case of Divorce', *Yale Law Journal* 88 (1979) 950–97.

Morris, M. *The Pirate's Fiancée: Feminism, Reading, Postmodernism* (London: Verso, 1988).

Morrison, T. (ed.) *Race-ing Justice, En-gendering Power: Essays on Anita Hill, Clarence Thomas, and the Construction of Social Reality* (London: Chatto and Windus, 1993).

Muir, K. *Arms and the Woman* (Sevenoaks: Hodder and Stoughton, 1993).

Mulvey, L. *Visual and Other Pleasures* (London: Macmillan, 1989).

Mushroom, M. 'Merrill Mushroom is a Jew', *Common Lives, Lesbian Lives: A Lesbian Quarterly* 7 (1983) 78–85.

NATFHE *Sexual Harassment at Work: What Is It: What Are Its Effects: What Can NAFTHE Do about It: How Can We Prevent It?* (London: NAFTHE, 1985).

Newburn, T. and Stanko, E. (eds) *Just Boys Doing the Business: Men, Masculinity and Crime* (London: Routledge, 1994).

Paglia, C. *Sex, Art and American Culture* (London: Viking, 1992 and Harmondsworth: Penguin, 1993).

Paludi, M. *Ivory Power: Sexual Harassment on Campus* (Albany, NY: State University of New York, 1990).

—— *Academic and Workplace Harassment: A Resource Manual* (Albany, NY: State University of New York, 1991).

Parmar, P. 'Hateful Contraries: Images of Asian Women in the Media', in Betterton, R. (ed.) *Looking On: Images of Femininity in the Visual Arts and Media* (London: Pandora, 1987) 93–104.

Pattinson, T. *Sexual Harassment: The Hidden Facts* (London: Futura, 1991).

Pattullo, P. *Judging Women: A Study of Attitudes that Rule Our Legal System* (London: National Council of Civil Liberties Rights for Women Unit, 1983).

Phillips, C.M. and Stockdale, J.E. with Joeman, L.M. *The Risks of Going to Work* (London: The Suzy Lamplugh Trust, 1989).

Pickard, T. 'Culpable Mistakes and Rape: Relating Mens Rea to the Crime, *University of Toronto Law Journal* 75 (1980) 75–98.

Poage, G. *In Garments All Red: The Story of Maria Goretti* (Washington, DC: Ave Maria Institute, 1971).

Pollitt, K. 'Canon to the Right of Me ...' *Nation*, 23 September 1991.

Prawer, S.S. *Caligari's Children: The Film as Tale of Terror* (New York: Da Capo,1988).

Pribram, E.D. *Female Spectators: Looking at Film and Television* (London: Verso, 1988).

Radford, J. and Russell, D. *Femicide: The Politics of Woman Killing* (Milton Keynes: Open University Press, 1992).

Read, S. *Sexual Harassment at Work* (Feltham: Hamlyn, 1982).

Reilly, T., Carpenter, S., Cull, V. and Bartlett, K. 'The Factorial Survey Technique: An Approach to Defining Sexual Harassment on Campus', *Journal of Social Issues* 38 (1982) 99–110.

Renvoize, J. *Innocence Destroyed: A Study of Child Sexual Abuse* (London: Routledge, 1993).

Reuther, R.R. *Womanchurch: Theology and Practice of Feminist Liturgical Communities* (San Francisco: Harper and Row, 1985).

Robbins, B. *Secular Vocations: Intellectuals, Professionalism, Culture* (London: Verso, 1993).

Robertson, C., Dyer, C.E. and Campbell, D. 'Campus Harassment: Sexual Harassment Policies and Procedures at Institutions of Higher Learning', *Signs* 13 (1988) 792–812.

Robson, R. 'Legal Lesbicide' in Radford, J. and Russell, D. (eds) *Femicide: The Politics of Woman Killing* (Milton Keynes: Open University Press, 1992).

Roiphe, K. *The Morning After: Sex, Fear and Feminism* (London: Hamish Hamilton, 1994).

Rose, J. *Sexuality in the Field of Vision* (London: Verso, 1986).

Ross, A. *No Respect: Intellectuals and Popular Culture* (London: Routledge, 1989).

Rush, F. *The Best Kept Secret: Sexual Abuse of Children* (New York: McGraw-Hill, 1980).

Russell, D.E.H. *Sexual Exploitation: Rape, Child Sexual Abuse and Work Place Harassment* (London: Sage, 1984).

Salmond, J. *Jurisprudence* (London: Sweet and Maxwell, 1937).

Sarat, A. and Felstiner, W.L.F. 'Law and Social Relations: Vocabularies of Motive in Lawyer/Client Interaction', *Law and Society Review* 22 (1988) 737–69.

Sarkar, S. *Modern India, 1885-1947*, 2nd edition (London: Macmillan, 1989).

Saward, J. *Rape: My Story* (London: Pan, 1991).

Schauer, F. *Playing by the Rules: A Philosophical Examination of Rule-Based Decision-Making in Law and in Life* (Oxford: Clarendon, 1991).

Schneider, B.E. 'Consciousness about Sexual Harassment among Heterosexual and Lesbian Women Workers', *Journal of Social Issues* 38 (1982) 75–98.

Schwendinger, J.R. and Schwendinger, H. 'Rape Myths in Legal, Theoretical and Everyday Practice', *Crime and Social Justice* 1 (1974) 18–26.

Scott, J.C. *Domination and the Arts of Resistance* (New Haven, Conn.: Yale University Press, 1990).

Scully, D. and Marolla, J. 'Convicted Rapists' Vocabularies of Motive: Excuses and Justifications', *Social Problems* 31 (1984) 251–61.

—— 'Riding the Bull at Gilley's: Convicted Rapists Describe the Rewards of Rape', *Social Problems* 32 (1985) 251-61.

Sedley, A. and Benn, M. *Sexual Harassment at Work* (London: National Council for Civil Liberties, 1982).

Segal, L. and McIntosh, M. *Sex Exposed: Sexuality and the Pornography Debate* (London: Virago, 1992).

Seidman, S. *Embattled Eros: Sexual Politics and Ethics in Contemporary America* (London: Routledge, 1992).

Shklar, J. *Legalism* (Cambridge, Mass.: Harvard University Press, 1964).

Smart, C. *Feminism and the Power of Law* (London: Routledge, 1989).

—— 'Penetrating Women's Bodies', in Abbott, P. and Wallace, C. (eds)*Gender, Power and Sexuality* (London: Macmillan, 1991).

Smith, A.M. '"What is Pornography?": An Analysis of the Policy Statement of the Campaign against Pornography and Censorship', *Feminist Review* 43 (1993) 71–87.

Smith, J.C. and Hogan, B. *Criminal Law*, 7th edition (London: Butterworths, 1992).

Smyth, C. *Lesbians Talk Queer Notions* (London: Scarlet, 1992).

Somers, A. 'Sexual Harassment in Academe: Legal Issues and Definitions', *Journal of Social Issues* 38 (1982) 23–32.

Soothill, K. 'The Changing Face of Rape?', *British Journal of Criminology* 31 (4) (1991) 383–92.

Sorella, M. 'Lies, Lies and More Lies', *Sinister Wisdom* 35 (1988) 58–71.

Sparks, R. 'Reason and Unreason in "Left Realism": Some Problems in the Constitution of the Fear of Crime', in Matthews, R. and Young, J. (eds) *Issues in Realist Criminology* (London: Sage, 1992).

Spender, D. *Man-made Language* (London: Routledge and Kegan Paul, 1980).

Spivak, G.C. *The Post-Colonial Critic: Interviews, Strategies, Dialogues* (London: Routledge, 1990).

Spring, J. *Cry Hard and Swim: The Story of an Incest Survivor* (London: Virago, 1987).

Stamp, P. 'The Uphill Battle for Equal Opportunities', *Spare Rib* 178 (May 1978) 35–8.

—— and Roberts, S. *Positive Action: Changing the Workplace for Women* (London: National Council of Civil Liberties, 1987).

Stanko, E. *Danger Signals* (London: Pandora, 1990).

—— 'When Precaution is Normal: A Feminist Critique of Crime Prevention', in Gelsthorpe, L. and Morris, A. (eds) *Feminist Perspectives in Criminology* (Milton Keynes: Open University Press, 1990).

Stanworth, M. *Gender and Schooling: A Study of Sexual Divisions in the Classroom* (London: Hutchinson, 1981).

Sumrall, A.C. and Taylor, D. (eds) *Sexual Harassment: Women Speak Out* (Freedom, Calif.: Crossing Press, 1992).

Sykes, G.M. and Matza, D. 'Techniques of Neutralization: A Theory of Delinquency', *American Sociological Review* 22 (1957) 664–70.

Tannen, D. *You Just Don't Understand: Women and Men in Conversation* (London: Virago, 1992).

Taylor, N. (ed.) *All in a Day's Work: A Report on Anti-Lesbian Discrimination in Employment and Unemployment in London* (London: Lesbian Employment Rights, 1986).

Temkin, J. 'The Limits of Reckless Rape', *Criminal Law Review* 5 (1983) 5–16.

—— *Rape and the Legal Process* (London: Sweet and Maxwell, 1987).

—— 'Sexual History Evidence – The Ravishment of Section 2', *Criminal Law Review* 5 (1993), 3–20.

Thomas, A. and Kitzinger, C. '"It's Just Something that Happens": The Invisibility of Sexual Harassment in the Workplace', *Gender, Work and Organization: An International Journal* (1994).

Thomas, D.A. *Principles of Sentencing* (London: Heinemann, 1979).

Till, F. *Sexual Harassment: A Report on the Sexual Harassment of Students* (Washington, DC: National Advisory Council on Women's Educational Programmes, 1980).

Tomaselli, S. and Porter, R. (eds) *Rape* (Oxford: Blackwell, 1986).

Toner, B. *The Facts of Rape* (London: Hutchinson, 1977).

Tong, R. *Women, Sex and the Law* (Totawa, NJ: Rowman and Allanheld, 1984).

Trades Union Congress *Sexual Harassment at Work* (London: TUC, 1983).

Transport and General Workers Union *Combating Sexual Harassment* (London: TGWU, 1984).

TUCRIC *Sexual Harassment of Women at Work: A Study from West Yorkshire* (Leeds: TUCRIC, 1983).

Tuttle, L. *Encyclopaedia of Feminism* (London: Arrow, 1986).

Twitchell, J.B. *Dreadful Pleasures: An Anatomy of Modern Horror* (Oxford: Oxford University Press, 1985).

Unger, R.M. *Law in Modern Society* (New York: Free Press, 1976).

Vogelman, L. *The Sexual Face of Violence* (Johannesburg: Ravan, 1990).

Walker, L. (ed.) *Cracks in the Pavement* (London: Sorella, 1993).

Wallace, M. and Dent, G. *Black Popular Culture* (Seattle, Wash.: Bay Press, 1992).

Ward, E. *Father–Daughter Rape* (London: Women's Press, 1984).

Weedon, C. *Feminist Practice and Poststructuralist Theory* (Oxford: Blackwell, 1987).

White, L. 'Subordination, Rhetorical Survival Skills and Sunday Shoes: Notes on the Hearing of Mrs. G.', *Buffalo Law Review* 38 (1990) 1–58.

Wilkinson, S. and Kitzinger, C. '"Whose Breast Is It, Anyway?": A Feminist Consideration of Advice and "Treatment" for Breast Cancer', *Women's Studies International Forum* 16 (3) (1993) 229–38.

Williams, G. and Hepple, B.A. *Foundations of the Law of Tort* (London: Butterworths, 1976).

Winkler, J.J. *The Constraints of Desire: The Anthropology of Sex and Gender in Ancient Greece* (London: Routledge, 1990).

Winship, J. *Inside Women's Magazines* (London: Pandora, 1987).

Winter, S. 'Transcendental Nonsense, Metaphoric Reasoning, and the Cognitive Stakes for Law', *University of Pennsylvania Law Review* 137 (1989) 1105–237.

Wise, S. and Stanley, L. *Georgie Porgie: Sexual Harassment in Everyday Life* (London: Pandora, 1987).

Wittig, M. 'The Straight Mind' in Hoagland, S. L. and Penelope, J. (eds) *For Lesbians Only: A Separatist Anthology* (London: Onlywomen, 1988).

Wollstonecraft, M. *A Vindication of the Rights of Woman* (1792).

Young, A. *Femininity in Dissent* (London: Routledge, 1990).

Young, J. 'Risk of Crime and Fear of Crime: A Realist Critique of Survey-based Assumptions' in Maguire, M. and Pointing, J. (eds) *Victims of Crime: A New Deal?* (Milton Keynes: Open University Press, 1988).

Index